Faces of Feminism

Foundations of Social Inquiry

Scott McNall and Charles Tilly
Series Editors

Faces of Feminism: An Activist's Reflections on the Women's Movement,
Sheila Tobias

Criminological Controversies: A Methodological Primer, John Hagan,
A. R. Gillis, and David Brownfield

Immigration in America's Future, David M. Heer

*What Does Your Wife Do? Gender and the Transformation of Family
Life,* Leonard Beeghley

Contact Westview Press for information
about additional upcoming titles.

Faces of Feminism

AN ACTIVIST'S REFLECTIONS ON THE WOMEN'S MOVEMENT

Sheila Tobias

WestviewPress

A Division of HarperCollins*Publishers*

Foundations of Social Inquiry

Copyright © 1997 by Westview Press, A Division of HarperCollins Publishers, Inc.

Published in 1997 in the United States of America by Westview Press, 5500 Central Avenue, Boulder, Colorado 80301-2877, and in the United Kingdom by Westview Press, 12 Hid's Copse Road, Cumnor Hill, Oxford OX2 9JJ

Library of Congress Cataloging-in-Publication Data
Tobias, Sheila.
   Faces of feminism : an activist's reflections on the women's
movement / Sheila Tobias.
      p.   cm.—(Foundations of social inquiry)
   Includes bibliographical references and index.
   ISBN 0-8133-2842-X.
   1. Feminism—United States.   2. Feminist theory.   I. Title.
II. Series.
HQ1426.T64   1997
305.42—dc21   96-40894
                                                                          CIP

Text design by Heather Hutchison

The paper used in this publication meets the requirements of the American National Standard for Permanence of Paper for Printed Library Materials Z39.48-1984.

10   9   8   7   6   5   4   3   2

To the people whose feminism shaped mine:

Kate Millett, Gloria Steinem, Betty Friedan,
Florence Howe, Catharine Stimpson, Sonia Pressman Fuentes,
Bernice Sandler, Dorothy Haener, Pauli Murray,
Eleanor Smeal, Lenore Weitzman, Vivian Gornick,
Sheila Ruth, Betsy Holland Gehman, Helen Astin, Alice Rossi,
Sylvia Roberts, Gerda Lerner, Berenice Carroll,
Amy Swerdlow, Jo Freeman, Cindy Cisler,
Mary Jean Tully, Bill Chafe, Linda Kerber,
Pat Graham, Leslie Wolfe, Mariam Chamberlain,
Yvonne Ozzello, Suzanne Taylor, Margaret Feldman,
Donna Shavlik, Emily Taylor, JoAnn Evans Gardner,
Alison Bernstein, Elly Anderson, Jessie Bernard,
Alice Cook, Barbara Richardson, Patricia Lamb,
Sister Joel Reed, Cynthia Fuchs Epstein, Barbara Bergmann,
Elizabeth Janeway, Carolyn Heilbrun, Myra Dinnerstein,
Jean Lipman Blumen, Harold Feldman, Wilma Scott Heide,
Joan Kelly, Shirley R. Bysiewicz, Catherine East, and Audrey Beck.

And in memory of my sister and first friend, Deanne Tobias Abedon,
1937–1996, in tribute to her love of family and her strength.

Feminism, appropriately enough, initiated the cultural work of exposing the gendered nature of history, culture, and society. . . . The category of the human—the standard against which all difference translates into lack, insufficiency—was brought down to earth, given a pair of pants, and reminded that it was not the only player in town.

Susan Bordo, "Feminism, Postmodernism, and Gender Skepticism"

History is always a combination of continuity and surprise.

Jan Romein, historian

Contents

Illustrations

Tables

Figures

Illustrations

Preface

THERE HAS BEEN MUCH LOOSE TALK of late about "postfeminism" in America. Critics of feminism, such as Phyllis Schlafly, Sylvia Ann Hewlett, and Elizabeth Fox-Genovese, have asserted that the majority of women—the kind they claim to speak for—find the feminist agenda contrary to their needs and values.[1] Worse yet, young women whose opportunities are the direct result of feminist efforts over the past three decades are generally unwilling—or too uninformed—to acknowledge that debt. And no wonder. There is no longer that thrilling unanimity that once characterized the movement. As one observer comments, "You put a foot into feminism these days and you don't know where you're stepping."[2] Like Marxism in its middle period, there are deviations to the right, deviations to the left, and far too much concern with what is "politically correct."

I believe, to the contrary, that a central core in the second wave of feminism still exists, a core that resides in the penetrating and at the same time immensely unsettling analysis of "sexual politics" that the writer Kate Millett taught us how to do twenty-five years ago. And I believe feminism still can unite around a single goal: the overthrow of the too-easy acceptance of male domination that, because it has been around so long, feels natural. Millett gave male domination a name. "Patriarchy," she called it, to the discomfort of many good men who did not recognize themselves either as exploiters or abusers of women. But patriarchy as she used the term meant much more than the sexist behavior of individuals. Patriarchy is a system by which men who would sincerely have it otherwise are advantaged just by being male. Since patriarchy comes in many guises, feminists have much to learn from earlier stages in the struggle against it. We risk losing the future, in other words, if we discount the past.

I first encountered Millett's thinking when she was invited in November 1968 to do a reading from her book *Sexual Politics* (still in manuscript) before a gathering of soon-to-become feminists at Cornell University, and I have never stopped drawing sustenance and stimulation from her work. Our group had not gone looking for Kate Millett—no one knew of her work at the time—and she had not gone looking for us.

Emerging exhausted from the politics of anti-Vietnam activism that had consumed us from 1964 to 1968, some of us were slowly shifting our focus to women. A group of thirty women on campus decided to organize a conference on women and pursued Ti-Grace Atkinson to be a speaker. Atkinson was also not yet well known, but she had been featured in an article about something called "the second feminist wave" in no less a publication than the *New York Times Magazine*.[3]

When I sought her out in early fall, however, Atkinson declined our invitation, explaining to me, with the patience reserved for the unenlightened, that she did not speak before "mixed audiences"—audiences, it took me a while to comprehend, that included men. So unless I could restrict the attendance, she recommended as a substitute the head of the nascent New York NOW (National Organization for Women) task force on education, a doctoral student in Columbia University's literature department named Kate Millett. Two years later, after *Time* magazine featured Millett and her book in a cover story remarkable for its attention to a movement as young as the "new feminism," everyone would be familiar with the broad outline of Millett's theories of patriarchy and "sexual politics." But as we soon-to-become feminists sat transfixed by her presentation in November 1968, we already knew in our bones that history was about to be made and that we were going to be a part of its making.

Some would say that Millett, to whom, among others, this book is dedicated, is no longer in the movement's mainstream; that, in the face of so many individual women's achievements since 1968 and the passing of so much new equal rights legislation in America, her stark rendering of patriarchy is obsolete. Others would maintain that her theory of sexual politics has been superseded by feminist thinking more sensitive to women's *differences* than to the *sameness* of their social roles. Some would say that. I would not. For me, the insights that cascade from the pages of Millett's work remain as fiery and as much a call to arms as Thomas Jefferson's "We hold these truths to be self-evident."

Millett came back to Cornell two months later to keynote our Conference on Women. In typical "movement" fashion, she persuaded us to let her trade in her prepaid airplane ticket for a rental van so that she could bring a small delegation of New York feminists with her to our rural campus. Among them were six radical women from New York City's self-styled cabal, the Women's International Terrorist Conspiracy from Hell (WITCH). We also invited Betty Friedan, who was still touring the country with her 1963 book, *The Feminine Mystique*, leaving protofeminists everywhere in her wake. In the persons of Millett and Friedan (although we had no way of knowing it at the time), Cornell would bring two strands of the emerging second wave of feminism together for the first time on a single platform. There, the feminists would confront—also for the first time—"experts" on women who thought they were unbiased and male student radicals who thought they were revolutionaries. Nothing at Cornell (or at the various colleges and universities where conferences like ours took place later on) would ever be the same again after these encounters.

Typical was an exchange between the feminists and a Cornell anthropologist on the subject of gender differences. "Yes, we do studies of behavioral sex differences," the anthropologist said. "We know that men play tic-tac-toe to win, women to tie." The WITCHes hissed, the crowd cheered (the hissing), and later, when the imported feminists pointed out that in men's "socialist heaven" women poured the coffee, ran the mimeograph machines, and played groupie, it was the radical males' turn to cower. A feminist critique of radical politics was long overdue.

But so was a critique of the curriculum. As the four-day conference wound down, students in our audience began to grasp that going to college was for women a kind of socialization for inferiority. Insofar as the curriculum mentioned women at all (and for the most part women's lives and accomplishments were omitted), it trivialized both their problems and their contributions to literature, history, the arts, and the behavioral sciences.[4] On a college campus, we began to realize, feminist politics clearly had a teaching function as well. But who would replace what was missing? Who could and would offer courses on women and women's issues? Who would critique the curriculum as a whole for its unexamined biases on gender issues? Questions like these haunted us conference organizers over the summer of 1969 and motivated us to offer in the spring of 1970 "The Evolution of Female Personality." So it was that our first lecture-sized women's studies course was born.[5]

In the late 1960s, women had to invent new ways of working together. Patriarchy, according to Millett, involved hierarchy; women's work need not. True to our subject, we course planners made ourselves into a collective, a team with no captain. The collective met regularly for ten weeks in fall 1969 and managed to create a course syllabus, reading list, and a series of lectures virtually out of nothing. To be sure, there were books about women, some biased, some good, but most dated. To our continuing surprise, the search for reading material made us realize that, although we came from disciplines as diverse as sociology, literature, and biology, we had read many of the same books. But there was no structure, no "story line," not yet any agreed-upon topics in women's studies. We had to sculpt a new field for ourselves and our students.

If material was scarce, colleagueship was not. All over the country in that first year of the 1970s, feminists who were scholars and scholars who became feminists were beginning to locate "lost women" in history and literature and to do important new research about women and men, employing and sometimes having to modify the techniques of social science.[6] Within a year, I located sixteen new courses at various other colleges about women and women's lives. I compiled these into what became the first of a series of course catalogs of women's studies.[7] Within a decade, there were four thousand college-level treatments of women's studies and six hundred programs. The Cornell collective and I had no way of knowing it, but our participation in that first course in women's studies was going to change our lives.

This book is the product of all that history. I think of it as an activist's recollection and analysis. Since it is history, it is partly chronological. But since it is also personal, it is highly selective, when appropriate, topical (such as the long chapter on lesbianism and feminism), and shaped by questions, the kind my students asked as I taught follow-up courses to "The Evolution of Female Personality" for the next twenty-five years. The topics also follow the contours of my own activism and scholarship as I moved from one set of issues, such as "What really happened to Rosie the Riveter?" in 1973, to *Overcoming Math Anxiety* in 1978, and then to *Women, Militarism, and War* in 1990.[8] In myself and others, feminist activism produced feminist thinking and feminist scholarship. I draw heavily on that thinking and that scholarship in the pages that follow.

At least as important to me are the even larger contours of change-making in America. One has only to glance at the *New York Times* reporting on the day after the anniversary of the passage of the suffrage amendment in 1960 compared to the coverage afforded that anniversary in 1970, 1980, and 1990 to be reminded of how quickly the ideas of the second wave of feminism caused a sea change in the way both women and men thought about women's rights. Feminists may think they led a unique revolution, but in fact theirs is a classic example of democratic reform employing multiple strategies against multiple targets. E. J. Dionne, writing in 1996, says of political democracy that it allows "ordinary people to do extraordinary things."[9] Indeed, the feminist movement, on balance, demonstrates this observation. One can remain critical of racism, classism, and other inequities in American life and still marvel at the degree to which, once organized, individual women moved into the mainstream. In the last chapter of this book, I consider whether the current feminist leadership is willing to bring the "movement" itself into the center—with all the compromise that mainstreaming entails. But as a case study of the possibilities of collective action and change-from-below, the story that unfolds in the pages that follow deserves a place in American political history as well as in feminist studies.

But this is not a scholar's book for scholars. In place of an all-knowing narrator, my voice is personal, my opinions openly biased, the asides frankly pedagogic and passionate. My goal is to make understandable not so much the flow of events as the bigger picture against which these events were taking place. We can ask—we must ask—to take one example, how it was possible that a decade of success between 1966 and 1976, when virtually the entire 1968 NOW agenda found its way into law and practice, could be nearly reversed by Phyllis Schlafly's StopERA. And in the service of that question, we can ask—we must ask—whether women's politics in the decade after suffrage in any way prefigured that comeuppance.

The bigger picture reveals that feminist issues are not fixed but evolving. In the period I trace, "first-generation" issues, issues such as equal pay and equal access to credit, were women's concerns that most Americans, once enlightened, could support. But "second-generation" issues, such as reproductive rights and equal access to sports, threatened age-old traditions about what it means to be "male" and "female" and so were hotly contested. On second-generation issues, feminists were united, but nonfeminists were fiercely opposed. Soon to come, however, were "third-generation" issues, issues on which even feminists do not all agree, such as pornography, surrogacy, women and the military, comparable worth, and the Mommy Track. The reason for this is not hard to locate: Issues get tougher and more complicated as patriarchy unravels. Is pornography "only words," or is it incitement to violence against women?[10] In battles against rape and incest, are women falling prey to "victim feminism"[11] or constructing the conditions for their survival? Debates on these issues would appear to outsiders as breakdowns within feminism. But to us, they are just part of the process of extending insights and connections previously overlooked.

My passion for feminism is wedded to my sense of urgency. A terrible staple in the history of feminism in this country is that every seventy-five years or so we have to start over from scratch. My generation did not know the history of the first wave of feminist activism in the nineteenth century. Perhaps that is why there had to be a second. I shudder to think this might happen again. For all these reasons, I want this basic narrative to be where it belongs: in every woman's head and in her heart. Men, too, I think will profit from a deeper knowledge about the play of sexual politics in our recent past. The story, as presented here, is intended to bridge, not to widen, the discordances among us.

Sheila Tobias
Tucson, Arizona

Acknowledgments

MY FIRST DEBT OF GRATITUDE IS, OF COURSE, to the feminist activists and scholars who were my teachers and friends throughout our shared involvement in the movement and in the field we all helped found, which we called women's studies. In the writing of this book, as in my teaching over the years, I returned again and again to their books and papers and to memories of conversations with them, always learning something new from their utterances and being forced to rethink my own analysis.

My second debt is to the nearly two thousand students who enrolled in my courses "Gender and Politics" and "Feminist Theory" at the University of California, San Diego, in the period 1984–1992 and to my trusted coinstructor, Pamela Vose. In the nine years we taught together, Pam gave me extremely valuable feedback that reshaped my own understanding of the movement and helped me convey its many nuances to undergraduates who could not know what it felt like to have been there. Without the additional support of the department's executive staff, the late Betsy Faught and Kathy Klingenberg, managing the course would not have left as much time for reconceptualizing each time it was taught.

My third debt is to my devoted research and editing assistants Jacqueline Raphael and Susan Newcomer of Tucson, Arizona, now themselves coauthors with Dawn Haines of *Writing Together* (forthcoming). Jacqueline began the construction of this book by sensitively transcribing tapes of the lectures that form its core and then stayed on to help me research and write the rest. Susan's critical eye kept us from veering off track and, in its later stages, helped enlarge and enhance the manuscript with freshly digested new material.

I am always grateful to my agent, Gloria Stern, who has been with me since my first book, *Overcoming Math Anxiety,* was conceived (first in her head, then in mine) in 1977 and to my new friend and editor Jill Rothenberg at Westview Press. Eileen Shanahan, who brought news of the feminist movement to the *New York Times* in the 1970s, allowed me to pick and choose among her personal files. Sonia Pressman Fuentes shared with me personal memories of the early days and filled in some of the gaps. Susan Koppelman, a literary scholar and "recoverer" of lost women short story writers; Arlene Scadron, a women's historian; and members of the editorial board of the *Clarion*, a feminist newspaper in Tucson, read parts of the manuscript and made some valuable suggestions. Sheila Ruth, professor of philosophy and women's studies at Southern Illinois University, Edwardsville; Leslie Wolfe of the Center for Women Policy Studies; Pamela Vose of San Diego; Anne Bowen of Tucson; Scott McNall of Chico State University; and Dominique Thiers, a recent graduate of American University in Washington, D.C., all reviewed it critically in its entirety. My particular thanks to Barbara Allen, Nancy Meyers, Paula Merrigan, Maida Tilchen, and Dorrie McClelland for commenting critically and helpfully on the chapter on feminism and lesbian rights.

The time I had to devote to this project over the past four years would have been much less had not Susan Seidl, my personal assistant, taken over in an executive manner the day-to-day managing of my lecture and consulting appointments. Finally, of course I am grateful to my husband, Carl Tomizuka, who provides the criticism a writer needs most: He points out what is not working and lets me figure out why.

S. T.

1

Gender and Politics Redefined

THE WOMEN'S MOVEMENT HAS CHANGED the way we think about both gender and politics in this country. In feminist theory, gender, unlike sex, is defined as a *socially constructed role*, which means that it is the result of political arrangements and is amenable to social and political analysis. To understand this idea, we have to think about roles the way social scientists do—not as God or nature determined, but as how and with what rationale a particular culture distributes certain tasks, certain privileges, and certain responsibilities.

We owe the original formulation of this radical idea to anthropologist Margaret Mead, who in a study of three primitive societies in New Guinea noticed that, even though in every culture certain tasks, responsibilities, and privileges were assigned by gender, those assignments were not identical. In one, the military task of protecting the village was assigned to males, but in another both sexes had to go to war if the village was threatened. In still another tribe, food production by agriculture was assigned to women, and the men who had to do hunting and gathering had much more free time. Hence, when the males were not away, they were home unemployed and able—indeed, expected—to sit around and indulge in what we Americans would call gossip. In that society, gossiping was considered a male privilege, whereas in our society such conversation is thought to be a frivolous female pleasure.[1]

Mead's analysis demonstrated that, although every society defined certain activities as either male or female, the gender designation of those activities varied from culture to culture. No universal role was either male or female. The societies Mead studied were interesting and important to her analysis because there was little contact among them; each had invented its own gender arrangements independently. Nevertheless, there was always gender definition, and one pattern everywhere held true: Whatever men did was more highly valued by the village than whatever women did. In modern terminology, males were assigned tasks that, by themselves, conferred higher status.[2] Thus, as we move into a discussion of sexual politics in America, we have to face the challenge of the universality of gender differences and the fact that, despite myths about matriarchies, almost everywhere males enjoy a socially constructed superiority over women.[3]

Why? That is the question ethnologists, anthropologists, sociologists, and political scientists have been asking for the past several decades. Some analysts believe it is because males are physically stronger. Can we infer that in all societies males have threatened women physically to maintain a superior status? Or is there something about the childbearing and childrearing functions that so debilitates women that they are unwilling or unable to compete with men for positions of leadership and power? Remember that in a world without contraception, a healthy female will be pregnant constantly during her adult life. The only natural contraceptive is mother's malnutrition.

Despite the difficulty of answering these questions definitively, the reason for women's inferior status has to be addressed. If biology is not women's destiny, then some other explanation of how women's destiny came to be defined this way, in culture after culture, must be provided by feminists.

Just as gender has been reconceptualized, "politics," too, has been expanded by feminists. In its narrowest definition, politics has to do with participation in government, party politics, and elective or appointed office. More broadly, however, politics has to do with power: getting people to do what you want them to do. This definition is still being challenged by academics, but feminists have refused to limit a political analysis to that of formal roles. Politics, feminists believe, includes relations in the world of work: for example, who is hired, who is fired, who is always boss, who is never boss. In *Sexual Politics*, Kate Millett's definition of sexual politics goes even further: Sexual politics, she writes, is the power relationship between men and women in formal groups and in the family.[4]

Thus, sexual politics must include the politics of motherhood. Although from one perspective, contraception and abortion pertain only to a woman and her pregnancy, the question of whether a woman is legally obligated to carry her fetus to term is, in most countries today, determined by society. In some, it is never appropriate to end a pregnancy, even if it is medically possible. In others, it is the decision of the husband and father because the fetus is considered to be his property. In the United States since 1973, the decision may be made only by the person who is pregnant, in consultation with her medical adviser—not the father of the child and not the state. But these are political issues, not issues determined by nature.

To take another example based on this broader definition of politics, child care today is considered a political issue, but in a different society or at another time, it might have been considered a family or a private matter. Politics impinges on the right to work, marriage and divorce, participation in the military, pornography, and even advertising, which, as feminists see it, affects people's view of women and women's view of themselves.

Feminists did not always define politics this way. In the nineteenth century at the beginning of the women's rights movement, women activists concentrated on bringing balance to the civil and political (in the narrow sense) rights of men and women, and in time their work focused on a complex, protracted struggle for the right to vote. To win this battle, our foremothers had to form strong organizations that could work across the nation concurrently for a common goal. This was hardly an accident of history, so we must ask ourselves, What led to the mobilization of so many women activists in this concentrated, all-out suffrage effort? Under what conditions, and through what small struggles, did the first wave of feminism emerge?

It is by asking these sorts of questions about the women's movement—about political expediency, the quirks of fate and circumstance, and individual leadership as well as theory—that we gain a useful understanding of how these fundamental changes in our thinking occurred. The new feminism (sometimes called the second wave of feminism) burst upon the American scene somewhere between 1967 and 1968 with, as far as the general newspaper-reading public was aware, no antecedents. Suddenly, as if planted by an extraterrestrial being, the words *sexism, male chauvinism,* and *patriarchy* were on everybody's tongue. In fact, the movement drew on the civil rights struggle of African Americans and was deeply embedded in our own 1960s countercuturalism. Nevertheless, the theory of patriarchy, first sketched out in Millett's riveting book *Sexual Politics,* is where the story of the new feminism has to begin.[5]

Patriarchy and Politics

Patriarchy has been defined as a state whose ethos reflects the characteristics of masculine gender. As Kate Millett used the term, it was meant to characterize a society dominated not just by masculinity but also by *men* whose primary purpose is to construct and maintain a certain power relationship over women. In such a society, much of what is taken to be traditional or even "true" is really an extended political maneuver to maintain the unequal power relationship between males and females. This does not necessarily imply a conspiracy in which every man colludes with every other man to keep women out of power. That would imply malevolent intention. It is rather the case, feminists believe, that in the enjoyment of privilege and individual advantage, all (or most) men accede to the system that is in place and have no particular interest in making change.[6]

This theory was first outlined by Kate Millett, who began with the observation that males and females are traditionally differentiated on three dimensions, dimensions she called *temperament, role,* and *status.*[7] Everyone in our society, from the man on the street to the professional psychologist, harbors certain cherished beliefs about sex differences. Women, they will tell you, are more passive; men are more active. Women are dependent; men are independent. Women are emotional; men are rational. So as an outgrowth of these temperamental differences, women are less comfortable with and less likely to seek a life of their own and more likely to rely on their feelings for truth, whereas men will concentrate on what is demonstrably true. Obviously, these sex differences—real or perceived—will have a significant impact on women trying to succeed in a world whose values are dictated by men.[8]

After temperament, Millett examined the prevailing views of adult roles. Patriarchs, she explained, want people to believe that adult role differentiation is natural and in fact grows out of temperamental differences. The desire to marry, to mother, and to make a home is as natural for females as is the male's need to make his mark in the outside world. Woman is a private entity, man a public one. And as a consequence of role differentiation, observed Millett, men enjoy higher status than women because what men like and do are given more social value than what women like and do.

Virginia Woolf, an early-twentieth-century British novelist and one of our inspirers, once wrote that Leo Tolstoy was considered a greater writer than Jane Austen because he wrote about war and peace, whereas Austen limited herself to the drama of interpersonal relationships. But who decides, Woolf asked provocatively in her book *Three Guineas,* that war is more important than interpersonal relationships?[9] Society, of course, she replied, the particular society in which the novelists write and are read. Since men derive status from what they do, the argument soon becomes cyclic: What men do is more important because men do it.

In the popular view, the causal chain of temperament-role-status begins with temperament and ends with status. Temperamental differences are supposedly present at birth and lead inevitably (no one plans or needs to enforce this pattern) to role and status differentiations. And since the key years of professional advancement in an industrial society are between the ages of twenty-five and forty, the years when "normal" women are fulfilling their home and motherhood yearnings, without conspiring to, men end up in higher status positions than women.

In Millett's view, that causal chain is reversed. Status really comes first in patriarchy, Millett argued, for patriarchy's most important goal is to maintain the superiority of males over females. Then in a direct effort to reduce competition from women, patriarchy assigns women roles that isolate them from other adults and busy them in caretaking.

How are these roles assigned? And what causes women to accept them without rebellion? In her most brilliant insight, Millett saw that the people professionals—social and behavioral scientists, therapists, and educators—directly contribute to patriarchy by defining what is normal and what is not. Let a woman declare the mother role to be constricting or want the kind of economic power usually enjoyed by men, and she is judged in need of "professional help." And that, Millett helped a whole generation of feminists to see, is the way women in our society are made to accept their social roles.[10]

Millett's analysis was unsettling both because it shed new light on so many previously accepted traditions and because it made women angry. Like the Copernican revolution that took the earth from the center of the solar system, where the ancients had thought it was, and put it in an orbit around the sun, Millett turned conventional assumptions about women's temperament, roles, and status upside down. Reading Millett or hearing her theories secondhand, women in the early 1970s began to look at the arrangements they had made in their lives, particularly in their relationships with men, and had what they called the "click!" experience, a sudden awareness of how political those relationships were.[11]

Sexual politics, as Millet defined it, bears heavily on women in our culture. It is clear that the temperament required for dedicated, original work—the staying-up-all-night kind of dedication, the I-can't-think-about-anything-else-darling-not-even-you-tonight-because-I've-got-those-things-growing-in-the-petri-dish kind of intensity—is, of course, antithetical to what is considered normal behavior for a female. So the American female finds herself in a double bind. Insofar as she experiences the ambitions of a careerist, she is not feminine, and insofar as she accedes to the needs of her feminine nature, she will not be taken seriously as a professional. As mentioned, those childbearing years, when a woman is healthiest and has the most energy for childrearing, coincide with the peak opportunity years in any profession. And to the extent that she is tempted to take a break, the cost to a woman's career, given the dominance of the male model, is high. Indeed, many of the reasons women give for leaving their careers and the reasons men give for not encouraging them to stay involve this double bind.

In the Millett model, only three roles have traditionally been appropriate for women in our society: the mother role, the wifelike role, the decorative role (only possible, incidentally, for women when they are young). Whoever does not naturally fit into any of those is dumped into the one remaining category: the witch-bitch trough. Careers that are considered most appropriate for women are precisely those that appear to be natural extensions of women's three approved roles. Working with children or the handicapped or the old in some nurturing capacity is an obvious extension of the mother role. Women who function as research associates, secretaries, lab technicians, or assistants all their lives are playing out a wifelike role for the men they serve. And women whose femininity is their strongest selling point are decorative objects.

Within the ideology of patriarchy, another bias inhibits women seeking work in the intellectual professions and the arts. This is the powerful idea that any really good work has to begin in youth. If a woman returns to university training to do science, for example, at thirty-five, even if she intends to spend the next thirty years in full-time research, her colleagues believe she is not likely to make a major contribution. Science and many other intellectual and artistic professions are considered to be young people's fields. The myth about science, the arts, and the professions comes from data culled from the eighteenth and nineteenth centuries when young men did not live as long. Most likely, another variable is at work besides the number of brain cells in youth: newness to the field.[12]

In the end, of course, knowledge is power, and so it is not surprising that any dominant group will try hard to keep subordinate groups away from knowledge. During slavery and beyond, African Americans were not allowed to learn to read, the first tool of knowledge; women in earlier centuries were forbidden formally to study art—the presence of nude models was thought to compromise women's purity.[13] In the same spirit, every colonial power has limited the education of its colony's native born. Increased knowledge brings with it not only increased status but also increased power, exactly what the entire patriarchal structure is designed to prevent.

Can a political movement change ideology? As with differences of opinion over religion, it is difficult to argue people out of a set of beliefs from which they have derived status and power. But theory can provide the glue that holds a movement together and can give it direction. First, theory offers a sense of shared identity. Second, by revising history, theory can give a group the knowledge of its past together with the possibility of a future that will be different from that past. Lastly, theory provides the group with a political agenda by which to get from here to there.

A feminist strategy, then, begins by taking back control over the meaning and interpretation of events. Millett offered one new way of thinking about the present and the past. So long as feminists shared that view, they rapidly achieved their first set of political goals. But even in feminist politics, gender is not the only influence on human behavior, and in time differences *among* women had to be dealt with both in feminist theory and feminist practice.

Race, Gender, and Class

Women are not just female. Like men, they are situated in certain economic and social classes. In America, with its history of slavery, its conquest of indigenous and border peoples, and its persistent racism, there is a caste-based set of issues and stigmas affecting women as well. Feminist scholars disagree as to whether race, class, or gender (sometimes called sex class) is the most fundamental of the oppressions women suffer. Socialist feminists see economic change (including the overthrow or substantial modification of capitalism) as a first step toward women's liberation. Even when women of color share white feminists' overall views, as numerous people have observed, the term *women* usually implies white women, and the terms *blacks, Native Americans,* and *Hispanics* generally mean men.[14] Thus, female members of groups already stigmatized may suffer hardship as well as isolation because of race, gender, and class.[15]

Women of color, immigrant women, and women whose families needed their financial support have always worked outside the home, many in low-paid service or manual labor, and so have different levels of experience of sexual harassment and gender discrimination on the job and different views of the relative value of marriage and work. Such experiences cause them to question whether employment outside the home is inherently meaningful, as so many white middle-class feminists assert, and whether it is innately liberating—issues that illustrate the intersection of class and race. As regards image, there are differences, too. African-American women, according to writer bell hooks (who spells her name with lowercase letters), are most negatively stereotyped. Speaking specifically for women of color, bell hooks argues that such stereotypes dehumanize black women—even more than black men, even more than white women.[16]

Nevertheless, most analysts agree that white women and women of color share many of the same degrading experiences in a sexist society—prejudice in the workplace (in terms of access and wages), sexual harassment, imposition of the "feminine mystique" (see Chapter 5), exclusive domestic responsibilities, and battering and the inability to protect themselves and their children from battering—but that women of color face different and greater limitations imposed by a racist and classist society as well. Hooks believes that women of color are deeply feminist but are reluctant to join the "white" women's movement because it is deeply racist.[17] As we see in a brief review of the nineteenth- and twentieth-century struggle for women's rights, many white women activists promoted gender equality while tolerating, and in some instances exploiting, racism as well.

The class issue also divides women differently than men. When is a woman working class? Is it when she holds a working-class job, or is it when she is married to a husband who does? The question is not just academic. As women divorce, they discover all too late that their class membership was tied to their husband's income and place in a community. As Wilma Scott Heide put it dramatically in a 1972 speech as president of the National Organization for Women (NOW), quoting Johnnie Tilmon, "Every middle-class married woman is one man away from welfare."[18] Friedrich Engels, coauthor with Karl Marx of *The Communist Manifesto,* claimed that in terms of "economic class," married women were not even operating in the same economic system as their spouses.[19] They were mired, Engels wrote, in a "preproperty" phase of economic development. Insofar as they exchanged their service for protection, they functioned in the marriage much as serfs did, farming the lord's land in exchange for his army's defense.

Differences in class account in part for differences in politics. During the nineteenth century, even though all women were deprived of certain civil and political rights, not all women felt the pangs of gender disadvantage in the same measure. In the 1970s, antifeminism on the political Right was fueled by fear among economically dependent women of loss of privilege. Class issues also contribute to the distrust some working-class women feel for women of privilege, even when that privilege is earned. Women today acknowledge what was only dimly perceived twenty years ago: that there are profound and unalterable differences among women. It has not been easy—indeed, it may not be possible—to forge a common agenda among women who work in low-paying, low-status fields; women who are in the higher reaches of personal career attainment; women who are disadvantaged by race or immigrant status; and women who do not want to give up dependency on men to compete in an economic race they feel they cannot win.

The Politics of Difference

Whether women can claim equal civil rights with men while retaining their different aspects is an issue that was born in the suffrage movement and remains unresolved even today. In a thoughtful history of the women's suffrage movement, 1890–1920, historian Aileen Kraditor points out that the arguments for suffrage oscillated between two views of women: one, that women are equal, virtually indistinguishable from

men in their political capacity—the "natural rights" argument
that women, being morally and socially more upright than m
when enfranchised, bring peace to the world and uncompron..omg rec-
titude to the task of governing.[20] Kraditor names the first of these asser-
tions the "argument from justice" and the second the "argument from
expediency." She notes that, whereas the earliest pioneers in the
women's rights movement held a radical position on women's moral and
political *sameness* with men, as the movement widened in its appeal, the
argument that women's differences would introduce new and higher
standards of civic behavior weakened the case for women's suffrage.

We can date the beginning of the reappearance of the "differences argument" to the publication in 1982 of Carol Gilligan's influential book *In
a Different Voice*.[21] In this work, based on interviews and a fresh interpretation of gender differences in children's moral development, Gilligan found young women's sense of morality to be different in interesting
ways from that of young men. In place of an almost impersonal, mecha-
nistic view of justice and fairness, Gilligan located women's moral values
in a more personal, contextual view of life. Women, she asserted, seek
wholeness and connectedness to others, and when faced with conflict,
they want to change the rules to avoid conflict, if at all possible, rather
than manage it (as men would do). Many women readers of *In a Different Voice*, finding themselves mirrored in the comments made by Gilligan's subjects, agreed. Not long after, a team of women educators carried the moral development argument further. In *Women's Ways of
Knowing*, Mary Belenky and her colleagues suggested that women learn
in different ways from men.[22]

Kraditor found, in the writings of suffragists, inherently irreconcilable
points of view. Gilligan, Belenky, and their followers may be said to have
created the argument anew, and much of feminist scholarship and feminist debate over strategy since the early 1980s has hinged on the equal-
ity/difference issue. The political implications of either side of the debate are just as divisive now as they were at the turn of the century. If
women are fundamentally different—and not just as a result of their socialization—they may never be interchangeable with men. And if
women have to become too much like men to compete for the power,
positions, and resources that men have heretofore reserved for themselves, in the end women's "victory" may be without meaning. As Betty
Friedan put it more than once, "Women don't want to be equal to unfree
men." What is the point of equality if women's specialness is to be compromised?

Issues of race, class, and women's specialness weave in and out of
feminist politics, especially after 1975. The possibilities afforded by military service, surrogate motherhood, the Mommy Track, and electoral office are simply not of equal value to all women. In the decade that wit-

nessed the rebirth of feminism, however—in the period 1967 to 1977—these divisions were not yet so obvious, and the problems women faced were far more pressing. Today, however, disagreements among feminists are not just theoretical but also present a challenge to the future of feminism itself.

2

The Emergence of Women's Rights as a Political Issue

IT IS IMPORTANT TO SET ANY STUDY of gender and politics in the context of the long history of the nineteenth- and early-twentieth-century women's rights movement because the second wave of feminism is in many ways cousin to the first. The earlier women's rights activists began their reform activities, as did their descendants in the 1960s, not as advocates for their own rights but as participants in campaigns to enhance the rights of others. Three such campaigns spawned the women's rights movement in the nineteenth century: temperance, antislavery, and social reform. From these movements, women emerged as competent reformers while experiencing frustration owing to their lack of power and influence in the parent movement—a similar experience, as I chronicle, to that of the women in the civil rights and anti–Vietnam War movements of the 1960s.

The nineteenth-century pioneers, much as twentieth-century second-wave feminists, were "radicalized" by their frustration. Lack of status, respect, and power drove them toward the position abolitionist Angelina Grimké expressed in 1838 when she said (speaking for all the women in her movement) that she could not make the contribution she was capable of making toward the emancipation of the Negro slave until and unless she achieved her own emancipation.[1] The problem was partly male unwillingness to share a podium with a woman speaker— even one as powerful and energizing as Angelina Grimké is reported to have been—and partly a result of women's restricted participation in the male-dominated worlds of politics and the law.

In nineteenth-century America, even "free" white women (as opposed to slaves and Native American women) inhabited a subcitizen's class.

According to common law, a married woman did not have property rights, which meant she could not own her own farm, have her own bank account, or do business as an independent contractor. Even the property she might inherit from her father or the income she earned if she worked outside the home did not legally belong to her but was, much as were her children, the property of the man she married. These indignities might have been addressed in the political arena had American women enjoyed legal, political, or even civil rights, but just as women were not empowered by property, so they were not empowered by the Constitution. Women could not sue in court, serve on juries, vote, or run for office. Legally, they could not even keep their own names once they married. The present-day tradition—now no longer legally required—of a female giving up her name upon marriage is a vestige of these long-standing limitations.

In the family, thought to be the province of women, rights were restricted, too. A mother's right to custody of her children took second place to that of her children's father, and even though abortion in the early years of the nineteenth century was not prohibited by law, the decision to terminate a pregnancy belonged to the male parent. The unborn child, like the wife herself, was his "property."[2] According to American civil law, which was based on English common law, a wife's marital status made her wholly dependent on her spouse. Upon marriage, a male and female became "one"—and that "one" was male. In legal terms, a married woman was a *femme couverte*, French for "a covered woman." Enclosed by her husband, a wife had no legal identity apart from his, and lacking legal standing, she was denied many of the other privileges of civil life.

In fact, in mid-nineteenth-century America, a white woman was freer if she was not married, and the most privileged legal status was reserved for widows, who as *ex couverte* were allowed some degree of independence regarding property ownership but still no civil or political rights. This was theory. In fact, with some exceptions, a widow's property would normally pass from her husband's control to her son's.[3]

Extending from these barriers were limitations on women's employment and professional rights. The only profession truly open to and welcoming of educated women in the nineteenth century was schoolteaching. (Midwives were, for the most part, self-educated.) Single women wanting to teach completed high school and then two years of teacher training in "normal college," after which they went into the classroom. It was, in fact, this artificially constructed labor force of women, underpaid and willing (because they could not do anything else legally), that gave America a public education system much sooner than most other countries.

Women's unequal status and power are not something one can blame on the founding fathers or any other villain in American history. The traditions were as old as Western civilization; British and later U.S. law had simply codified them. But beginning in midcentury, some of this code began to change. Lobbied for by fathers eager to protect their daughters' right to the families' property, particularly when they were married to irresponsible husbands, the first of a series of Married Women's Property Acts was passed in New York State in 1848. These statutes permitted women who had personally inherited property from their families to own and dispose freely of that inheritance. The laws went far in protecting women, but they did not yet incorporate women's own earnings. Females who went to work outside the home still owed that income to their husbands, and it remained their husbands' so long as they were wed. It is important to note that the Married Women's Property Acts were not initiated by women themselves. Although there did exist a feminist awareness before midcentury, there was no organized women's movement. These acts were the gift of moneyed fathers seeking to preserve their families' property. Their daughters were powerless to lobby for any change in their own status.

So why, the political analyst must ask, did women in the middle of the nineteenth century suddenly begin to challenge their political powerlessness? The answer to this question lies in a combination of conditions and the work of some remarkable human beings. Most Americans have heard of Susan B. Anthony and Elizabeth Cady Stanton and perhaps of Lucy Stone and Lucretia Mott as well. The vision and leadership provided by these and other women, people of extraordinary intellect, energy, and confidence, partly explain the birth of a women's movement during this period. But how they met, what brought them together, and why, after decades of quiescence, these women dedicated themselves to women's rights are interesting examples of the intersection of time and circumstance in history. The answer is that all of them were already politically active before they became "feminists."[4] Like Angelina Grimké, they cut their political teeth on other people's causes.

Nineteenth-Century "Reformism"

The first of the nineteenth-century movements from which these leaders emerged was temperance ("prohibition" in a later era), the drive to criminalize the sale of alcohol. On the surface, temperance might not seem fertile ground for women's rights. Temperance was a "do-gooder" Christian movement, stubborn in its belief that liquor was associated with sin. Employers, too, were eager to stem the absenteeism caused by drink. But because married women lacked control over their own and their husbands' earnings and because alcohol then, as now, was known to contribute to domestic abuse, temperance appealed to wives and mothers as a means of curbing their husbands' spending. So much was temperance linked to women's interests that substantial and sometimes effective campaigning against women's suffrage lasted well into the twentieth century, paid for by the so-called liquor interests. Manufacturers of "bottled spirits," dealers, distributors, and owners of bars united in their determination to keep women from getting the vote, fearful that they would vote to prohibit the manufacture and distribution of alcohol at the first opportunity.

Temperance was Susan B. Anthony's movement. But she and many of her cofounders of America's first women's rights movement were also active in opposing slavery. Antislavery attracted moralists, Northerners and Southerners who, knowing slavery firsthand, could expose it passionately in print and at meetings. Some of the most powerful speakers against slavery were southern women or women who had studied America's "peculiar institution," and, like the Grimké sisters and Harriet Beecher Stowe, author of *Uncle Tom's Cabin,* could discuss it with knowledge and with emotional force as well.[5] Slavery contradicted America's Judeo-Christian heritage and spoke particularly to women's values and their instincts for taking care of the dispossessed. Eventually, women activists in antislavery would find themselves conflicted when, thirty years later, the Negro male would be given the rights of citizenship and suffrage that American women, white and Negro, were denied. But in the 1830s and 1840s, American and British antislavery societies welcomed and made good use of their women members.

The third source of women's activism in the nineteenth century was a reformist tradition, one that found response among privileged women for the downtrodden, the mentally ill, and the immigrant. Many of these activists did not become women's rightists; doing good was more satisfying than doing well.[6] The next generation of reformers made social history: Florence Nightingale, founder of the nursing profession; Jane Addams, leader of the Settlement House movement; and Florence Kelley, labor organizer on behalf of working women. Like their sisters in temperance and antislavery, many of the women reformers of the earlier era discovered their lack of power and influence in the course of seeking money and support for their other work. Elizabeth Cady Stanton and Lucretia Mott provide us with a dramatic cameo of how women activists, struggling to be useful on behalf of other people's movements, finally dared to start their own.

Stanton and Mott were united by their abolitionism and by their association with Quakerism, which was more egalitarian as regards gender than any other religion of their time. Stanton grew up in one family of antislavery activists and married into another; Mott was a minister in a Quaker meeting. As the story goes, in 1840 the two women traveled as official U.S. delegates to the World Antislavery Conference in London and found themselves relegated to the nonvoting section of the meeting. They had been duly selected by the American Antislavery Society to attend the meeting in London, but because they were women, they were not allowed to sit with their delegation, to speak to the assemblage, or to vote on any of the resolutions. It is important to think back to that time. Traveling to an international meeting was exhilarating and exhausting; the issue of ending slavery was of paramount importance to our nation and to the world. The women had been laboring side by side with antislavery men for many years. They had earned their delegate status. But simply because they were women, such rights were denied them.

Think, too, of the contradictions. The movement that had begun in Britain as an effort to end the slave trade in the British colonies was dedicated to the elimination of slavery; yet politically, that same movement (or at least its English branch) was unwilling to fully credential its own female delegates. Not surprisingly, as the story continues, Stanton and Mott sat in the balcony for this weeks-long conference, fumed, and one day nudged each other and (may have) said, "The issue of slavery may be too important to be diverted by any other. But when this business is over, we must turn our attention to women's rights." The antislavery struggle, according to the editors of the *History of Woman Suffrage in America*, was "the single most important factor in creating the woman's rights movement in America."[7]

There is a parallel in the story of the origins of the second wave of feminism in the 1960s. Student activists joined women's liberation groups because, however valiantly they fought alongside their "brothers" in the 1960s battles for civil rights and peace in Vietnam, "radical" men turned out to be traditional when it came to sharing power with radical women. As countless memoirs from the 1960s have documented, women in the various student movements were assigned to the mimeograph and coffee machines, while their menfolk planned and executed the "revolution."[8] In caucuses and consciousness-raising, 1960s women no doubt echoed Stanton and Mott: "Civil rights and the war in Vietnam are too important to be diverted by the issue of our rights and status. But when this campaign is won, it will be our turn." And, indeed, when the anti–Vietnam War campaign came to a temporary halt in the aftermath of Richard Nixon's election in 1968, a movement for "women's liberation" began.

Forging a Women's Rights Movement

Those who populated the first generation of women activists were not always in agreement as to what should be the scope or the dominant strategy of a women's rights campaign. Some had a far-reaching agenda—modern, we might say—involving women's social roles and restrictions, as well as their legal and civil rights, and therefore advocated wide-ranging reforms. Others wanted to focus exclusively on the right to vote, arguing that once women were a political force to be reckoned with, all else would follow. Some were "radical" in their political philosophy and style of protest; others were more conventional. And so the years of activist campaigning were marked by splits and conflict, not least over what we would call today different "lifestyles."

Susan B. Anthony, a single woman, was able to inherit her father's property. Not having to be *couverte* to any husband, she was free to dedicate herself first to temperance, later to campaigning around the country on behalf of women's rights. Lucy Stone, in contrast, did get married but not under the "old rules." Although she lived in conservative Boston, she refused to take her husband's name upon marriage. The couple also, in anticipation of many modern couples' preference, wrote its own wedding vows. Elizabeth Stanton was an uncoventional mother of seven. The movement also included pioneers in male-dominated fields such as Dr. Elizabeth Blackwell, the first woman to struggle through medical school, beating all odds and professional prejudice.

In 1848, true to that whispered promise, Lucretia Mott and Elizabeth Cady Stanton convened two hundred like-minded women and forty men in a meeting in Seneca Falls, near Stanton's home in upstate New York, to initiate discussion of women's rights and to pass some resolutions on the subject. Aware of the historic significance of what they were doing, they employed a full-time (male) parliamentarian and called themselves "delegates," as if to some constitutional convention. In the course of those meetings, they hammered out, much as our founding fathers had done, a declaration of principles using much the same language—"We hold these truths to be self-evident, that all men *and women* are created equal and are endowed by their Creator with certain inalienable rights"—and they delineated those rights in a "declaration of sentiments" extremely radical for its time. An acknowledgment that women as a class had needs and problems might have sufficed. But the women and men at Seneca Falls pushed further, declaring that women were in all civil aspects equal to men, deserving of the rights and privileges of full citizenship.

They also devised a strategy at the convention. Stanton provided the intellectual analysis and vision in the form of essays and tracts that traveling organizers such as Susan B. Anthony turned into eloquent speeches to rouse and educate an audience. Given the times—antebellum America did not provide safe and comfortable means of travel—Anthony's nonstop campaigning for women's rights has to be admired and credited with the propagation of these radical ideas.[9] Typically, Anthony would be invited by a reform-minded minister of a church or by a church women's group to visit a town. Bounding through snow, sleet, rain, and heat, in horse and buggy, the indefatigable Anthony would arrive a day early and distribute printed flyers (or handbills, as they were called), sometimes hanging these on trees, inviting townspeople to attend her lecture on "women's rights." A sizable audience would gather, among them the curious, the gaping, and the hecklers, to listen to Anthony talk through the analysis that Stanton had constructed. Not content just to talk and educate, Anthony would attempt to organize some women's rights effort locally before moving on to the next town. Those of us who traveled the United States in the 1960s and 1970s lecturing and organizing grassroots caucuses and task forces can relate to Anthony's existence very well.[10]

The 1850s were an important time for the women activists, fighting for the first time in their country's history for their own, not other people's, interests. We have no audio records of Anthony's speeches, but those who heard her (and we have their letters) wrote that she was an energetic, extremely fluent, and inspiring speaker who left her audiences dazed and excited. Activists communicated by letter, and the historical material available to scholars tells much about their organizing efforts.[11] Those letters also testify to the enormous passion and commitment these women leaders brought to and drew from their movement.

When civil war broke out in 1861, nearly all women's rights activity stopped for the five years' duration of the conflict. The Civil War was important in many respects, but for the new women's movement, particularly so. When the war ended, a crisis developed that led to an important turning point for the women who had entered women's politics by way of antislavery.

The Status of Women of Color

The women in the preceding description were mainly white, educated, and middle class. Such women were deprived only in comparison to their fathers, brothers, and husbands. But compared to women of color,[12] women of recent immigration, Native American women, and, above all, to the 1.5 million women who were slaves and indentured servants, these women were privileged. It is a historical truism that the most downtrodden in any society rarely initiate the battle for their rights. They are usually too powerless—in Marxist terminology, too oppressed—even to contemplate a change in their status. Rather, revolutions occur in thought and in deed with rising expectations. That is why, prior to their emancipation, only a few African Americans who escaped to freedom returned to the South to lead their other slaves out of bondage.[13] Even had they known about it—and slaves had little access to the news— slave women could hardly have been expected to feel any affinity for what from their vantage point was a white women's movement.

African-American men and women were not the only people denied basic human rights in the young republic. Another blemish upon our history occurred with the Indian Removal Act, signed in 1830 by President Andrew Jackson—an act that arranged for the federal government to "purchase" Native American land east of the Mississippi River, land desired by white settlers and traders. The Native Americans were simply supposed to agree to move West. But five tribes—the Cherokees, Choctaws, Creeks, Chickasaws, and Seminoles—refused to turn over their communities, including well-cultivated farmland, to the U.S. government in exchange for land they had not even seen. So the government forcibly removed some one hundred thousand Native Americans from their land, marched them across the South, many in chains, and relocated them in territory in Oklahoma. Up to 25 percent of the Native Americans herded along what became known as the "Trail of Tears" did not survive, many of them women and children. Even when they resisted, it was to no avail. The Seminole tribe fought for its land in Florida for seven years, only to be defeated in 1839 by U.S. troops.

Thus, while white women were wondering why they had no claim on their husbands' or fathers' property rights, Native American women and men were being robbed of what had been theirs long before the settlers arrived from Europe. In a final affront, in 1912 the U.S. government opened to white settlers the territory that had been given to the Native Americans in Oklahoma, reneging on every aspect of the "business arrangement" instigated in 1830.

The relation of women to men and both to mainstream America among Mexican Americans during the nineteenth and twentieth centuries is also very different from the social and economic milieu from which white activists were drawn to the women's rights movement. The year 1848 is a case in point. For the native-born white woman, 1848 marks the Seneca Falls Convention and the first (New York State's) of the new married women's property acts. For Mexican-American women and men, 1848 was the year of the war against Mexico, after which, by way of the Treaty of Guadalupe Hidalgo and the Gadsden Purchase, the territories of Texas, New Mexico, Arizona, and California were annexed to the United States. With this annexation came thousands of new inhabitants who were not asked whether they wanted to immigrate.

Thereafter, many poor Mexican Americans had the worst of both worlds, exploited as "natives" by their privileged conquerors and treated as "immigrants" (even, when it pleased their employers, as "illegal immigrants") by the authorities. The women in these communities, as Chicana historians and anthropologists write, like African-American women, were active in labor and community organizing but did not separately pursue women's rights. On the contrary, reports anthropologist Marta Cotera, the white women's movement was perceived by Chicanas in both the nineteenth and twentieth centuries as "anti-labor, anti-socialist, anti-slum, and anti-immigrant," leaving little reason for Chicana labor organizers to join, even if they had been invited.[14]

Women of color, compared to white women, were politically invisible.[15] Yet women of color were affected by their gender as well as stigmatized by their race. Take slavery, for example. All African-American people were dehumanized under slavery, but women were especially terrorized. Racism enslaved them, but sexism made the lot of women especially harsh. Women worked in the fields beside men (although only men were elevated to positions of relative authority) while bearing additional domestic and childrearing responsibilities. By their white male owners they were raped, beaten, and forced to breed new slaves. Although much has been written in recent years about the "emasculation" of African-American men, bell hooks asks us to consider how much African-American women were "masculinized" by constant threats to their survival and that of their families during slavery. Even books written about slavery draw predominantly from the experiences of slave men, as if theirs were somehow more significant than the experiences of slave women.[16]

The relationship of white Southern women to their own personal female slaves and to slavery more generally has been much studied and, among modern feminists, much lamented. Many Southern white women saw, in the cruelty of their husbands and sons toward African-American women, that they had better mind their place in Southern white society. Others, like activists Angelina and Sarah Grimké, were moved by the plight of their slaves to leave the South to work full time for abolition. Some white women distrusted their female slaves, were taught to see them as "sexual savages," and were forced—as a modern political scientist would put it—to participate in a sex-race caste system not of their own making. Others, it is said, envied African-American women the richness of their emotional and spiritual lives and what appeared to white Southern ladies to be their considerable influence over slave husbands and sons.[17]

Yet as scholars have now documented, African-American men and women, even during slavery, absorbed some of the ideology of white society. Slave men learned, by watching their white slave owners, to feel possessive of slave women, and their women, in turn, coveted the privileges Southern ladies seemed to enjoy. Calvin Herndon, a perceptive sociologist writing about the links between sex and racism in America, concludes that white slave owners maintained their patriarchy by putting white women on a pedestal and emasculating African-American males.[18] Meanwhile, women of color were the means, the instruments, and the objects of the system. Thus it was that black women, during and after slavery, as feminist historian Karen Anderson expresses it, "found themselves caught between competing and unstable systems of male domination."[19]

After the freeing of the slaves, first in the border states in 1863, then overall with the Thirteenth Amendment to the Constitution, ratified in December 1865, a number of African-American women began to organize around an agenda of their own. "For the Black female activist," writes historian Paula Giddings, "the choice was not so much race *versus* sex, as of finding the best means to secure their own well-being."[20] In the next several decades, excluded from the organizations of white women in the North as well as in the South, African-American women (who called themselves "colored women") formed volunteer associations to take care of their own. The National League for the Protection of Colored Women, for example, was established primarily to protect young women migrating north. The Colored Women's League, the National Federation of Afro-American Women, and the National Association of Colored Women were all involved in community building or betterment.

In the last two decades of the nineteenth century, a wave of so-called Jim Crow laws set de facto segregation in place all over the South. African-American males who had voted and had even sent representatives to federal and state legislatures during Reconstruction were thrown out of power as the Old South reasserted itself. With the withdrawal of Northern forces from the South after 1876, African-American men and women became dependent on themselves to provide the social benefits that government was beginning to provide elsewhere to white Americans: care of the sick, homeless, and aged and health and education benefits.[21] In addition, writes Eleanor Flexner in *Century of Struggle,* "the southern Negro woman faced wanton assault and the danger of prostitution on a scale unknown to her white sister."[22] Under such circumstances, the colored women's clubs were not alien from but deeply devoted to the survival needs of their communities. In the twentieth century, Mexican-American women's organizations would do the same.[23]

Personal threats to black women were only one aspect of the violence of the post–Civil War South; lynching was another.[24] In the 1890s a brilliant African-American woman journalist and newspaper publisher, Ida B. Wells, launched a crusade against lynchings through her newspaper, the *Memphis Free Speech*, and after her offices were attacked by a mob and her paper closed by threat of further violence, she continued to lobby against lynching through columns in other papers, on lecture platforms, and in colored women's clubs, which she helped found, in Boston, New York, Chicago, and the Midwest. Antilynching activities required large-scale organization and cooperation with white men and women. And so in the next decade, the National Federation of Afro-American Women was organized (with Mrs. Booker T. Washington as president), which in time merged with the Colored Women's League to form the National Association of Colored Women (NACW) under Mary Church Terrell. Historian Giddings sees the founding of the National Association of Colored Women in 1896 as a watershed in the history of black women.[25]

Within twenty years, the NACW represented fifty thousand women in twenty-eight federations and one thousand clubs. Like white women mobilizing for social reform, the Colored Women's Club Movement saw itself as especially progressive; the world was "needing to hear [its] voice."[26] Even though most of the participants in these organizations, like white women in temperance, antislavery, and social reform, were middle class and educated (and to the extent their race did not bar them, upwardly mobile as well), there were differences between the two movements. Educated African-American women might experience all the professional and legal restraints that barred white middle-class women from personal fulfillment, but in addition they felt a greater concern for and identification with poor women forced to work to support themselves.[27] For African-American women, Giddings reminds us, helping the poor was more than a "socially sanctioned activity." These women understood well that, because of race, their fate was bound up with those who had fewest resources and least opportunity.[28] One NACW leader, Fannie Barrier Williams, expressed the difference between black women's and white women's organizations at the time as follows: "Among colored women the club is the effort of the few competent in behalf of the many incompetent [of both sexes]. . . . Among white women the club is the onward movement of the already uplifted."[29]

This is not to say that the black women's organizations, any more than Chicanas organized in Texas, New Mexico, and California during this period, did not favor women's causes. In segregated or economically exploited communities, their reports showed, 75 percent of the African-American women were overworked and underfed. Moreover, as was not yet the case in white America, African-American women contributed as much to family income, then as now, as did their men. Hence, when women were out of a job, the whole family suffered. This explains the National Association of Colored Women's motto, "Lifting as We Climb," and why the organization spent more of its energies on setting up kindergartens, founding schools, and training teachers than on advocating for women's legal and political rights. Sixty years later, for much the same reasons, African-American women and white women would develop parallel but separate activisms on behalf of their gender during feminism's second wave. This is not to say that African-American women are not feminist. It is simply that in a society as racially defined as it is gendered, it is extremely difficult and even morally questionable for African-American women to distance themselves from and to lobby against their own people—even if they are men.

1865–1870: The "Negro's Hour"

In 1865, Congress debated three amendments that were intended to make the freeing of the slaves a permanent part of the Constitution. The Thirteenth Amendment declared slavery unlawful in the United States. The Fourteenth Amendment provided that civil rights may not be rescinded or abridged by state governments except by means of due process, guaranteeing former slaves their citizenship. The Fifteenth Amendment gave voting rights to former slaves, but, like the Fourteenth Amendment's guarantee of citizenship, only to African-American *men*.[30]

It is a little known fact that citizenship was not explicitly reserved to males in the wording of the original Constitution. For this reason, the addition of the term *male* in the amendment gave women's rightists cause for alarm. So traditional was the notion that governing is a male prerogative that the founders did not think it necessary to say so. Voting rights were in any case reserved to the states, and some states and territories had occasionally allowed propertied women or widows of propertied men to vote in local elections. This is why the Fourteenth Amendment's establishment of citizenship and the Fifteenth Amendment's establishment of voting rights explicitly to former slave *men* triggered an acrimonious debate among women's rightists, resulting in the first formal split in the (white) women's rights movement.[31]

From the point of view of some already deeply devoted to the suffrage issue, so long as gender was not specified in the Constitution, suffrage could one day simply be extended to women. But if only African-American males and not females were enfranchised, it would be harder to achieve women's suffrage in the long run. Approval of the Fourteenth and Fifteenth Amendments, then, many white and black women concluded, would postpone indefinitely the legal participation of women in government.[32] At the same time, the women's rights movement had been deeply wedded to abolition. For the majority, 1865 was deemed, in the words of Wendell Phillips, "the Negro's hour." It was not right to quibble over the word *male* when it had taken thirty years and a brutal five-year war to achieve the abolition of slavery. Those in the proamendments camp refused to do anything to threaten ratification. Because Stanton and Anthony were opposed to sacrificing women's rights to ratification, the proamendments faction broke away and formed a new organization in 1869, called the American Women's Suffrage Association, to push for swift ratification. African-American club women were also divided over this issue. Frances Harper supported it, while Sojourner Truth expressed the fear that giving more power to men (even African-American men) would add to the oppression of African-American women.[33]

Stanton, Anthony, and their followers, however, would not compromise on suffrage. They formed a competing women's rights organization, which they called the National Women's Suffrage Association, or the NWSA, and lobbied intensely against ratification. Their argument was that passage of the Fourteenth and Fifteenth Amendments would make the struggle for women's rights twice as difficult and twice as long. Moreover, the "Nationals" were eager to move on from suffrage to other social, familial, and religious issues. Those of us reading their broadsides 140 years later cannot help but admire their radicalism on these other issues. In a time when divorce was rare, the NWSA took a strikingly modern position on women's right to initiate divorce and separation. In a time when women's sexuality was still associated with sin and temptation, the NWSA supported a notion of "free love."[34] Yet on the issue of the Fourteenth and Fifteenth Amendments, there was to be no compromise. Even though all three amendments were ratified by 1870, the two women's rights associations remained separate for twenty-five years.

Eventually, in 1890, the two organizations combined into the National American Women's Suffrage Association (NAWSA), but not without great loss. Although the radicals in any political organization can be difficult to manage, they contribute to its energy, its vision, and its conscience. As we shall see, when the NAWSA became a 2-million-member organization by 1912, its size, its willingness to make political compromises, and eventually its success in winning the vote for women in 1920 took their toll.

1890–1920: The Final Struggle for the Vote

After the two suffrage organizations merged, the radical agenda was cut out in favor of an all-out campaign for voting rights. Recall that for its time, the Mott-Anthony-Stanton vision of women's emancipation was comprehensive. It did not include abortion, pornography, or "comparable worth"—issues to be taken up later—but it encompassed rights within the family (marriage, divorce, child custody); economic rights, if not economic equality; the right to organize; and civil rights, including the opportunity for jury duty, the right to testify, and the right (as lawyers) to stand before the bar.

But by the turn of the century, the vote had become the dominant issue. If women voted, so the argument went, males running for office would have a new constituency to serve and would have to adopt at least some of the issues of the women's program. It was easier for women activists to work on this one critical goal, one without which women could hardly expect to proceed in other directions, than to fight for many subsidiary prizes at the same time. By building on the drama of the newly passed Fourteenth and Fifteenth Amendments and by concentrating on the vote, suffragists could mobilize more women and launch a more powerful campaign. Besides, some of the obstacles to women's professional advancement were disappearing. Women were beginning to attend law school, and a few medical schools for women opened, such as the famous Women's Medical College in Philadelphia. As the nineteenth century came to a close, even though Stanton and Anthony were still alive and active, mainstream suffragists focused almost entirely on the vote.

Given women's absence from electoral politics, the campaign for the vote had to be two-pronged. At the national level, the NAWSA had to lobby members of Congress—eventually even President Woodrow Wilson himself—and on the state level they had to try influencing local legislatures and governors around the country. But the two efforts were very much entwined. If the campaign could get some states to enfranchise women, then the members of Congress from those states would vote favorably on the suffrage amendment when and if it came up in Congress. At least that was the theory behind the two-pronged strategy. Once Congress legislated suffrage, then the groundwork done at the state level could be reactivated to get the amendment passed. (Then, as now, three-quarters of the states have to approve an amendment before it becomes part of the Constitution.)

If we count back from the first women's rights convention to list suffrage as its goal (1852),[35] it took nearly seventy-five years of hard work to win the vote for women. It is wrong to think that suffrage, like the Married Women's Property Acts, was an overdue "gift" from men in power. If ever there was a *battle* for women's rights, this was it. Historian Eleanor Flexner cites a total of 480 campaigns in thirty-three states, 17 referendum votes, and only 2 victories in the entire period from 1897 to 1910.[36] The few victories were in the West because women there were highly valued in the settlers' economy as community builders. Colorado was the first (in 1893) to allow women to vote; Idaho, Wyoming, and Utah followed soon thereafter. In the last fifteen years of the suffrage fight, however—from 1905 until 1920—suffragists were at times running twenty different campaigns in as many different states *at the same time.* Some campaigns were more important than others, notably the New York State campaign, because New York led the nation in population and opinion-making. Some campaigns overlapped, but in others, as in the more recent battle for the Equal Rights Amendment (ERA), activists frequently found themselves spread thin to counter intense antisuffrage lobbying.

The cost of this double strategy was enormous. First, the state campaigns had to be maintained while another arm of the movement worked on Congress.[37] Finally, in 1916, lobbying focused on President Wilson, who had always been a difficult man for the suffragists to nail down. It is interesting how past (and present) leaders, revered for their liberalism and far-sightedness on issues such as Wilson's League of Nations, could (and can) be so traditional on women's rights. But the suffragists had one last winning card: Women war workers had made a difference during World War I. Nevertheless, Wilson hesitated. Carrie Chapman Catt, NAWSA's last president, writes in her voluminous record of the struggle how the leaders still were not sure, even moments before Wilson came out in favor of suffrage, whether they had his support.[38] They did, and finally, as a result, the U.S. Congress passed the Nineteenth Amendment—the women's suffrage amendment—to the Constitution in 1919.

A final hurdle remained. Three-fourths of the states had to ratify the amendment, and in this case it happened quickly. Unlike the battle for ratification of the Equal Rights Amendment, all the needed states quickly lent their support, and in less than a year the Nineteenth Amendment sailed through ratification. The speed of victory was due in large measure to the multilevel strategy of NAWSA's organization, which had suffragists, with a campaign base and well-trained long-term activists, in every critical state. Thus, the first wave of American feminism ended with a decisive victory won by a strong, politically organized army of women.

Unfortunately, the Nineteenth Amendment no more guaranteed suffrage for all women than the Fifteenth Amendment had for all men. However inspired and inspiring the nation's beginnings, America in 1920 was a society divided in its privileges by race, class, and immigrant status. Barriers to voting, such as the poll tax and education and property qualifications, effectively blocked racial minorities from voting, especially in the South. It is for this reason that most radical historians (along with feminists of color) regard the passage of the 1974 amendments to the 1965 Voter Registration Act, which guaranteed access to the polls for all citizens in all sections of the country, of far greater import than the women's suffrage amendment passed fifty-four years before.[39]

Seeds of Conflict

In the first decades of the women's suffrage movement, the argument for women's rights was rooted in the natural right of all people, regardless of gender, to participate as citizens. This argument simply took the claim in the Declaration of Independence—that all men are created equal and possess certain inalienable rights—and applied it to women. But by the turn of the century, although many suffragists maintained the original natural rights argument (the argument from justice, in Aileen Kraditor's formulation),[40] other suffragists justified the vote in terms of the benefits (because of their "differences" from men) that women, once they voted, would bring to the nation as a whole (the argument from expediency, as Kraditor defines it).

Why the fuss? If nineteenth-century women's rights advocates had found it useful to argue that woman's suffrage was a natural right,[41] does it matter that early-twentieth-century suffragists rested their claims instead on the pragmatic benefits of women's enfranchisement? The reason this mattered then (and theoretical arguments matter just as much today in the evolution of a feminist agenda) is that, in time, the issues became not just matters of theory but also issues of strategy, alliance, and politics.

This is not to say there is not room for different views in any women's movement. In more than sixty years of campaigning for women's rights, Elizabeth Cady Stanton, initially a "justice" advocate, made frequent reference to the benefits women's enfranchisement would bring society as a whole. The suffragists never claimed that men and women were exactly the same. They recognized that since only women could be wives and mothers, their nature and their role in society inevitably made them more vulnerable. Thus, the need for self-protection became another argument for the vote. Once women voted, it was thought, they could protect themselves by advocating stiffer penalties for rapists, argued Lucy Stone. Florence Kelley, eager to improve working women's lives, thought enfranchisement would protect women from physically and morally dangerous working environments. Women involved in the temperance movement saw the vote as a first step toward national prohibition.

In the course of their many campaigns, some suffragists were so blinded by the these arguments that they began to see women as almost uniquely qualified to have the vote. And to win friends and influence men of very different political colorations, they often employed arguments that were inconsistent with the principles on which the movement had been founded.[42]

Some suffragists went much further than they needed to. One Mary A. Stewart, testifying for women's suffrage before the Senate Judiciary

Committee as early as 1880, said of the fact that African Americans could vote and women not, "The negroes are a race inferior, you must admit, to your daughters, and yet that race has the ballot."[43] And later in the struggle, Kate M. Gordon, a Louisiana suffragist, devised a plan that she hoped would win women's suffrage first in the South, then in the nation: to play the "Jim Crow" card against southern Democrats (vote for women's suffrage, and women will support segregation in the South). The 1890s brought "nativism"—opposition to the enfranchisement of foreign immigrants—into the equation as well.

It was perhaps inevitable that southern suffragists would complain that they were being "ruled" by former slaves and for their northern sisters to feel "indignant" that they were governed by laws made by nonnatives, but Kraditor assures us that the growing conservatism of many suffragists was not universal. Some of the movement's pioneers, such as Susan B. Anthony, continued to oppose all educational and/or property qualifications for the vote.[44] Carrie Chapman Catt (to her credit), last president of the NAWSA from 1916 to 1920; the northern wing of her organization; and many southern suffragists did not endorse either an anti-Negro or an anti-immigrant strategy. But the struggle holds numerous lessons for feminist activism and prefigures later splits over ideas and strategy.

In the end, contends historian William O'Neill, the suffragists "oversold the vote" by promising a better society with women at the helm and, in the course of their many campaigns, made too many compromises. Practical politics made these choices essential, O'Neill concedes, but "expediency tarnished the moral quality that was the movement's most precious asset."[45]

3

Feminism in
the Postsuffrage Era

HISTORIANS NO LONGER BELIEVE that the organized women's movement "fell apart" after suffrage.[1] Historian Estelle B. Freedman blames mainstream chroniclers for misrepresenting what actually happened to women during the 1920s, 1930s, and 1940s and for not taking seriously enough women's continuing involvement in state and national politics. Older, more traditional assessments of that era note the absence of a women's voting bloc after suffrage was won and conclude from this fact—wrongly, says Freedman—that the long anticipated women's voice in politics had somehow been stillborn. Others believe that the flapper era, which witnessed an increase in sexual freedom and personal mobility, shifted interest among younger American women away from the group politics of the presuffrage era and toward a more individual independence.[2] Never mind that women were still barred from many of the professions and most centers of power; they were seen by most historians—to borrow the words of the Virginia Slims advertisement—to have "come a long way."

The reason we know more about this period now than we have known before is that feminist scholars are in the process of revising that history. Women's experience, individual and collective, had been (and still continues to be) largely left out of historical writings. But feminist scholars, paying closer attention to those experiences, have unearthed new findings and reconceptualized mainstream history as well. In the thirty years since "women's history" was reborn, they have provided us with different interpretive lenses through which to look at women's political, domestic, and social activities—lenses more appropriate to women of the interwar period. Now that women's experience is becoming better understood, the decades in which they were presumed to have been inactive politically are becoming better understood as well.

There is no question that women's overtly political work after suffrage changed direction. However, feminist historians such as Gerda Lerner, James Stanley Lemons, Estelle Freedman, William Chafe, and Jo Freeman trace a continuing women's movement from the period after suffrage to the Great Depression, one that changed character and agenda but remained progressive. Their new scholarship reminds us that even the definition of politics sometimes has to change. The fight for the vote involved one definition of politics—in its lobbying; its statewide campaigning; its marches, parades, and public demonstrations; and, above all, in its particular goal: to give women the same voting rights as men. The social reform activism that would attract the majority of postsuffrage women was political in another sense. Its purpose was to better society, particularly but not exclusively on behalf of women.

As we shall see in this chapter, social reformists were not nearly as unified, nor were their victories as spectacular as woman's suffrage. Besides, the movement divided as "social feminists" parted with "equal rights feminists" over the Equal Rights Amendment. Further complicating the postsuffrage era, some of the political compromises that had been made to get suffrage passed in male-only legislatures—compromises on race, on nativism, and on principle—returned to haunt the movement's followers in the next decades.

It would be wrong to blame Carrie Chapman Catt, the last head of the NAWSA, for not better preparing the ground for postsuffragism. It would be just as wrong to blame the flappers for their apparent indifference to politics or Alice Paul and her National Woman's Party (NWP) for devaluing laws that gave women special protection.[3] Two political realities cannot be ignored. First, even though American women may have agreed on their right to vote, they were not necessarily going to agree (any more than American men have ever agreed) on what to vote for; second, in the period immediately after suffrage, as in all periods following women's gains, a strong conservative reaction took hold.

Only feminist historians have taken seriously the fact that discrimination against women in the workplace and in the political arena persisted well after suffrage was won. Nor is it widely appreciated how determined those in power in the 1920s were to convince themselves and others that suffrage for women was all that women wanted. Suffrage, as the nineteenth-century pioneers had originally intended it, was to be the first, not the last, step to women's emancipation. No wonder conservatives felt threatened by the idea that women's rights might be extended beyond suffrage. Social and economic arrangements were at stake that depended on women's lesser roles and lesser status.

So, eager to discourage further social change, an antiwoman reaction set in during the first decades after suffrage. At first male politicians took the lead. Then sociologists and historians of the era weighed in with their "evidence" and rationalizations. In rhetoric remarkable for its anticipation of the arguments of Phyllis Schlafly in our own day, commentators of the period worried in print that the "new woman," who had supposedly come to power with suffrage, was causing a rise in divorce and a weakening of parental authority. Other contemporaries linked working women (i.e., the poor, the nonwhite, those who *needed* to work) with the decline of the American family and lauded women who chose to remain in the home (i.e., middle- to upper-class white women)—without acknowledging that they inhabited different economic worlds. These combined prejudices—against women, against feminism, and against the working class—would continue to characterize the politics and the scholarship of the period well into the Depression era. "From the mid-1930s through the late 1940s," historian Freedman tells us, "feminism was not a popular subject among historians. A country struggling through a prolonged depression viewed woman's emancipation and her entry into the job market in a very different light than had an earlier, more prosperous society."[4]

Nevertheless, it behooves feminists of the second wave to consider how and why the first wave of suffragist feminism came to an end. There is no question that a younger generation chose not to join the 2 million older women who had struggled valiantly and successfully to win the vote and that the older generation did not participate in politics to the extent that was expected.[5] Some of those women were what we would call today "burned out." Carrie Chapman Catt observed in the early 1920s that the victors were "disappointed . . . because they miss the exaltation, the thrill of expectancy, [and] the vision which stimulated them in the suffrage campaign."[6] The majority of those who stayed active, historians appear to agree, turned back to social reform.

The Social Reformers

After enfranchisement, the collective suffrage coalition split into two camps, one more reformist and the other more radical in its views. Reformers and radicals shared a common desire to improve women's status, but they disagreed as to the roles and nature of women, as well as how to achieve even the goals they shared. The majority of suffragists focused their activity on legislative reform within the states and at the nation's capital. Political historian Jo Freeman feels that even feminist historians sometimes fail to recognize the *political* character of women's advocacy during the 1920s because so much of their legislative work took place in state legislatures and was not national in scope. Perhaps the reason for the retreat from national politics is that their issues—child labor and protective labor legislation—are determined at the state level.

Take, for example, the activities of the newly formed League of Women Voters. In the last decade of the NAWSA's existence, the association had a membership bordering on 2 million. There were chapters in all states with women at the helm whose collective political savvy had been cultivated in the fight for the vote. In 1920, Catt reasoned that since the NAWSA was a *nonvoters'* organization, a new voters' organization ought to be founded in its stead, which she named the League of Women Voters.

The League of Women Voters, a nonpartisan organization, introduced and worked to pass important legislative measures in the states throughout the 1920s. Its work was accomplished primarily through women's legislative councils coordinated by state chapters. By 1925, the league claimed that 420 state laws had been passed with its support since suffrage. Of these, 130 concerned child welfare, but 86 (the next largest number) removed legal barriers to women's equality. The league also supported laws that improved social hygiene, education, government efficiency, women's conditions in industry, women's living costs, antilynching, and "the repression of vice."[7]

As we look back on that era of social reform, we cannot help but be struck by the extent to which some kind of women's political network was still operating. Even though its members worked with men—mainly former Progressives from the movement of that name, which was also in decline during the 1920s—when it came to large-scale organizing, the league turned mainly to women's groups. Soon after 1920, the league created a loose coalition called the Women's Joint Congressional Committee (WJCC), for which league president Maude Wood Park served as chair. The *Ladies Home Journal* described the WJCC as the "most highly organized and powerful lobby ever seen in Washington."[8] It included members of the General Federation of Women's Clubs, the National Consumers' League, the National Federation of Business and Professional Women's Clubs, the American Association of University Women, and, eventually, twenty-one organizations with wide-ranging financial and political support.

Three organizations, the League of Women Voters, the National Consumers' League, and the Women's Trade Union League, were most influential in the WJCC, which, by its own description, acted less as an independent women's organization than as an information clearinghouse. The way the coalition worked was this: Subgroups of three to five women's organizations from the WJCC roster would band together to lobby for bills that their members especially wanted to see passed. The women in these separate organizations obviously had different agendas and often different reasons for supporting these measures, but the WJCC managed to collapse these differences within the coalition. Jo Freeman maintains that the WJCC's success, which was especially strong in its first five years, was largely due to the "persistence and thorough organization" its members had learned in the long battle for suffrage. For example, she tells us, "the League maintained a card file on every important office holder in Washington down to the name of his grandmother and the kind of face powder used by his wife," and when a bill was about to be voted on, members would swamp their legislators with letters, telegrams, and personal visits at strategic moments.[9]

Over the years since its founding in 1920, the League of Women Voters has held itself to high standards of independence in research and brought many new women voters a level of confidence and political literacy they might not have otherwise obtained. It certainly helped maintain the sanity of many unemployed mothers who liked political research and conversation. Their evening meetings gave many women a place and space to exercise their minds. But by the time I came to know it during the years of the "feminine mystique," it had ceased to be "radical" in any sense of that term. By calling itself "nonpartisan," the league meant it would not support specific candidates in city, state, or federal elections, not even those candidates who favored women's issues—not even women. Nor would it support an existing party or candidate. It would not, in other words, advocate for women in any electoral sense. Rather, in the spirit initially enunciated by founder Carrie Chapman Catt, the League of Women Voters began to see itself exclusively as a teaching organization, educating women voters about politics. In a way, it was demeaning to suggest that just because women had not voted before 1920, they needed to be taught how to understand the issues—as if men, just because they had voted before, knew everything they needed to know about political choice.

The social reform work of enfranchised women reached into areas of particular concern to women, such as pre- and postnatal care and women's citizenship, and in the area of child labor laws, issues on which women such as Florence Kelley had long been working. One success story is that of the Sheppard-Towner Maternity and Infancy Protection Act, first introduced into Congress in 1918 by Representative Jeannette Rankin (R–Mont.), elected to Congress in 1916 and the first woman member of that institution.[10] Her bill provided funds to the states for "pre- and post-natal care, instruction in infant hygiene, and consultation centers for mothers."[11] Rankin's motive was to lower the high maternal and infant mortality rate in the United States. Although neither the Democratic Congress nor President Wilson originally supported her bill, once suffrage was won women's organizations rallied around it. By means of a barrage of telegrams, letters, and petitions, with a Republican Congress in power in 1921, the Sheppard-Towner Act was passed. Funds appropriated were meager, however, and when a women's voting bloc failed to emerge in the mid-1920s, Congress was able to discontinue with impunity the Sheppard-Towner Act (stigmatized by critics as "the women's law"). So long as Sheppard-Towner was law, however, obtaining matching funds, state by state, became a major activity of the WJCC's state legislative councils.

In addition to pre- and postnatal care, a second goal for the social reformers was to change the laws introduced in 1907, during an anti-immigrant fervor, that compelled a woman who married a foreigner to take on her husband's citizenship, even if the couple lived in the United States. Since citizenship was required for civil service jobs and elected or appointed office, these laws effectively disenfranchised certain married women. Worse yet, with the entry of the United States into World War I, some of these women, though born in and residents of the United States, found themselves classified as enemy aliens and their property seized. Their numbers included several militant suffragists, as well as many other prominent women married to foreigners.[12] The WJCC's Maude Wood Park and Representative John Cable (R–Ohio) worked together on a bill to rectify these problems, and through vigorous WJCC advocacy, the Cable Act passed in 1922. The statute now guaranteed a woman's nationality independent of her husband's, although these women were not given full citizenship until the 1930s.

Child labor was the third arena for social reformers—and the most difficult. Exploitation of children had been a concern of women's organizations for over two decades. In 1922, Florence Kelley, head of the nongovernmental National Child Labor Committee, asked the WJCC for help in pressing for a constitutional amendment that would give Congress the power to regulate the labor of workers under eighteen. In June 1924, Congress passed the amendment and sent it to the states for ratification. Not unexpectedly, serious opposition came from manufacturers and farmers. But somewhat surprisingly, the Roman Catholic Church weighed in on the side of nonregulation as well, arguing in a paper promulgated by the Boston Archdiocese that the measure would "set aside the fundamental principles of states rights, and at the same time would destroy parental control over children."[13] By 1930, only six states had ratified the amendment.

Freeman suggests that a powerful claim made during the suffrage campaign—that women would use their votes to enforce moral purity—both strengthened and weakened the WJCC. Congress, she reminds us, genuinely feared what the "women's bloc" would do. Suffragists had predicted that women would use their voting power to "improve the political system." They were, so it was claimed, more pure and more selfless than men. And while suffrage was being debated in Congress, in those states where women had already won voting rights, they did appear to vote differently from men. In Illinois, women were voting en bloc for reform candidates. In other states, they joined together to defeat antisuffrage legislators.

But by the end of the 1920s, it appeared that women's enfranchisement had somehow "failed." Writing in *Everyone Was Brave: The Rise and Fall of Feminism in America,* William O'Neill says this was due in part to the fact that the Progressive movement declined just when women began to vote. He observes that for many suffragists, fighting for the vote had been more rewarding than getting it.[14] The push and pull of party politics did not fit their dreams. The experience of Winifred Starr Dobyns, first chair of the Republican Women's Committee, was typical. O'Neill describes her experience: "While the parties were willing to give women symbolic appointments, they were carefully shut out of the decision-making process. This was not so much because they were women as because they were amateurs who did not share the regulars' passion for office. The professionals reasoned correctly that once in the organization [women] could be controlled. [Their] nuisance value was gone. Not only that, [their] power for good was gone."[15]

Feminism in the Interwar Period

There are always exceptions to every generalization in politics, and in the postsuffrage era there were women who eschewed social reform in favor of equal rights for women, most notably the women who gathered around Alice Paul to press for an equal rights amendment. It could be argued—depending on one's preferred definition of feminism—that the National Woman's Party was the only postsuffragist organization that kept the "pure feminist" faith. Unwilling to undertake yet another state-by-state struggle to extend suffrage to a broader guarantee of equal rights, the Woman's Party offered a more radical solution to the piecemeal work of the reformers. It would be better for women to channel their votes into a political party of their own, argued one of the NWP's founders and benefactors, philanthropist Mrs. Oliver Belmont, than to become "servants to men's parties."[16]

Every year, beginning in 1923, the National Woman's Party introduced a constitutional amendment that called for equal rights regardless of sex. Unlike the NAWSA, however, the National Woman's Party did not garner wide-ranging support. It remained largely a lobbying group throughout the interwar period and on into the 1960s. Donations from benefactors such as Belmont, and legacies from other rich women, kept this early ERA advocacy group going. What the National Woman's Party lacked in numbers, however, it made up for in single-minded devotion to its cause and in perseverance. Alice Paul herself was of privileged background, elitist, often racially biased in her views. But she has to be credited for her understanding of the significance of a constitutional guarantee of women's rights and for her lonely leadership of a small rump group for nearly fifty years. Paul was still alive in the 1970s when some of us new feminists were beginning to celebrate the winning of suffrage with annual August 26 marches and parades. In Washington in 1970, I had a chance to meet her in person. I found her, in her ninth decade, as feisty as ever.

The difference between reformers and feminists became even more pronounced after 1923, when the Equal Rights Amendment was first proposed. It was not the first time in American feminist history, as we have already seen in Chapter 2, that women's rights advocates would disagree not just on strategy and goals but also on what it means to be a "feminist." And it would not be the last. Indeed, the argument over the ERA would surface again in the 1970s. In the 1920s, one side wished to extend *protective legislation* to working women; the other wished to establish *equal access* for those women who could take advantage of it. In the 1970s and 1980s, the issue was joined by those who thought that the Equal Rights Amendment would undercut the social protections afforded wives and mothers.[17]

Extending the arguments from justice and expediency, the National Woman's Party never considered disbanding. "It viewed suffrage as a step along the way to full equality, not an end in itself," according to Freeman.[18] In addition to lobbying for an ERA, the National Woman's Party pressed for state laws to give women equal rights in jury service, in domicile (the right to claim their own home as their legal residence wherever their husband might be living), in officeholding, and against laws restricting women's workload. But success in the states was rare; indeed, out of several dozen bills introduced into twelve state legislatures, only Maine and New York enacted laws giving married women their own domicile. Only Wisconsin passed the Equal Rights Act, one of the "blanket" equal rights bills designed by attorney Sue Shelton White of the National Woman's Party. Even so, the Wisconsin law included an exemption for "the special protection and privileges which [women] now enjoy."[19]

Such exemptions turned out to be the focal point of almost all the debate about the ERA from this time on because of the different interpretations, by feminists and women's advocates, of how this protective clause—and of how any kind of special legal consideration based on gender—would be used (and abused) by those in power. National Woman's Party members, equal rights feminists by and large, believed that such exemptions would be used to limit women's equality. And indeed, in 1929 the Wisconsin attorney general used the "special protection" clause that limited women's workload to exclude females from all legislative positions, the Wisconsin Equal Rights Act notwithstanding.

Thus, in addition to the state campaigns throughout the 1920s, the National Woman's Party believed it had to introduce a federal equal rights amendment into Congress. The party's logic was unassailable. ERA advocate Emma Wold put it this way: "If Equal Rights for men and women are to be secured during our lifetime, they must eventually be obtained through the only logical and permanent method, the amendment to the National Constitution."[20] What the NWP well understood and what social reformers pursuing individual women-friendly legislation did not is that legislative statutes can always be overturned by later statutes. If a floor of women's rights were to be enacted, it would have to take the form of a constitutional amendment.

But the 1920s were not favorable to sweeping equal rights legislation of any kind. Although World War I (like World War II) was presented to the American people as a way to extend freedom and democracy to the world's peoples, that war brought in its wake political backsliding and repression. Partly in response to the 1917 communist revolution in Russia (by 1923 the Union of Soviet Socialist Republics, the world's first all-communist state, had been established in Russia), partly because of a natural swing of the political pendulum, 1920s America turned to the right, and the movements that had been friendly to the feminists' cause also suffered decline. In many ways, the 1920s were like the 1980s, with "get rich quick" replacing social activism. And when the "bubble" burst with the stock market crash in 1929, the nation was too paralyzed to worry about women's rights.

Paranoia about Soviet communism played a major role in setting back women's emancipation. Typical was the publication in 1924 of a "spider web chart" purportedly originating with the Department of War (later the Department of Defense). The chart showed a malevolent spider (Communist Russia) infiltrating progressive organizations in America. In an accompanying article entitled "Are Women's Clubs 'Used' by Bolsheviks?" the text suggested that under the "generalship of avowed socialist Florence Kelley," the Soviets were using such fronts as the Children's Bureau to advance the purposes of the Kremlin. A month later the WJCC complained to Secretary of War John Wingate Weeks and threatened reprisals from 12 million women. Weeks admitted the chart had errors, insisted the librarian had not published it in her official capacity, and ordered all copies destroyed.[21] Although the WJCC won the round, redbaiting, as it began to be called, had more lasting consequences for women's organizations and women's causes. Funding under the Sheppard-Towner Act came to an end, and the child labor amendment was not ratified. Organizations began to withdraw from the WJCC, and their support of the child labor amendment dropped off even before the amendment was defeated. That fight exhausted the funds of the most prominent organization in the WJCC, the National Consumers' League, which then left the coalition.

Another link, then, between the first wave of women's rights activists and the second-wave feminism of the 1960s is the dependence of both on a climate of reform. Both movements were born during periods of change, when people were willing to look critically at slavery in the one instance, at social injustice in the other. But in periods of regression, especially when accompanied by political repression, the women's movement does not fare well. To the contrary, just as the first wave of women's activism grew out of temperance, abolitionism, and social reform, the second wave would emerge out of counterculturalism, the anti–Vietnam War movement, and civil rights. Reversals came when progressivism was no longer in vogue.

Flappers

Nevertheless, we must ask ourselves why young, college-educated, middle-class (white) women, women who would have been supporters of women's suffrage ten or twenty years earlier, did not identify with the movement for women's rights in any of its guises. For the truth is that younger women joined neither the League of Women Voters nor Alice Paul's NWP. They were not looking to become "educated voters" or to join any picket lines—not on behalf of birth control or the child labor amendment, not even on behalf of themselves.

Many younger women opted, instead, to be flappers—the 1920s version of the "liberated woman"—putting their personal sexual and social freedom ahead of their own and their sisters' civil empowerment. In the 1920s, women started smoking cigarettes, going out on dates without chaperones, and driving cars. The Roaring Twenties, as they are called, were also the decade in which the sexual revolution began in earnest in America. That revolution had a lot to do with the unchaperoned mobility provided by the automobile, and it signaled, as far as researchers can document, the beginning of the end of premarital virginity. No one who studies the 1920s can doubt that an extensive shift in customary habits was in the making. Instead of restricting the intake of alcohol, Prohibition loosened morals. Otherwise law-abiding young people frequented illegal bars called "speakeasies." For them the term *scofflaw* was coined, meaning someone who deliberately flouted the law.

Flappers got high, one might say, on personal freedom, fashion, and travel, and those who were unmarried started going to work, which enhanced their personal freedom and enlarged their personal resources still more. In Chapter 4 I examine working-class women, women whose opportunities were expanding but whose politics did not yet encompass women's issues. For now, it is sufficient to note that young, economically privileged women began to experience superficial equality, enough perhaps to account for their shortsighted unwillingness to unite politically to maintain it.

The 1920s also ushered in a period when college became a more common prenuptial experience for the middle-class girl. Indeed, more women were achieving educational distinction in proportion to men in the 1920s than for decades afterward. But for the most part, the high achievers chose not to marry, and, as we shall see, the Depression and World War II eroded women's rights as well as women's accomplishments. How much that slippage has to do with the disappearance from history of suffrage activism we can never know. But as far as the next generation was concerned, within twenty years of the passage of the Nineteenth Amendment, the entire struggle was virtually erased from American history. Locate a high school or college history text published between 1940 and 1975, and count the number of historically significant women described. Chances are there will be only four—Betsy Ross, Amelia Bloomer, Carrie Nation, and Eleanor Roosevelt—and the choice tells us as much about America's view of women as about these women's lives.[22]

The Great Depression

Another factor affecting the survival of equal rights feminism between the wars was, of course, the economic depression precipitated by the 1929 stock market crash but also fueled by the environmental disaster of the Dust Bowl. The Great Depression brought a decade of bankruptcy, farm foreclosures, poverty, and unemployment in its wake. A crisis of this magnitude makes all other matters appear trivial in contrast. When millions of people of both sexes are unemployed, standing on bread lines, about to lose their homes and farms to unpaid mortgages, they will not have the time or the sentiment to worry much about equality of rights between the sexes.

In like manner, feminists found it difficult to defend their issues during the 1980s even in progressive circles when nuclear war seemed just one international crisis away. As we see in a discussion of women, militarism, and war in Chapter 11, women's issues are quickly made to appear trivial in the face of national emergencies. The political truth is this: To launch and maintain a successful women's movement require not just passion and people but also *circumstances* that favor progressivism but do so in a period of relative national security and well-being. This is not to say that women's rights are a luxury. No feminist would allow that.

Rather, how political movements fare depends greatly on history as well as leadership.

A number of measures were taken during the Depression that cost women many of their earlier gains. Professional married women were the first to lose their jobs after factory workers whose plants went bankrupt and farmers who lost their land to indebtedness. This was due to Section 213 of the National Economy Act of 1932, the first of several bills initiated by the Roosevelt administration to deal with the economy. Section 213 made it illegal for both husband and wife to work for the federal government at the same time. Soon school boards and some private industries followed suit, laying off women who were married to working men. Called by the women in Roosevelt's own party the "one black mark" against the administration (which otherwise had a good record on women), the act forced sixteen hundred married women to leave government service between 1932 and 1937, when the act was finally repealed.[23] Franklin Roosevelt, as it turned out, was more in tune with public sentiment than with the women in his party. In 1936, a Gallup poll showed that 80 percent of those questioned believed a wife should not work if her husband held a job.[24]

Women and World War II

The 1940s brought with them World War II, which ended the Great Depression but was otherwise a mixed legacy from the point of view of American women and women's rights. On the one hand, young single women were recruited for military service as uniformed personnel and nurses. Women who remained on the home front could compete (absent men) for liberating and well-paid wartime jobs. With 12 million men lost to the workforce because of war, noncollege women were temporarily able to leave female job ghettos in laundering, waitressing, household work, short-order cooking, and farm labor (in the case of minority women) and enter the well-paid, secure, unionized positions that opened up in manufacturing. Many professional women enjoyed newfound opportunities in law, medicine, government, and management. Many wives tasted economic independence for the first time. On the other hand, American women who came of age in the 1940s experienced a kind of existential inferiority because they missed the searing experience of their generation: to have served directly in World War II.[25] Excluded categorically from an event that took on mythic proportions in the minds of the public, they would find it difficult to compete in the postwar world with the men who had served.

After the war, in novels, in movies, in the news, and in the ranks of government, men who fought in World War II—no matter whether they had played poker behind the front lines, as Richard Nixon had, or risked their lives to save their buddies, as John Kennedy made sure everyone knew he had—were bonded by an experience women could not match. Women's lives changed, too, in their work and in the demonstration of their capacity for sacrifice and for valor. But nothing in their experience was mythologized as was life on the fighting fronts. In the long run, the absence of women from the theaters of World War II would postpone for a generation their integration into public life.[26]

Not just John Kennedy and Richard Nixon, but Gerald Ford, George Bush, Robert Dole, Joseph McCarthy, and hundreds of other men, of all parties and political persuasions, emerged from World War II with a leadership experience that translated easily into political capital. Immediately after the war, though younger than their political opponents, they had and used a compelling argument in their campaigns for office: If they were grown up enough to have risked their lives for their country, they were grown up enough to run it.[27]

Conclusion

Even though there was more feminist activity in the 1920s, 1930s, and 1940s than has been previously documented, equal rights feminism lost credibility as a progressive movement among the working class, social reformists, and younger women—without whom, under some kind of unifying political umbrella, there could be no feminist activism after the Depression and the war. Indeed, when we pick up the story of feminist activism beginning again in the 1960s, we see that the old arguments—equal rights versus protection—and the old divisions between white women and women of color, and between the classes, continue to exist. But before leaving the postsuffrage period, I want to convey to those who started school after 1970 what it was like to grow up during World War II in what ought to have been the afterglow of the first wave of feminism but which, because of limited access to that history, virtually disappeared from public view.

In 1947, at age twelve, I joined an organization of young women that, among other services, tried to provide a little Christmas cheer for poor children. As part of our training for a lifetime of volunteering, we were encouraged to collect used toys around our city, repair them, and then distribute them. It is clear to me now, although it was not then, that ours was a do-good activity, as opposed to a more political one that would have gone to the root of the reasons we had poor children in our community. In any case, we worked on the toys and stored them in an old, seemingly abandoned building, mysteriously called the Women's Institute.

For me, working in the Women's Institute was like coming upon an archaeological find. Why, I wondered, was it called the Women's Institute? And why had it been abandoned? Something important must have happened there, for the place seemed haunted by history. I must have spent a great deal of time (it was my first women's history project, one might say) sniffing around and looking for remnants of the building's past. I asked everyone who came in and all the neighboring merchants what it had been used for. Who had built it? Who had paid for it? But nobody knew. For as long as anyone remembered (and this was the late 1940s), it had been vacant.

I have since learned that the Women's Institute of Yonkers, New York, was part of, if not the suffrage movement itself, then that enormous, energetic social reform movement that women had spearheaded during the Progressive era at the turn of the century. I would have loved to have known this in 1947. I would have loved to have studied the history of these women, of their projects, and of their building, but no one—not even my American history teachers—gave me access to their story. There was not even a plaque in the building reading, "Dear little girl, if you should happen upon these rooms, here's a story you should know." I could have learned much from such as plaque, but it was not there for me or for my friends to read, and I think that absence caused me, much later, to study women's history and politics.

What we children did know of the movement for women's suffrage was caricature. Typical were Marx Brothers comedies that often featured an old and always unattractive suffragist as a figure of derision. Groucho would lean his head on her ample bosom in his funny way, as if it were a shelf. Altogether, the suffragist was a parody of a bullheaded female, oversized in every respect, pounding on a table to make her now comic point about women's rights. Any young woman growing up in the 1940s who had ever had a glimpse of those women would have wanted to distance herself from them and from their movement. Was this a plot to erase honor from early feminism? Or was this just the consequence of feminism's being out of style?

We know now that the women's movement did not fall apart after suffrage, but we do not yet understand fully the dynamics of its near total eclipse, why two decades later all that energy and accomplishment had virtually disappeared from public memory. Was it *backlash*, a term Susan Faludi employs in describing the conservatism of the 1980s?[28] Or *counterrevolution*, the term Kate Millett prefers? Whichever, it is urgent that we understand this, lest it happen again.

4

Women at Work

POLITICAL ACTIVISTS DO NOT LIKE TO ADMIT IT, but sometimes the most profound changes in the course of human events are not political at all. That is, they are not driven by new visions, crafty leadership, political organization, or any particular political action. Rather, "metaforces" may be driving history forward, metaforces that, like rising or ebbing tides, make historical change inevitable. Sometimes these metaforces consist of nothing more than technological innovation, such as the availability of birth control in the early twentieth century. Sometimes, they involve a massive shift in how people live and work. When Karl Marx offered his theory of "dialectical materialism" in the mid-nineteenth century, he intended to overturn his contemporaries' cherished notions of how and what causes historical change. In place of the "idealism" of prior thinkers—the notion that ideas shape human events—he found historic significance in the daily "materialism" of life. By materialism, Marx meant how property is defined and distributed, what people do for a living, how and by whom they are compensated, and who benefits from the "surplus value" of their labor.

Historians of the future may conclude that, despite the enormous effort that fueled both the "old" and "new" feminist movements in America, the most significant improvements in women's lives and options came about not because of the *ideas* of the women's movements or the battles for suffrage and equality with men, but because, through contraception and readily available abortion, twentieth-century women (at least in the industrial West) gained control over reproduction and with it, control over their lives. A second factor—driven more by industrialization, urbanization, and modernization than by any particular political agenda—gave first working-class and then middle-class women economic independence by making it possible and acceptable (and now, necessary) for them to work outside the home. Although as a political historian, I resist the oversimplification that the development of birth control and the availability of labor force participation *by themselves* emancipated women in our times, I must concede, as must any observer, that their significance is undeniable. If not by themselves, then certainly in conjunction with politics, they made a difference. In this chapter I trace the influence of one of those factors—women at work.

What we notice first when we leave the political arena and concentrate on how women made a living is that even in periods of low political activity—in the postsuffrage era, for example—women continued to make gains in employment. Between 1880, forty years before suffrage, and 1940, women's participation in the American labor force increased steadily, culminating in a precipitous influx of women into manufacturing and other male-dominated industries during World War II. Their participation dropped off sharply after that war but began to rise again in the 1950s. One question that concerns us in this chapter is how to account for the steady increase both in women's employment opportunities and in women's willingness to go to work.

Definition of Work

Women have always worked—inside the home. They took in laundry, farmed and privately sold the produce from their barnyards and gardens, took care of children—theirs and other people's—made clothing, put food by, took care of elderly parents and relatives, sewed, ironed, cleaned, and cooked. But the official definition of labor force participation is "work outside the home for pay or profit," and thus the bulk of women were not included in the labor force in the decennial censuses for a long time.[1] In other words, the "labor force" is an arbitrary categorization designed for keeping a census and for keeping track of who's "working" in America, but this definition effectively excludes women from many privileges associated with "work," such as unemployment compensation. Because the housewife has been considered merely an economic and social appendage of her husband, explains economist Barbara Bergmann, she was not taxed and therefore not eligible, like other workers, for social security and health insurance.[2]

It is one thing to exclude from labor force participation the work women do in their own homes; it is quite another to exclude the work women do as "domestics" in other people's homes, a job category that historians think may have accounted for as much as 60 percent of African-American women's nonfarm employment until 1940.[3] Nevertheless, even under the government's strict definition of work, more and more women were entering the workforce incrementally, for different reasons and for different kinds of work.

Let me add one further note about data gathering in labor force analysis. There are two ways to understand labor force participation. One statistic concerns the *percentage of all women* (usually counted between the ages of sixteen and sixty-five) who are working outside the home. Another statistic concerns the *percentage of the workforce* that at any one time is female. The first statistic could approach 100 percent if all women were working. The second will probably never rise much above 50 percent since women are about 50 percent of the population. The discussion that follows refers mostly to the *percentage of all women* who are working outside the home.

Who Works: Debunking the Myths

The best way to describe women's participation in the labor force from the late 1880s to the present is as a slow revolution, but a revolution nonetheless. Not all women entered or stayed in the labor force for the same reason or for the same amount of time. Thus, the first question we must ask is, Which women are working? To answer this question, it is useful to sort adult American women into three categories: (1) American-born women of color and immigrant women, (2) single white women under the age of twenty-five, and (3) married white women age twenty-five and older. We do not distinguish between single and married women of color and poor women because they have been more likely to work outside the home whether married or not.

After slavery, African-American women, both single and married, often became tenant farmers (called sharecroppers) with their husbands.[4] From the farm on which they were working, they might move into the household as domestic help. Later in the nineteenth and early twentieth centuries, it became possible for a young black woman to attend an all-Negro college and teach in a segregated southern school; there was also employment in the growing service or food industries. Immigrants, especially northern Europeans, might also become domestics; southern European women tended to do factory work in textiles or tobacco.[5]

Single white women usually had greater opportunities as a result of their higher-class status. By the mid-nineteenth century, for example, young white women were entering the nursing profession or graduating from teachers' colleges and going on to teach in the public school system. With the invention of the typewriter in the 1880s, office work was revolutionized. We now think of the office work as a "pink-collar ghetto,"[6] but before the 1880s the office was usually populated by males. Because (it was argued) the typewriter had small keys to suit a woman's smaller fingers, it was an appropriate female instrument, and this technological innovation by itself opened up office work to women. What used to be a dark and dingy place for scribes and clerks was billed as a pleasant place for females to work. The so-called Gibson Girl, a turn-of-the-century pinup, was dressed not in a bathing suit but in a long woolen skirt, with the cuffs of her long-sleeved blouse covered in a kind of "dainty" to protect her and her blouse from the ink stains of office work. The Gibson Girl was the "emancipated woman" of her time.[7]

The next change involved an increased labor force participation on the part of white, middle-class, *married* women, who beginning in the 1920s would work after their children went to school. Married white women's employment pattern—work-motherhood-work—would stamp itself upon employers' perception long after women began working for longer periods of their lives. (The point is that it is never correct to talk about "working women" without specifying their race, class, age, level of education, immigrant status, and time period in which they worked. Nevertheless, some generalizations can be made. such as this one: As the twentieth century wore on, more and more women began to work outside the home for longer and longer periods of their lives.[8]

Labor Force Participation

If one generalized about women at work, the facts would look like this: In 1900, about 20 percent of women (age sixteen to sixty-five) were working as defined by the census. In 1920, that figure grew to 23 percent; in 1940, 28 percent; and in 1945 (the height of World War II), 36 percent. In 1947, it was back down to 32 percent. In 1950, the figure was back up to 34 percent; in 1960, 38 percent; in 1970, 43 percent; in 1980, 52 percent; and in 1994, 60 percent.[9] These figures document the trends I have described: (1) the percentage of women working outside the home increased steadily from 1900 to 1940; (2) there was a steep increase during the war years both in the number of women in the labor force and in the percentage who must have been married; (3) even before the war about 25 percent of all women were working, more than was generally reflected in the popular culture of the day; and (4) within ten years after the war more women were working than ever before. These data challenge the prevailing myths about women that they were always part-time workers and that they worked for little extras (what used to be called pin money).

Women at Work

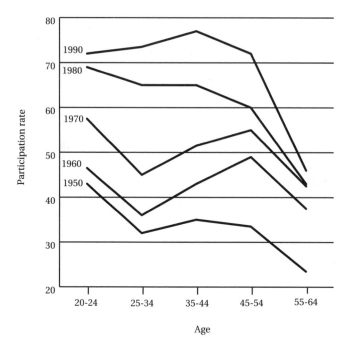

FIGURE 4.1   Female Participation in the Labor Force by Age, 1950–1990.
SOURCE: From Sheila Ruth, *Issues in Feminism: An Introduction to Women's Studies,* 3rd edition (Mountain View, Calif.: Mayfield Publishing Co., 1994), p. 324.

If we look specifically at the age at which most white women worked, we note that until at least World War II, except for women who never married, most married women worked before marriage, took time off to bear and raise children, and then returned to the workforce at least until their husbands retired (see Figure 4.1 for a graphic description).[10] The reason for this pattern appears to be obvious: Women between twenty-five and forty-five are more inclined to stop working to raise families. But if we look at this pattern over several decades, we discover that for the past half century American women who "retired" for childrearing stayed home fewer and fewer years. This was in part because they had smaller-sized families as birth control became more available from the 1920s to the 1990s, in part because work became increasingly appealing to women and women became increasingly appealing to employers. The problem, however, is that employers still believe that women will take off long periods of time for childrearing, even when the statistics no longer support this assumption.

Where Women Worked

During the pre–World War II period of gradually increasing employment for women, the one sector in which women were *not* finding jobs was in large-product manufacturing. Immigrant and poor working women were always welcome in the textile and tobacco trades (largely situated in Massachusetts and Georgia) because of their nimble fingers. More likely, it was also because these industries did not pay well, exploited their workers, and were not easily unionized. Chivalry in nineteenth-century America stopped at the factory door. Women received no special compensation or arrangements for their "delicacy," except that they earned lower wages.[11] In mining and heavy manufacturing, of course, the barriers to women were the degree of strength and stamina required for physical labor and the sheer brutality of the working conditions. But another reason women were not welcome, not even those willing to (or having to) work hard to support themselves and their families, was that mining and heavy manufacturing were the first to unionize, which in turn forced their management to pay higher wages and provide benefits and job security. From a working person's point of view, these were the best jobs available, but entry was highly competitive, and women did not successfully compete.

Traditional accounts rarely depict manufacturing jobs as the best jobs. Historians (like their readers) tend to bring the prejudices of their own middle-class origins to their work. So manufacturing jobs are seen to be dirty, repetitive, and unattractive. However, from a working person's point of view, unionized factory work used to provide job security, relatively high pay that increased with job seniority, benefits, and the chance to engage in collective bargaining with management. The American people were made to think that women had to be coaxed into factory jobs during World War II. My research suggests this was not the case. Working-class women, employed as laundresses, short-order cooks, sharecroppers, and domestics, flocked to manufacturing jobs once they became available. The question is not *why* they went to work in manufacturing but what the circumstances were that caused them to "voluntarily" leave those jobs when the war was over.[12]

Supply and Demand for Women Workers

How is it that so many women came into the workforce over a sixty-year period (1880–1940) and that there were jobs for them to fill? In many ways, women's increased labor force participation was a matter of simple economics. The nation was growing, and there was a *demand* for more and more workers that not even an open-door immigration policy (until 1921) could quench. As the nation's output grew, sales at home and abroad followed, fueling a demand for even more workers. Also, as the century progressed, increased automation (up to and including today's computer operations) made it possible for more and more women to find work in industries that had once required hard, physical labor. Finally, there is in our American economy a steady shift from manufacturing to service industries. Today, 52 percent of America's gross national product (GNP) is derived from the service industries that are particularly welcoming of women directly serving customers: health care, food preparation, education, hospitality-related businesses, financial services, communications, and information management. Only 48 percent of the nation's GNP is still derived from manufacturing. So from the "demand side" of the labor-economic equation, it appears that in the past one hundred years America changed the way it made its living, and women were as well or better suited to the newer industries as men. This was not yet the case on the eve of World War II. But with the drafting of most nonfathers under the age of thirty-five—12 million males at the height of that war—a burgeoning economy needed even more women to work.

The other side of the supply/demand equation has to do with increasing supply. Why were women suddenly more available to work outside the home?[13] One overriding need, of course, was for additional income. With the likelihood of divorce increasing steadily over the past sixty years, women were becoming heads of households, and in an increasingly urbanized society where errant fathers could simply "disappear," women needed to work simply to support themselves and their families. Another factor that contributed to the increasing supply of women workers is what economists call the "opportunity cost" of not going to work. Women who were able to complete a career-oriented education found the "cost" of staying home, that is, the "income forgone," hard to justify. Two additional societal changes also played a role: smaller families were more common, and the work that full-time mothers had traditionally performed in the home, like clothes production and food preparation (from basic materials), were being taken over more and more by industry (in economists' language, being displaced to the market).[14]

So in classic economic terms, the *supply* of women willing and able to work and the *demand* for their labor were increasing in tandem. Moreover, supply to some extent contributed to demand, and demand to some extent contributed to supply. Massive dislocations—such as the Great Depression in the 1930s and World War II in the 1940s—perturbed these trends, but the trends were there nevertheless. From this point of view, the recruitment of women to war work was less "unnatural" than the country was made to believe.

Society's Response

Despite an increase in the numbers and the percentage of women working outside the home—from 1.2 million to 12 million by 1940—little public recognition of the gradual but revolutionary influx of women into the workforce made its way either into popular culture or (with the exception of protective legislation) into public policy. The "head of household" was still a man, and "wives" were nonworking "helpmates" of their husbands. In one sense, government and the media simply refused to acknowledge this "evolutionary revolution."

A new pastime in the 1920s was the movies. In Molly Haskell's book-length review of the roles women played in film, she finds that, even though young women were shown to be working outside the home, for the most part neither they nor anyone else took their work seriously. And the more glamorous the leading lady was, the less likely she was to be employed.[15] Then, as now, working-class women (and men) were rarely portrayed at all, certainly not as heroes and heroines. This denial in popular culture continued (with some interesting exceptions that Haskell documents in her book) right up until the 1960s.

Even as women took shorter and shorter midcareer retirements from the workforce, working women still had difficulty convincing their employers that they were serious about their work. In the perception of their employers and in popular culture, despite wage-earning status or satisfaction from work, women would always put family responsibilities ahead of work responsibilities and may in times of stress stop working altogether. A woman might be bright, skilled, and committed, with much employment potential, but in the mind of the typical employer she remained for decades a temporary worker and not worth on-the-job training, employer-sponsored off-site schooling, or any other kind of long-term investment.

To some extent, the assumption of women's temporary status in the workforce reflected both fact and perception, even though these gradually diverged. Insofar as women did take time away from their jobs, they lost significant career advantages, especially if they were absent or only partially employed between ages twenty-five and forty, when important career moves are made or solidified. One of the early arguments for social security, for example, was the concern on the part of middle-class men that their widows might have to work at low-level entry jobs (or worse yet, as domestics) to support themselves. This prospect was so awful to contemplate that Congress was willing to establish federally guaranteed survivors' benefits for widows and dependent children as early as 1935. There was little recognition that some women did work as domestics every day, and there was even less regard for the economic welfare of women who became heads of households through divorce.[16] Widows surely deserved society's support, but if a woman was divorced or indigent, our policies suggested, it must in some way have been her fault.

The lag in perception of women's contribution to the American economy continues to this day. According to Alice Kessler-Harris and Karen Brodkin Sacks, writing in 1987, the single most important structural transformation in the American economy is increased female employment and increased male unemployment. (This is both the result and, social scientists would argue, the cause of the breakdown of families because it alters the power structure within families.) With 8 million American families headed by women, the issue of women's employment is no longer peripheral either to their lives or to that of the nation.[17] But that is getting ahead of our story.

Protective Legislation

Although America between the wars was "in denial," one might say, of women's increasing labor force participation, there was recognition that women who were working needed some protective legislation that regulated the conditions of work, such as hours, rest periods, and lifting limits. It was a long-standing American tradition that private business not be regulated. The due process clause in the Fourteenth Amendment was interpreted for decades by the Supreme Court to mean that corporations, as well as individuals, could not be denied their rights. Among the corporate rights was freedom to negotiate any labor contract. From this perspective, laws that protected women and children from exploitation and from egregious working conditions on the job were unconstitutional. But beginning in the 1870s, a number of states began passing laws limiting hours children could work and forcing corporations to limit weights lifted and night work of women employees. The Supreme Court under Justice Louis Brandeis, in a series of historic decisions handed down between 1907 and 1914, allowed these laws to stand. And thus a climate for protection was put in place.[18]

Increasingly, more states passed laws regulating, for example, the number of hours that women could work or requiring that couches be provided for women's "monthlies" in ladies rest rooms and seats for women's "tender pelvises" on the assembly line. Other laws mandated that women not be asked to lift more than thirty pounds (though this amount varied by state) and, if they worked a second or third shift, that women be driven or accompanied home at the employer's expense. Most of this legislation was rooted in the perception of women's vulnerability, both to excessive physical demands on their bodies and to threats by men. Protective legislation did indeed protect women, but it was also used to lock women out of better-paying jobs, particularly in manufacturing. In other words, women were discriminated against by the very laws that were supposed to protect them. Protective legislation cut both ways.

When the Equal Rights Amendment was introduced in Congress for the first time by Alice Paul's National Woman's Party in 1923, it was immediately perceived to threaten protective legislation. If there were an equal rights amendment, or so it was argued, all those special considerations that protected women on the job would be invalid. Equal rights would be taken to mean equal risks and equal responsibilities. It was for these reasons that the League of Women Voters and other organizations in the reformist tradition opposed the Equal Rights Amendment *on behalf of women.* In the 1970s and 1980s, some women leaders would oppose the elimination of protective laws on these same grounds. Myra Wolfgang, for example, vice president of the Hotel and Restaurant Workers Union, responded to the reintroduction of the ERA in 1970 in classic terms. "Working overtime may be fine for lady lawyers and other members of the [Business and Professional Women's Clubs]," she said, "but it isn't fine for women working the laundries in the hotels, restaurants and on the assembly line." For members of Wolfgang's union, hour limitation laws protected them against obligatory overtime so that they could have time at home.[19] In 1925 quite as much as in 1970, many saw the ERA as a class issue: a middle-class piece of legislation meant to be exacted at the expense of, or on the backs of, working-class women.

As regards women at work, then, two contradictory phenomena persisted throughout the interwar period. One was the general politics of denial: More and more women were working, but society was not acknowledging this as involving any kind of cultural or role change. The other was the issue of class, dividing those who wanted to protect women from the harshness of working-life conditions from those who wanted equality for women in wages and job access. So began a conflict that would be played out over the next few decades.

The War Years, 1941–1945

By the time the Japanese bombed the American naval base at Pearl Harbor on December 7, 1941, called "a day that will live in infamy" by President Franklin Roosevelt, 12 million American women were already in the workforce and 25 percent of all American workers were women.[20] Most of these women were single, divorced, widowed, or older—mothers with young children were still not a major component of those working outside the home for pay or profit—having to work, not working for "fun."[21] Yet the war, with its nearly insatiable appetite for workers on the home front as well as soldiers in the field, would change the lives of previously employed women quite as much or more than it would change the lives of the previously unemployed men—but not necessarily, in the long run, for the better.

The tragedy—and the story that needs to be told—is that, contrary to popular myth, World War II may not have been the boon for women it is generally assumed to have been. Certainly for some women, ballooning paychecks, union membership, and job security in wartime manufacturing were welcome, and while women of color decreased their share of domestic service, large numbers of them were able to flee farm labor, kitchen, and laundry work to those centers of war production where jobs and, even more important, training could be had.[22] War work brought more money and more job satisfaction than these women had ever believed possible. One African-American woman who had gone "clear across the country" to be trained as a pipe fitter to work in the shipyards remembers the "thrill" of watching a ship she had helped build go down the plank and pass the test of seaworthiness. She and her coworkers "launched" three ships during the war, but she was unable to keep her job or get a comparable one, despite her training, once the war was over. And she was not unique.[23]

As feminist historians have now incontrovertibly documented, women war workers were the first laid off and the last rehired as the war drew to a close. Fear of postwar unemployment meant that the demobilization of the nation's 12-million-member armed forces had to be accompanied by separation of women war workers from their jobs. Many of the women war workers did have job seniority by dint of years worked and union membership, and they were promised postwar employment if not at the same job, certainly for an equivalent salary at the same company. But after the war, management, state government, and the women's own unions combined to drive the women out of the well-paying jobs they had come to cherish.[24] What was "best for the boys" was for the "ladies" to give up their jobs to returning soldiers and go back to their homes as they had promised to, according to a union leader in a collage of Pathe News clips from the 1980 film *In The Life and Times of Rosie the Riveter*. "We were never his *workers*," complains one "Rosie" of her wartime boss, in the same film. "We were only his *girls*."

The entry of women into industries and occupations previously reserved almost exclusively for men was the most striking labor-market development of the war period.[25] One indication that women entering war work were not from the "idle middle class"—as the propaganda movies portrayed them—but from lower-income populations instead is that as openings for women in wartime jobs increased, the overall numbers of women in domestic service showed an immediate decline. But many of the lower-level jobs that African-American women were able to vacate during the war were filled in certain sections of the country by Chicanas. Mexican-American families in the Southwest who had survived the wave of deportations initiated during the Depression years now sent their wives and daughters to work in nonunion manufacturing or as domestics. Marta Cotera draws our attention to the wholesale removal of the garment manufacturing industry to the Southwest during the 1940s, done largely to capitalize on the availability of low-priced female labor.[26]

The question, then, of why so many women went to work during World War II is the wrong question to ask. Many women were working all along, just not in manufacturing jobs. But it was the question that tended to be asked—and answered by women's "patriotism," their "loneliness" with husbands and sweethearts away, or their having "nothing better to do." The real question is how the women who had benefited from access to industrial jobs fared after the war when these jobs were no longer available.

Standard history books afford us a glimpse of the era's third favorite stereotype (after GI Joe and the leggy pinups with which GIs used to adorn their barracks and their fighter planes). She is "Rosie the Riveter," with movie-star looks, hair pulled up in a colorful bandanna, sleeves rolled high, ready to take rivet gun in hand. Everyone knows Rosie. She had not worked before the war. With "her man away fighting," however, and "not much else to do," she was cajoled into taking one of those dirty wartime jobs—out of patriotism and boredom (or both). Attired in new-found overalls and bandanna, she riveted away for the duration of the war, dreaming of a time when she could return to her home and tend to her domestic chores (see Illustration 4.1).

This was the image promoted by the government and the media. The film *The Life and Times of Rosie the Riveter* exposes the image-making regarding working women during the war. In an expert interweaving of excerpts from wartime newsreels, the film makers contrast the mythic "Rosie the Riveter" with six real-life Rosies, three white women and three women of color. As the film editors make quite clear, 1940s newsreel clips intend to give the incorrect impression that the government had to actively recruit women to war work. The clips show recruiters breaking up idle women's bridge games to remind them of their patriotic duty. The real Rosies report on film that they had to be recruited not because they were idly playing bridge, as the newsreels display, but because they had never before thought that they could be trained for and employed in manufacturing. In view of the urgency of the war, many state governments relaxed or simply did not enforce the protective legislation on their books that would have kept women from taking industrial jobs.

Illustration 4.1   Rosie the Riveter. Courtesy of the Smithsonian Institute.

This, together with some federally supported child care centers, enabled women to move into skilled labor that had previously been out of their reach.

The newsreels and magazines of the day portray the mythic Rosie as a nonworking housewife or, if working, as a baby nurse or a store clerk. She had to be cajoled into factory work either out of guilt for "our boys' wartime sacrifice" or in competition with her neighbor. Above all, the ads and brochures go out of their way to assure women that war work, particularly work in factories, will not impinge on their femininity. "Washrooms will be provided, and you will leave your place of work looking like 'business girls'"—a reference to office personnel. Conspicuously absent from the newsreel propaganda is any reference to money. Yet as the real-life Rosies tell the film maker in the live interviews that make up the bulk of the film, good pay and job security (and not washrooms and pretty overalls) were what made war work attractive.

With hindsight and the benefit of feminist historiography, the film makers help us see what was really going on in the 1940s. First, there was more denial of the very existence of a working class of women who were permanent members of the labor force and, like men, were always looking for a better-paying job. Second, there was little acknowledgment of the importance of money to women as a means of self-emancipation.

What Really Happened to Rosie the Riveter?

The myth of Rosie the Riveter continued to be cultivated even after the war was over. Women were supposed to have been grateful that they no longer had to work in industry, happy to be able to return to their homes and to "make babies," as one of the real-life Rosies says in the film. Certainly, they were not supposed to keep those wartime jobs and most definitely not supposed to make trouble. My research, done with Lisa Anderson, indicates that women were laid off when wartime production stopped and, by means of collusion among management, their own labor unions, and state government, effectively kept from returning to high-paying industrial employment.[27]

Government and the media launched a powerful campaign to persuade women to return to their homes. The Pathe newsreels of the time again provide the evidence. Women were told that "this job belongs to a soldier." They were constantly reminded that returning soldiers had been defending the country overseas, and now they deserved their jobs back. Second, most wartime plants closed in the months immediately after the war to retool for a peacetime economy. Almost all employees were laid off—they were told "temporarily"—while the owners made this transition. Employees collected unemployment insurance and expected to be rehired, but when rehiring began, women war workers were not welcome.

At first, the women were not suspicious. They were certain they would be rehired because of their "seniority"—an important benefit won by unions prior to the war. But a new kind of seniority superseded theirs, a seniority awarded veterans based on their time in service. Although such policy was understandable in terms of the nation's gratitude to its returning soldiers, nothing was done then or later to compensate women war workers for the loss of their jobs. Immediately after the cessation of hostilities in 1945, governors and state legislatures moved to enforce or tighten protective legislation that had been relaxed between 1942 and 1945 because of the demands of wartime production. Thus, women who had done heavy work during the war were suddenly informed they were not strong enough to do the same work after the war; women who had welded and riveted were no longer "qualified" because of lifting or second-shift scheduling.

In fact, returning veterans were given three advantages over the women who stayed behind. First, anyone working on a job before Pearl Harbor was treated as though he had worked without interruption for the duration of the war, accruing seniority no woman war worker could match. Second, for men who decided to change jobs or even to relocate after the war (and the great migration to California began in 1945), veterans were given preference in hiring (a kind of affirmative action). They were awarded extra points, for example, on civil service exams. And finally, Congress passed the GI Bill of Rights, giving veterans free postsecondary education and a monthly stipend if they returned to school.

As much as these initiatives rewarded returning soldiers and helped the economy, they also had the effect of locking working women out of better-paying jobs after the war. Worse yet, because of the prevailing wartime myth that Rosie the Riveter had not wanted to work anyway, there was no acknowledgment of wartime workers' plight. No one was asking questions about the real Rosie the Riveter—the working-class woman who needed to keep on working—because as far as popular culture was concerned, she had never existed.

Why did women not fight back? This was the question that took Lisa Anderson and me to union grievance files at the United Auto Workers (UAW) Union archives as we tried to piece together the story of what had really happened to Rosie the Riveter. In examining those files, we discovered that, indeed, forcibly demobilized women did try to fight back, but even where a local union official was sympathetic, the women's parent union (in the cases we studied, this was the United Auto Workers) defended the rights of working men over working women.[28] In addition, there was no organized, aggressive feminist movement to take up Rosie's cause. Few laws on the books had even been violated by the forcible layoffs of women or the preferential hiring of male veterans after the war. Absent a feminist movement poised to defend the rights of working women, Rosie the Riveter was doomed to fall back on the work she had done before the war. As one African-American woman in the film observed ruefully of her return to kitchen work in an airport restaurant after the war (referring both to her gender and her race), "I could always get a job in a kitchen; they save those jobs for us." Finally, there was a return to "normalcy." In the minds of most Americans, normalcy meant men at work and women in the home. Women were still assumed to be not serious about employment.

The 1940s represented an era in which American women were more active in the world of work than ever before, but although they had some limited opportunities, most women did not experience America at war the way men did. They had not fought. They had not risked their lives (in great numbers). They had not died in defense of their country. Thus, they achieved only temporary acceptance both in the world of work and in the corridors of business and government. In the 1950s, as we see in Chapter 5, there was a return to earlier values, a reinvention of a "feminine mystique," which would prevail until, with its exposé by Betty Friedan, a second wave of feminism exploded into national consciousness.

5

Betty Friedan and the Feminine Mystique

ALMOST EVERY WOMAN OF MY GENERATION can remember where she was the day she first came across Betty Friedan's book *The Feminine Mystique*.[1] Judith Saidel, executive director of the Center for Women in Government at the University of Albany in New York, recalls that in 1963 she was completing her senior year at Wellesley College. In her course on the social and intellectual history of the United States, her professor had invited the students to choose one book from a list of end-of-course readings for a final discussion. On that list was the just published *The Feminine Mystique*, a blistering account of how American women had been stymied in their progress toward equality in the years after World War II. The professor did not recommend the book especially strongly, but the title intrigued the graduating senior, so she bought it and took it with her for a weekend of reading and study at a friend's house north of Boston. "I was lying on a hillside," she recalls,

> enjoying the spring weather, occasionally gazing out at the ocean, thinking only vaguely of what I would do after I graduated, when I began reading *The Feminine Mystique*. I couldn't put the book down. I almost forgot I was supposed to read it for a course. It was riveting. As I worked my way through Friedan's chapters on Freudianism, on "sex-directed educators," and on the "selling" of marriage and motherhood, I realized that much about my life that hadn't made any sense could be explained by her theory. My view of myself and that of all the people I was until then trying to please was caught up in a "feminine mystique." My sense of life's possibilities changed that day, and they have never been the same.[2]

Friedan's was not the first book in the postwar period to describe how women's lives and their perceptions of their lives were shaped by a gendered society. Shortly after World War II, Simone de Beauvoir, a French intellectual, had written *The Second Sex,* an analysis of how, in the cultural tradition of Western culture, women were objectified by male writers, sometimes as "angels," sometimes as "sirens," sometimes as "witches," always as something "other" than humankind.[3] That experience of "otherness," de Beauvoir argued in brilliant critical prose, shaped women's views of themselves, sapped their creativity, and denied them a legitimate "voice" in Western culture. In certain intellectual circles on both sides of the Atlantic, de Beauvoir's book was known and much discussed. But the average American woman was not familiar with her analysis. Friedan's book, with its focus on the American woman's experience, spoke more directly to millions of women in this country, changing their understanding of their lives as it did Judy Saidel's and mine and Friedan's herself.[4]

The "feminine mystique," as Friedan defined it, was an ideology perpetrated (*intentionally,* she argued) in the post–World War II period to return women to what a male-dominated society liked to think of as their "rightful place." Sold to the American public by the media, by social and behavioral scientists, and by sex-directed educators, this ideology caused women to be brainwashed into believing that success and happiness lay only in their traditional wife and mother roles and that the adventure of workforce participation during the war was a deviation from the norm. "Norm" in sociological terms means typical, average, or approved; "norm" in the period of the feminine mystique, said Friedan, was extended by the newly popularized Freudian psychology to mean "normal." Any woman who resisted the pressure to return to hearth and home was deviant, abnormal, sick.

History is often cyclic, and it can be argued (and has been) that after a war as extensive and brutalizing as World War II had been, there is a desire on the part of a nation's population to return to "normalcy"—that is, to the political and domestic arrangements that predated the war. Add to this our nation's determination to avoid the economic dislocations and unemployment that had accompanied the Depression in the 1930s, and one could argue that it was necessary for the mental health of the men who had fought in World War II, and for the economy as a whole, that women free up jobs for returning GIs and soothe their troubled warriors' brows. Thus, the consumerism that first appeared as an "ism" in the postwar period, along with a celebration of the family, can be seen as an inevitable consequence of the sacrifice and deprivation caused by four years of war.

Nevertheless, as noted in previous chapters, women's rights were expanding in the years before and during the war and need not have been stunted after 1945. The need to produce war matériel brought to working-class women (and especially women of color) industrial opportunities they had never had before. Equal pay became common in those industries where women ably took over "men's jobs," and the "career woman" was celebrated in fiction and film. Women made steady gains in higher education, the professions, and government from 1920 onward. During the sixteen years of Franklin and Eleanor Roosevelt's stewardship, women moved into advisory positions, and thirty-three prowomen bills were passed by the wartime Congresses.[5]

Five to 6 million women had joined the workforce during World War II, 2 million in high-paying heavy industry. Even if women did not organize afterward to fight for their jobs or to gain compensation from the federal government for their wartime efforts, even if they did not retain their margin of opportunity in labor, in 1950 twice as many women were working as had been in 1940, and by 1952 women's labor force participation—albeit in lower-paid clerical and administrative jobs—exceeded what it had been during the peak of the war. And the majority of these working women were married. All this was new and could have signaled the real revolution ahead.[6]

But it is also true that most women had been on the home front instead of the battlefront during World War II and therefore could not lay claim to the heroic experience many soldiers used later to win jobs and congressional, and even presidential, bids.[7] Nevertheless, the 1950s could have brought advances to women in politics and industry. No longer were there the pressing social dilemmas that had marginalized the suffrage movement after 1920. The Roaring Twenties were over. The country had been humbled by a depression and a second world war more devastating than the first. Finally, firmly beyond the tumult that discouraged women from bringing their charges out in the open, one might have expected some positive changes after the shock of World War II wore off.

But that was not to be the case. As Friedan documented, and as every young woman growing up in that period knew well, within fifteen years of the end of World War II the realities and the perceptions of woman's place had reverted to a norm closer to that of the Victorian period than to that of the early twentieth century. To give just a few factual examples: There were more American women, proportionate to men, graduating from college in the 1920s than in the 1950s, and there were more women in Congress in the 1940s than in the 1950s. Not only was the extension of women's rights decelerated in the period after World War II. It was also as if something had thrown the whole process into reverse.

So powerful was the feminine mystique, and so effectively was it "sold" to the American public, that a collective amnesia seemed to settle over the nation, obscuring all the previous history I have sketched so far. In a history textbook I was assigned to read in college in the mid-1950s, the entire women's suffrage movement was compressed into a single chapter called "Prohibition and Other Events." A whole generation of postwar children grew up without any knowledge of the struggle for the vote or for other rights. Women in the 1950s enjoyed more legal rights than their foremothers, and the availability of birth control devices (not yet the pill) presented more opportunities for women to shape their lives. But without knowing the history of the struggle, young women could assume, as most of us did, that an enlightened country had simply *given* women the vote in 1920 and that there were no more battles to be fought.

Quite the contrary was true. Women were still denied equality before the law in employment, in pay, and in access to professional schools. There were quotas on women students in most medical schools. The nation's most prestigious law schools did not admit women at all, and women journalists, with few exceptions, were relegated to the "women's pages" or to women's magazines. There was hardly any scholarship on women that did not fit neatly into "home economics," and even though women were recruited to companies dealing with household products and cosmetics, the independent woman business owner could not be competitive in a world where banks could deny women credit simply for being women or for being married.

None of this was being addressed in the 1950s and 1960s, and had Friedan not provided her critique and her later leadership of a nascent new feminist movement, who knows how long it would have taken American women to realize they had been backsliding. On the eve of my graduation from college, the 1956 Christmas issue of the then widely read *Life* magazine, dedicated to "The American Woman," said it all: The ideal American woman was white and middle class and frivolous and spoiled and fun loving and materialistic and beautiful and boy crazy and—if not already living it—dreaming of wifehood and motherhood in middle-class heaven, the envy of her sisters all over the world.

Bringing long hours of scholarship and a highly intuitive sensibility to the reality of the life of "privileged" American woman, Betty Friedan reported in her book that women in the 1950s were suffering a problem—the "problem that had no name," she called it—that they could neither identify nor deal with. How was it possible, she asked herself, that women were complicit in their own disempowerment? Where did this new "feminine ideal" come from, and who had a vested interest in perpetuating it? These questions brought her to the New York Public Library and to the field, where she conducted interviews. Once she had answers to her satisfaction, she began promoting her ideas. And the consequences were enormous. A population of women that had been virtually depoliticized was made to look again at the choices it had made, this time in political terms. Her analysis became part of the dogma and one of the founding themes of the second wave, and her energy, as promoter and later cofounder and first president of the National Organization for Women, gave the movement its first victories in the legislative arena.

Thus, Betty Friedan is crucial to a certain class of women who came of age in the 1950s and 1960s and not just because she wrote a book that many women read and were moved by.[8] Her analysis actually changed the course of American women's history, first by identifying a phenomenon—the feminine mystique—no one had previously isolated or described, then by providing an analysis of how such a set of beliefs came into being, and finally, by giving the feminine mystique a limited place in history.

I personally responded to being of the "second sex" by leaving the country after graduation from college. In 1963, I had just returned and was trying to figure out why I was not more successful either as a journalist or as a graduate student. For me, reading *The Feminine Mystique*, handed to me by my mother in summer 1963, only a month or so after Judith Saidel had discovered the book on her reading list at Wellesley, the message was loud and clear: The set of beliefs that had begun in the aftermath of World War II and held sway while I was a college student did not have to be. Betty Friedan's book would change my life, too.

The Story of the Book

As is often the case with germinal thinkers, Betty Friedan did not set out to write *The Feminine Mystique* but simply to collect some survey data about her graduating class of 1942, which had left college in the middle of World War II. The occasion for her report was the class's fifteenth reunion. The year was 1957, and Friedan had been struggling for some years to maintain a career as a freelance writer while being married and bringing up three children. Battling what we would later call sexism in the feature-writing field, she found the women's magazines to which she was relegated unwilling to assign her articles of general interest. So when *McCall's* magazine asked her to write an article about what had happened to her Smith College classmates in the fifteen years since graduation, she accepted the assignment with alacrity.

She had not set out to be a freelance writer. She had studied psychology at Smith College and thought for a while of graduate school in that discipline but did some freelance writing instead. When she married and became a mother, she brought her full complement of intelligence and energy to that role. As Friedan recounts her history, she bought an old house in Westchester County, New York; fixed it up; bought another home and fixed up that one, too; and was in every sense a "supermom," all the while trying to work as a freelance writer. She found writing compatible with her domestic responsibilities. She could interview people over the telephone and work at her typewriter while the children slept.[9]

Her preference was to write serious features about women, if that was what the women magazines wanted, and about world news, science, and culture. But as she would document in her book, the women's magazines of the time were not just reflecting women's interests in the late 1940s and 1950s; they were defining women's interests for them. Unless she wrote about homemaking, travel, toddlers, beauty, self-help, or self-improvement, she had no market for her work. Query letter after query letter to *Better Homes and Gardens*, *Vogue*, *Family Circle*, and other women's magazines came back rejected. Unwillingly but pragmatically, Friedan learned to write what the women's magazines wanted.

The *McCall's* assignment appeared, at first, not too different. The magazine gave her the title and the article's theme: "The Togetherness Woman," expecting, as did Friedan herself, that in her survey and interviews with her classmates, she would find them knee-deep in "togetherness" (a catchphrase for 1950s family life), privileged, satisfied, and happy. Friedan agreed to the assignment and, well in advance of the reunion, sent her female classmates a detailed questionnaire asking about what life had been like for them, about marriage, about the birth of their children, about what had surprised them most about life after college, and about what they expected of the rest of their lives.

From their returned questionnaires, however, Friedan noticed a tantalizing pattern, nothing she had been looking for or had expected. Despite privileges and the protection provided by a middle-class family income, many of these women were deeply dissatisfied with their lives. It was not that they said so directly. But as a sometime student of psychology, Friedan recognized clues that all was not well in the suburbs. Later, in her follow-up interviews with classmates, she noted more serious symptoms of depression such as unexplained fatigue, lack of hope for the future, and lack of interest in the world outside their families. When she confronted her women subjects with her observations, they could not themselves articulate the cause of their distress.

Although the women she interviewed tried hard to repress this truth, taking care of husband, home, and children was not a fulfilling role—postwar propaganda notwithstanding. Friedan concluded that these women were suffering from more than "housewife's fatigue"—a syndrome the women's magazines occasionally wrote about. It was, Friedan thought, not at all physical in origin but a psychological response to being entrapped in a life and lifestyle supposedly the envy of the world (certainly the envy of America's less privileged races and classes), but not in itself fulfilling for "overeducated" women. The women Friedan surveyed and interviewed could not admit to any of this because if they did, the whole fabric of their lives would unravel. Society had placed such a strong emphasis on the role of wife and mother that to suggest one wanted *more* than that was abnormal—a virtual taboo.

And so Friedan's book began to take shape. It began with the problem that has no name and proceeded to name it—the feminine mystique—to document it, and to analyze its manifestations and its cause. In one stroke, Friedan took the problem from the realm of inner traits, where it could be dismissed as just another female neurosis, and exposed it as an ideology—that is, an artificially created belief system grounded (in good measure) in myth. Indeed, myths that are social in origin may be (and usually are) internalized by large numbers of people living in some common group, but they are only "true" so long as they are believed. Furthermore, as anthropologists know well, myths are neither accidental nor purposeless. Their function is to establish social control.

How did society come to believe that modern women, having been liberated from the physical hardships of preindustrial life and the exigencies of constant pregnancy, still belonged full time in the home? Juliet Mitchell, a British philosopher and social critic writing eight years after Friedan, proposed one answer to that question.[10] Mitchell wrote that in preindustrial times, adult women had had four time-consuming home functions to perform: production (of food, household goods, and the family's clothing), reproduction (six to eleven pregnancies over a lifetime), childrearing (of four to eight children), and the duties of helpmeet and wife. The Industrial Revolution and the shift of the population in Western industrialized countries from rural to urban areas, wrote Mitchell, had displaced production of food, household goods, and clothing from home to store; had reduced reproduction from full-time childbearing to the birthing of four or fewer children; and had limited childrearing to a shorter time span. To replace the lost functions, and to keep women from exploring their other capabilities, society had created new norms by which childrearing (even of a few children) and the companionate function (continuing to attract and please a husband) were elevated to represent the full-time fulfillment of a modern woman's femininity.

In the face of such pressure, what else could a modern woman do, whose husband was succeeding in the world of work, except turn her two remaining functions into life-fulfilling goals? Children would be fussed over, ferried around, and invested with their mother's own frustrated fantasies. Husbands would be seduced, cajoled, expected to provide a lover's attention. It is not surprising that in this setting, elixirs that promised "eternal femininity" found willing customers and that a $2 billion cosmetic industry began to flourish in America.[11] Meanwhile, the wife whose husband, either because of race or class discrimination, was not able to provide material-based "togetherness," not even to properly support a family, was made to feel deprived that she had to go to work. She, too, bought into the feminine mystique, wishing to enjoy the full-time wife-and-mother role and blaming her husband when his income made it impossible for her to do so.

Friedan (and Mitchell after her) documented what had been a sea change in American women's values and behavior in the short period from the end of World War II until the beginning of the 1950s. Two out of three privileged college women were dropping out to marry, according to a Mellon study of Vassar students; college had ceased to be a launching pad for a meaningful career. By 1956, Vassar women were defining themselves exclusively in terms of family. "They do not expect to achieve fame, make an enduring contribution to society, pioneer any frontiers, or otherwise create ripples in the order of things."[12] Marriage rates went up significantly during the period of the feminine mystique, just as the average age of marriage for women was going down. In the 1950s, for the first time in American history, the typical bride was twenty. Was this just a "return to normalcy," as the women's magazine editors claimed? Or was something more sinister at work?

The "Happy Housewife Heroine"

How much is our behavior shaped and constrained by the movies we see and the fiction we read? Being a writer and somewhat of an expert on women's magazines, Friedan had a hunch that the women's magazine editors had been major players in the effort to send American women back into the home. She began *The Feminine Mystique* with a content analysis of women's magazine fiction and general interest articles, contrasting story titles and plots, topics, and reader response to articles published before the war with those published afterward.

She looked at advertisements, how-to articles, photo stories, and profiles, but it was in fiction and general interest features that she located a 180-degree shift in emphasis. Sometime just after the end of the war, the women's magazines had turned domestic. Serious fiction by some of America's best fiction writers was replaced by formulaic stories, and the heroines, who had once included high-flying aviators, intrepid foreign correspondents, and interesting nonconformists, were suddenly either "happy housewives" or wanna-bes. Where current events and analysis of international affairs had once had their place in *Mademoiselle, Redbook,* and *Woman's Home Companion,* after the war "Life Adjustment," "Marriage and the Family," and "How America Lives" took over.[13]

The change in magazine fiction and general interest articles led Friedan to an in-depth exploration of how the expectations of what it meant to be a woman had become focused more on the home and less on "public" life. She reviewed the writings of prominent anthropologists, sociologists, and psychologists—those of Margaret Mead, Talcott Parsons, and Sigmund Freud in particular—and continued her interviewing of media and business leaders, educators, and even more women. In time, Friedan was able to trace a general shift in society's view of woman from active participant in all aspects of life to "specialist" in the home.

But the mystery remained. Why had the shift occurred? And who benefited from the feminine mystique as Friedan described it: Husbands who did not want their wives competing with them for status? Employers who could exploit their able women workers and pay them less, all the while telling them that their real purpose lay not in providing financially for their family but in putting a good dinner on the table? Whoever it was profited from women's passive acceptance of a segregated and second-rate status at work. Indeed, a European describing life in America in the 1950s said that the whole system rested on the "artificial buoyancy" provided by occupational segregation by race and sex. No matter how meager one's skills and incompetent one's overall performance, this observer said, if a person was white and male, he could not sink to the bottom because the bottom was fully occupied by women and non-whites.[14]

One other explanation, not entirely rejected by Friedan, is a quasi-Marxist one—namely, that capitalist society, particularly after demobilization, needed a full-time consumer class to drive up the demand for goods. What better "consumer" was there than a full-time homemaker and mother to buy the goods manufacturing plants produced? In fact, the 1950s did see an enormous upsurge in the manufacture and purchase of durable goods—automobiles, homes, home furnishings, appliances—goods that had been unavailable during the war years. Was that not stimulus enough? Friedan thought not. The feminine mystique, she concluded, was an artificial construct made up by manufacturers, in cooperation with advertisers and the media, to sell to the American public an ideal woman constantly available for shopping. "In a free enterprise economy," she quoted one unidentified market researcher as saying, "we have to develop the need for new products. And to do that we have to liberate women to desire these new products. We help them rediscover that homemaking is more creative than to compete with men. . . . We sell them what they ought to want."[15] Hence, Friedan concluded, the feminine mystique was the result of a conspiracy.

Alternatives to Conspiracy

It is tempting to try challenging Friedan's conspiracy theory. As mentioned, anthropologists tell us that after a war there is an almost atavistic urge to repopulate. America lost fewer soldiers than other countries in World War II, but the deaths of even three hundred thousand, together with the life interruption of nearly five years of war, could, by itself, have generated some kind of conservatism in gender roles. Men dreamed of home in their foxholes or on their warships, and women dreamed of having them home. This explains (even without the profit motive) the proliferation of single-family homes in the years after World War II and the emergence of the suburbs. That a great many men and women could not afford even the lowest-priced houses, and that many women had to provide sole support for their dependents, did not fit neatly into the American Dream is indisputable. But winning the war gave our country the right to dream its dream, however fanciful it might be.

Another explanation for the postwar reversion to prefeminist values is that American women won the right to vote with corresponding access to education and certain occupations without a thoroughgoing nationwide debate on men's and women's social roles. Given the complementarity of men's and women's roles in our society, there was no way to further women's rights and opportunities without calling into question the basis on which men claimed theirs. From this perspective, the achievement of the woman's suffrage amendment was but the first act in a drama that had to play itself out over time.

Women in Eastern Europe and the Soviet Union also found their "equal rights" to be hollow. There, equal rights for women had to be introduced from above by the conquering communists: in 1923 in the Soviet Union, in 1945 in Eastern Europe. Although women benefited much from freedom to divorce, abortion rights, equal access to employment, and more or less equal pay, many of those privileges were taken away when the government had other priorities. Abortion is a case in point. Abortion was eliminated altogether during the Soviet Union's labor power buildup for World War II. Afterward, Communist Hungary restricted abortion, too, when the government became concerned about low birthrates among Hungarians compared to Gypsies in that country.

Access to the professions and to powerful government positions also shrank in these countries as a postwar generation of men came to maturity. And, as everyone knows, Soviet and Eastern European men never took "equality" beyond the kitchen door. In *Soviet Women*, Frances du Plessix Gray makes quite clear that women never ceased doing double duty there because the introduction of women's "equal rights" was not accompanied by a true, far-reaching sex-role debate.[16]

From this perspective, the era of the feminine mystique was an important reminder of how little distance American women had really covered despite their suffrage victory. The new feminists' agenda picked up where the old feminists had left off: with an analysis and a bill of rights aimed at changing sex roles. Betty Friedan knew this intuitively. How else could we explain the central place in her book of her criticism of Sigmund Freud?

The Attack on Sigmund Freud

A centerpiece in Friedan's analysis of the origins and social control function of the feminine mystique was her treatment of the impact of Freudianism on postwar thinking about women and gender roles. Betty Friedan was the first but by no means the last of a whole line of feminists to take on Freud and his theorizing about women. What was the reason for this focus? Friedan and others believed that Freudianism, the popularization of the ideas of Sigmund Freud, was a key factor in the construction and enforcement of the feminine mystique.

Every society makes arbitrary (but politically useful) judgments about the distribution of tasks, responsibilities, and privileges to certain groups. These distinctions do not simply affect gender definitions. Roles, privileges, and handicaps are typically assigned to higher and lower "castes," as in premodern India; to conquerors and "natives," as under colonial rule; and to slave owners and slaves, as in the antebellum South. Historians have always understood that these distributions are enforced by the powerful over the powerless and are reinforced by beliefs—beliefs that African Americans, for example, were intended by God to be hewers of wood and drawers of water, beliefs about who is "primitive" and who is not, beliefs about "God's grace," beliefs about the biological basis of sex differences, and beliefs about what is "natural" and what is "against nature." In turn, these beliefs are woven into religious teachings and further enforced by religious leaders.

Friedan reasoned that as modern societies became more secular and religion lost its hold, something or someone else had to fill the vacuum. In the place of religion, she said, came the behavioral scientists, psychologists, and sociologists. Their arguments were couched in new language but were familiar nonetheless. Only the justifications and the punishment for nonconformity were new. In place of God's will came mental health and social stability. And in place of damnation came social ostracism, neurosis, and family instability. Coming from "experts," whom secularists respected in matters other than ethics more than they do religious leaders, the new belief systems were powerful, indeed.

Two of America's behavioral gurus were attacked in *The Feminine Mystique:* psychoanalyst Sigmund Freud, who found sex differences not just in biology (the phrase *biology is destiny* came to be a shorthand for a superficial reading of his views of women) but also in children's "natural" personality development from infant to adult, and sociologist Talcott Parsons, who believed sex-differentiated roles made for family stability.[17] Freud and Parsons had had their critics before, other experts who had disagreed with some of their findings or who had disputed some of their technical detail. But, except for Karen Horney, a Freudian disciple who had offered a more complex view of women's psyche, not before Friedan was Freudianism exposed as essentially conservative regarding sex roles.[18]

Among the earliest writings of the new feminists, Naomi Weisstein's famous paper "'Kinder, Kuche, Kirche' as Scientific Law: Psychology Constructs the Female" circulated in the feminist underground as early as 1968 and expressed with no holds barred the feminists' objection. Psychology, said Weisstein, did not just study women; it actually *constructed*, she said, a female psyche that fit with the discipline's self-serving view of how it wanted females to be.[19] Quoting psychologists whose writings influenced researchers and clinicians alike, she reminded her readers, who might never have heard of Bruno Bettelheim, Erik Erikson, or Joseph Rheingold, of what the "experts" were saying about women. Like Friedan's analysis, Weisstein's quotations informed and enraged her readers. For the Bettelheims, Eriksons, and Rheingolds were not just telling women how to behave; they were also telling women that anything less (or more) than their traditional behavior was inimical to society's health.

It had all started with Freud, who, as Friedan read aloud from passages of his work on platform after platform, saw the "motive force" of women's personality in "penis envy." The girl child's discovery of the anatomical difference between herself and her brother, according to Freud, caused her to feel that she and all other women (including her mother) were lesser beings, incomplete males. The wish for a penis was central to the Freudian view of women and girls. It explained why the "normal" female wanted a husband and (male) child as compensation, and it accounted for everything in her personality: her neuroses, her self-absorption, and her "lack of originality" and sense of justice.[20]

Accepting her penis envy as inevitable was bad enough for a woman. Not accepting it was worse. If she tried to compensate for her missing part by mimicking the life or ambitions of a man, she was then in the throes of a "masculinity complex," doomed to a life of sexual immaturity and frustration. Freud missed the point, said Friedan and other feminists. Girls and women *do* feel inadequate, but not because of a missing penis; rather, they see themselves as deficient because of missing privileges and opportunities for self-fulfillment outside the home—typical in the kind of male-dominated society in which Freud himself grew up.[21] Freud never wanted to change society; he sought to help adult men and women adjust to it. Hence, he was essentially conservative when it came to women and women's roles.[22]

But this still does not explain why Freud's theory had such a powerful influence on American popular culture decades after he had first published his "findings." Not many Americans read Freud; fewer still met directly with a Freudian analyst. But beginning in 1940, after Freud died, his ideas found their way into books people did read or at least heard about. One popularization, *Modern Woman: The Lost Sex,* a best seller in the 1940s, applied Freud's view of women to American feminism.[23] "Normal female traits are receptivity and passiveness," wrote the authors, "a willingness to accept dependence without fear or resentment . . . a readiness for the final goal of sexual life—impregnation."[24] It was the error of feminists to take women off "the female road of nurture."[25]

Reading Freudians on women today makes us realize how much feminism's second wave changed popular culture.[26] Forty years ago, respected and much-sought-after American disciples of Freudian psychology could make pronouncements such as these: "We must start with the realization that, as much as women want to be good scientists or engineers, they want first and foremost to be womanly companions of men and to be mothers."[27] Or, "Woman's . . . somatic design harbors an 'inner space' destined to bear the offspring of chosen men, and with it, a biological, psychological and ethical commitment to take care of human infancy."[28] As Friedan and Weisstein knew so well and helped the rest of us understand, this was no longer a science of human behavior. This was wishful thinking on the part of men in power presented as if it were religious dogma: "When women grow up without dread of their biological functions and without subversion by feminist doctrine, and therefore enter upon motherhood with a sense of fulfillment and altruistic sentiment, we will attain the goal of a good life and a secure world in which to live."[29]

The great failure of clinical psychology and the theories of personality on which it rested, said Weisstein, was that the "experts" were looking for inner traits without considering the influence of social expectations.[30] The question remained, as with the construction of the feminine mystique altogether: Why? Was it flawed thinking, too much reliance on clinical experience and not enough on experiment? Or were the experts merely doing their part in a centuries-long conspiracy to keep women in their place?[31] Betty Friedan thought she had an answer.

6

The Origins of the
Second Wave of Feminism

THREE STRANDS AND AN ACCIDENT

IT USED TO BE THOUGHT THAT THE SECOND WAVE of feminism in America burst upon the political scene out of the 1960s counterculture, having no particular links to our past. Terms such as *patriarchy, sexism, women's oppression,* even *women's liberation,* seemed to be original and without antecedents either in suffrage history or in any other kind of radical or progressive thought. But slowly we are learning much more about the origins of the second wave and are in the process of revising our understanding of how it came to be. First, we know now that the long period of feminist quiescence was not entirely without activism and that many women (in the 1930s, 1940s, and even 1950s) found their way into left-wing and labor politics, where they championed peace, international cooperation, desegregation, unionism, and even equal pay.[1]

Second, at least three different groups of women were brought to a similar consciousness of women's secondary status in America during the 1960s—thanks to three very different sets of circumstances—so that within a decade there was a sizable population poised to take part in feminist politics. And third, many activists from the 1930s and 1940s, the Women's Bureau's Esther Peterson, Representatives Martha Griffiths and Edith Green, Eleanor Roosevelt's protégée Pauli Murray, and labor union leaders such as Dorothy Haener and Myra Wolfgang lived on into the 1960s to provide experience and encouragement when it was needed most.

Aided by the almost accidental passage of a powerful new federal law (Title VII of the 1964 Civil Rights Act) forbidding discrimination on the basis of sex in employment, the new women's movement was able to capitalize on the breadth and depth of its initial support, on its connections to other progressive movements, on a remarkable display of sisterhood across the generations, and on spunk.

The first of the three groups that would come together to populate the second wave were the older, professional women, whom President Kennedy and later the governors appointed to the various Commissions on the Status of Women. These women were most likely not feminists to start out with, not radical, not revolutionary either in lifestyle or politics. But as they themselves have testified, they were radicalized by their own investigations.[2] The second strand was composed of Betty Friedan's housewives and mothers—previously nonpolitical and largely white—who read and responded to *The Feminine Mystique* and provided a potential membership in the tens of thousands for the new women's organizations. And the third strand came out of the student Left late in the 1960s. In a curious replay of the first wave of feminism, radical young women invented "women's liberation" as a way of venting their frustration at the roles assigned to them in the student movement.

The story is as significant as it is fun to tell (especially the part about the legislative "accident") because it illustrates the somewhat haphazard way in which diverse groups of 1960s women came together to transform gender and politics in America. In truth, members of the three strands would not ordinarily have perceived themselves as having much in common. The upper-strata professional women (and some men) who were appointed, first by President Kennedy, then by their respective state governors, to formally investigate the status of women in America were not the kind of people who started movements or, for that matter, participated in them. We need more research on the commissions and their members, but of some things we can be reasonably sure: These women would not have been comfortable striking, sitting-in, or participating in the "guerrilla theater" that would characterize new feminist politics in the late 1960s and 1970s.[3]

Nor could anyone have predicted that economically secure but frustrated housewives would find much in common with the radical younger women coming out of the 1960s "free speech" and student movements. Yet thanks to the popularity of Friedan's book and her nonstop traveling during the mid-1960s, millions of American housewives were readier than they might have been to consider themselves "oppressed"—a new concept brought into political parlance by the civil rights and student movements—and not simply "discriminated against."

The Status of Women Commissions

When John F. Kennedy was inaugurated in 1961, he was proud of the fact that he was the first president to have been, as he put it, "born in this century." And to make the point he brought to his cabinet and to his inner advisory circles other young and (he thought) brilliant men— "Men of the New Frontier," he called them. The New Frontiersmen later became known less for their brilliance than for their bungling (they were the group that got the country deeper into the quagmire in Vietnam), but at the time of Kennedy's inauguration, they were the "best and the brightest" at hand—and they were all men.

"Where are the women on your New Frontier?" Eleanor Roosevelt is purported to have asked the president shortly after the inauguration, and as a way of redirecting her ire, he is supposed to have agreed to establish a president's commission on the status of women with her as chair. There is some controversy over whether it was, in fact, Eleanor Roosevelt who pushed Kennedy to establish the Commission on the Status of Women. But if, indeed, she put that question to Kennedy, Roosevelt was way out in front of most of us women, who were too caught up in the magic of "Camelot" to notice its essential machismo. Certainly Eleanor Roosevelt was then, as often during her late husband's presidency, far ahead of her time.

The story is probably not that simple. More likely, it was Esther Peterson, head of the Women's Bureau in the Department of Labor, who, in her eagerness to retain protective legislation for working women, wanted to stall any revival of the ERA. Historians Leila Rupp and Verta Taylor have found a letter written by Peterson to the secretary of labor urging the creation of a presidential commission that would, she hoped, "substitute constructive recommendations for the present troublesome and futile agitation about the 'equal rights amendment.'"[4] Pro-ERA women, in fact, saw through this ploy and denounced the commission as anti-ERA.[5]

There is no evidence that John F. Kennedy knew or cared much about either equal rights for women or protective legislation. Perhaps establishing the commission was his way of assigning others to investigate an issue that he did not wanted to think about himself. But what matters is this: With a presidential commission in place, there would be, for the first time since World War I, an executive task force with a mandate to study any and all aspects of the condition and the status of women in America.

The fifteen women who were appointed to the president's commission (along with eleven men) were women leaders but not—and this is an important distinction—leaders of women. Rather, with some exceptions, they were among the small minority of American women then in their forties and fifties who had beaten the odds, one might say, to become lawyers, economists, social workers, senior professionals in child welfare agencies, and, through their commitment to public service, political appointees. Despite the absence of an organized feminist movement in this period, small groups of women in every part of the country enjoyed high status and even personal power.

The kind of women who eventually populated the commission were not revolutionaries. They were "over thirty"—the threshold at which the counterculturalists of the 1960s used to characterize people they could not trust—highly educated and, for the most part, well off. There would be significant differences in age, style, appearance, and class between Kennedy's commissioners and the women on the political Left who would flock to women's liberation some years hence. For the commissioners, men as well as women, promulgating an "equal rights" agenda was not as important as combating the disabilities women suffered as a corollary of their sex, disabilities such as poverty and abandonment. Most of the commissioners did not (yet) acknowledge that "equality" would remove the disabilities suffered on account of sex. Having described those disabilities, they were reluctant to take the next logical step and challenge women's traditional roles.[6] Their first report, in fact, while calling for "an amelioration of the several disabilities suffered by women," at the same time reaffirmed the "primacy of women's maternal role."[7]

But I am getting a little ahead of the story. The commissioners' first order of business was to become informed. They had a great deal of work to do because little factual information was routinely collected about the status and condition of women in America. Apart from the Women's Bureau in the Department of Labor, no federal or state agencies were responsible for gathering data about women. And the Women's Bureau was not aggressively feminist in its orientation. Women's employment and pay records, for example, were routinely compared (by education and skills level) by the bureau to those of other women's but not to men's; the cost of sex discrimination in employment, as in professional entry quotas, was never calculated.

Everyone knew that quotas limited women's access to professional schools and training, but government neither recorded nor proposed a lifting of those ceilings. Later, the very suggestion of a "quota" in the implementation of affirmative action would be met with hostility. Nor did the nation have any sense as to what percentage of women (and their children) were living in poverty. The social security system, erected during the 1930s, took reasonably good care of widows and orphans but not of women made single or children made poor by broken marriages. Remember, the Kennedy commission began meeting in 1961, a period still steeped in the feminine mystique, which maintained that "good women" married and stayed married; only "bad women" got divorced. Why should government take care of women who had brought poverty upon themselves?

The commissioners and their staff worked diligently until 1963, collecting data that would find its way into a final report to the president.[8] Customarily, commissions close their offices when their final report is done. But in 1963, instead of closing down, the President's Commission on the Status of Women recommended that the president appoint a permanent citizens' advisory council on the status of women and that the states create comparable commissions to continue the work. Eventually, fifty parallel commissions were formed that extended the investigation and documentation not just of women's "disabilities" but also of women's "unequal status."

This scenario is not unusual in Washington. One commission decides that it needs fifty more commissions, and bureaucracy proliferates. But in this case, proliferation meant that where there had been about one hundred commissioners and staff working on women's issues in the period 1960–1963, now there might be more than one thousand nationwide. Besides providing an agenda for change, the commissions brought "visibility and legitimacy to women's concerns," Susan Hartmann writes in her history of this period, and, more important still, provided an intensive "consciousness-raising" experience for most of the women involved.[9]

The state Commissions on the Status of Women worked until 1966, when they were called to Washington—all fifty of them—to compare their findings. By 1966, a new antidiscrimination law, Title VII of the 1964 Civil Rights Act, was being only halfheartedly implemented on behalf of women. When called upon during the meeting to pass some resolutions on the matter at hand, some—but not all—of the state commissioners wanted to move to a more activist agenda; others, deferring to their official mandate, balked. The conference divided, and resolutions were not admitted, but it was obvious to all that the commissioners had been stirred by their own findings. Nevertheless, most were not ready to step out of role. They would leave Washington once their reports had been filed and wait for a beneficent president to take care of the problems they had described. On the surface, they appeared to be good and obedient workers, but with hindsight we can see that even those who voted not to admit resolutions in 1966 returned home like so many hundreds of time bombs waiting to go off.

We have already met the second strand, the housewives that Betty Friedan wrote to and about, mostly of the middle classes, ten to twenty years younger than the commissioners and not nearly so prestigious or professional. Still in the throes of childbearing and childrearing, many of them, in reading Friedan's book, became aware of how confined their lives were within their socially approved roles as housewives and mothers and of how the "experts," the media, and their own trusted educators and psychotherapists had conspired to limit their options. Friedan's message was well understood. The feminine mystique was not universal but was rather a historical phenomenon with a beginning (circa 1946), a middle (the 1950s), and one day, possibly, an end. Women were not to blame themselves for the problem that had no name, but, Friedan all but said it, they were to find ways to liberate themselves. But these women did not yet know what to do or how to begin. They were just another set of time bombs waiting to be sparked into political action.

Women's Liberation

The third strand called itself women's liberation, but as the media began to report feminist activity more generally, the name became attached to the rebirth of feminism as a whole. One reason for the confusion is that women's liberationists—or, as they came to be known, derisively, "women's libbers"—tended to dominate the public's perception of the movement. They were never as organized as the other two strands, but they got more than their share of publicity, partly because of their "actions," partly because of their youth, partly because of the public's and the media's voyeurism. (Women's liberation was associated with "bra burning.") Although not coextensive with the movement as a whole, women's liberation was perhaps its most critical component.

The transformation of "movement women," as activists in the various organizations associated with the civil rights movement, the anti–Vietnam War movement, and the Students for a Democratic Society (SDS) called themselves, into active feminists has been ably chronicled by Jo Freeman, Sara Evans, Pamela Allen, and other contemporary historians and sociologists.[10] Sara Evans locates the first stirring of women's liberation among women civil rights activists from the northern student movement who went South to participate in voter registration and public accommodation sit-ins in the 1960s. Evans was herself a white activist in the Student Nonviolent Coordinating Committee (SNCC), an organization of young people founded in the South in 1960 by African Americans to protest civil rights violations in their region. Martin Luther King Jr. had already emerged as a leader of the older generation, having conceived the Montgomery bus boycott in 1955. His work and the organization he founded—the Southern Christian Leadership Conference— eventually led to a sizable nonviolent movement for change among southern blacks and their supporters. King came to national attention at a stirring march for civil rights on Washington in 1963. His prominence and the publicity garnered by the Montgomery bus boycott brought thousands of young people South to help desegregation. Starting in the late 1950s and extending into the 1960s, northern teachers and their students spent summers riding interstate buses, registering voters, teaching in alternate "Freedom Schools," and serving as out-of-state buffers between black activists and local police.[11]

The mass migration of northern students to the South had a searing effect on the white women students who had volunteered. In 1962, the target was Greensboro, North Carolina, where there were sit-ins—white students accompanying African Americans to previously segregated lunchrooms. The sit-ins spread throughout the South and provided organization and activity for more northern (and southern) students who wanted to "do something" for civil rights. While working with local leaders, hundreds of white women involved in these activities had their eyes opened to the realities of activism and of police retaliation. During Freedom Summer in 1964, when eight hundred white student volunteers went to Mississippi and hundreds more to other states to assist with voter registration, three activists were killed, allegedly by the sheriff and deputy sheriff of Neshoba County. Many of the female volunteers returned to the North "seared by an experience that marked a turning point in their lives," writes Sara Evans.[12] The first casualty was their naive expectation that as women they would be protected by local authorities even as they were challenging that authority. A second shock was their discovery of sexism in SNCC, a sexism exaggerated by racial and sexual competition between black and white volunteers.

Northern white female volunteers were in awe of their black sisters in the movement, especially such larger-than-life figures as Fannie Lou Hamer, cofounder of SNCC and of the Mississippi Freedom Democratic Party. But because the white and black women had different priorities, they had different experiences. "Most of the white student volunteers were given little responsibility and were assigned to do office work or to teach. . . . That may have been partly because it seemed safer to give [whites] less visible jobs," writes Flora Davis.[13] However, female volunteers "were often judged on their looks—and some were rejected for being too outspoken."[14] Racial and sexual tensions between white and black volunteers finally resulted in SNCC's decision to ban whites altogether from its organization. These issues foreshadowed later conflict between white feminists and women of color as "women's libbers" sought to organize in the late 1960s.

In the North during this same period, further stimulated by the nation's growing involvement in the war in Vietnam, activist students organized, first in defense of free speech at the University of California at

Berkeley, then for more general political change. The organizations that benefited most from this growing disaffection among America's college population were SDS in the North and SNCC in the South. By the mid-1960s, there was a massive migration under way of college-age men and women wanting to participate in antiestablishment political actions—the closest America has ever come to hosting a youth movement.[15]

But the experience was not a positive one for all. Beginning in the mid-1960s, Sara Evans writes, groups of movement women began to experience alienation largely because of their secondary status within the movement—most especially because of the kind of public and private roles they were being assigned. Bear in mind, these young women had joined what they thought was a democratic revolution, one that would attempt to destroy all oppressive institutions in America, from segregation to the draft (in some quarters, it was hoped, even capitalism). Yet male domination of females in the student movement resisted change, even acknowledgment, even in the face of females' complaints.

As movement women began to circulate their thoughts on paper—some of them as early as 1965, when Casey Hayden and Mary King distributed a memo about sexual inequality within the movement at a staff retreat in Mississippi—movement men retaliated.[16] That memo, says historian Flora Davis, "may have done as much to ignite the women's liberation branch of the movement as Betty Friedan's book did to spark liberal feminism."[17] Indeed, when asked what position there was for women in SNCC, Stokely Carmichael, then head of SNCC, shot back in a phrase that was instantly quoted and requoted around the country, "The only position for women in our movement is prone!" And when draftable men began burning their draft cards at great personal risk, a bumper sticker appeared in university parking lots advertising the fact that "Girls don't say 'no' to men who won't go." As one movement male acknowledged in Sara Evans's tracing of the roots of women's liberation in the civil rights movement and the New Left: "Women made peanut butter sandwiches, waited on tables, cleaned up, got laid. That was their role."[18]

Soon papers were giving way to meetings (the women called them women's caucuses) and then requests for time at national meetings for consideration of women's concerns. But radical men—even men of great devotion to the dispossessed—were not willing to provide time at their meetings for "womentalk." In a move that may have eventually cost them half the membership, radical men hooted women off their platforms and drove them into organizations of their own. Jo Freeman remembers that the first paper, "Women's Liberation—a Step Beyond Rights," offered at an SDS convention in 1965, was laughed off the floor. Typical was the formation in 1967 of the "Chicago Women's Liberation

Group," perhaps the first in the country to use the term. The group had
tried to bring up a resolution on women at a "new politics" convention
and was told it was "too insignificant" to be worthy of the conferees' attention. The same treatment was afforded a women's group at an SDS
meeting in Seattle, and similar events began occurring elsewhere. Black
women in SNCC did not join these women's liberation groups as frequently as white women, according to Paula Giddings, because "most of
them saw the race issue as so pressing. They had little attention to spare
for the question of sex."[19]

Unlike the women in the first and second strands who were relatively
new to the concept of oppression and the politics of grassroots organizing, movement women, once aware of the contradictions in their organizations on the Left, knew exactly what they had to do and in what
order: They had to analyze and organize. Every bit of the analysis they
had absorbed of racism and imperialism could be applied to their own
situation. Books and articles with titles such as "Woman as Nigger," *off
our backs, Up from the Pedestal, Bread and Roses*, "The Politics of Housework," and *Our Bodies, Ourselves* spoke volumes to women trapped in
domestic or secondary roles.[20]

Women on the Left discovered that men were in charge of the antiwar
and desegregation movement's all-important debates on theory and
strategy and that only men were permitted to lead overall. The women's
role was to service the men. The irony was suddenly all too clear. However distant the women might have imagined themselves from the suburban middle-class households for which they had only contempt, here
they were, underground women, playing out those same wifelike roles.
As Sara Evans tells it: "Superficially it seemed that women had never
been more invisible [in SDS]. All of the working papers and documents
for the conference were prepared by men. Hardly a woman spoke in ple-
naries and only a tiny number in workshops. [Once a woman] chaired
one tumultuous session, and as she attempted to gain control she was
booed and hissed."[21] In local work, too, women were assigned clerical
tasks, while the men got on with the real business of organizing.

I had such an experience while working for Eugene McCarthy's
anti–Vietnam War campaign for president in 1968. As a volunteer in New
Hampshire helping to open storefronts for the McCarthy campaign, I,
too, was struck with how tasks had been assigned. Males who were a
decade younger and had far less political experience than me were out
in front planning strategy; we women were in back turning McCarthy's
off-the-cuff talks into press releases. It was not that our work was not
important. It was simply that age and experience made no difference;
every male activist saw himself quite naturally in charge and had little
respect for women's input.

Women's liberation contributed significantly to the theory and politics of the second wave of feminism. First, the New Left provided a training ground—movement women were already organized and knew how to organize others. Second, it provided a set of metaphors—"woman as nigger," "woman as underclass," "woman as object," "woman as minority" (in terms of status, not numbers). Finally, women's liberationists brought from the barricades a taste for bottom-up, collective political action and a talent for guerrilla theater—a way of making themselves heard that would enlarge, enhance, and leave its stamp on feminist politics forever after.

An "Accident"

Human events, as experienced political activists know well, are hard to fathom, hard to predict, and even harder to control. A case in point occurred one year after passage of the 1963 Equal Pay for Equal Work Act. In 1964, debate began on a major civil rights bill that was meant to rectify some of the injustices of racial segregation. John F. Kennedy did not live to participate in the congressional debates on his administration's wide-ranging civil rights initiative. He was assassinated in November 1963. But his vice president and successor, Lyndon Johnson, committed himself and all his political skills to its immediate passage. The bill, later to become the 1964 Civil Rights Act, had many diverse sections, called titles, each of which was designed to rectify long-tolerated segregation and discrimination on the basis of race, in particular. It was hoped that the act would eliminate ethnic and religious injustices as well. One title had to do with equal opportunity in education, another with equal access to public accommodations—the kind of issues the student activists had gone South to promote. But by far the most important and far-reaching title in terms of equalizing economic opportunity was Title VII, the section of the bill that made it illegal to discriminate in employment on the basis of race, religion, or national origin.

Not surprisingly, a number of legislators—particularly Democrats from the still largely segregated South—were opposed to the bill, and many conservative Republicans joined them in lobbying particularly against the employment section. Relations between employers and their workers were considered "privileged," and the "long arm" of the federal government was not supposed to enter into the hiring policies and practices either of corporations or small businesses. Of course, the privacy of those labor-management relations had already been compromised—by fair labor standards legislation, by the official recognition of collective bargaining, by the requirement that businesses contribute to unemployment insurance, by workmen's compensation, and by social security, all of which had been legislated as part of Franklin Delano Roosevelt's New Deal in the 1930s. But thus far, individual hiring and wage policies had remained, even through the Roosevelt years, untouched by regulation.

During the congressional debate on the civil rights bill, to make the point that businesses should not be required to meet equal opportunity standards in hiring, Representative Howard W. Smith, a Democrat from Virginia, introduced an amendment to Title VII that would have included "sex" as one of the prohibited categories. There is one (hotly contested) view that Smith may have been sincere in wanting to extend the "chivalry" of protection to white women employees, but most of his contemporaries and most historical accounts describe his amendment as intending to demonstrate the "ludicrousness" of the whole idea of applying equal rights to jobs.[22] If that was his motive, then he was outplayed. Despite the fact that there were only thirteen women in the 1964 House of Representatives and only one woman, Margaret Chase Smith, in the U.S. Senate, this group included some savvy parliamentarians, women of remarkable standing and perspicacity, who recognized in Howard Smith's amendment an opportunity to write a prohibition of gender discrimination in employment into the act.

Most of the liberal, pro–civil rights legislators, including one woman, Edith Green, a Democrat from Oregon, opposed Smith's amendment outright. Women might be deserving of employment protection, they argued, but in a remarkable replay of the debate over the Fourteenth Amendment, this was the "Negro's hour." A decade or more of civil rights activism, including the 1954 landmark Supreme Court decision that desegregated schools, was supposed to come to fruition in the 1964 Civil Rights Act. The act was President Kennedy's legacy. It should not be diluted by other issues. But other women disagreed. Martha Griffiths, a Democrat from Michigan, led four other congresswomen in a successful battle, first to pass Smith's amendment—not as a joke, but as a serious addition to the act—then to get the entire Civil Rights Act passed intact. Griffiths and her allies succeeded. The Smith amendment passed in the House of Representatives 168 to 133; and the bill itself, 290 to 130. Smith's strategy had backfired.

In putting forth her case, according to one scholar, Griffiths allowed herself an argument that foreshadowed problems when race and sex were in competition. Without the prohibition of discrimination on the basis of sex, she said, employers might hire black women over white women as a way of avoiding charges of racial discrimination.[23] But, as it turned out, Title VII would serve women of color quite as much as white women in its implementation.

The addition of sex to the prohibited categories of discrimination in employment was a great victory for women. While the handful of women in Congress must be given credit for the parliamentary maneuvering that made it happen, it was not a feminist victory. In 1964 (except for the continued lobbying of the National Woman's Party), feminism had not yet reemerged in any organized fashion. Rather, Title VII would be "on the books" for feminists to use once they arrived on the political scene. And until they did, the sex provision would be virtually ignored.

Victories in politics are not really won even when the desired law is passed. When Congress passes a bill, regardless of its length, the bill is not yet as specific as it needs to be in order to be enforced. An important next step is the writing of detailed regulations (called regs by insiders) that will set some agency in charge and guide enforcement. The congressional act is taken to reflect the will of Congress, but it is left to the executive branch to designate the procedures by which the goals of the act will be realized. Sometimes, as in the case of Title VII of the 1964 Civil Rights Act, the act or one of its titles is so far-reaching and complex that an altogether new agency must be created to act as regulator and enforcer.[24] Congress anticipated this in the case of Title VII and authorized the creation of the Equal Employment Opportunity Commission (EEOC), first to hold public hearings on what should be the regs for Title VII, then to conduct investigations, and finally, to enforce the new law.

In the beginning, for understandable reasons, the EEOC saw itself as responsible primarily for the enforcement of the racial discrimination aspects of Title VII. The head of the EEOC and some of the newly appointed commissioners viewed the addition by Congress of the sex provision as a distraction from the main provisions of the act. The thousands of sex-discrimination claims that flooded the EEOC in its first months of existence were left untended. Sonia Pressman (later Fuentes) applied to the Office of General Counsel at the EEOC in 1965. She immediately saw the potential of Title VII to ameliorate the problems of professional and nonprofessional working women and chafed at the commissioners' clear preference for race cases. As she puts it, "We had an agency [EEOC] with a mandate to prohibit sex discrimination . . . in a country that was not conscious of the fact that women were the victims of discrimination. After all, while the creation of the EEOC was in direct response to the movement for black rights in this country, there had been no similar movement immediately prior to 1965 for women's rights."[25]

One issue of importance only to women and not to racial or ethnic minorities was given particularly short shrift at the EEOC. This was the issue of sex-differentiated want ads. It was a long-standing tradition among U.S. newspapers and other journals to separate "Help Wanted—Male" from "Help Wanted—Female" in their classified pages in recognition of the fact that hiring and employment in this country were largely segregated by sex. But was this not an infraction under the new law? And why was the EEOC not writing regs to outlaw segregated want ads, asked

"Hire him. He's got great legs."

If women thought this way about men they would be awfully silly.

When men think this way about women they're silly too.

Women should be judged for a job by whether or not they can do it.

In a world where women are doctors, lawyers, judges, brokers, economists, scientists, political candidates, professors and company presidents, any other viewpoint is ridiculous.

Think of it this way. When we need all the help we can get, why waste half the brains around?

Womanpower. It's much too good to waste.

Illustration 6.1   Public service announcement denouncing gender-specific classifieds. Courtesy of the NOW Legal Defense Fund.

Pauli Murray, a member of the President's Commission on the Status of Women, at a meeting of the National Council of Women on November 12, 1966, in New York City. The want ads were not trivial. Not only did they reinforce existing discrimination, but also, since they were widely read even by young women not yet on the job market, their content lowered expectations and contributed to female socialization. (For an ironic response to these ads, see Illustration 6.1.)

Murray and Mary Eastwood from the Department of Justice had already written an article on sex discrimination and Title VII, provocatively entitled "Jane Crow and the Law."[26] Franklin Delano Roosevelt Jr., head of the EEOC, was not much interested in sex discrimination. His view of Smith's amendment was that the congressman had wanted to create "ridicule and confusion." Since the amendment had no legislative history (no hearings, no research, no public discussion), Congress's intent was unclear.

As for want ads, the EEOC initially ruled that employers could continue to run sex-segregated ads so long as an announcement appeared in the same section indicating that segregation by sex was done for the convenience of the reader. Fuentes describes this ruling as "ludicrous." Despite resistance from newspaper publishers claiming First Amendment protection against interference with the free press, pressure from outside forces eventually got the EEOC to view sex-segregated want ads as discriminatory.

But in 1966, the agency stonewalled, and Fuentes, Eastwood, and Catherine East, executive director of the now permanent Citizens' Advisory Council on the Status of Women (the coordinating arm of the states' commissions), solicited the help of Congresswoman Martha Griffiths, who had been instrumental in the passage of Title VII. Griffiths again came to the fore, delivering in Congress a scathing attack on the EEOC for its indifference to the "human rights of women."[27] The speech was circulated at the national commission conference in 1966, which led some of the state commissioners to draft a resolution demanding across-the-board enforcement of Title VII. When officials at the national conference told the commissioners they could not introduce such a resolution, some of them concluded that women needed an organization outside government, comparable to the National Association for the Advancement of Colored People, to lobby on behalf of women's rights. In fact, this was not the first time anyone had thought about such an organization. Fuentes had already made the same suggestion to Betty Friedan, and in what *The Feminist Chronicles* calls another "of the many historic linkups," Friedan had been following the problem of the want ads and had already made phone contact with Pauli Murray.[28]

The Founding of the National Organization for Women

Betty Friedan took time off from her nonstop lecturing on *The Feminine Mystique* to attend the 1966 state commissioners' national conference. It was in her hotel room that fifteen women decided to press the state commissioners to pass a resolution on Title VII enforcement and to demand the reappointment of Richard Graham, the only one of the four male commissioners who could be called feminist. In fact, the women had heard a rumor that Graham was not going to be reappointed because of the seriousness with which he took discrimination against women. The next day, officials of the state commission convention voted not to bring such a resolution to the floor. That afternoon, during one of the official luncheons, some of the women who had been meeting with Friedan passed notes to one another across the lunch table about meeting separately to take action. Days later, thirty women and men gathered to officially found the National Organization for Women to play just the role that Fuentes and other insiders had asked for: to press government from the outside to better enforce the regulations that were on the books. The willingness to admit men who were sympathetic to women's rights was the reason the founders chose the phrase *for women* for NOW's name instead of *of women*. Friedan's vision from the outset was that NOW's purpose was "to bring women into full participation in the mainstream of American society . . . in true and equal partnership with men."[29]

Of the thirty founding members, none was a member of women's liberation. Several had been active on the presidential and state commissions, others came from the federal government or from women's committees of the large labor unions, and one was a member of the NWP—providing a thin link to the past. The housewives Friedan was igniting with her book and her talks around the country would provide the new organization with a jump start in membership. At NOW's first formal meeting six months later, Friedan could take satisfaction from the fact that three hundred women had already joined. One year later, membership had quadrupled to over twelve hundred men and women, and there were NOW chapters in California, Illinois, Wisconsin, New England, New York, the nation's capital, and the South.

There is no question in my mind, having lived through these events (and having been a founding member of one NOW chapter in upstate New York),[30] that, although the women involved in the state commissions and the founders of NOW were angry and impatient with the EEOC's foot-dragging, they were not yet the "radical feminists" they would eventually become. Two of the founders left NOW soon after its founding in disagreement over an extension of the NOW agenda to include abortion, and they founded another, "less controversial" women's organization, the Women's Equity Action League (WEAL).[31] Others saw Title VII as a "mixed bag" for women. If protective laws were in conflict with the provision for "equal opportunity," would women workers be better off without them? Union women were not sure and retained their class-based preference for legislation that honored women's "difference" from men over legislation that promoted raw, unprotected "equality."[32]

When at our Cornell Conference on Women in winter 1969, Betty Friedan encountered Kate Millett and other New York–based feminist activists for the first time, there were clear differences in both the style and the substance of their respective agendas. Nevertheless—and this would remain the source of the power of feminism's second wave—for the most part they agreed to work together, and in time they united with older women, professional women, disgruntled housewives, and women renegades from the student Left to press for an ever more comprehensive and radical set of goals.

An example of the merging of these women's different styles is a process called consciousness-raising, a major contribution made by women's liberation to the women's movement generally.[33] In 1968, in meetings held by a group called New York Radical Women, women began talking about their personal lives in light of the oppression and limitations they were enduring because of their gender. Many of the women's basic assumptions about what it meant to be female were challenged by this discussion process, and their personal reflection led them to became more ardent and activist in their feminism. By better recognizing patriarchal oppression, women were more able to fight it. Consciousness-raising changed many women's beliefs, and even though it did not necessarily lead to man-hating, as some of the more conservative feminists feared, it lead to a more willful self-determination. In fact, consciousness-raising in time became the most common first step on a path to activism for women who had not previously been involved in politics.

Although the women who started NOW were ingenious at attracting media attention for their protests—such as throwing bundles of newspapers tied with red ribbon on the steps of the EEOC to protest the sex-segregated want ads and staging sit-ins at bars and restaurants that refused to serve women—it was the tactics of the third strand, the activists from the New Left, SDS, and the civil rights movements, that catapulted the second wave of the women's movement into the consciousness of all Americans. The same group that started consciousness-raising, New York Radical Women, staged a protest against the Miss America pageant in 1968 that both helped publicize and would later haunt the women's movement. Almost two hundred activists came to Atlantic City to underscore the dehumanizing effect of that contest on American women's sense of themselves. They stood on the boardwalk, where the pageant was being held, and crowned a live sheep "Miss America" to make the point that American women ought not have to meet or compete over prurient male standards of beauty.

Then the protesters did something no one would ever forget. They threw curlers, underclothes, and high-heeled shoes into a "freedom trash can" to symbolize their rejection of their status as sex objects. The press blew up one inaccurate report that protesters had "burned their bras" (though as one participant said later, "Bras were not the problem; girdles were"). There was, in fact, never a fire; but the negative image of "bra burners" thereafter haunted the women's movement. This made it possible to depict feminists not just as militantly antimale but also as militantly antifeminine, and the movement had to work hard to overcome all of this. However, the women's audacity in protesting the Miss America contest caused all the major newspapers to take notice. Throughout the 1970s, women's liberationists continued to stage dramatic, often humorous, protests that made their way into the press. The press was not seeking to support the movement, but because women were involved, the stories were seen to be titillating.

Although it is tempting to draw causal lines between America's civil rights movement, the President's Commission on the Status of Women, and the women's liberationists to explain the outburst of feminist activity beginning in 1966 in the United States, there were multiple appearances of feminism in other countries, especially in the English-speaking world, in that same period. The first national women's liberation conference was held in Great Britain, for example, in 1970, and Australian feminists began making headlines around this time, even though Australia's civil rights movement was not as mature.[34]

Early Victories

A sweet and ironic triumph of the women's movement was that some of the stereotyping in women's magazines that Betty Friedan had so ably uncovered and explained to women in *The Feminine Mystique* raised consciousness among women reporters and editors themselves. Starting in 1970, the nation's presswomen began to protest both the slanted coverage and the content of stories written about or for women on television and radio and in newspapers and magazines.[35] They complained that the realities of women's employment (more than 50 percent of all women were working at this time) were not reflected in the media and that on TV and in the women's magazines, adult females were always depicted as housewives—and not very bright ones at that. It was a tradition in most newspapers that even professional women would be described by their physical characteristics ("a slim brunette"), and this, feminists argued, reinforced the objectification of all women.[36] Within one week in 1970, sit-ins protesting discrimination against female workers at *Newsweek* and *Ladies' Home Journal* were staged, the latter including women from NOW and New York–based women's liberation groups.

These battles were rooted in women's changing understanding of their personal potential and of the restrictions they had grown up with simply because of their gender. The power of patriarchy rested with women's internalizing and "buying into" male ideas of women's potential, as illustrated in one of NOW's first victories with the EEOC. Starting in the 1950s, stewardesses at different major airline companies were fighting, with some support from their unions, to end the airlines' policy of "retiring," that is, forcing female flight attendants to quit at age thirty-two (or thirty-five, depending on the airline) or upon marriage. As Flora Davis writes in *Moving the Mountain*, "In the hierarchy of 'glamour' jobs open to white women in the early sixties, stewardesses ranked right after movie stars and models."[37] In fact, for every woman hired as a stewardess, more than one hundred applicants were turned away. Those who were chosen embodied the American image of the wholesome "girl-next-door," which meant white and attractive in a feminine, youthful sense. To project this image, stewardesses took classes in make-up, grooming, and social skills, in addition to flight safety, at "charm farms." They were required to keep their skirts, hair, and heels at specified lengths, and they could be fired for gaining too much weight. Despite all this, most women did not dispute the airlines' uniform definition of attractiveness or their right to base employment strictly on these criteria. Such women were as yet "unradicalized."

This was a time when 70 percent of American women were married by age twenty-four and the average American woman got married at age twenty, earlier than in any other generation since the turn of the century. Davis explains that "most stewardesses themselves assumed when they were hired that they'd marry within a few years. In fact, at American Airlines the gold wings presented to a woman after five years of flying were known as 'your failure pin,' because they signified that she had so far failed to marry."[38] What did the airlines have in mind—that a woman over thirty was not attractive enough to be a stewardess or that her marriage automatically rendered her unfit? Although the airlines may have maintained that the issue was image and tradition, others believe, among them Flora Davis, that money was their bottom line. The airlines did not want to have to pay stewardesses higher wages, and because of enforcement of these restrictions, the average stewardess had a tenure of only three years. The airlines also avoided paying extra fringe benefits this way, as well as cutting down on their health insurance bills.

Two American Airlines stewardesses, Nancy Collins and Dusty Roads, were trying to use their union, the Airline Stewards and Stewardesses Association, to change these policies, but it was not working. They and other angry stewardesses saw their struggle as a unique issue between themselves and management, not as part of a national problem. Davis writes, "Stewardesses fought to be treated as workers, rather than as sex objects, at a time when the term 'sex object' hadn't yet been invented."[39] When at some time in the late 1950s, Dusty Roads discussed the situation with Representative Martha Griffiths, Griffiths helped her see that the airlines' policy belonged to a troubling pattern of sex discrimination in many fields across the country.

With Griffiths's encouragement, Collins and Roads brought their case to the EEOC in summer 1965, soon after the commission had opened its doors. By 1966, there were ninety-two separate claims by stewardesses. And although Fuentes recalls the agency holding hearings and devoting attention to this issue, Aileen Hernandez resigned from the EEOC because of the agency's indifference to women's issues.[40] As soon as NOW was formed, it issued a press release supporting Hernandez and the stewardesses' claim of sex discrimination. NOW went on to lobby the EEOC relentlessly on behalf of these women.

The unions did contribute to this work as time went on. They brought a separate case concerning the stewardesses' marriage restriction to the EEOC and won a ruling in their favor in 1968; at the same time, the age limit was declared in violation of Title VII. By 1985, the average flight attendant (so called since the 1970s, when men began to be hired for the job) was serving ten years and enjoying an annual salary as high as $40,000. Today, female flight attendants do not have to retire until age seventy, and, in a happy ending to this story, Roads and Collins were still flying in 1991.[41]

Reactions by Women of Color

Davis points out that the early second-wave feminists largely ignored the fact that nonwhite women were rarely hired as stewardesses, an example of the legacy that led to the complex, difficult, and sometimes painful relationship between early white feminists and women of color. This is not to say that minority women were not welcomed into the women's movement. Many found their way into NOW, and several became national leaders, among them Aileen Hernandez. Although she was not present at NOW's founding meeting, NOW members elected Hernandez executive vice president soon thereafter, and in 1970 she became NOW's second president. Other early supporters of mainstream feminism included African-Americans Pauli Murray, a protégée of Eleanor Roosevelt, an Episcopal priest, and a lawyer who wrote the brief for *White* v. *Crook* arguing for jury participation of women; Fannie Lou Hamer, leader of the breakaway Mississippi Freedom Democratic Party; lawyer Florynce Kennedy of New York; and Addie Wyatt, vice president of the Amalgamated Meat Cutters Union. When the National Women's Political Caucus (NWPC) formed in 1971 to assist women in getting elected to political office, that organization attracted, among other women of color, LaDonna Harris, an Indian rights leader, and Dorothy Height, head of the National Council of Negro Women.

Chicana activists were doing parallel work during this same period in organizations of their own. Their priorities were the wages and working conditions of migrant and indigenous farmworkers and welfare rights. Dolores Huerta was a leader in the farmworkers' movement, and Alicia Escalante lobbied for welfare rights. Locally, such as in Texas, Chicanas began to run successfully for political office not to further women's rights but to extend their community work. Nevertheless, despite many shared goals, relations between the new feminism and the most disadvantaged women in our society remained cool.

In *When and Where I Enter: The Impact of Black Women on Race and Sex in America*, historian Paula Giddings provides a perspective on why many African-American women distrusted the rebirth of feminism in the 1970s, holding the movement in disdain. For one, the white women's movement was competing for media and political attention with the black movement. Indeed, as feminism succeeded, black activism receded, and it was tempting to see a causal link between the two events. As an example of such competition, Giddings notes that in 1968, the year of Martin Luther King's assassination, the Poor People's March organized by the grassroots National Welfare Rights Organization was given little publicity, while feminists' bra burning at the Miss America pageant claimed a lot of public attention.[42]

But more important, Giddings thinks, were the ideological schisms. The women's movement is rooted in the claim that it is male supremacy, rather than race or class supremacy, that is the cause of women's oppression. African Americans must put race first, and white feminists frequently do not understand this. When Angela Davis, a black philosophy instructor at the University of California, found herself on the FBI's Ten Most Wanted List, black feminists and others rallied around her cause. Yet when New York feminists organized a march in 1970 to celebrate the fiftieth anniversary of the ratification of the suffrage amendment, the Third World Women's Alliance, a black feminist group under Frances Beal, was told that its sign "Free Angela Davis" could not be displayed.

Still smarting from the pictures of white women threatening black children at the Little Rock schoolhouse in 1957, as writer Toni Morrison described it, African-American women and their leadership sensed continuing racism among white women.[43] In a 1971 article provocatively entitled "What the Black Woman Thinks About Women's Lib," Morrison wrote, "Black women look at white women and see the enemy, for they know that racism is not confined to white men."[44] If Angela Davis had no place in a feminist march, the feminist movement had no place in black women's lives. Ida Lewis, an African-American editor and publisher, expressed the irrelevance of the new feminism even more baldly: "The

Women's Liberation movement is basically a quarrel between white women and white men."[45]

Giddings and other African-American contemporaries do not deny that sexism and male supremacy were on the rise in black civil rights movements. Black Power represented a resurgence of African-American male aggressiveness. The Black Muslim movement prescribed rigid roles for women, requiring that they wear long white garb and dedicate themselves to reproduction. What these women argue is that since race was a bigger issue for them than gender, if African-American women were to organize at all, separate from their men, they would do so alone. In 1973, a national black feminist organization was established, but within a decade it was nowhere to be found.[46]

Gloria Joseph and Jill Lewis, the one African American, the other white, see the relations between the African-American and the white women's movements more positively. Writing in 1981 in their book *Common Differences: Conflicts in Black and White Feminist Perspectives,* Joseph and Lewis state without reservation that "the sexual politics of the Women's Movement has [connected] to the struggles of women of different classes and races as no feminist movement has ever done before."[47] What has impressed them is the evolution of the feminist agenda from a narrow list of grievances to a more inclusive analysis. One example they give is the shift from a single proabortion strategy, defined as a "woman's right," to one promoting choice and, above all, opposing forced sterilization. Another is a replacement of a single-minded "anti-housewife" trend with a more class-oriented analysis of the role of domestic labor under capitalism. Joseph and Lewis applaud as well the "space" for lesbians in the women's liberation movement and the evolution of its thinking from a celebration of "sameness" of all women's experience to a greater appreciation of cultural and racial differences.[48]

Within the minority communities in America, as we see in later chapters, the debate as to whether white women's feminism is relevant to women of color goes on. Whether the primary focus or not, there is no question that large numbers of African-American, Hispanic, and Native American women, along with poor white women, did benefit from the consequences of feminist actions. The bitterly fought case against the American Telephone and Telegraph Company (AT&T) involving occupational segregation by job category was resolved in favor mainly of the lower-paid women in that company (details in Chapter 7), and most of the $15 million settlement went to women in the lowest pay scales. As educational and occupational barriers fell, women of color, who are more likely to work and on whose shoulders the economic burden of family support is more likely to fall, were able to pursue nontraditional careers and take home the higher wages that accompany them. The emerging feminist focus on "the feminization of poverty" brought national attention to the material conditions of welfare recipients, and the introduction of the phrase *displaced homemaker* gave women abandoned by divorce a certain status.[49]

Despite all this, Chicana anthropologist Marta Cotera, writing in 1980, faults feminists for putting the needs of professional women over those of clerical staff whenever there was a conflict.[50] This is why historian William Chafe, who studies race as well as gender issues, concludes from his study of this period that race, gender, and class continued to intersect in ways that made gender solidarity difficult, if not impossible.[51]

Even if the new feminism was mainly populated by middle-class white women, the new focus on women helped rekindle the self-help organizations that minority women had already pioneered in the nineteenth century. In 1970, only four years after the founding of NOW, women from forty-three tribes organized the first North American Indian Women's Association. A year later, six hundred Chicanas convened the first national Chicana conference, followed in 1972 by the first conference of Puerto Rican women. Working-class women active in labor unions managed to do what the labor union movement itself had never achieved—namely, to unite workers across industries and ethnic boundaries. The Coalition of Labor Union Women (CLUW), founded in 1974, was openly feminist in its orientation and embraced the full spectrum of working women from the public and private sectors, white-collar employees to farm labor women. Such organizations, of course, had their own priorities not always in synch with the feminists'. For CLUW, equal pay, pregnancy benefits, and occupational safety and health were of utmost importance; the image of women in advertising and reproductive freedom were less so. But as long as these organizations were willing to work in coalition with feminists, the broader issues relating to women and work would remain in the spotlight.

7

The Women's Movement Goes to Work

ROLE EQUITY ISSUES

THE WOMEN WHO WERE ATTRACTED TO FEMINISM went to work almost immediately on the wide range of issues that seemed to be of common interest and urgency. Some of those issues, such as sex discrimination in employment, housing, and credit, would result in new or more power- fully enforced legislation at the federal and state levels. Some, such as the issues of pregnancy, abortion, and the extent to which the federal government could enforce equal employment opportunity, would re- quire rulings by the courts, including the Supreme Court. Still others would be achieved by executive order of the president, in those matters over which the chief executive has sole control. Thus, the history of the new feminism at work also chronicles how movement politics was to make its mark.

I have found it useful to distinguish three classes of women's issues that roughly correspond to three generations or agendas embraced by the women's movement.[1] The first generation is characterized by "role equity" issues, those rooted in the moral imperative that all people, at least as far as government is concerned, ought to be treated the same. Everyone knows that when the founding fathers used the term *equal* in the eighteenth century (as in "All men are created equal"), they knew full well that all men were not *identical*. There were shop owners and farm- ers, entrepreneurs and laborers, people who were "well born" and poor people. But there was in the establishment of our republic a sense that all people have value and that their value is equivalent, even if people are not the same. As applied to the new feminists' agenda, role equity issues do not involve any change in women's nature or in their social roles. They simply extend the tried-and-true American view that all people should be able to vote and be welcomed into the political process, that their abilities should be fairly judged and taken seriously, and that they should have "equal access" and "equal opportunity." Role equity issues, then, as feminists pursued them and as a majority of Americans perceive them, ask for and expect equal treatment for women without challenging the notion that men and women are different. Examples of this kind of legislation include pay equity (equal pay for equal or identical work) and equal access to jobs.

A second category of laws, court rulings, and executive orders falls under the rubric of "role change." Anything that suggests interchangeability of roles involves the far more radical notion that, apart from gestation, women can and ought to be able to do anything men do in the private and public arenas; and the reverse, that men could be assigned the same tasks and obligations as women, obtains as well. Such issues are, obviously, much more controversial than role equity issues. Whereas role equity falls within a hallowed American tradition of equality of opportunity, role change threatens an older set of practices and traditions. In my reading of the legislative history of the period 1968 to 1975, it seems to me that, once enlightened as to the many legal privileges men enjoyed over women, the majority of the American people were quite willing to legislate those privileges away. But the kinds of change inherent in the battles over reproductive rights, equal access to sports, and affirmative action were more threatening to role assignments and as a result much harder to win. This helps explain why the Supreme Court's ruling on abortion and the statute requiring the opening of school and college sports activities to girls—two second-generation issues—were so much more controversial than the Equal Credit Opportunity Act, which passed almost without opposition in the same time period.[2]

We might speculate as to why, in mid-twentieth century America, men (and some women) would be so loathe to give up women's "specialness" in favor of role interchangeability. Part of the reason was simply tradition—the kind of tradition Kate Millett sketched out so well in her book *Sexual Politics*. Psychologists might argue that it is much easier to find one's way in a culture where roles are highly differentiated. Each of us knows what is expected of us, how to behave in single-sex and mixed-sex situations. We have scripts to follow and therefore do not have to deal with ambiguity in our relationships with one another. Feminists would retort that, comfortable as assigned roles might be, the situation in the 1950s and 1960s, as well documented by Betty Friedan and others, gave men many advantages. Simply legislating equal opportunity and not dealing with different expectations for men and women would not bring real justice to women. And so the battle lines were drawn.

At least, all feminists agreed pretty much on the role change issues. This was not to be the case as regards what I call third-generation issues (which we come back to in Chapter 11). These include pornography and how to deal with it, women and the military (particularly the issue of combat), sexual harassment, surrogacy (the arrangement by which one woman's womb is used to gestate the child of another), and comparable worth, a form of pay equity whereby women would not simply be paid the same as men holding similar or identical jobs but would get "equal pay for work of equal value." There are at least two (sometimes three) sides to each of these issues. And not all feminists agree on which would be the fairest, most sensible, most realistic, or even most "feminist" position on each.

Take, for example, an issue that emerged in the mid-1980s as well-educated women, who had benefited from the opening of higher education to more and more female students, suddenly entered the professional job markets in large numbers. Some of these young women had taken role interchangeability seriously by preparing themselves at great expense for the "big jobs" that awaited them, all the while postponing childbearing in the hopes that, once established, they would be able to take some time off and have their babies. It is one thing for a woman in a traditional pink-collar job to get time off for childbearing and, after the children are born, to get additional leave for family emergencies. Her work is interchangeable with that of others. But in a busy law firm or banking establishment, where each member of the professional staff has his or her own clients to serve, time away from work (even when it is legally permitted, as it was eventually by the Family and Medical Leave Act passed in 1993) is much more costly to the professional and to her firm. What, then, is the best and fairest policy for women who are not interchangeable with anyone else?

Felice Schwartz, a feminist with high-level corporate connections, created a fair amount of controversy on this issue by suggesting that it might be better for some women, especially mothers, to select a separate and parallel career track.[3] The Mommy Track, as others called it, was for women willing to trade professional benefits and opportunities for a lighter and more manageable workload. A female lawyer would be free to tend a sick child or to stay nearer home during the summer months but, in exchange, would not make partner in the normal time frame (or not make partner altogether). A banker on a Mommy Track would be assigned less demanding clients and so on.

The Mommy Track divided the feminist community almost immediately. It seemed to some that this was just a new excuse for not promoting able women and that, when widely implemented, some women would be forced to accept lesser pay and privilege against their will. Others saw this as a creative way to facilitate a combined professional life and mothering. A like division occurs whenever the issue of child care is raised. Ought stay-at-home mothers be paid out of the federal Treasury for doing the nation's child care for their own children? Or should federally sponsored child care be reserved only for women who work outside the home? In the same way, comparable worth causes divisions among feminists. Some see it as "fair" in the same way that affirmative action is just compensation for previous discrimination against racial minorities. Others see it as one more way to keep women in their place. The issue of surrogacy raises the same kinds of questions: For some feminists, surrogate motherhood is but a humane extension of adoption as some other person's biological child becomes one's own. But for other feminists, surrogacy is "womb rental," a pernicious form of prostitution and exploitation when a poor woman's uterus is used to gestate rich people's offspring.

To summarize, role equity policies are those that most Americans, once made aware, are willing to support. Role interchangeability issues are ones that feminists are likely to support but that people outside a feminist framework (both men and women) typically oppose. Third-generation issues are ones over which even feminists disagree. Certain commentators say the last phase of disagreement shows that the feminist movement is disintegrating, that it cannot even agree any longer on a single policy agenda. I would say simply, along with Confucius, "One barrier down, next one higher." With time, the issues get tougher and more complex. But at the time we pick up the story in about 1967, these more complex issues were far in the future.

Factors in Feminist Success

Not only was feminism an unfamiliar factor in American politics; also, in some measure, the kinds of issues that feminists began to work on were usually not debated in the public arena—issues such as contraception, childbirth, child care, advertisers' images of women, gender-differentiated toys and activities, and access to sports. What is remarkable is not just how much of the 1968 NOW Bill of Rights made its way into law and public practice in the next decade, but also how much the public was willing to accept the radical notion that, for women at least, the personal was political.[4] Even more remarkable is that feminists managed to do so much so quickly. By 1975, job access, the right to a medically assisted abortion, and equal access to credit for single and married women alike were on the books, and quotas, men's-only scholarships, and restrictions on benefits due to pregnancy were all disappearing. Virtually everything the NOW organization had laid out in its 1968 Bill of Rights had come to pass.[5] What made this possible was that feminists used every means at their disposal to get the changes they wanted.

In addition, second-wave activists benefited from four other factors. First was the size of their following. Tens of thousands of women found their way into women's liberation "cells," half a million subscribed to *Ms.*, another half a million (with some overlap) joined NOW, and countless others organized around particular problems, such as marching against rape or fighting locally to open Little League to girls, or specific projects, such as beginning a feminist bookstore or establishing a feminist think tank.[6] A second important factor was visibility. The media found the whole feminist movement, particularly after the Miss America protest in 1968, sexy. They gave a lot of play to physically attractive spokeswomen such as Gloria Steinem and Germaine Greer, until, a decade later, they decided feminism had gone far enough.[7] A third factor was the inordinate amount of untapped talent and womanpower available to the movement, including a virtual underground of underemployed and undervalued women working in the nation's capital. These women knew the legislative, litigative, and regulation processes as well as the men they worked for and were delighted to put their skills at the service of feminism. And the fourth factor was a social climate in the 1960s and 1970s that was unusually favorable to change.

And there was work to be done. First, the feminists had to lobby Congress for the statutes they wanted passed. Then, they had to lobby (or picket or sue, as the case might be) the executive agency that was to enforce the new statutes to get the regulations they wanted. Very often, as in the case of Title VII of the 1964 Civil Rights Bill, the agency assigned to the job, in this case the Equal Employment Opportunity Commission, had to be prodded to do its work. Sometimes, prodding was not enough. In the course of NOW's and WEAL's first fifteen years, the two organizations not only lobbied Congress and the president but also filed claims on behalf of aggrieved groups of women and, when necessary, sued corporate and nonprofit organizations. When the federal government moved too slowly, they targeted the errant agency (at one point the Department of Health, Education, and Welfare) with a suit in federal court.[8]

Lobbying was accompanied by massive "public education" on issues that only a few years before would have been laughed out of the public arena. Employers, broadcasters, political analysts, and, eventually, even opponents of the new feminism learned not to comment on a woman's appearance in professional settings, not to ask about her marital status, and, above all, not to trivialize the feminists' agenda. Men sputtered at first, but soon nearly everyone was saying "chairperson" or "chair." More important, a series of books and "speak-outs" on rape caused evidentiary practice in rape trials to be completely overhauled. No longer would rape be tried as a "sex crime," with the victim's previous sexual history displayed and her veracity challenged by the defendant, the jury, and the judge. Rape was redefined as "aggravated assault," and the plaintiff (who was, of course, also the victim in a rape case), quite as much as the defendant, would be protected from first arrival in the hands of the police to final verdict.[9]

To accomplish the full agenda, second-wave feminists evolved a number of different legislative strategies (reviewed in this chapter and the next), resulting in a remarkable amount of new law and new practice. This review sets the stage for the subject of Chapter 9—namely, how, only a decade later, in a stunning reversal of feminist fortune, the Equal Rights Amendment failed to be ratified.

Victories in Congress: Equal Pay

The rebirth of feminism is usually dated as of 1966, with the founding of the National Organization for Women. It could just as well be dated with the publication of Pauli Murray and Mary Eastwood's article on sex and the law; the appearance of the Washington-based newspaper *off our backs;* the publication of *Notes from the First Year,* a collection of writings and reports on radical feminism; the call to Atlantic City initiated by Redstockings to protest the Miss America contest in 1968; or the first Women's Equality Day, organized by Betty Friedan in 1970. The point is that after a long hiatus thousands and then hundreds of thousands of women suddenly were attracted to feminist goals and feminist organizations. There was no end of legislative and litigative issues for them to pursue and, given the decentralized nature of the movement, no end of large and small organizations for them to join.

To tell that story in any depth, we have to go back in time and remind ourselves that prior to the establishment of NOW, two pieces of important anti–sex discrimination legislation were already on the books. I have discussed the employment discrimination protection provided by Title VII of the 1964 Civil Rights Act and how it contributed to an awakening feminist consciousness. But even earlier, in 1963, Congress passed the Equal Pay Act, which was intended to guarantee that for equal work—work of exactly the same description (title, responsibilities, and working conditions)—men and women would be paid the same amount. Prior to 1963, it was not illegal to pay men and women differently for the same work done. In a "gendered" society, by which feminists mean a society in which gender differentiation is taken for granted, unequal pay for the same or identical work was taken for granted, too. The myths about why women worked continued: Men worked to support a family; women worked briefly at certain convenient times of their lives for pin money.[10]

In the immediate aftermath of World War II, it was not feminists, not even the Women's Bureau, but male members of Congress—Ohio's Republican senator Robert Taft and Florida's Democratic representative, later senator, Claude Pepper—who introduced an equal pay bill, which would not be passed for eighteen years. Taft and Pepper were motivated to put equal pay for equal work into federal law partly because a hodgepodge of equal pay acts were ordered during the war that needed to be standardized, partly as a way of saying, "Thank you" to women war workers. For the next seven years, because there was no organized women's rights or feminist movement, little happened. There were hearings, debates, occasional votes in committee, but not even the Department of Labor could see its way clear to support the bill. One might say the country was not ready for equal pay for women, except in wartime. Finally, in 1952, under the leadership of Esther Peterson of the Women's Bureau, the National Committee for Equal Pay (a nongovernmental lobbying organization) was established. It took another eleven years (imagine the endurance of supporters), but in 1963 the Equal Pay Act was passed without much public outcry, for or against.[11]

Like all federal statutes originating in Congress, the Equal Pay Act had to be enforced by a federal agency. In this case, responsibility for writing regs and for handling enforcement was assigned to the already existing Wage and Hours Division of the Department of Labor, which, it was believed, could handle equal pay cases along with its other work. But the Wage and Hours Division was already a busy agency with many other complaints and investigations to handle. Therefore, the funds and human resources that could be used to implement the Equal Pay Act were restricted. Another limitation on this (and all federal employment legislation) is that the law did not apply to all enterprises, only those "within the federal reach," that is, having twenty-five or more employees or engaging in interstate commerce; nor, as written, did the act cover administrative, executive, or professional personnel. Nevertheless, for those stuck in sex-differentiated wage systems, the bill could be a potent remedy.

It would be wrong to imagine that the passage of the 1963 Equal Pay Act meant that henceforth the pay of men and women doing identical work would be the same. Complaints had to be brought before the Wage and Hours Division. Interpretation of the statute would have to be made after cases were brought to the courts. And once certain businesses recognized that to equalize wages, they would have to pay women more—that is, increase their total wage bill—they dug in their heels.

I participated in some of the equal pay actions in the 1970s and was constantly surprised at how often occupational segregation by job category was the vehicle by which women were paid for similar work substantially less than men. In certain insurance companies, for example, women and men were typically designated "raters" and "underwriters," respectively, even though they did essentially the same kind of work. Both dealt with customer inquiries, except that men answered questions about contracts and premiums on the telephone (their voices were presumed to be more authoritative) and women responded by typing letters. When salaries were compared, raters earned $2,000 less a year ($6,000–$8,000 in today's currency) than underwriters. The raters were women, the underwriters were men, and transfer possibilities were nil. It was not so different at the newsmagazines where college-educated women were fact-checkers (researchers), while their male classmates started out in reporter positions at considerably higher pay; transfer opportunities were also nil.[12] By 1970, 150 cases of equal pay violation had been brought before the Wage and Hours Division by individual plaintiffs and groups like ours, and 52,000 women had been awarded equal pay.[13]

I spent the bulk of the 1970s as a university administrator in Connecticut, where, among other actions, a group of us founded a statewide feminist newspaper we named *Alert,* intending for it to act as a spur to state legislators when it came to enacting feminist-friendly laws.[14] How did we make ourselves seem more powerful than we were? We printed ten thousand copies of each issue, placed one each in every state legislator's mail box, mailed multiple copies to the media, and gave the rest away. The strategy was to have the legislators wonder how many of their constituents were also reading the issue. We called this "exposure" or "penalty" politics: "If you don't vote our way, we will let all your constituents know." In time, other single-issue groups used the same technique to up the political ante absent an overlarge staff.

In the course of our feminist organizing in that state, we were joined by a group of women attorneys who saw the need for a feminist legal defense fund, one that could spur plaintiffs to bring suit under existing antidiscrimination law. Together we founded CWEALF, the Connecticut Women's Education and Legal Fund, to provide the research and, if needed, professional assistance to women in business, teaching, and industry. Among the early victories for CWEALF was a state department of education ruling that overturned the decades-old requirement that female teachers leave the classroom (and their jobs and forgo their medical benefits) in their fifth month of pregnancy.

Nevertheless, nothing would have happened had not equal pay and anti–job discrimination legislation been on the books. However accidental or incidental its origin, nothing forces change in the workplace as effectively as federal law. Once legislation is enacted, it pulls human resources, money, and the full power of the justice system into an arena that had previously been entirely unregulated. That is why the battles over legislation in Congress are so fierce.

Gains in the Courts: The Case Against AT&T

Once legislation is in place, it often has to be interpreted by the federal courts. A case in point was the situation at the nation's then telephone and telegraph monopoly, now dismembered by another federal ruling. At the time, the American Telephone and Telegraph Company was the largest corporation in America, with as many employees as the Pentagon. So what happened in one of its subsidiaries, Southern Bell, in terms of equal pay and job opportunity, would act as a signal for the rest of the nation.[15] The telephone company, as AT&T was known locally, had long been an important employer of women for the comfortable, relatively unchallenging jobs; reasonably good benefits; and security of employment it provided. As long as anyone could remember, in the days before direct dialing, women joined the telephone company as telephone operators, and men of the same age and educational background started work at better-paying "linesman" positions.

Operators were less well paid than linesman and more closely supervised. Indeed, their stock responses, their voice quality, and their handling of irate customers were strictly controlled and closely monitored by their supervisors.[16] The operators' upward mobility was severely limited compared to that of linesmen since middle managers at the telephone company were recruited from lines personnel. Rarely did an operator move up except to become a senior operator. In defending the system in one of the first and hardest-fought cases in the industry, Southern Bell argued that the company had to employ females as operators because users of the telephone system preferred the female voice. (Note how the insurance industry argued just the reverse: that it had to employ male underwriters because people took what men said on the telephone more seriously.) The upward mobility issue was joined when Southern Bell argued that it just so happened that in their organization operators became "senior operators," supervising other operators, while linesmen became middle managers. And linesmen (we now call them linespersons) would, of course, have to be male. Who would expect women, with their tender pelvises, to shimmy up telephone poles or to work outdoors when it rains?

Loreen Weeks, an employee of Southern Bell, wanted to be a linesman. When she was denied the position solely on the basis of her sex, Sylvia Roberts, an experienced Louisiana civil rights lawyer, brought suit under Title VII on behalf of Weeks and her "class" of women employees who were similarly excluded from these better-paying positions. After a long, hard fight, during which time Roberts's expenses were covered by the NOW Legal Defense and Education Fund, the U.S. Fifth Circuit Court ruled that under Title VII, Southern Bell had to prove that there was a bona fide occupational qualification that Weeks could not meet. Roberts successfully convinced the court that not only was differential entry wage at stake, but also Weeks's opportunity for advancement was foreclosed given the opportunity structure at the company.[17]

Once the case was won, Southern Bell settled for $15 million in back pay to the class of women Loreen Weeks represented and $23 million in immediate pay raises. Illustration 7.1 illustrates AT&T's subsequent attempts to correct its past discriminatory hiring practice. Even more far-reaching was the impact of the suit on other companies. Distribution of jobs on the basis of gender, even if these distributions were hallowed by tradition, would not be tolerated by the courts.[18]

An Executive Order: Affirmative Action

Another avenue for action, apart from legislation and litigation—of which there was much in the period 1969–1975—was the executive order, essentially a presidential decree. There is much in our system of government that the chief executive can do on his or her own. In the 1980s, President Ronald Reagan eliminated fetal tissue research as one of the medical research areas the National Institutes of Health could fund—with just the stroke of a pen. In January 1993, President Bill Clinton rescinded that restriction—with the stroke of another pen. This is one example of executive power. Another is in the so-called power of the federal purse. The federal government is a large purchaser in our economy; in fact, it is the largest purchaser of all, buying everything from military uniforms and equipment to school lunches and supplies for government offices. Thus, even before a congressional statute is available that mandates certain standards for American businesses, the government can demand that higher standards be met among those companies wanting to sell products and services to Uncle Sam.

President Roosevelt was the first to employ so-called federal contract compliance to encourage equal opportunity in employment. It was the eve of World War II. African-American leaders, aware that the federal

Illustration 7.1   AT&T promotional campaign.
Courtesy of AT&T.

government was going to have to become a large purchaser of war-related equipment if it was going to pursue the war, were determined to take advantage of the opportunity to force through equal employment measures. J. Philip Randolph, then president of the (all African-American) Sleeping Car Porters Union, which represented workers in an entirely racially segregated industry, led a march on Washington in 1941 to bring to the president's attention the inequities in employment opportunity for African Americans. In response, Roosevelt signed an executive order authorizing the federal government, as procurer, not to purchase anything from a company that did not provide equal employment opportunities to minorities.

This was no statute. It would have been impossible, in a southern Democrat–dominated Congress, to get anything like the 1964 Civil Rights Act passed in 1941. Roosevelt knew that, and he was not one to waste his time on the impossible. Instead, companies that wished to continue discriminating against minorities in hiring, promotion, and job assignment could go on doing so, but they would not be able to do any business with the government.

Twenty-five years later, in 1966, faced with continuing occupational segregation by race, especially in the skilled trades, President Lyndon Johnson took a leaf out of Roosevelt's book and signed Executive Order 11246, which required that all companies wishing to do business with the federal government not only provide equal opportunity for all but also take *affirmative action* (defined as extra steps) to bring their hiring in line with the available labor pools by race (and later gender). Affirmative action had already been required of companies found by the courts to have historically discriminated against minorities. As part of their court-ordered settlements, such companies had to meet certain guidelines and even institute temporary hiring quotas to compensate for past practices. With Johnson's order, affirmative action would henceforth be required even of companies not proved to have discriminated. This and the very mention of "goals" and "timetables" (which detractors translated into "hiring quotas") made the executive order controversial. When efforts to meet goals and timetables resulted in de facto hiring quotas or in so-called set-asides for minority- and women-owned businesses, certain white workers and businesses were disadvantaged; in time they sued. By the mid-1980s, during the Reagan years, affirmative action would become harder and harder to implement. But these reversals were in the future.

At the time Executive Order 11246 was signed by Johnson in 1966, feminists just getting organized recognized that the power of the federal purse would be a potent instrument for rectifying past unfair hiring practices in regard to women as well. Hence, they lobbied President

Johnson, already weakened by his Vietnam War policy, for an extension of 11246 to include "sex" as a protected category. In 1967, Johnson did just that. He signed Executive Order 11375. Revised Order 4 of that directive required that affirmative action be taken to bring hiring of women into line with their availability in relevant labor pools.

Enforcement of these executive orders was given to the Office of Federal Contract Compliance (OFCC) in the Department of Labor. But as with the EEOC's enforcement of Title VII, the OFCC was not particularly eager to deal with women's issues. For one, women were being discriminated against in different occupational sectors from minorities and in industries where there was not much of a federal presence.[19] For another, the minority issue was by far the more urgent, or so it was thought. A little later, during President Nixon's administration, Bernice Sandler, an officer of the Women's Equity Action League and a psychologist who had personally suffered employment discrimination, decided on behalf of WEAL to test the reach of Executive Order 11375. Would the OFCC rule that universities doing "business" with the federal government had to have an "affirmative action plan"? That is, would the executive order apply to institutions that had not products to sell but the kind of high-level services involved in research? There was only one way to find out, and that was to sue a sizable number of universities and research institutions (350 of them) under Executive Order 11375 and wait for a ruling.

In a ruling that made history, the OFCC concurred with Sandler: The patterns of employment in the nation's colleges and universities did not reflect the existing labor pools of women. Research universities, like all prestigious institutions, had until then considered themselves exempt from the executive orders. After all, when a laboratory is seeking world-class talent, any restriction on its freedom to hire will, it can be argued, compromise the work.[20] That may be, conceded the OFCC, but as long as that laboratory receives funding support from the federal government, the entire university has to meet contract compliance goals. Sandler's action and the accompanying ruling from the OFCC have changed the way colleges and universities do their hiring. Where once word of mouth and personal contacts (the old boys' network) kept faculty and postdoctoral appointments outside the purview even of university administrators, today women and minority scholars can enjoy a more open process of application and employment, and universities have to monitor their hiring according to a long-term affirmative action plan.

The implementation of affirmative action in time gave rise, as mentioned, to backlash among white males who claimed to experience reverse discrimination as municipal police and fire departments, medical schools, and other public employers scurried about trying to meet affir-

mative action goals. In some, perhaps in many, cases, companies implemented quotas in their desire to keep federal contracts, to stay out of
court, or even to sabotage affirmative action. But it is indisputable that
the occupational inroads women have made, especially in the high-
prestige professions, would not have taken place without mandated affirmative action and the threat of lost contracts.

More Legislative Gains:
Equal Credit Opportunity

The classic role equity issue, according to Joyce Gelb and Marian Palley,
who invented the category, is the Equal Credit Opportunity Act of 1974,
which sailed through Congress with little opposition from the powerful
banking industry and the Federal Reserve Board, charged with oversee-
ing that industry.[21] The 1973 Congress was favorably inclined toward
women's issues. It had passed the Equal Rights Amendment, which
would have eliminated discrimination on the basis of sex in federal and
state law. Thus, it was fitting that the same Congress attend to discrimi-
nations on the basis of sex (and marital status) in the private sector.

Equal credit opportunity was long overdue. Women attempting to
borrow money to start or to expand a running business were often denied bank loans that a man running the same business would have gotten with ease. Banks are in the lending business. That is how they make
their money. As long as the balance sheet and the business plan meet
their standards, there ought to be no reason to deny credit. But in the
decades prior to 1974, chances of getting business loans were significantly less for women. Women were seen as part-timers, as malingerers
(feigning or being more vulnerable to illness), as lacking in good business sense and in any "real" commitment to working outside the home.
That an individual woman business owner had no such failings was not
as important as what the sociologists would call her latent status, the
very fact that she was a woman.

Prior to 1974, even women with a good personal credit history would
be denied consumer credit after they were married. If they were told
anything at all about the reason for the denial (and many were not), they
were advised to get their husbands to put them on their credit cards instead. To be sure, the debt of one spouse is often held to be the responsibility of the other, but statistics would probably show that as many (if
not more) men defaulted on loans and on personal credit as did women.
Nevertheless, the stereotypes from a much earlier era were in force. And
women, unable to get home mortgages, initiate business expansion, or
even purchase disability insurance for the long term, were the losers. As

in the early nineteenth century, widows were exempt from many of these restrictions, although they found it difficult to establish credit once their husbands had died, not having built any credit history of their own. Female-headed households suffered most of all.

From the beginning, NOW established a task force on credit issues that, although not as prominent as some of its other committees, did attract experts in finance and business to develop the research needed to make the case for an equal credit bill. In 1972, President Nixon established the National Commission on Consumer Finance, whose report did much to bring inequities in the credit industry to the public's attention—particularly the unequal treatment of men and women in the credit realm. By 1974, according to a Virginia Slims American Women's Opinion Poll, 57 percent of American females were aware that women suffered credit discrimination. In short order, Congress held hearings and a markup of the Equal Credit Opportunity Bill began to make its way through committee in both houses. The attractiveness of the bill was enhanced by the fact that it would not involve any outlay of federal funds, as other provisionary acts and programs do. On the eve of a midterm election, Congress was looking for ways to do "good" without any cost attached. The credit industry, too, Gelb and Palley tell us, recognized some of the advantages of extending credit to eligible women. Its own credit market would be enlarged, and support for this legislation would enhance the industry's public image.[22]

Bella Abzug, the newly elected Democratic representative from New York, was one of 100 cosponsors of the bill in the House of Representatives. But it was not just a liberal issue. In the Senate the bill's sponsor was William Brock, a moderate Republican from Tennessee, whose membership on the National Commission on Consumer Finance made him a supporter. The bill's passage showed how far women activists had come since the timidity of the 1966 convention of state commissioners. Women provided expert testimony in the marking-up phase of the act and then lobbied effectively outside of Congress once it was through committee. Feminist organizations had spawned permanent lobbyists able to raise funding on their own. The Center for Women Policy Studies (still in operation) attracted a number of feminist economists and what today would be called "policy wonks" to work on issues of importance to feminists. In the end, the inside/outside strategy paid off. A bill prohibiting "discrimination on the basis of sex or marital status with respect to any aspect of a credit transaction" passed the Senate by a voice vote and was approved by the House, 355–1.

Next came the writing of the regs. Here the banking industry was not as cooperative. What if a bank did discriminate and a woman had to sue for her rightful credit? Who would pay court costs? Did a woman denied credit have the right to receive in writing an explanation for that decision? And if so, how long would banks have to maintain those records? Those writing the regulations—the Federal Reserve Board—at first caved in to the banking industry's demands on several of these matters. But the board had not counted on feminist vigilance. Calling the regs a "sellout to the banking hierarchy," Karen DeCrow, NOW's president in 1974, wrote to all members of Congress that their intent in passing the bill was being undermined. NOW gathered a coalition of other women's organizations for a renewed fight for credit equity.[23] In a strategy that would pay off again and again in lobbying for legislation, the feminists succeeded in demonstrating to Congress that until a bill was fashioned into a law with regulations they could live with, the feminists were not going to let up on the pressure.

The final regs on the credit bill were favorable to women, partly because the Federal Reserve Board contracted with the Center for Women Policy Studies to help write the regs. Part-time work and even alimony could be counted by women as income. Mortgages would be calculated on the basis of both spouses' earnings. In time, the credit industry even agreed to provide a written explanation for credit denial when gender or marital status was at issue.

The success of the Equal Credit Opportunity Act demonstrates how much the new feminists learned about politics between 1966 and 1974. It also shows that Americans were quite willing to extend "fair play" to women. By emphasizing the fairness issue, feminists were able to deflect the incipient fear that women would become more powerful and independent as a result of their credit lines. It may have been clear to NOW and the Center for Women Policy Studies, but it certainly was not bandied about that, just beneath the surface of the classic role equity issue of credit fairness, lay much potential for role change.

From Protest to Participation: All Roads Lead to Houston

By 1976, the new feminism had made enormous inroads into patriarchy. Thanks to unusual (and, as I have noted, sometimes puerile) interest on the part of the media, the ideas of the movement were widely disseminated. Also, much important new legislation and new regulations were on the books. Conservative Phyllis Schlafly's forces were poised to block approval of the Equal Rights Amendment, but feminists did not know that yet. The year brought wider and wider circles of influence and even international activity. Feminism, like democracy at the end of the 1980s, seemed to be catching fire.

The United Nations had designated the 1970s worldwide as the "Woman's Decade," launching the decade with a first international women's conference in Mexico City in 1975, a follow-on in mid-decade in Copenhagen, and an end-of-decade meeting in Nairobi. Others have written about the heady experience American feminists had in meeting their counterparts (not always called feminists but feminists at heart) from other countries, particularly from the Third World. While the United Nations and its member governments sponsored many of the "main events" at these meetings, there were dozens of other exhibits, mounds of materials, and, above all, thousands of participants who came as members of so-called nongovernmental organizations, of which, of course, America's National Organization for Women, the Women's Equity Action League, the National Abortion Rights Action League, and others were major players.

In the middle of the U.N. Women's Decade, Jimmy Carter followed Richard Nixon and Gerald Ford as president of the United States. Although not yet prepared to honor the feminists' agenda in quite the same measure as Bill Clinton would be sixteen years later, Carter and his independent-minded wife, Rosalynn, were willing to lobby extensively for the ERA and to bring a number of feminists into his inner circle of advisers. Among these were Sarah Weddington, who had brought the nation's first abortion case to the Supreme Court; Midge Costanza, an outspoken women's rights mayor from Rochester, New York (who managed a community liaison office down the hall from the president's in the White House); and former Representative Bella Abzug, whom Carter appointed to the special National Commission on the Observance of International Women's Year. Abzug soon set about getting congressional backing for a national gathering of women and women's groups in Houston in 1977, organized by paid employees of the administration and funded—and this would turn out to be controversial—from the national Treasury.

The conference presented the second-wave feminist movement, in effect, with its first official recognition. Although not feminist in name or official status, with Abzug at the helm and funds to spend, it was as if the new feminists had finally come of age and could employ government organizations, government personnel, and government moneys to further their cause. The plan was to convene delegates at fifty state grassroots assemblies and bring those delegates to Houston to vote officially on some national resolutions. This gave Houston a quasi-official character that the women's movement in the United States had not had since 1920.

Feminists cheered Carter's appointment of Bella Abzug and Congress's commitment to the Houston conference. It was an exhilarating time, and Houston promised to be a celebration of how much the new movement had been able to accomplish and how fast. Eventually, however, antifeminist women would challenge many of the state delegate assemblies and bring busloads of hecklers to the 1977 convention. I remember being alerted by friends in Connecticut that the delegate selection meetings had been unexpectedly conflict ridden, thanks to efforts by antifeminist forces to push through their own antifeminist slates and antifeminist platforms. Like so many feminists, however, I did not take seriously enough the sudden appearance of antifeminism among women and made my own way to Houston as an appointed "delegate-at-large."

More than two thousand people came to the conference as invited guests, official observers, and resource people and almost that same number as reporters, writers, photographers, and broadcasters. The woman's movement was by then hard news, not just fillers for women's pages, and the fact that 60 percent of the people requesting press passes were women attested to how responsive the media had become on the subject of their own personnel policies and their image. The delegates and official invitees came to lead workshops, give lectures, run exhibit booths, and provide entertainment. About one hundred women from other countries were also official guests.[24] More important, feminists were represented by a coalition of more than forty organizations. The movement had come a long way in terms of role equity. How far would the nation permit it to go in terms of role change?

8

Second-Generation Issues

CONFLICT OVER ROLE CHANGE

FROM 1968 THROUGH ROUGHLY 1975, legislative and enforcement victories came swiftly to feminist activists. Part of the reason was the reality of sisterhood—the convergence of so many different populations of American women and the apparently widespread support for feminism's goals. But another was that the surface inequities between women and men (what I have been calling first-generation issues) were easy to identify and not so difficult to fix. Second-generation issues were going to provoke much more opposition from the public at large because they questioned widely shared assumptions about sex and sex roles.[1]

Typical of the shift in response to the feminists' agenda was the enormous resistance generated to Title IX of the 1973 Civil Rights Act. Title IX sought to enforce sex equity in education. It was not opposed for its promise of equity in regard to access, scholarships, and hiring in public schools and universities—these guarantees fell nicely into the role equity category. But when Title IX challenged the privileges of men-only athletics on college campuses, it struck a nerve. That women students desired, qualified for, and deserved equal access to and equal funding for varsity sports challenged popular conceptions of what was normal and appropriate for men and women to do.

Comparable reactions occurred when women were fully integrated into the U.S. military after the draft was abandoned and when affirmative action was used to ease women into traditionally all-male occupations.[2] And even though no equity-conscious American (not even the red-blooded kind) would publicly condone forcible rape, feminists' insistence on redefining rape as a crime of assault, rather than one of passion run amok, challenged age-old prejudices. With date rape and sexual harassment added to the feminists' list of grievances and pregnancy defined—for the sake of workplace benefit payment plans—as just another illness or disability, the political fault lines were drawn anew. Throughout this period, feminists rarely wavered from their support for these issues, but provoked by growing concerns over legalized abortion, the deleterious effects of no-fault divorce, and illegitimacy—all constituting a perceived threat to "family values"—a vocal minority of politically conservative Americans began to see feminism and its efforts to ratify the Equal Rights Amendment as a threat.

The Equal Rights Amendment was passed almost unanimously by both houses of Congress in 1972 and should have been received by the American public as the ultimate equity issue. But by the time the ERA made its way through what was expected to be (but turned out not to be) a rapid ratification process, alliances were being forged among groups that found themselves in opposition to one or more of the feminist causes (see Chapter 9). The Equal Rights Amendment's guarantee, "No law shall be passed that abridges rights on the basis of sex," was presented by conservatives to state legislatures as a slippery slope, at the end of which would be homosexual marriage, unisex restrooms, and, most important, a loss of age-old certainties as to what men and women are supposed to be.

Rape

One would not have thought that the reclassification of rape as a crime of assault would be controversial. But when second-wave feminists extended the idea of rape to other relations between the sexes, rape became an issue that some thought feminists were taking too far. At first, the rape issue served to bond women who were victimized twice, once when they were assaulted, again when they prosecuted their assailant. Between 1971 and 1974, New York Radical Feminists put rape squarely on the feminists' agenda by organizing three public speak-outs on a subject all too often hidden from view. The speak-out was a new kind of event, a public sharing of an experience and a way of expunging misplaced shame and guilt. But along with the personal, the political came into play: Rape law, including evidentiary requirements (indications of a struggle, presence of a witness), was sorely in need of reform.

The prevailing theory, embedded in law, was that "stranger rape" was something out of the ordinary, that only men whose sexuality was pathological would commit rape, that it happened to women who were "asking" for it by their provocative dress or "contributory behavior," and that since "bad" or masochistic women often cried "rape" after the fact, the law and evidentiary procedure had to protect innocent men as far as was possible.

Thus it was that rape became, as historian Susan Brownmiller wrote in her groundbreaking book *Against Our Will: Men, Women, and Rape* in 1975, "the only crime of violence in which a victim is expected to resist."[3]

The impact of Brownmiller's book is hard to overstate. I was present at a meeting of feminists in 1973 when she read aloud from her chapter in progress on the history of rape. Rape had not previously had a history. Indeed, when researching the subject of rape in various libraries, Brownmiller had found little cataloged under rape per se. But through her feminist lens, a story unfolded that was not pretty: rape as the theft of one man's property by another, rape as a spoil of war, epidemic rape of slave women in the antebellum South, rape of "gal-boys" in prison. Most striking was her conclusion, resisted by the wider public: "Rape is not a crime of irrational, impulsive, uncontrollable lust, but is a deliberate, hostile, violent act of degradation and possession on the part of the would-be conqueror, designed to intimidate and inspire fear."[4] The fact that some men rape provides a sufficient threat to keep all women in a constant state of intimidation.

Once educated to this thesis, feminists proceeded to go to work on several fronts. The New York City speak-outs were memorialized all over the country in "Take Back the Night" marches, which marked sidewalks where a woman had been raped to raise consciousness among passersby of the pervasiveness of the threat. On the legal side, there was also much to do. At the time Brownmiller was conducting her survey of rape law, three kinds of "proof" were required for conviction: corroborating evidence, resistance on the part of the victim, and proof of the victim's past sexual "innocence." Victims of other kinds of assault were never expected to produce all three.

Thus, the feminists' political agenda was cut out for them: Reform rape law such that women's previous sexual history would be inadmissible in rape trials, reduce the requirement of third-party testimony to prove guilt, train police personnel to respect the rape victim and to take her testimony seriously, redefine rape as a crime of assault rather than a sex crime, and, above all, rid the populace of the "Boys will be boys" or "Soldiers will be soldiers" notion that served to mitigate crimes against women in certain circumstances. Ten years later, the world would view with horror the double jeopardy with which the women of Bangladesh had to contend. First they were raped in their civil war, and then their husbands refused to take them back because they were "unclean." More recently, the global community has had to come to terms with the wholesale rape of the women of Bosnia as an intentional strategy of ethnic cleansing. Phyllis Chesler, writing about Bosnia in 1996, argued (as it turns out, successfully) that since rape was used as a weapon in that war, it should be considered a war crime.[5] Three months after her article ap-

peared, for the first time in history, a U.N. tribunal indicted eight Bosnian Serb military and police officers in connection with rapes of Muslim
women during the Bosnian war, setting a precedent in giving "gender-
related crimes . . . their proper place in the prosecution of war crimes."[6]

Twelve years after Brownmiller's book appeared, Susan Estrich, a professor of law and herself a victim of stranger rape, created a stir with another pathbreaking book, which added "acquaintance" or "date" rape to
the analysis.[7] In her 1987 book *Real Rape*, Estrich argued that in date or
acquaintance rape, where the woman has known her rapist and where
extraordinary force may not have been present, police tend to find a
case "unfounded."[8] Part of the problem is that society encourages men
to be the aggressor; another is the belief that women mean "Yes" when
they say, "No," even that they desire forced sex. The issue brought out
the big guns on the other side. Conservative Norman Podhoretz saw
date rape as overblown, as "nothing less than a brazen campaign to redefine seduction as a form of rape."[9]

The issue for Podhoretz and others was in part what they took to be a
wild exaggeration of the numbers, the claim that one out of four American college women has been the victim of date rape.[10] Among feminists,
the issue was also problematic. For some, the campaign against date
rape looked like a retreat from the sexual revolution and a revival of Puritan constraints. For others, the campaign put women in the victim's
corner, unable to withstand sexual advances or to effectively exercise
their power to choose.[11]

In the workplace, exploitation and intimidation of women were exposed as sexual harassment. Again, unlike first-generation issues, sexual
harassment was at first vigorously denied and then hotly debated. With
more women entering the workforce, bringing with them an expanded
consciousness of their rights, women in greater numbers (and by no
means all of them young) felt freer to express their anger—in some instances, their rage—at behavior that men had assumed for a long time
to be "within bounds and no big deal."[12]

Sexual Harassment

"Economic power is to sexual harassment as physical force is to rape."
So wrote feminist legal scholar Catherine MacKinnon in her 1979 book
Sexual Harassment of Working Women, a call to action in the workplace
that corresponded to Susan Brownmiller's call to action on rape.[13] There
had never been any legislation specifically against sexual harassment.
Feminists did not feel that was necessary. The feminist argument was
that sexual harassment is covered under Title VII as a pernicious form of

sex discrimination in employment (see Illustration 8.1). Indeed, feminist lawyers such as MacKinnon started bringing sexual harassment cases to federal courts as early as the mid-1970s. But it fell to the Equal Employment Opportunity Commission to add sexual harassment to its "Guidelines on Discrimination," which it did in 1980. Under "unlawful, sex-based discrimination," the new EEOC guidelines read:

> Unwelcome sexual advances, requests for sexual favors, and other verbal or physical conduct of a sexual nature constitutes sexual harassment when (1) submission to such conduct is made either explicitly or implicitly a term or condition of an individual's employment or academic advancement, (2) submission to or rejection of such conduct . . . is used as the basis for employment decisions, . . . or (3) such conduct has the purpose or effect of unreasonably interfering with an individual's work or academic performance or creating an intimidating hostile or offensive working or academic environment.[14]

Sexual harassment appears to be pervasive among working-class and professional women equally. Since the publication of these guidelines in 1980, on average four thousand to five thousand sexual harassment claims have been brought to the EEOC annually.

From a feminist perspective, it is appropriate that sexual harassment has made its way from the personal to the political. In the past, women suffered silently, wondering whether they had perhaps invited unwanted advances, worrying that outright rejection would cost them their jobs. With the promulgation of the EEOC guidelines and much publicity on the subject, sexual harassment has become "the most recent form of victimization of women to be redefined as a social rather than a personal problem."[15]

Except for employees who suffered and employers who were brought up on charges, sexual harassment might still have remained in the shadows of feminist politics had not two cases burst upon the American scene in the 1990s that exposed how men holding public office are capable of sexual harassment and intimidation of their staff. The first was a searing exposure in October 1991 on the eve of the confirmation for Supreme Court justice of Clarence Thomas. The issue pitted the former EEOC director against Anita Hill, a soft-spoken African American, like Thomas, who in 1991 was a professor of law in Oklahoma but who from 1981 to 1983 had worked for Thomas at the Department of Education and had followed him as his special assistant to the EEOC.[16]

Hill claimed to have endured continuing sexual invitations, innuendos, and intimidation from Thomas during the twenty-three months she worked for him. She had remained silent for nearly a decade, but when his nomination was announced, she felt obligated to send an unso-

Illustration 8.1 Public service announcement to raise awareness about sexual harassment. Courtesy of the NOW Legal Defense Fund.

licited negative evaluation to the Senate Judiciary Committee, a letter that alleged (in some detail) many incidents of sexual harassment. When the committee took its time responding, Hill's allegations were leaked to the press. This forced the committee to schedule an extraordinary televised hearing. Although millions of Americans watched the Hill-Thomas duel, in the end the committee endorsed Thomas's nomination, the Senate confirmed it, and eight days later he was sworn in.

As in many less publicized confrontations between a woman employee and her boss, the issue boiled down to his word against hers. Anita Hill had not brought charges against Clarence Thomas at the time of the alleged harassment, and fearful and embarrassed that she might be perceived to have solicited his alleged advances, she had never recorded them, nor had she told many people about her "hostile work environment." Fearing for her job and her professional advancement, she had tolerated behavior that more than a decade later she believed disqualified her former boss from sitting on the Supreme Court.

The issue appeared to be one on which feminists had no reservations both as to the credibility of Anita Hill (despite punishing cross-examination by the Judiciary Committee) and the unworthiness of Clarence Thomas. Feminists responded with empathy to what Hill had to go through to make her case against Thomas. Calls to Nine to Five, a feminist office workers' organization, quintupled after the hearings, almost all favorable to Anita Hill, revealing raised consciousness about women's own experience with sexual harassment. After the hearings, women's residual anger about the Hill-Thomas case brought new money into feminist political causes.[17] Hill got a standing ovation at the National Forum for Women State Legislators a few months after she testified, and *Ms.* magazine published her speech.[18] For *New York Times* columnist Anna Quindlen, the lessons of the Thomas case were unambiguous: "I learned that if I ever claim sexual harassment, I will be confronted with every bozo I once dated, every woman I once struck as snotty and superior, and together they will provide a convenient excuse to disbelieve me."[19]

But not all Americans viewed the case the way feminists did. On the eve of the Judiciary Committee's vote, polling revealed that 49 percent of women believed Thomas (who denied the charges), not Hill, as did 55 percent of men.[20] Complicating the politics of the issue was the fact that both the alleged perpetrator and his victim were African Americans and that Hill, despite her race, was perceived by working-class women (or said the pollsters) as "privileged" (she was a Yale Law School graduate). Even though most civil rights leaders took Hill's side, in nationwide polls a majority of African Americans, too, favored Thomas's appointment.

A year later, opinion had shifted, partly the result of the Navy's Tail-hook scandal, in which a group of naval aviators were charged with assault and lewd behavior toward women naval officers at their annual convention.[21] As journalists Jane Mayer and Jill Abramson report, by October 1992 a *Wall St. Journal*/NBC News poll of registered voters showed 44 percent were now persuaded that Anita Hill had told the truth, and only 34 percent still sided with Justice Thomas.[22] But by then, of course, the case—though by no means the issue—was history.

Shortly after the 1992 election, a group of women who had worked for Senator Robert Packwood of Oregon accused him of years-long sexual harassment of his staff. Four years later, despite every effort to save his seat, Packwood was forced to resign. One of the several reasons the Senate was not able to treat Packwood's behavior (as it might have a decade earlier) with a slap on the wrist was that the Hill-Thomas hearings had awakened Americans to the fact that sexual harassment by powerful people was not improbable. Even so, the Packwood case might have been buried in an internal ethics committee report had not a California woman senator, Barbara Boxer, elected to the U.S. Senate in 1994, insisted on public hearings. Faced with having to answer charges publicly and risk expulsion (and the loss of his lifetime pension), Packwood chose instead to leave the Senate.

That sexual harassment is a problem for even the highest-placed professional women was further documented in 1991—shortly before the Hill-Thomas exposure—when Frances Conley, a Stanford University neurosurgeon, resigned her position due to what she described as unrelenting sexual harassment from colleagues at the Stanford Medical School and to the unwillingness of the university administration to do anything about it.[23] She later rejoined the faculty when she felt convinced her action had led to changes. Meanwhile, Bernadine Healy, President Bush's appointee to head the federal government's largest research agency, the National Institutes of Health, told in many interviews of unceasing sexual harassment when she was a research associate in cardiology at Johns Hopkins University years before. Unlike Anita Hill, Healy went immediately to the provost to complain. But like Anita Hill, she was not taken seriously.[24]

Thanks to all this publicity, by the mid-1990s the courts and most Americans were willing to acknowledge that sexual harassment exists and that it may have as much to do with power as with sex or sexual gratification.[25] Anita Hill told the Senate Judiciary Committee that she found Clarence Thomas's behavior to be an expression of *hostility* rather than lust. "I never felt he was genuinely interested in me; only in coercing me."[26] And her experience was probably typical. The broader issue, that of a hostile work environment for women, is beginning to be better understood.[27] Here the courts appear to be ahead of the population. They have recognized sexual harassment to be a punishable offense when it is "pervasive" and severe enough to affect the psychological well-being of the accuser. However, since such effects are hard to document and harder yet to attribute, the burden of proof (as in rape and wife abuse) still falls on the accuser. Complicating matters is a generation gap. Older men, who came of age in a prefeminist era, can commit sexual harassment unknowingly. That is why, in addition to public discussion, one feminist strategy has been to develop training programs for businesspeople and professionals so they will recognize sexual harassment and stop it early.

Nevertheless, most sexual harassment goes unreported. As many as one out of every two women will experience sexual harassment at some point during her academic or working life. Studies put the figure at 42 percent in the federal workforce and 66 percent in the U.S. military; others claim it could be as high as 70 or even 90 percent.[28] And the most likely to be victimized are working-class women, women who "invade" previously men-only job categories, white-collar secretaries and assistants who work closely with their bosses, and professional women. Meanwhile, popular films such as *Fatal Attraction* and *Disclosure* and the David Mamet play *Oleanna* presented reverse scenarios: women aggressing men or accusing them falsely of sexual harassment. These fictional accounts had the effect of taking the focus off women's nearly universal experience and blaming feminism for having unleashed women's aggression.

Some believe, as author Susan Faludi and others have pointed out, that sexual harassment may be the price women have to pay for workplace equality. "You wanted equality. I'll give it to you with a vengeance," says Faludi in interpreting men's resistance to being held to a higher standard of behavior. For feminists, however, there can be no compromise. Sexual harassment is a "slow, relentless accumulation of slights and insults that add up to . . . 'we don't want you here, and [to prove that to you] we are going to make you uncomfortable.'"[29] A way out of the division between men and women on this issue might be this: Once sexual harassment is understood to be only one form of more general economic intimidation of all workers, whatever their sex or race, it is possible that feminists will find more allies for their campaign.

Marriage and Divorce

At least as troubling for Americans who did not share feminist assumptions about egalitarian marriage was the specter of no-fault divorce. As we will see in the next chapter, Phyllis Schlafly, the organizer of women against the ERA, gave voice to ordinary women's fears that, among other unwelcome changes, divorce was becoming too easy and that women's libbers were to blame. When we look back on the period, it is easy to see how the link might have been made. In 1970, just at the point when the second wave of feminism was becoming a force, California became the first state to adopt a "no-fault" divorce law, and by 1980, all but two states had some form of no-fault divorce. Simple (but incorrect) logic would suggest that feminism had been behind no-fault. But in fact, feminism was only one of many parties. Rather, beginning in the 1960s, a marriage and divorce law reform movement was initiated by the American Bar Association as a way of standardizing and simplifying what had become a crazy quilt of divorce laws that sent lawabiding citizens to divorce mills in Reno, Nevada, or to the Virgin Islands, where the laws were more lax, or, if that was not possible, forced them to perjure themselves in court.

The reason for the subterfuge is that prior to the 1970s, in all fifty states, a partner had to establish both grounds and "fault" to obtain a divorce. Thus, even if both parties consented to the end of the marriage, there had to be an innocent and a guilty party.[30] Since financial support was linked to guilt or fault, there was a certain amount of bargaining or out-and-out lying at the time of divorce. In many states, adultery, itself a crime, had to be established to obtain legal separation from a spouse. Given the law, both parties found it necessary to hire lawyers, who then with typical lawyerly enthusiasm engaged in adversarial proceedings that took a further toll on the unhappy couple and the children.

As Lenore Weitzman recounts the history of the reform that produced no-fault divorce, change in divorce law was supported—for different reasons—by liberals and conservatives alike. Conservatives were concerned about preserving marriages and thought that the establishment of "family courts" designed to mediate between warring spouses would be preferable to fighting or fabricating "fault." Liberals, too, wanted to lessen the harmful consequences of divorce proceedings. Even the Catholic Church originally supported the no-fault reform, counting on family court to save troubled marriages and facilitate nonadversarial divorce when it became absolutely necessary. The fact is that it was the American Bar Association's Task Force on Marriage and Divorce, not any feminist organizations, that invented and promoted the no-fault option.[31]

Under the California law—the model for other state adoptions—three groups of women were supposed to be assured of support and special treatment even without their husbands being "at fault" in the breakup of the marriage: women who had been homemakers all their lives, mothers of young children, and mothers needing transitional support. Under the old "fault" system, if one spouse opposed the divorce, the other had to bargain. With no-fault, of course, wives lost this tool. Their continuing support was left for judges to determine. Unfortunately, many judgments ignored the value to the divorcing husband of his pension and continuing earning power (his mobile property), assigning the divorcing homemaker only transitional payments. Instead of lifetime alimony, she got only half of the couple's accumulated assets—by Weitzman's 1972 calculations, about $13,000, on average, per household.[32] The annual income for a divorced woman in the immediate year following separation goes down on average by 30 percent; her ex-husband's goes up by 15 percent, according to another national study.[33]

Less the result of no-fault divorce than of judges' naïveté, according to Weitzman's decade-long study of the impact of no-fault on California couples, women and their children (even with child support) suffered a substantial decline in their standard of living after divorce. Divorce may have changed, but gender role stereotypes of traditional marriages had not. Some ex-wives were occasionally awarded alimony, based on age, limited employability, and the duration of the marriage, but since alimony had been tied in judges' minds to "fault," it was no longer considered an automatic right of the "wronged" wife.[34] In fact, if the woman had supported her husband during marriage and he was financially in need at the time of divorce, he might be awarded regular support payments from her.[35]

What did not change was mothers' passion to retain custody of their children. In this sense, divorcing husbands now had the bargaining power divorcing wives had lost. "Women," Weitzman found, "are more likely to forego their claims to support and property if threatened with the loss of custody or other arrangements harmful to their children."[36] Add to this an increasing reluctance on the part of fathers to pay even court-awarded child support (40 percent of all divorced, separated, and single women have never received any money from the fathers of their children),[37] and one can see that no-fault divorce was a two-edged sword.

States can hold fathers criminally liable for nonsupport if the nonsupport is "willful" and the wife or children live in "destitute" conditions. In 1975, Congress adopted a provision making federal employees' salaries subject to garnishment for child support and alimony,[38] and Public Law 93-647, passed in 1993, established a federal service to locate delinquent parents, thereby providing incentives for states to enforce support and for the IRS to collect back support in certain circumstances. Nevertheless, the economic consequences of divorce continue to drive many previously married women into poverty.

Those who were not reading feminist literature on the economic consequences of divorce did not know that it was the Congressional Women's Caucus that was lobbying for child support enforcement and for protection of "displaced homemakers," ex-wives left with neither

support nor earning power. It was simpler to link no-fault with feminism, to link both with the erosion of marriage, and to see divorce as a
consequence of the twin evils of the sexual revolution and women's liberation.[39]

Even though feminists were not behind no-fault and not naive about
its consequences, there was, of course, a vast difference between feminists' view of marriage and divorce and that of a large portion of the
American population. Feminists did not look upon divorce as inherently
"evil." It was better to divorce than to be unhappily wedded for life. For
feminists, the negative economic consequence of divorce was the symptom, and enforced dependency in marriage was the disease.[40]

Title IX

As noted in Chapter 6, the addition of sex to the employment section of
the 1964 Civil Rights Bill was done in haste as a result of parliamentary
maneuvering on the part of certain members of Congress who wanted
to cut out the bill's employment provisions altogether. There were many
other "titles" of that landmark bill that these congressmen did not think
they had the power to alter, however, titles having to do with race discrimination in public accommodations (the lunch-counter issue) and in
education. For feminism, the 1964 Civil Rights Act came early. It would
take several years for a full-fledged women's movement to become politically active. As a result of this tortuous history, the other titles to the
1964 Civil Rights Act were never expanded to include sex as a protected
category.

Of the unamended titles, Title VI prohibited discrimination in all federally assisted programs. Feminists made a strategic decision in the mid-
1970s not to open Title VI to amendment for fear Congress would repeal
it altogether. Instead, in 1972, they lobbied for two new bills: Title IX of
the 1972 Educational Amendments and the Women's Educational Equity
Act. Title IX was particularly important. It forbade discrimination on the
basis of sex in all publicly funded educational programs but did not provide any funds to augment programs for girls. The Women's Educational
Equity Act provided some of the funding needed for schools and other
organizations to, as the act read, "counter sex-role socialization and
stereotyping" in educational materials.[41]

While Title IX was being debated in Congress, there appeared to be little popular opposition. Nevertheless, Representative Edith Green
(D–Ore.) discouraged feminists from lobbying too publicly for the bill
lest attention be drawn to its wide-reaching powers. She was right to do
so. As enforcement details were hammered out after passage of the bill

in the Office of Civil Rights of the Department of Health, Education, and Welfare (HEW), the male sports establishment discovered that the enforcement of Title IX potentially threatened the privileged place of male varsity athletics in U.S. colleges and universities and began to lobby to weaken the title. It was not that varsity sports would become coed. Contrary to some opponents' claims, feminists never demanded the right to play football or men's basketball.[42] Rather, the issue was equal or proportionately equal *funding* for school-based sports for women. As written, Title IX provided that "no person in the United States shall, on the basis of sex, be excluded from participation in, be denied the benefits of, or be subjected to discrimination under any education program or activity receiving federal financial assistance." Girls and boys under age twelve might play on integrated teams. But it was understood that from middle school onward, girls' and boys' sports could be separate so long as there were equal athletic opportunities for each.

The cause of the intense lobbying against Title IX, then, was not coeducational sports but equal funding for men's and women's sports (see Illustration 8.2). Title IX's enforcement provisions, at least on paper, were serious. If any educational institution was found to discriminate in any of its programs—including admissions, athletics, financial aid, counseling, facilities, and employment practices—federal funds would be cut off.[43] The employment provision was a particularly important victory for feminists since under Title VII of the 1964 Civil Rights Act, women who held professional jobs (nonexempt, in the jargon of labor legislation) had previously not been covered either by Title VII or by other antidiscrimination legislation. For ten years, school janitors could sue for employment discrimination under Title VII; teachers could not.

The equal admissions section of Title IX, however, was no less crucial. The amendments put a long-desired end to caps on the admission of women students in medical, law, business, and other professional schools; America would no longer participate in the Rhodes Scholar program unless the British agreed to make it available to qualified women. But, again, admissions were seen as a role equity issue for which most Americans were ready to give up male privilege. Sex equity in college athletics, however, went further than many Americans were willing to go. And there was a ready lobby in the National Collegiate Athletic Association (NCAA) eager to represent that point of view. At first, the NCAA did not attempt to repeal Title IX; rather, its strategy was to slow the title's enforcement by lobbying the Department of Health, Education, and Welfare. That strategy was so effective that at one point women's groups had to sue HEW and the Department of Labor to get the federal government to enforce Title IX altogether. And with good reason: As of this writing, no funds have ever been cut off because of noncompliance with Title IX.[44]

Title IX of the 1972 Education Amendments guarantees equal rights in education to your daughter

BUT here is her share of school sports' budgets!

©NOW LDEF. Concept & design by Jane Trahey.

did you know that your daughters get just 20% of sports budgets in the public schools?

did you know your daughters get just 15% of all athletic scholarship dollars?

did you know that in at least 50% of school districts coaches of girls' teams are paid less than coaches of boys' teams?

did you know that girls' trophies are not the same size and do not have the same importance as boys' trophies?

did you know that practice time for boys far exceeds practice time for girls?

did you know that award dollars for girls' athletic excellence differ substantially from those for boys?

did you know that seven times as much press is given boys' sports as is given girls' athletic events?

did you know that there is a serious imbalance in the number of games scheduled for girls vs. games for boys?

did you know you have every right to challenge your own school to see that a fairer apportionment of sports budgets go to your daughters? Do something about it today!

YOU CAN IMPROVE THIS PICTURE. For more information write
NOW Legal Defense & Education Fund (C) 132 W. 43rd Street, N.Y., N.Y. 10036

Illustration 8.2 Public service announcement to raise awareness about discrimination in public schools. Courtesy of the NOW Legal Defense Fund.

Nevertheless, there was some voluntary compliance on the athletics issue in elementary and middle schools as parents pressured Little League and local school boards to add sports programs for girls. Women's participation in women-only college sports also benefited from the challenge to outdated notions of "femininity" initiated by the feminist movement more generally. And even as the NCAA was fighting Title IX's enforcement provisions, the regulations of the title made it possible to collect data. Thus, we know that before Title IX, there were about 16,000 women participating in college athletics annually and that by 1984 that number had risen to 150,000. More important, there was now new money for women's athletics. Before Title IX, about 1 percent of total college spending on athletics was assigned to women's sports; by 1984 that figure was 16 percent. Of the 150,000 college women participating in varsity sports, 10,000 held athletic scholarships.[45]

The federal government's legislative reach is limited, of course, to "federally assisted educational programs." Technically, colleges and universities are either private or state supported. Apart from the military service academies, there is no national school or national university in the United States. But many institutions were (and are) in receipt of federal funds in the form of research grants and contracts for special educational programs, and all receive federal aid in the tuition their students pay that is supported by federally guaranteed student loans. The legal (and, of course, political) question that the Supreme Court eventually tried to settle was this one: Must educational equity be assured in programs *not directly* funded by the federal government (such as varsity sports) or only where federal funds were specifically involved (such as student loans)?

In 1984, a small private college in Pennsylvania sued the then secretary of education (Terrence Bell) on that very question. In *Grove City College* v. *Bell*, the Supreme Court decided in favor of the college, ruling that only those programs funded directly by federal money had to provide sex equity. After *Grove*, Title IX enforcement languished for four years. But by the late 1980s, there was sufficient congressional support to enact a new bill (the 1987 Civil Rights Restoration Act), even over President Reagan's veto, that essentially overturned the Supreme Court's earlier decision and restored Title IX coverage in full.[46] Much of the success of the Congressional Caucus on Women's Issues in passing the Civil Rights Restoration Act was due to a broad coalition of women's and civil rights groups working together.[47]

There were still limitations, however, which further legislation and court decisions sought to overturn. The 1987 Civil Rights Restoration Act exempted admissions to private and even public undergraduate institutions that had been continuously and traditionally single-sex and to the nation's military academies. In 1976, Congress opened West Point, Annapolis, and the Air Force Academy in Colorado Springs to women students. But private military institutions were still exempt. In 1994, a young woman with the unisex first name of "Shannon" applied and was admitted to The Citadel, a private South Carolina military academy. When the college discovered that she was female, it promptly rejected her. Under advice from her lawyers, Shannon Faulkner sued the academy under the equal protection clause of the Fourteenth Amendment.[48] Faulkner's claim and that of the young women who in June 1996 won from the Supreme Court the right to be admitted to the all-male Virginia Military Institute are rooted in the same philosophy that undergirded Title IX and the 1954 anti–school segregation decision in *Brown* v. *Board of Education*: namely, that separate programs and separate facilities for whites and blacks or for men and women will forever stand in the way of equal opportunity.

Today, Title IX enforcement has been extended to include ageism and protection from sexual harassment—all of which, say some, water down its original intention. What is interesting is that the athletics issue will not go away. Football remains a sticking point. At times, the regulators have tried to exempt football by creating a special category called contact sports. But feminists buried that strategy with an unforgettable one-liner: "Dancing is a contact sport; football is a collision sport." In 1995, the regulations were being revised once again by the Office of Civil Rights in the Department of Education. Even after twenty years, three acts of Congress, and a Supreme Court decision, the idea of sex equity in collegiate athletics is still only grudgingly accepted.[49]

Affirmative Action

While struggling under Title IX to eliminate quotas on women's access to higher and postgraduate education, feminists were mobilizing support for what their opposition called quotas in affirmative action hiring. Supporters of affirmative action insist that these are not quotas but "goals and timetables." But the problem is more than semantic. Affirmative action was meant to compensate women and minorities for the prior collective disadvantage of either gender or race (or both). But in so doing, it set group needs against individual rights in ways that made even well-meaning Americans uncomfortable. I have already traced the series of executive orders beginning in World War II that required firms doing business with the federal government to provide equal opportunity for minorities in employment. When "equal opportunity" did not go far or fast enough in eliminating sex and race segregation in employment, activists wanted the federal government to pressure public- and private-sector employers to take the next logical step and *favor* members of previously excluded groups.

The legal justification for the extra efforts (or preferences, as the opposition would call these) was grounded in court-ordered "remedies" applied to businesses where discrimination had been unequivocally established. The remedies were in essence punishment not for the *country's* past wrongs but for the *company's*. So long as affirmative action was limited to such companies, the practice generated little opposition. The sticking point came with the extension of such remedies to employers not found by the courts to have intentionally discriminated but whose employment rolls showed severe "underrepresentation" of certain "affected groups."

Affirmative action was never voted by Congress as statute. Rather, it took the form of Department of Labor regulations and executive orders issued by the president, and it meant to use the government's purchasing power as the "carrot" rather than the courts' remedies as the "stick." Requiring more than equal opportunity of those from whom the federal government purchased goods and services could have a great impact on the economy as a whole. At any one time, as many as 325,000 firms do business with the federal government, which together employ anywhere (depending on year and contract renewal) from 16 to 25 million workers (out of a total workforce of 110 million). Thus, between 20 and 30 percent of all workers could be affected by affirmative action requirements if they were comprehensively enforced.[50] But as affirmative action requirements were adopted by the states and applied to municipal fire and police departments, nonprofit cultural institutions, and universities (adding 18 million more workers to the total covered), the carrot came to look more and more like a stick, and support for affirmative action by the American people as a whole eroded.

Feminists' support never wavered, even during affirmative action's rockiest periods. From the moment feminist activists persuaded President Lyndon Johnson to amend Executive Order 11246 in 1967 to include women (Executive Order 11375), the pressure was on to get large employers to develop affirmative action plans. These plans involved four critical steps: first, to do a race/gender count of persons employed in various job categories in the company itself; second, to determine the size of the supply pool—by job category—from which minorities and women might be recruited for the next available job by job group (a national pool in the case of a professional search, a local pool in the case of the search for an office employee); third, to compare the size and race/gender ratio of the supply pool to the existing race/gender composition of the company's workforce—again by job category; and fourth, from that ratio, to tally a score card as to how the company's workforce corresponded to the potential supply. Only if minorities and women were underemployed (given the score card) would the company be asked to select a "reasonable" set of "goals" and a "timetable" to achieve racial and gender "balance" in the near future.

At the stage of recruitment and hiring, at least in theory, only a "good faith effort" was called for to locate candidates from the enlarged labor pool for every job opening. Competition among candidates was supposed to remain fair. But under pressure to meet affirmative action goals, employers sometimes compromised fairness or (as a way of expressing their opposition to the process) publicly advertised that they did.[51] This only incensed workers and their families who were denied employment or promotion.

Simply stated, there was a problem, and not just one of perception. Two federal policies—equal opportunity and equal proportional outcomes—were in conflict. Title VII of the 1964 Civil Rights Act expressly forbids preferential treatment to remediate any imbalance. Indeed, the law is unambiguous on this point: "Nothing in [this law] shall be construed to require an employer ... to grant preferential treatment to any individual or any groups ... on account of any imbalance that may exist with respect to the total number and percentage of persons of any race." But President Johnson's executive orders required companies to accelerate their hiring of women and minorities in order to meet affirmative action goals. Not surprisingly, "goals" were often treated by management and seen by employees to be nothing less than quotas, and the hiring of women and minorities in positions where there had previously been only whites or only men were considered "preferences." No wonder the controversy over affirmative action continued unabated through six administrations.

As it turned out, affirmative action did not change the ratio of women to men in the occupations in which they were underrepresented (the trades, for example, or the airline pilots association) (see Illustration 8.3). That would require other kinds of strategies. But for women already trained and poised to take advantage of new jobs, affirmative action turned out to be an extremely effective method of moving in and moving up.[52] For this reason, even though support for affirmative action lost to feminism many of its original equity-based allies, feminists have stuck with it. The irony, however, not lost on them (and a continuing source of political discomfort) is this: A policy originally designed to compensate African Americans for the enormous injuries suffered under slavery, segregation, and residual racism has disproportionately benefited white women.

Evidence for this is in the increase of women in corporate management. At this writing, women hold 40 percent of all corporate middle management positions and between 5 and 7 percent of senior manage-

**"When
I grow up,
I'm going
to be
a judge,
or a senator
or maybe president."**

Oh, no you're not little girl!

Your chances of making it into public office are very slim. Only 23 of 657 FEDERAL JUDGES are women. Only 2 of 100 SENATORS are women. No woman has ever been PRESIDENT. But you do have a 99% chance to be a NURSE. (You'll earn less than a tree-trimmer.) Or a 97% chance to be a TYPIST. (You'll earn less than the janitor.) Or a 60% chance to be a SCHOOL TEACHER. (You'll earn less than a zoo-keeper.)

Concerned mamas and daddies are asking how they can help their female children to get an equal crack at vocational training —training that opens doors to non-stereotypical, better paying jobs. Parents want their female children to get the same kind of coaching in sports and physical education as boys do.

Parents want the kind of counseling that will encourage wider career options for girls. (Most young women graduate without the science and math credits they need to exercise full options for higher education.) If your female children attend a federally supported public school in this country you can and should help them get a more equal education.

YOU CAN HELP TO CREATE A BETTER FUTURE.
Write NOW Legal Defense & Education Fund (H) 132 W. 43rd Street, N.Y., N.Y. 10036

Illustration 8.3   Public service announcement illustrating women's limited employment opportunities. Courtesy of the NOW Legal Defense Fund.

ment positions, up from 1.5 percent in the mid-1980s. Equal credit legislation, along with small business set-asides that the federal government has required (contracts reserved for women- and minority-owned businesses), has contributed to a 57 percent increase in the number (not, however, in the total value) of women-owned businesses in the last decade.[53] In contrast, African Americans' share of middle management and professional positions went up only 1.5 percent—from 5.6 to 7.1 percent in that same period.[54] The reason is that there is continuing discrimination against people of color in education and training.

Nevertheless, the majority of women workers remains locked in pink-collar ghettos, segregated by their own and other people's perceptions of what is appropriate work for women to do.[55] Women's entry into the male-dominated trades has been the least successful of the many employment strategies pursued by feminists. Despite a federal "goal" of 6.9 percent, women never managed to fill more than 2 percent of construction jobs. And women in the entry-level jobs that dominate the retail service sector have hardly benefited at all. Their problem is not low numbers but low pay and limited mobility once employed.

"If you have only an imprecise conception of affirmative action, you are not alone," wrote Carol Carson and Faye Crosby in their update on affirmative action published in the Smith College *Alumnae Quarterly* in winter 1989, twenty-two years after Lyndon Johnson's executive order for women went into effect.[56] Intended to advance equal opportunity, affirmative action appears to contradict it. Equal opportunity is supposed to be sex and race blind. Affirmative action, in contrast, requires an organization to take account of sex, race, and ethnicity.

Indeed, feminists and other advocates for affirmative action hiring shifted the argument in the mid-1990s from "compensatory fairness" to "diversity." But countless white males feel they have lost out, and many middle-of-the-road Americans are of the opinion that, even if affirmative action has been effective in moving some women and minorities up the job ladder, it is no longer fair (if it ever was) and certainly not efficient.[57]

Mirroring the nation's ambivalence on the matter, the Supreme Court itself has gone back and forth on affirmative action, sometimes restricting it, as in the famous *Bakke* decision, where a white male (Allan Bakke) was not admitted to the University of California Medical School at Davis, although "less qualified" minorities were. The Court took a middle ground: Bakke had to be admitted, race could not be used as an exclusive criterion (the way the university "reserved" 16 percent of its openings for people of color was declared illegal), but race could be a "plus" factor in admission.[58] At other times, the Court let programs stand because they removed "manifest imbalances in traditionally segregated job categories."[59] The Court, like many Americans, is unwilling to countenance reverse discrimination even to correct past inequities.

In the mid-1990s, thirty years after affirmative action was first promulgated, it remains controversial. But feminists are still in favor, even after Republican presidential candidate Robert Dole publicly changed his position on affirmative action in 1995—he is now opposed—and his party declared it the "wedge issue" in the 1996 elections. In response, Kathryn Rodgers, executive director of the NOW Legal Defense and Education Fund, reasserted NOW's view: "[Affirmative action] says: a woman should apply; if she applies she will be considered on her merits; when she's hired she can be trained for advancement; and when a promotion is available, she will be considered on her merits. None of these things was true only 30 years ago—remember those sex-segregated want ads?"[60]

Many women are too young to remember the want ads or the admissions quotas or the employment ghettos, and many more feel uncomfortable with a policy that can be characterized as giving them preference.[61] So do "angry white males," who, ever since the Reagan years, have been pitted against women in the currying of political favor. Antifeminists claim that "average women" do not want equality in the workplace if it means interchangeability with men, and African Americans feel cheated when white women are preferred, complicating the politics of affirmative action still more.

But perhaps the most serious challenge to affirmative action remedies has come from those who feel that, in its emphasis on race and gender, affirmative action has failed to open doors and to compensate the most educationally and occupationally disadvantaged group of all: the poor. America, it appears, has been more willing to talk about and to compensate race and gender discrimination than to deal with the issue of class.[62]

Abortion and Pregnancy

Even though abortion was legalized by a remarkably swift and comprehensive Supreme Court ruling in *Roe* v. *Wade* in 1973—an earlier and more complete victory than the new feminists had any right to expect— abortion was and remained for decades the consummate second-generation issue.[63] Rattled by the sudden demise of hundred-year-old state laws that had criminalized abortion in all but cases where the mother's life was in danger, and shocked by the numbers of legal abortions that were being performed (1–1.5 million per year beginning in 1973), a "right-to-life" movement gathered its forces to work on every front to overturn the Supreme Court's decision. Throughout the 1980s, an antiabortion amendment to the Constitution was frequently introduced. Had it passed Congress and been ratified by three-quarters of the states, the fetus would have had the legal standing of a "person," making abortion murder.

Although the amendment never made it out of Congress, several times it came very close. More successful were antiabortion amendments to various budget authorization bills from 1976 onward, which prevented poor women from taking advantage of their constitutional right to abortion by preventing federal funds from being used to pay for the procedure.[64] With the presidency in the hands of out-and-out abortion foes from 1980 to 1992 and a Republican Party ever more dependent on support from right-to-lifers, the abortion issue could be said to have galvanized the "silent majority" and, worse yet, threatened to roll back all of feminism's successes. The story of the Supreme Court's backtracking on abortion rights belongs to Chapter 14, but the power of the issue to generate votes for right-to-life candidates caught the feminist leadership by surprise.

Less volatile but no less central to the feminist agenda was a reassignment of pregnancy from its unique, almost mystical place in the American firmament to the status of a "temporary disability" that could be treated (and paid for) like any other disability as far as workplace benefits and health insurance coverage are concerned. Recall that in the "bad old days" public school teachers in most states had to resign their positions when they became pregnant, lest the children in their charge be made uncomfortable by their condition. With their resignations went their health coverage, which meant that only the *wives* of male teachers had access to pre- and postnatal medical reimbursements. Maternity leave in other occupations was deducted (if it was allowed at all) from a woman's personal sick days; and women who left for six weeks or more to nurse and care for infants risked losing their jobs completely. Meanwhile, men with hernias (which took about as much time to heal) or heart attacks (which took longer and often reduced the workplace efficiency of the patient) retained all of their benefits (including retirement and seniority) and got their expenses reimbursed. It would have been considered heartless (if not illegal) not to give them their jobs back when they recovered.

Could one make the case that "pregnancy discrimination" is a form of "sex discrimination," even though only women can get pregnant? The Equal Employment Opportunity Commission was developing guidelines to this effect in the early 1970s, but the General Electric Corporation (GE) thought not. Its benefits package did not cover pregnancy-related disability and illness for *anyone;* hence, GE's lawyers argued, it was nondiscriminatory. When one of its unions representing a woman employee sued the company under Title VII, the Supreme Court bought the company's argument that its policy was gender neutral and ruled in

General Electric v. *Gilbert* in December 1976 in favor of General Electric. Clearly, an amendment to Title VII was due.

Again the issue was not the constitutionality of any statute but rather what had been the intent of Congress in adding sex to the employment provision of the 1964 Civil Rights Act. Absent a historical record (recall that the addition of sex to Title VII had been a parliamentary maneuver—an "accident"—so there had not been hearings or any significant debate on the issue of women and employment), there was no way the Court could know what Congress had intended in regard to pregnancy discrimination. But after 1976, Congress could act to clear up the confusion. A campaign to end discrimination against pregnant workers, with labor union support, succeeded in getting the Pregnancy Discrimination Act passed in 1978.[65] The act, as Joyce Gelb and Marian Palley report it, went beyond health insurance coverage. Its intent was to "prohibit discrimination against pregnant women in all areas of employment including hiring, firing, seniority rights, job security, and receipt of fringe benefits. It also required employers who offered health insurance and temporary disability plans to provide coverage to women for pregnancy, childbirth, and related medical conditions."[66]

A sticking point was whether elective abortions would be covered by the bill's requirements. Antiabortion forces supported the bill because it protected mothers but balked at the possibility that the ending of a pregnancy and its attendant medical costs and possible consequences would be included. Eventually, a compromise was reached whereby companies would be permitted but not required to cover abortion. But they could not discriminate by firing or demoting an employee because of either.

Pregnancy was not abortion, and so the discussion of "pregnancy rights," though new, was never as intemperate as that of a woman's "right to choose" to end a pregnancy. Nevertheless, the new language challenged the significance of reproduction-related sex differences and indirectly of motherhood itself. Since pregnancy is presumed to be intentional, it did not seem to fit under disabilities, which are not sought. A snide colleague of mine commented at the time that such a "disability" would be like a football injury: "You didn't play to get hurt, but you wouldn't have gotten hurt if you hadn't played." Discussions like these erased some of the magic of motherhood. Equality was moving closer to interchangeability in the eyes of many. And these portended role changes many Americans were not yet willing to contemplate, much less to accept.

9

Antifeminist Women on the Right

THE BATTLE OVER THE ERA

THE EQUAL RIGHTS AMENDMENT WAS FIRST introduced into Congress in 1923 by Alice Paul's National Woman's Party, which took the position that the next logical step after women's suffrage had to be a constitutional guarantee that "no rights would be abridged on account of sex"—that is, an equal rights amendment. Quite early in the lobbying for an ERA, however, it became clear that this amendment would be far more controversial than the Nineteenth, which had given women the right to vote. The ERA was opposed by "social feminists," who had taken upon themselves the task of protecting women, most particularly working-class women at the lower end of the economic scale.[1] For many postsuffrage activists, an equal rights amendment that eliminated gender differences in the law threatened the minimum hours and other protective legislation that social feminists had lobbied for in the late nineteenth and early twentieth centuries. Indeed, protective legislation rested in theory and in practice on the fact that there are fundamental physical and emotional inequalities between men and women and on women's greater vulnerability.

Right away, supporters and opponents of the ERA divided along class lines. Those who saw women's interests as benefiting from equality split off from those who saw women as needing protection. And the divisions reemerged along similar lines—thanks in large measure to the work of Phyllis Schlafly's anti-ERA campaign—fifty years later. In short, the opponents feared that an equal rights amendment would, by itself, undo all the workplace protections that had been upheld under the Brandeis Court. Since a large majority of women politically active in the 1920s shared this point of view, those who had promoted the ERA in the years before and immediately after World War II found themselves isolated from the mainstream.

The idea remained in the background during the decades of economic depression, war, and the return to "normalcy" after the war, nurtured by the tiny rump group that maintained the NWP throughout this period. After World War II, many of the formerly fascist countries in Eastern Europe fell under Soviet domination and adopted constitutions incorporating something like an "equal rights for women" clause. But it was only after the revival of feminism in the United States in the late 1960s that the ERA resurfaced here. In the early tentative coalitions that brought Kennedy commissioners, unemployed housewives, and radical younger women together as "feminists," only the labor union women remained attached to protective legislation and retained the old doubts about the ERA. For newcomers to women's rights issues, the arguments for an equal rights amendment to the Constitution seemed irresistible, and as early as 1968, the newly formed NOW organization put the ERA high on its agenda. As that agenda made its way through the legislative process, the Equal Rights Amendment was introduced in the House and Senate and finally passed both houses in 1972, with no exemptions.

That there were no exemptions in the final wording of the ERA was the feminists' first major achievement in the renewed battle for the ERA. Most previous versions of the amendment had included a qualifying clause that read, "Nothing in this Amendment shall be construed to deprive women of any of the rights, benefits, or exemptions [such as from the military draft] they now possess." Many men in Congress were still not prepared to contemplate a comprehensive implementation of gender equality without some restrictions. The story of their attempts to amend the amendment is an interesting and important prologue to the impassioned debates that were to follow during the failed attempt at ratification from 1972 to 1982.

It is tempting to view the men in Congress who wanted to amend the ERA as having an antiwoman bias. But what motivated someone such as Senator Sam Ervin, an elderly southern gentleman who had served the state of North Carolina with distinction for many years and who just a few years later was to make a memorable contribution in the Watergate investigation, was more complicated. To Ervin, "women's rights" signified privileges and protections—not only at work but also in the family—and the privilege Ervin was most concerned not to lose was women's exemption from military service, the most macho and dangerous of male-only enterprises. But he was just as determined to protect wives, mothers, and widows from the economic consequences of an entirely "liberated" society. Other opponents to the amendment were not so pure of heart.

Among them were Henry Hyde (R–Ill.), who would later be a fierce opponent of federal funding for abortion, and Emmanuel Celler (D–N.Y.), whose position as chair of the House Judiciary Committee made it impossible for the ERA even to get onto the floor of the House without a clever maneuver designed by Representative Martha Griffiths.[2] Together, eleven amendments to the Equal Rights Amendment were proposed in the course of the congressional debates on the ERA.

But to ERA supporters in the early 1970s, still riding high on the media's rapid acceptance of the basic premises of the new feminism, such exemptions were not to be tolerated. As Griffiths argued, "What are called protective laws have become in fact restraints which keep the wife, the abandoned wife, and the widow alike from supporting their families."[3] Women belonged in the military, it was argued, because if women were to enjoy the rights and privileges of full citizenship, they were going to have to pay their dues, as men do. ERA proponents also feared that any exemptions in the Equal Rights Amendment could lead to negative adjudication later. With *some* exemptions in place, it would be hard to argue that *other* exemptions had not been intended by Congress. There was, then, a general theoretical objection to any amendment to the amendment and a specific objection to the military service exemption. Indeed, as the ERA wound its way through the House and Senate, feminists began to lobby for the shortest and least ambiguous of all possible wordings, one that would permit no limits on equal rights for women.

The wording of the Equal Rights Amendment that finally passed was short and unambiguous, indeed: Article I, "Equality of rights under the law shall not be abridged by the United States or by any state on account of sex." Article II, "The Congress shall have the power to enforce by appropriate legislation the provisions of this Article." Article III, "This Amendment shall take effect two years after the date of ratification."

So on October 13, 1971, in the House and on March 22, 1972, in the Senate, with the requisite two-thirds majorities, the Equal Rights Amendment overcame its first major hurdle to passage. Since the Constitution requires that three-quarters of the states ratify within seven years, ahead were thirty-eight state campaigns. Looking back on that period, some feminists now believe that they misled themselves by thinking that Congress would provide the most serious opposition. With the congressional victory in hand, they fully expected the thirty-eight states rapidly to follow suit. Indeed, one month later (and this often happens with amendments to the Constitution), there was a "rush to ratify." Several states wanted to go down in the history books as having been first. With an eye on history, the new state of Hawaii voted immediately in favor of the ERA—twenty-two minutes after passage in the Congress—

and thirteen others followed suit soon after. Not all state legislatures meet annually, so there were expected delays. Nevertheless, one year later, in 1973, thirty states were on the "yes" side of the ERA balance sheet, and none was yet on the negative side.

With only eight to go, it seemed in 1973 that the ERA was certain of ratification. But in the next six years, only five more states voted to ratify, and five others rescinded their earlier approval.[4] After 1977, despite twenty-five more votes taken (a total of fourteen alone in the Illinois legislature), the final approvals never came. Even after the deadline had been extended from 1979 to 1982 by dint of heavy lobbying by feminists, the ERA ultimately failed. The question as to whether the five rescissions would have counted never had to be tested in the courts. But by the acts of rescission, several states indicated substantial reversal of sentiment, at least on the part of their legislators, if not their constituents, on the issue of the ERA. What happened?

The task of a feminist analysis is to try to account for this political turnabout. Why did it happen? How much was the demise of the ERA the work of anti-ERA lobbying, most particularly by one person, Phyllis Schlafly, who worked tirelessly for more than a decade to expose what she and her followers came to believe would be the negative consequences for women and their families if the ERA was ratified? How much was failure due to an inability on the part of the pro-ERA forces to make their case stick? And how much was due to the political tide turning to the Right in the United States toward the end of the 1970s?

All of these played a role. But however much her detractors would like to deny her capability, the impact of Phyllis Schlafly has to be acknowledged. Almost single-handedly, Schlafly formulated an anti-ERA position that tens of thousands of her women followers could relate to, and with it, she energized the forces that together brought the ERA to a halt. Without her, the ERA might have sailed through ratification by the mid-1970s, before the Reagan era.[5] To examine this interpretation, we must do what contemporary feminists were loathe to do during the long battle over ERA—namely, to look closely at the politics of the ratification process and to examine objectively the impact of Phyllis Schlafly and her work.[6]

The Schlafly Phenomenon

The story of Phyllis Schlafly's opposition to the ERA begins in irony, for the forces that shaped Phyllis Schlafly's life were not so different from the forces that shaped Betty Friedan's.[7] Born about six years later than Friedan, in the mid-1920s, Schlafly grew up in much the same era and with many of the same privileges and expectations. She attended college during World War II (Friedan graduated in 1942) and married after the war, as did Friedan. She had her six children in the 1950s and 1960s, at the same time Friedan was bringing up her three. While Friedan was trying to make a living as a freelance writer, Schlafly was collaborating on a number of political books. Both women were unquestionably accomplished, energetic, and certainly as ambitious as any in their generation. Yet, even though Schlafly tends not to dwell on her failures or frustrations (she likes to portray herself as master of her fate), the failures are there in her biography, and a startling conclusion is waiting to be drawn: Like Friedan and most of her female contemporaries, Schlafly did not do very well in a male-dominated world.

Consider the following three examples. Schlafly, as her biographer tells us, was an important contributor to Barry Goldwater's campaign for president in 1964. She was, in fact, the person who formulated the theme of that campaign. When her book *A Choice, Not an Echo*, which favored the senator and his program, sold 2 million copies, Goldwater appropriated the title and used it as the motto of his campaign. Yet, although she was crisscrossing the country on his behalf, not only did the candidate keep her from playing any major role in his campaign; he also did not even mention her contribution in his memoirs. Nor did he appreciate how much her political loyalty to him cost her. Goldwater's nomination in 1964 had set off tremendous divisions within the Republican Party. Many thought him too far to the right of the American mainstream, and, in fact, after the 1964 Republican debacle his supporters were excluded from party power until they reemerged with the Reagan forces in the 1970s. Schlafly's support of Goldwater cost her dearly with the Republicans, and her own political career among Republicans went into decline. One could argue that, like so many women of her generation, Schlafly's talents went unrecognized, and her contributions were undervalued because of her gender. But Schlafly chose not to draw this conclusion from these events.

After the Goldwater campaign, Schlafly became the vice president of the National Republican Women's Federation and in 1966 ran for president of that group. But her candidacy soon foundered on the opposition of Ray Bliss, then head of the Republican Party. In her retelling of the events that led to her defeat, Schlafly cites two reasons for Bliss's lack of support: first, that she was associated with the Goldwater faction of the party (1966 was, of course, but two years after the losses of 1964); second, that Bliss and the party hierarchy in general found her "abrasive." Interestingly, the same kinds of epithets were being hurled at feminists such as Betty Friedan, Bella Abzug, and others in the 1960s. Today, none of Schlafly's devoted followers finds her "abrasive" (though her feminist opponents do). More likely, Bliss's perception resulted from his expectations of how a female ought to behave. When Schlafly chose to play "hard ball" in her campaign for the presidency of the federation, she violated the "Nice girls don't . . ." code of behavior.

The third example of Schlafly's failure to succeed in a man's world (my assessment, not hers) is that she twice ran unsuccessfully for Congress, once in 1952 and again in 1970. Although her gender was not the chief reason she lost those races (but one of her opponents demeaned her candidacy by saying that "Mrs. Schlafly ought to be at home minding her family"), we can conclude that as of 1970, this energetic, highly politicized woman had failed to achieve three of the major political objectives she had sought: She had never won recognition for her part in the Goldwater conservative alliance within the Republican Party, she had lost two races for Congress, and she had not achieved the one big job she had really wanted as president of the National Republican Women's Federation.

So why did Phyllis Schlafly not become a feminist? In terms of her personal and professional experience, she might well have done so. As late as 1970, we have evidence that she was neither pro- nor antifeminist but was, rather, indifferent to the whole issue. She refused an invitation to debate a "well-known Connecticut feminist"[8] that year, her biographer tells us, because she was simply "not interested in the subject." Her antifeminism, then, was late in blooming. In that period of "indifference," might she have come close to accepting a feminist version of her life? Given her background, the answer is no. Schlafly is, essentially, a conservative and as such would have been put off as much by the arguments as by the agenda of the second wave of feminism. Simply because a woman is female or a housewife or has a problem that has no name does not mean she will become a feminist *unless*—and feminists took a long time to understand this—she leans toward a progressive agenda.

Evidence of Schlafly's conservatism goes well beyond her support of Goldwater. During those same years when she was running for Congress and for the top position among Republican women, she was writing five books on defense and national security issues in collaboration with a retired admiral. The starting point of these books was that in the face of relentless aggrandizement on the part of the Soviet Union, America's only hope lay in readiness for war (even nuclear war). Schlafly and her coauthor were so suspicious of the Soviets that they found fault even with the 1963 Atmospheric Test Ban Treaty, a treaty driven by citizen concern with radioactive fallout. Today, nearly everyone believes that the treaty was as valuable to world health as to arms control. But so deep was her distrust of the Soviet Union that to this day Phyllis Schlafly would rescind the Atmospheric Test Ban.

In addition to her promilitarism and her belief in a "strong" United States, there is Schlafly's Catholicism and midwestern roots. Writing about Schlafly in *The Hearts of Men,* Barbara Ehrenreich describes Schlafly's father as a role model for the conservative daughter. Although the Depression caused him prolonged unemployment, he continued to rail against President Roosevelt and the New Deal.[9] And although her mother worked to keep Phyllis in an elite Catholic girls' school, the young Schlafly "had no intention of following in her mother's footsteps and becoming—even voluntarily—a career woman."[10] Nor did Schlafly appear to experience the personal frustrations as a married woman that drove Friedan's generation into the streets. While Friedan's suburban housewives, trying to manage two to four children, found themselves drowning in diapers and buried in their homemade bread, Schlafly brought up six, all the while finding time for writing and politics. How? Her husband, a successful lawyer, provided the means to purchase household help. But another factor has to be her energy and her talent for organization. Schlafly's presumption, frequently expressed in her speeches and writing, that all women can accomplish as much with less is flawed, but her own capacity for hard work may well be, as she describes it, enormous.

If her underlying conservatism contributed to Schlafly's *resistance* to feminism, her passionate *anti*feminism still needs to be explained. Why, in the midst of a career pursuing other conservative issues, did she throw herself into the antifeminist camp and provide the theoretical and organizational leadership to oppose the ERA, which was barely in formation? Her refusal to debate feminist issues in 1970 provides a tantalizing clue to the rapidity of her evolution into antifeminism. In February 1972, only two years after she had turned down the Connecticut invitation, she dedicated an entire issue of *The Phyllis Schlafly Report* to the question "What's wrong with the ERA for women?"; soon thereafter she founded StopERA, an organization dedicated to halting the ratification process.

What attracted her to the ERA controversy was her opposition both to the theory and practice of feminism. But frustrated as she must have been with her lack of political success so far, anti-ERA also offered her a political opportunity to exploit. It is her opportunism, even more than her conservatism, that explains why Schlafly suddenly shifted in 1972 from lobbying generally for conservative causes to pursuing an almost single-minded opposition to the ERA.

One view of her anti-ERA campaign, then—the cynical view—is that it was nothing more than a vehicle for a politically ambitious woman. Unable to "make it" in other arenas and having a tremendous drive to wield power and hold office, Schlafly was clever enough to realize that of the range of issues available to a conservative in 1972, the ERA could be her own. Recall the politics of that era. In 1972, Richard Nixon, a Republican who was willing to embrace détente and even to recognize "Red" China, was in office. So Schlafly's political-military point of view was out of sync with that of her own party. According to Ehrenreich, Schlafly was keeping "one foot in the right-wing of the Republican Party and the other in the nether world of paranoid, evangelical organizations which made up what was then known complacently as the 'lunatic fringe' of American conservatism."[11] Looking for an issue, Schlafly found one where other male conservatives failed to look. And quicker than most, she was able to appreciate the potential of a grassroots group of women who felt "cheated" by women's liberation.

Frightened about their future, such women were dimly aware that the "deal" they had made with their husbands when they had got married many years before was being eroded. Changes in sexual mores made divorce more common and easier to get, and women who wanted to be at home were having trouble withstanding pressure even from their own children to work at a career. Like it or not, Schlafly captured and gave voice to an inchoate women's politics on the Right that no one else appreciated. In that sense, she was able to forge an issue out of an emerging constituency whom neither the feminists, the Democrats, nor the Republicans were bothering to cultivate.

Where did she find this constituency? In the course of running for president of the National Republican Women's Federation in 1966, Schlafly had collected a following of devoted women supporters who, when she lost that fight, were willing to follow her out of the federation. In 1966, she and they essentially seceded from Republican women's politics and began to compete with their earlier allies. In time, Schlafly did a kind of end run around the National Republican Women's Federation altogether, stealing its members and outflanking its policies. The organization, which in 1967 boasted a membership of 500,000, was reduced to 280,000 by 1980, and the blame (or credit) is given Phyllis Schlafly. What she built from 1967 to 1972 and then enlarged after 1972 was a separate grassroots network of Republican women on the Right.

At first it was just a mailing list of women, later subscribers to a newsletter, *The Phyllis Schlafly Report*, in which the founder/writer/editor picked the issues she thought should interest, even ignite, her followers. Then came a tax-deductible foundation called the Eagle Forum Trust, which permitted Schlafly to do more serious fund-raising, and finally, she established the Père Marquette Press to publish her own and others' writings. By the time she created StopERA in 1972, she was ready to shift her attention from the myriad of family and foreign policy issues that had been featured in her *Report* to the subject of the ERA.

Schlafly found a willing audience for her views among religious and anticommunist conservatives, some of whom thought feminism would weaken the "trinity of 'God, Family and Country.'"[12] Communism was and remains a vital enemy of the Far Right, and as early as 1969 the John

Birch Society, of which Schlafly was at some point probably a member, went so far as to call the women who demonstrated at the 1968 Miss America Pageant "communists." Ehrenreich explains:

> Communism would abolish the family, and conversely, any loosening of traditional sex roles would weaken our defenses against communism. So you did not have to believe in the natural inferiority of women, or in the necessity of their confinement to the high-tech purdah of American middle-class kitchens, to see that there was something menacing about feminism. When the far Right first caught sight of the women's movement, they saw—predictably—red.[13]

In 1972, George Wallace's American Party denounced the ERA as a "socialist plan to destroy the home," and the John Birch Society flatly declared that the ERA fit into "communist plans . . . to reduce human beings to the level of animals."[14] So Schlafly was not alone in her opposition. What was unique about her anti-ERA campaign was that it politicized *women* on the Right first against the amendment, then against the entire "liberal" agenda.

Schlafly's Opposition to the ERA: The Theory

We have seen how issues involving role equity inevitably lead to issues involving role change. Schlafly parted company with feminists precisely at this juncture. She claimed for herself the right to run for office and never wavered in her support for women's suffrage. But for Schlafly, equality for women meant being treated differently from men. Women would always need protection because wives are more dependent than husbands, widows are more vulnerable than widowers, and mothers cannot provide their families with the financial security that fathers can. The use of the word *sex* in the wording of the amendment suggested to Schlafly a gender-free or "unisex" society, which could not and should not be realized.

Schlafly never fully joined the most reactionary position (she is, after all, herself a working woman), arguing, for example, for unequal pay for equal work. But she doubted women could or would *want* to do the work of men. In the classic speech she gave again and again around the country, she called a "ridiculous premise" the idea that there was "no difference," for example, between "talking on the telephone in a comfortable office and repeating numbers clearly the first time they are given and climbing up telephone poles in all kinds of weather." After letting the two images sink in for a while, she would intone: "Any normal person can see that one job is better suited to women and the other to men."[15]

Her reference was, of course, to the costly and long-litigated AT&T settlement in which the company had to open all job classifications to women. Schlafly "knew" (she spent a lot of time on the telephone making long-distance calls, as she would say) that those "good" operators' jobs were now going to men, while few women sought positions maintaining lines. Schlafly also must have known, though publicly she had nothing but ridicule for affirmative action at the workplace, that the pay differential between operator and linesman was considerable and that what had strengthened the case against AT&T in the early 1970s was the fact that the all-female job categories never led to management.

More serious by far than redefining job categories for Phyllis Schlafly was the effort to integrate the military—worse yet, to draft women into combat. Here she drew both on the nature argument and on that of tradition. Moreover, as a committed student of military history and policy, she could assert that integration of the U.S. armed forces would most likely "weaken" the military, particularly vis-à-vis the Soviets, who, she told her listeners, limited their recruitment of females to 1 percent. But the full force of her argument centered on the draft and on women in combat. From a classic 1970s speech on the ERA:

> The military is an area where the American people have never wanted to treat men and women the same. . . . In the entire 200-year history and in the nine wars that our country has fought . . . no woman has ever been assigned military combat duty. No mothers . . . said, "If you take my son, I want you to take my daughter, too." . . . The ERA would absolutely require that men and women be treated the same. . . . I can think of nothing more contemptible than to put our young women into military duty.[16]

The unisex theme in Schlafly's speeches was always good for eliciting some guffaws and for establishing her opposition to women's liberation, but far more serious was the second point she would develop as she built her case against the ERA. "Women's liberation is really men's liberation," she would sometimes say quite baldly, meaning that the sexual revolution and all that followed from that revolution threatened to rend that "web of obligation that holds a man to his family." The ERA would be but the final tear. Let us examine this conclusion more closely because, even though her all-female audiences would not have been able to articulate these sentiments, they certainly understood what she was saying. What Schlafly expressed for them was "what every woman knew"—namely, that men could not be trusted to play out their grown-up roles in the absence of social controls. Urbanization, geographical mobility, no-fault divorce, and easy access to "safe" sex and abortion had already taken their toll. The ERA would finish the job.

Inside every "patriarch," Schlafly implied—and her listeners understood what was unvoiced—was an adolescent male itching to get out.

And so "liberation" was not what women (or men) needed more of; what they needed, rather, was a reinstatement of that "delicate balance of rights and responsibilities which is differently assigned to men and women."[17] "This is the delicate balance that ERA upsets," Schlafly would say, and the women in her audience knew exactly what was meant: There would be no *hold* on husbands once the ERA and the unisex society were in place. More specifically, she would predict: "ERA will not make your husbands do the diapers and the dishes. ERA will not stop husbands from beating their wives. ERA will not make the father send his child support payments that he hasn't been sending. [And most ominously] ERA will not keep your husband from divorcing you."[18]

This play on her audience's fears makes sense if we apply the social conservative's view of human nature, as expressed by Rebecca Klatch, to men in particular: They are "creatures of unlimited appetites and instincts. Left on their own, they would turn the world into a chaos of seething passions."[19] Left on their own—that is, without ties to the family or church—men would leave marriages. As Ehrenreich quotes Schlafly (from her book *The Power of the Positive Woman*): "Some ERA proponents argue that husbands support their wives only because of love, not because of the law." This is foolish romanticism, says Schlafly. Love "is not apt to survive all those years 'for better or worse.'" What is essential for long-term marriage is "duty."[20] Thus, as Ehrenreich puts it, "while the feminist analysis spoke to the housewife's anger and frustration, the antifeminist analysis spoke to her fear—fear that she might, after all, be a parasite whose support rested on neither love nor accomplishment, but only 'obligation.'"[21]

About midway in her speech, Schlafly would finally move in on her arguments against the ERA. She would cause her audiences to consider what no one else was saying—namely, that the ERA was not designed for "women" at all. The word *woman*, in fact, as she would painstakingly instruct her listeners, "is not even mentioned in the wording of the ERA," only the word *sex*. And sex, as her audiences knew well, had many levels of meaning, such as the sexual revolution or sexual disease or a unisex society. Absent an explicit definition, she would warn, "we will be giving a blank check to the Supreme Court to tell us what [sex] means after it's been ratified." What the ERA would *not* do is protect women. What it *would* do is "put all our laws into a computer which will spit out the 'sexist terms,'" like *man, woman, father, mother, male, female, husband, wife,* and replace these with terms like *parents, spouse,* and *tax-payer*."[22]

But (she would continue), the Constitution is already sex neutral. It does not talk about men and women but about "persons" and "citizens," "residents" and "inhabitants," "taxpayers," "electors," and "Presidents." So what is the big deal? she would ask. The big deal is upsetting the "delicate balance," the threat to hearth and home, the tearing of legal and moral obligations on husbands to stay home—a very big deal for the audiences she addressed.

Finally, she would stand back from the issue and argue "linkage." If the legal impact of the ERA was so trivial ("persons" instead of "men" and "women"), then why the enormous pressure to ratify? The answer lay in NOW's hidden agenda, she would say. "NOW wants to overturn legislation and court decisions that threaten the rights of lesbian and gay people who work with children," for one. For another, NOW wants "abortion on demand." For a third, NOW wants "to elect Senators and Congressmen who believe in the NOW program." NOW wanted an increase in federal power, pornography, busing, black power, to undo— she would say after the 1980 election that brought Ronald Reagan to power—"everything our President stands for."

It was not that the classic speech was heavy going. Schlafly's vocal delivery was monotone and her accent twanged, but she never condescended to her audience. She brought the kind of facts and insight that her listeners would have no trouble taking home. She had the speechmaker's skill of orchestrating reaction. There would be the reference to "husband Fred," whom she would regularly thank for "letting me come to [Georgia]. . . . I am very fortunate to have a husband that lets me spend *my* time and *his* money fighting ERA." And she had ready analogies for her points. In 1979, after the ERA was granted a three-year ratification extension, Schlafly added a whole segment on "rule chicanery" to her speech:

> Just suppose you were watching your favorite football team and it was winning the game, and in the last quarter, the coach of the losing team demanded that a fifth quarter be played to give them time to catch up; and furthermore demanded that in that extra quarter only the losing team would be permitted to carry the ball. . . . The Equal Rights Amendment was given seven years and so they demanded extra time, not extra time for both sides, but extra time for their side, to continue their battle.[23]

The extension enraged her and drove Schlafly back on the circuit. Even after the ERA was finally laid to rest (by failure of passage in 1982), she remained vigilant. Once in 1985 as NOW was gearing up for a statewide ERA referendum in Vermont, she pulled out the old StopERA red stationery and wrote to her network:

> Dear Eagle Friend:
>
> I really thought I'd never write you another letter using my red letterhead, but . . . I need your help to make sure that the fraudulent ERA with its hidden agendas doesn't spread to any other states.

The message was pretty much the same as it had been for thirteen years, with only one addition, a reference to acquired immune deficiency syndrome (AIDS):

> ERA does not directly lead to AIDS. But it would prevent communities from enforcing public health regulations to protect healthy citizens from contact with high-risk AIDS victims. . . . That's because ERA would prohibit all differences of treatment on account of sex; and AIDS is a sex-related disease.

Other Conservative Opposition

Schlafly's was not the only movement on the Right to oppose the ERA. But she provided the first indication that women were divided on the issue and that there was a way to link the "New Right" with the "religious Right" by way of "family values." During the 1977 National Women's Conference in Houston, Schlafly held a counterconference there and formed a new conservative coalition called the Pro-Family Movement. Schlafly's followers were typical social conservatives, so it did not take much to persuade them that the deterioration of traditional morality— the kind associated with God, family, country—was a consequence of the breaking of the bonds of faith, common values, and obedience.[24]

Two years after Houston, in 1979, the New Right was joined by the evangelical Right when television evangelist Jerry Falwell founded the Moral Majority. Falwell's followers were especially opposed to the 1973 Supreme Court decision on abortion and angry about the banning of prayer in schools. Other religious zealots, even orthodox Jews, became involved in evangelical politics when the tax-exempt status of religious schools was threatened. Ronald Reagan's presidency succeeded in forging a new conservative majority from these. It was symptomatic of Schlafly's effectiveness in galvanizing the opposition that it was at the convention that nominated Ronald Reagan in 1980 that the ERA was dropped—for the first time in forty years—from the Republican platform.

Not all women on the Right were antifeminists. There were free-marketers, or laissez-faire conservatives, who wanted to limit government intervention in individual lives, which meant reducing or dismantling welfare, taking back affirmative action, and so forth. These conservatives tend to advocate individual liberty above all else and believe that if government left individuals alone, human society would flourish, morally and economically. Laissez-faire conservatives think individuals are blessed and bettered by the active use of their free will; social conservatives, in contrast, want to rein in human nature.[25] Klatch quotes a laissez-faire conservative woman—not the pro-family, prochurch type who followed Schlafly—who was not threatened by the ERA: "Who really cares about the ERA? Do you think it would really make one bit of difference one way or the other? . . . It's not like it's the economy. There are so many more important issues. . . . Not that many people are going to get all hot and bothered about it. . . . But she [Phyllis Schlafly] *got* them hot and bothered."[26]

From Theory to Strategy: StopERA in Action

Indeed, Schlafly's purpose was to get conservatives, and especially women conservatives, "hot and bothered" over the ERA. Her politics was grassroots. Schlafly's typical follower was not an experienced activist like many (but not all) of the women who joined NOW. Generally, she was a housewife whose home was her home base. That housewife may have had a car of her own, but if so, she used it for marketing. She did not take herself to national or regional meetings, and she did not readily imagine herself having an impact on the national scene. Her telephone was an extension of her personal and social life, not her link to other activists, her congressional delegation, or her local media. If she was politically motivated at all, and many of these women were active volunteers, her focus would be on local issues by way of the PTA or her church. What Schlafly managed to do was to teach these women how to be politically effective on a few key issues that she selected for them.

Once StopERA got going, Schlafly designed organizational strategies to suit her constituents. For example, she relied on the "telephone tree" for her get-out-the-masses campaigns. Telephoning gave her network something tangible to do and something it could do well, as well as saving the costs of printing, mailing, and updating computer lists. Someone from StopERA headquarters (always identified to outside callers, at least, as "Mrs. Schlafly's home") would call five women; each of them would call five women; and each of them five more. Within hours, hundreds, even thousands of women could be notified of an upcoming event or of the need to send letters to representatives or to take some other kind of action.

The system, however, works only if no one breaks the chain. So the key to Schlafly's successful telephone tree was absolute loyalty. According to biographer Carol Felsenthal, women in her network would do *anything* for Schlafly. Women who had never gone to Washington, even as

tourists, rode for three days and two nights to march on the Capitol because "Mrs. Schlafly wants as many people there as possible." Schlafly
gave inspiration, shape, and direction to a group of people who previously did not know how to do any of this at all.

Her second strategy was to show power. She was skilled at getting
media attention because she understood the media and planned her
events to maximize coverage. Illinois legislators still talk about the first
time Schlafly's "girls" moved into the Illinois state legislature to lobby
against the ERA. They were wearing long white dresses, strewing flowers,
and carrying homemade loaves of bread to their delegates. Schlafly
readily borrowed the techniques of guerrilla theater from civil rights and
women's liberation. To get on the local evening news, she would schedule her events before 4 P.M. and make them as visually interesting as
possible.

She herself was particularly effective on television and seemed to get
more than her share of media attention, partly because she was taking
the unexpected point of view. In the face of her opponents' claim that *all*
women were oppressed and wanted equal rights, Schlafly, looking very
much like a "liberated lady," would disagree. "On behalf of the 15,000
women who are marching out there," she would say in the midst of a
demonstration, "I say to you, they are not oppressed." Moreover, she had
no competition for attention. While the women's liberation movement
was "trashing" its own leadership for becoming media "stars," Phyllis
Schlafly's followers were content to let her have all the fun. It fit with
their patriarchal concept. In a way, Phyllis Schlafly was the patriarch.

Nevertheless, she showed signs of "sisterhood." She wanted her lieu-
tenants to become every bit as effective on television as she was, so she
ran frequent training sessions for her team in dressing for television—
appearance was, of course, important for her and her group—and in
handling the video medium. Her ability to politicize her grassroots following and to effectively manipulate the media created the impression
that her following was even larger than it really was. As early as January
1973, less than one year after the ERA passed the Senate, Schlafly was
crowing (to *New York Times* correspondent Eileen Shanahan, no less)
that StopERA had several thousand members and was active in thirty-six
states.[27]

The third strategy she brought to perfection was an ability to target
races in certain states and on certain issues. It is difficult to get voters exercised over an entire party platform. By creating StopERA—even
though her interest in military and foreign policy, pornography, and
prayer in school continued—she was able to focus political energies.[28]
State legislatures are on different schedules, so when Florida had the
ERA on its agenda, Schlafly was able to bring all her forces down to

Florida to make the case. Then Illinois would schedule a hearing or debate on the ERA, and everyone would move back up North.

Schlafly's Impact: An Assessment

Phyllis Schlafly's first contribution was her critique of the ERA for conservatives. Bear in mind that the conservatives in the House and Senate had not opposed the ERA when it came up for congressional votes in 1971 and 1972. The only opposition had come from the "die-hards" who wanted exemptions for military service and continued protections in those areas where they felt women would be unable to compete with men. The conservatives in Congress did not initially see the ERA as a "liberal" (versus conservative) issue. After Schlafly, they did.

Her second political contribution was to alert the still largely male-dominated power structure to the fact that not all women were women's libbers, as she insisted on calling them. It would have been difficult for any male in the 1970s, conservative or liberal, to stand up and speak *for* women. That much had been accomplished by the women's movement. But when Schlafly delivered "15,000 followers marching on your Capitol this afternoon [who] do not share the goals of women's liberation," conservatives began to take notice. If Schlafly's women would march against the ERA, what else might they march *for?*

Her third contribution was to focus on Article II of the amendment, which nobody else had done. The first article is the substantive part: "Equality of rights under the law shall not be abridged . . . on account of sex." Article II is the boilerplate article. It simply states, as most second articles of amendments to the Constitution do, that "the Congress shall have the power to enforce . . . this amendment" once it is ratified. Schlafly pointed out that earlier versions of the Equal Rights Amendment had called upon "Congress and the several states" to share enforcement. But the "several states" had been eliminated from the final version. The final version, she would assert, violated the principle of states' rights and the original intention of the framers of the Constitution. The framers, she insisted, wanted to *reserve* to the states precisely these kinds of jurisdictions.

The effect of the ERA, Schlafly argued, would be to gather under federal control all those domestic, personal, and *private* issues that until now had been outside the reach of government. On the one hand, the states would lose their traditional jurisdiction over school policy, marriage, divorce, and child welfare; on the other hand, individuals would lose control over their own personal lives. Parental control was of partic-

ular interest to Schlafly and to her followers, for whom "children's
rights," quite as much as "women's rights," tore at family life.

Antifeminism and the Failure of ERA

Phyllis Schlafly discovered and drew on a great deal of latent antifeminism that feminists either ignored or decided did not exist. The women
to whom she appealed were threatened not only by sex-role reversal but
also by any role change. Respect, authority, and security for these
women resided in their position in the family and in the community and
as a reflection of their husbands' status and their children's loyalty and
success. Given all the media attention to women's liberation and an initial ambivalence about the roles of housewife and mother that feminists
allowed the media to exaggerate, these women sensed that women's liberation, if not the cause, was surely the symbol of everything they had to
lose.

By far, the majority of Schlafly's followers were housewives without
careers. In most cases, they had interrupted their schooling to marry
and have children. There was no way they could expect to acquire by
working the kind of financial security that they could have as housewives at home (so long as their husbands did not leave them). Women's
liberationists would counterargue that such women were naive. They
were, after all, as Johnnie Tilmon said, but "one man away from welfare."[29] The women Phyllis Schlafly appealed to knew that in their gut,
but their strategy was to hang on to what they had (their husbands) and
not to venture forth on their own. They believed—and as we have seen,
Schlafly addressed this incessantly in her talks—that the NOW agenda
would make it easier, and more socially acceptable, for their husbands
to leave them. Ehrenreich says it plainly: "From the vantage point of the
antifeminists, the crime of feminism lay not in hating men, but in trusting them too well."[30]

Because of this latent antifeminism, Schlafly was able to forge the
most unlikely coalitions, coalitions that experts in American politics
would have thought impossible. She got urban Catholics to join forces
with southern fundamentalist Baptists and orthodox Jews. Religion,
after all, was important to all of them, and they were looking out on a
godless, "humanistic" America supposedly promoted by feminists,
which threatened them more than someone else's orthodoxy. This
"Silent Majority . . . came to feel that their morals, their standards, their
religion, indeed all those things they held dear, were under attack from
the counterculture" of the 1960s, secular humanism, and the growing
power of the feminist movement.[31] Catholics and Protestants, funda-

mentalists and orthodox Jews, did not have similar Gods or similar litur-
gies, but they did share similar values: the patriarchal family, parental
control over children, and opposition to pornography and to the sexual
revolution.[32] For Schlafly and her followers, then, anti-ERA was more
than a campaign; it became a mission, which accounts in part for why
her followers were willing to phone incessantly and to get on buses to attend her rallies. In her victory speech after the ERA was defeated,
Schlafly said she would focus next on fighting sex education because she
believed "it was the cause of teenage pregnancy," and she would fight
the feminists who were trying to take gender stereotypes out of school
textbooks because, as Schlafly put it, "the way it is now, you can't show a
picture of a woman washing the dishes."[33]

   If all this latent antifeminism and fear of change were out there in the
population, then we might be tempted to conclude that even if Phyllis
Schlafly had not existed, some other political leader would have eventually pulled together the same kind of coalition against the ERA. But history is not like experimental science: We cannot run the events over
again, absent Phyllis Schlafly's activism, and see what would have happened. We can only ask why the feminists were unable to respond.

The Feminists' Response

Why were the pro-ERA forces not able to discredit and defeat those who
opposed the amendment? One reason is that in retrospect the contest
appears to have been an unequal one. For feminists, the ERA was one of
several issues and not as passionately supported as it was passionately
opposed. Another is that feminists did not expect to have to fight this
hard for ratification. Passage in Congress had been almost too easy.
Feminists and their followers who worked doggedly for ratification of
the ERA during this period were simply caught off guard by the power of
the Schlafly opposition. Their initial strategy was to assume Schlafly
could not be working alone and to investigate her operation to find out
where her money and support were really coming from.

   By the late 1970s, active feminists knew their history. They remembered that the liquor interests had dominated the antisuffrage campaigns prior to passage in 1920. Could liquor, insurance, banking, small
business—each with its own reason for opposing equal rights for
women—be behind the innocent-looking Schlafly? But most of the investigations proved fruitless. Schlafly's power was not in the money but
in the people she attracted to her cause. Also, remarkably, there did not
seem to be any *men* in the leadership of her camp. For once, Phyllis
Schlafly could rely on women, and she did so with success.

The feminists' mistake was to take Schlafly's opposition to the ERA at face value and not to take as seriously the real anxieties of the women who were flocking to her camp. Both pro- and anti-ERA forces could have agreed that the key issue was women's vulnerability in the family and in the workplace. But as in past times, a strategy based on "equality" and a strategy based on "difference" allowed for little compromise.

Nevertheless, pro-ERA spokespeople ought to have been better able to counter Schlafly's arguments and her movement. All throughout the 1970s when Schlafly was operating most successfully, polls showed growing public sentiment in favor of the ERA.[34] But the pros had other issues to deal with. By mid-decade, the feminist agenda had been significantly enlarged. Although NOW would regularly drop everything to work exclusively for the ERA, particularly during the fight for extension of the deadline and in certain thorny state campaigns, after 1979 NOW and other feminists members were unwilling to give the ERA their full attention for any span of time.

The reason is that the ERA ceased to be as meaningful as it once had been. Schlafly was correct in pointing out that the ERA would have no immediate impact on job opportunities for women. That had already been established by Title VII of the 1964 Civil Rights Act and Executive Order 11375 (see Chapters 6 and 7). The Supreme Court was becoming more willing to consider sex a "suspect classification" under the Fourteenth Amendment (though not nearly as automatically as race), which meant more cases against sex discrimination were being won in the courts. Schlafly could argue, What more would the ERA accomplish? And women's new problems—child care and welfare, the feminization of poverty, date rape, comparable worth, and reproductive freedom in the wake of new reproductive technologies—were not the kinds of problems the ERA was going to solve.

Indeed, if one looks back at a 1972 list of the kinds of corrections in state law that the ERA would have made, had it been approved within a year, one realizes how much was accomplished in a decade by ordinary statute and court interpretation. Laws (such as those in California at the beginning of the 1970s) that imposed greater restrictions on women to buy and sell property or to conduct a business were pretty much overruled by Title VII and the Equal Credit Bill. Laws setting different ages at which men and women attain legal majority or have the right to marry or become eligible for tax-supported retirement plans were being rescinded because of women's local lobbying. Different admission standards for women and men in tax-supported educational institutions had been taken care of by Title IX, which also outlawed different facilities and curricula (e.g., shop) in public schools. Laws establishing different jail sentences by sex for identical offenses were being overturned.

Laws giving preference to mothers in child custody cases and laws granting alimony to women without reference to need, and imposing the burden of child support on fathers regardless of relative economic situations, were being interpreted as appropriate on a case-by-case basis by the courts. Indeed, the NOW Legal, Defense, and Education Fund was reeducating jurists on these matters in all but mandatory "Schools for Judges." Regulations denying unemployment compensation to pregnant women still willing to work or those that treated pregnancy differently from other temporary physical disabilities were taken care of by federal statute (the Pregnancy Discrimination Act of 1978), and military rules setting higher entry standards for women volunteers than for men might have been exempted from the ERA anyway because of a national security override.[35]

As it turned out, feminists never satisfactorily addressed the issue of the military (see Chapter 11). There was a natural division among them as to the value of a woman's draft. Some feminists were antimilitarist; others were eager to achieve equal rights even in combat.[36] But was it an issue after all? With a little bit of homework, historian Jane Mansbridge argues, the question of the ERA and combat could have been dismissed as a red herring. The Constitution already allows for the exclusion of any particular group of people from combat—even the draft—by means of the "war powers" exemption. Mansbridge concludes that feminists made a strategic error in permitting Phyllis Schlafly to misrepresent the issue of women and combat without being publicly corrected.[37]

One powerful argument in support of the ERA was never made to stick—namely, that all the legislation won in the period 1963–1980 in favor of women's equality might be eroded during some future economic emergency since what Congress *gave*, that body could legally *take away*. Only with a constitutional amendment in place could women have avoided the kind of employment discrimination in jobs and job opportunities and the kind of arbitrary layoffs that women suffered during the Great Depression and after World War II. Phyllis Schlafly herself supported economic and job equality, and as a sometimes frustrated observer of congressional vagaries, she could not, in good conscience, have been able to counter that rationale (though she might have argued the point in any case). Whether such arguments would have impressed her followers is not that certain. But presenting the ERA as the only certain guarantor of a gender-equal body of law would have made converts elsewhere.

Toward the end of the 1970s, feminists reassessed the family issue, and certain thinkers began to question the appropriateness of "androgyny" and interchangeability as desirable goals. Fundamental "differences" in women's interests and concerns were discovered (or reasserted) in the writings of Adrienne Rich on motherhood, of Mary Belenky and Carol Gilligan on women's ways of knowing and thinking about morals, of Jean Elshtain and Betty Friedan on the family (in Friedan's third book, *The Second Stage*).[38] But by then ERA was dead or dying. The uproar over the Hill-Thomas affair and the picking away by the Supreme Court of women's abortion rights in the 1980s suggest that the ERA has been decoupled from women's progress, even women's liberation. Twelve years of conservative Republican government failed to undo much of women's progress. Perhaps history will show that Phyllis Schlafly's effort was but a detour on the road to gender equity and that StopERA battled only a symbol that meant more to people who opposed it than to the people who had initiated it in the first place.

10

Feminism and Sexual Preference

LESBIANS AND LESBIAN RIGHTS

WHEN I ASKED PHYLLIS SCHLAFLY IN 1988 when she thought she had won the fight against the ERA, her answer came quickly. It was during the 1977 International Women's Year Conference convened in Houston, she said, when the "libbers" voted for the sexual preference plank, extending the feminist platform to include lesbian rights. Lesbians had been lobbying the conference from inside (130 delegates to the convention were said to be lesbian) and outside during the heated debate on that issue. Many older feminists, fearful of being tarred with what some called the "lavender menace" (after the color lavender, associated with lesbianism), at first argued strenuously to exclude lesbian feminism from the platform. Others argued just as strenuously, and won the day, that a feminist agenda that did not include equal rights regardless of sexual preference was a contradiction in terms.[1]

After the vote—and Schlafly gloated as she retold the story—lesbian activists waiting outside the conference joined their friends in the bleachers where some of them had been sitting throughout and, snake-dancing across the floor, cheered "Thank you, sisters." Many lesbians, but not all, were dressed in mannish garb. Some had motorcycles parked outside. They were unaware or indifferent to the Schlafly forces that had been bused to the Houston conference to protest its feminist "bias." And after the vote in favor of the gay rights resolution, they were happy. Hooting with delight at the way the vote had gone, they let loose balloons that read, "We are everywhere."[2] Their rush into the conference arena, their balloons, and their cheering were all recorded on television, and that footage made its way around the country.

In the years that followed Houston, Schlafly would use that footage to recruit people to the antifeminist cause, displaying it on television as part of her paid advertisements against the ERA.[3] In her view, expressed to me eleven years later, the display of feminist solidarity with lesbians that day in Houston clinched her victory.

The Emergence of Gay Rights as a Feminist Issue

Feminism did not invent lesbianism, and lesbianism is not coextensive with feminism. There were lesbians and nascent, if somewhat closeted, lesbian rights organizations long before the second wave of feminism coalesced in the late 1960s. Logically, there ought to have been a natural alliance between the two: feminists fighting for every woman's right to her personal sexual preference[4] and lesbians recognizing how important the achievement of even a bare-bones feminist agenda would be for all women.[5] Nevertheless, there were initial resistance, suspicion, fear, and even paranoia lurking where the two movements overlapped: "How can you sleep with the enemy?" was one crude way of insisting that no *true* feminist would choose to be heterosexual;[6] and, on the other side, the lavender menace, it was thought, threatened to divide American women just as they were beginning to come together.

The most frequently told story of confrontation along these lines is lesbian-feminist Rita Mae Brown's: that at a 1969 New York NOW discussion, Brown demanded to know why issues relating to lesbianism were never raised at NOW meetings. Her question was met with a stony silence, she remembers. When Friedan warned the NOW National Executive Board that same year of the "dangers" to the feminist cause if lesbianism was perceived to be too closely linked to NOW, Brown and two others resigned from the board, explaining in the New York NOW newsletter, "Lesbianism is the one word which gives the New York NOW Executive Committee a collective heart attack."[7]

The point is that women's liberation, in all its many variants, attracted lesbians as members and some, such as Del Martin, one of the founders of the lesbian organization Daughters of Bilitis (DOB), became valuable officers of the organization. Martin was secretary of the NOW chapter in San Francisco in 1970 when she wrote to Friedan and Kay Clarenbach, then chair of the NOW National Board, asking that NOW take a stand in support of lesbian rights. Friedan never replied, and Clarenbach's response was negative. Soon after, Dolores Alexander, a supporter of certain lesbian stands within NOW and the national organization's first professional executive director, was fired. This firing and Brown's resignation from the National Board are often called NOW's first lesbian purge.[8]

Brown and others moved on to a more radical women's liberation group called Redstockings, which in turn was affiliated with the Gay Liberation Front. But where these women were overly sensitive to the lesbian issue, they found that the gay men who dominated the front were not sensitive enough. Eventually, they formed Radicalesbians, with an activist offshoot provocatively named the Lavender Menace Group, and prepared a position paper to be delivered to the second Congress to Unite Women in May 1970. Their intention was to initiate a discussion as to how lesbianism relates to the women's movement. But, as Sidney Abbot and Barbara Love described that event a year later, their appearance was electric:

> At the opening Friday evening session of the congress, the lights in the public auditorium suddenly went out. When they flashed on again, there were thirty "Menaces" in lavender T-shirts boldly lettered with the derisive name they had taken for their own. Much as the blacks had taken "Black is Beautiful" as a slogan to reverse their image, lesbians now said "Gay is Good" and used the words "lesbian" and "dyke" in a positive, fun-loving manner. Signs they carried read "Take a lesbian to lunch" and "Super-dyke loves you." The "Menaces" liberated the microphone for the evening and led an open forum on sexism within the movement.[9]

One cannot help observing how profound this challenge was to the nascent new feminist movement. "Sexism," after all, had just been coined to reflect negative stereotyping and isolation of women by men; here it was used to denote the same kind of stereotyping and isolation of women—*by women*. Sexism ought to have been the common enemy of lesbians and feminists.[10] And yet along with this charge of sexism, there was a deep search for common ground. Alice Echols, in her chronicling of the period, believes that the most important idea to emerge from the 1970 Congress to Unite Women was that women, whatever their sexual preference, could join together as "women-identified women." If lesbianism could be seen as "the quintessential act of political solidarity with other women," then lesbianism was a *political choice* rather than a *sexual alternative*. This argument, embedded in a paper written by the Menaces, was intended to assuage heterosexual feminists' fears by giving them a way of thinking about sexual preference politically.[11] As Echols remembers, the ploy succeeded in setting up two new categories: male-identified women, who wanted the power and privilege that males enjoyed, and women-identified women, who wanted to put some distance between themselves and "contaminating maleness." Thus, in terms of commitment and solidarity, feminism needed lesbianism quite as much as lesbianism needed feminist victories in the courts, in the legislatures, and in the war against stereotyping.[12]

The recasting of lesbianism as a political choice actually convinced some otherwise heterosexual women to become "gay," at least during the heady start of the women's movement. Some were attracted by the danger and forbiddance of the lesbian lifestyle, according to historian Flora Davis. And others sought the comfort of a purportedly feminist "utopia" where "women's values" would prevail.[13] Although the shift to a political definition angered some older lesbians who had grown up lesbian in a society prejudiced against homosexuality, it contributed to the lesbian community's evolving understanding of its own identity.

However, for Betty Friedan, president of NOW and chief spokesperson of the middle strand of the women's movement, the "lavender herring," like the "red herring" of the McCarthy era, was more than an epithet. Friedan feared that before the National Organization for Women had time to properly establish itself, its members would be tarred, as their suffragist foremothers had been, as not just misguided but abnormal. Friedan was not one to flinch from confrontation. Why did she not join arms with homosexual women from the outset and welcome them into NOW, as she would after 1971? Friedan knew history: how lesbianism had to remain hidden through so much of America's past and how much and how often America's suffragist forebears—indeed, any American woman who chose to be outspoken and nontraditional—had to defend herself against sexual innuendo.[14]

Friedan also might simply have been wishing to buy time, to protect the tendrils of her young organization until it grew strong enough to embrace still more radical issues. She knew, as feminist Ti-Grace Atkinson would later articulate, that "lesbianism" had always been a kind of "code word for female resistance."[15] Eventually, she and other liberal feminists would come to recognize that "sex," as well as "gender," was a feminist issue. But in the late 1960s and early 1970s, the lavender herring was the lavender menace. "For me," Friedan wrote in her 1976 retrospective, "the women's movement . . . had nothing whatsoever to do with lesbianism . . . or giving up, renouncing, denouncing, the love of men."[16] Friedan and others preferred to fashion their movement around gender discrimination and hoped that the issue of sexual preference would be left out of the debate.

But there was not to be any time for thoughtful consideration of the pros and cons of an alliance with lesbians, feminist or not. As is so often the case in politics, debate was overtaken by events. Hardly had the movement given itself rebirth when Kate Millett, its best-known theorist and the first of the second-wave feminists to achieve national attention (if not respectability), admitted publicly to being bisexual. She told a Columbia University audience on November 12, 1970, that, even though she was married, she was also a homosexual. *Time* magazine, which had celebrated Millett only months before as the chief theoretician and spokeswoman of the new movement and had called her book *Sexual Politics* "remarkable," responded to this announcement on December 8 with an article entitled "Women's Lib—A Second Look."[17] The article fueled Friedan's and others' worst nightmare. *Time* wrote: "The disclosure is bound to discredit [Millett] as a spokeswoman for her cause, cast further doubt on her theories, and reinforce the views of those skeptics who routinely dismiss all liberationists as lesbians."[18]

It would be wrong to conclude from the drama of these events that all heterosexual feminists were as fearful of or hostile to the lavender herring as was Friedan. In response to *Time*'s "Second Look," feminists Ti-Grace Atkinson of New York NOW; Gloria Steinem, who in 1970 was on the verge of founding *Ms.* magazine; Susan Brownmiller, who would soon become famous for her book on rape; and Florynce Kennedy, a black lawyer and activist, joined Representative Bella Abzug from New York, second NOW president Aileen Hernandez, and third NOW president Wilma Scott Heide in holding a press conference to respond. Feminism and gay liberation, they told the assembled media, were "struggling toward a common goal," and *Time* was just trying to "divide and conquer."[19] Nonetheless, the divisions between homosexuals and heterosexuals and between middle- and working-class women were real in the early 1970s and led some observers to call the second Congress to Unite Women the "Congress to Divide Women" instead.[20]

In January 1971 there was a second New York NOW chapter purge in which lesbians and straight supporters of lesbians were voted out of office. But only a few months later, the storm abated, and at NOW's 1971 annual convention a large majority voted in favor of a prolesbian resolution, admitting that NOW had been "evasive and apologetic" about lesbians and that "lesbian oppression" was of great concern to *all* feminists.[21] Even Betty Friedan changed her mind. She conceded that some of "the best, most hard-working women in NOW" were lesbians. Her fear had been that the "sexual issue," about which there was so much fear and loathing (later called homophobia), would keep the average American from supporting the feminist agenda. She was not necessarily interested in a radical critique of sexual preference. But she had come to realize, in the short space of two years, that a movement dedicated to the eradication of gender discrimination without addressing the sexual issue would be neither true nor successful in the long run.[22]

The Love That Dares Not Speak Its Name

If one looks for origins of fear and hostility to same-sex love,[23] one must start, of course, with the writings of Judeo-Christianity, which shower invective on all nonreproductive sex and sexuality. As regards female homosexuality in particular, the medical and psychological professions, until a 1985 reversal of this view, were of the opinion that female homosexuality is either a "gross abnormality" or stems from "arrested development."[24] In the writings of Sigmund Freud, lesbianism need not even involve a sexual object so long as gender behavior is "unnatural." A woman's failure to be passive, the presence of ambition, or her athletic interests were proof enough of latent homosexuality.[25] For Freud's less sophisticated followers, same-sex love was simply "sick."

Lillian Faderman, Michel Foucault, and Carroll Smith-Rosenberg, all historians of homosexuality, understand that, like all other cultural artifacts, "sex" has a history.[26] Indeed, Faderman and Smith-Rosenberg both link the "discovery" of lesbianism by nineteenth-century scientists and medical doctors with the emergence of taxonomy—a passion to classify everything—and of Social Darwinism. Once sexologists could put a label on same-sex attachments—"deviance," they called it—they could even theorize that lesbians, like criminals, were "degenerate" by virtue of bad genes.[27] Rather than "sinners" (the preferred classification in more religion-dominated periods of American history), people in same-sex relationships were now thought to be "congenital inverts" or victims of inborn "contrary sexual feeling."[28]

These theories became particularly popular after World War I (earlier in Europe), when people began to think there might be "latent sexuality" in same-sex friendships. Smith-Rosenberg and other feminist historians have unearthed and analyzed "romantic friendships" among women in the nineteenth century but conclude that these were a response to the intense segregation of women and men during that period into "separate spheres." The male sphere was intended to embody "muscular" or "rational" values, the female sphere to encompass family, morality, and "feelings."[29] Once education and the settlement movement brought some women together in meaningful and shared work, some women rejected these traditional roles, fearing that marriage and children would interfere with their goals and careers. Such rejections fueled the notion that, as one religious magazine of the time lamented, education would make the "female character . . . masculine."[30]

Until the twentieth century, however, romantic friendships between women were not regarded either as grossly abnormal or as developmentally arrested so long as women did not dress "mannishly" (cross-dressing was prohibited by statute in most states) or in other ways display "inappropriate" behavior. But once women began pressing for greater social freedoms, asking to be treated "equally" to men, friendships between women became suspect.[31] Faderman writes movingly of older women engaged in romantic friendships in the early twentieth century who were caught in a vise of suspicion. Some carried on innocently enough, and others decided in self-defense to join the attack on lesbianism. One of the latter was Mary Woolley, president of Mount Holyoke College, who lived for fifty-five years with Jeannette Marks, a professor there. Despite this long-term liaison, President Woolley wrote threateningly in 1908 of "unwise college friendships" that were "unpleasant or worse."[32]

It is surprising that nineteenth-century sexologists found women to have sexual appetites at all since Victorian views of women had denatured them into entirely nonsexual beings. They were not supposed to experience sexual pleasure whether a man was present or not. So long as women were nonsexual, same-sex friendships could flourish, and did. But these emotional involvements became suspect after women's and even infants' sexuality was "discovered" by sexologists Richard von Krafft-Ebing and Freud. Thus, it was not until well into the second wave of feminism—in the wake of another sexual revolution—that lesbians began to publicly "reclaim their own experience," that is, look at their love of women outside the doctors' categories and challenge the labels that had been invented by men. Today, homosexual women consider themselves to be as diverse as heterosexual women. Whether lesbianism is entirely a "political choice," as some lesbians believe, or congenital in its origins is still debated.[33] But in periods of heightened homophobia, lesbians have learned that they must seek political allies if they are to survive.

Homophobia

The term *homophobia* is relatively new, but antipathy to persons of homosexual leanings or behavior is not. Nevertheless, in twentieth-century America homophobia appears to have ebbed and flowed depending on more general conservative or liberal trends. During the more experimental 1920s, for example, especially in the larger cities, Americans showed more tolerance for female bisexuality even among the working classes. But by the 1930s, lesbians had begun to be regarded as "pathetic creatures cut off from the rest of womankind."[34] During this period, some lesbian clubs sprang up, Faderman tells us, but always under veil of secrecy, and it was behind that same veil of secrecy that a lesbian subculture was established. During World War II, with women working and living without men in same-sex environments, female independence and love between women became more common and were again better tolerated.[35] The late Audre Lorde, a black poet and a lesbian, describes in her autobiography, *Zami*, coming out with another woman she met working in a Bridgeport, Connecticut, factory during World War II.[36] At first, the military was lenient toward lesbianism. Many lesbians had joined when the services created women's branches in 1942. But after the war, once discovered, lesbians were immediately discharged.

At the end of World War II, society took a conservative turn, and "curing lesbians" on the (Freudian) couch became big business in America. Many young women languished in therapy or were sent to institutions. If the 1940s labeled lesbians "sick," the 1950s saw an escalating persecution of all homosexuals. This, despite the widely quoted Kinsey Reports that found half the men and a quarter of the women in America to have had some kind of homosexual experience when young.[37] "Perverts" were thought to have infiltrated government, putting America at risk, and during the McCarthy era the mere accusation of lesbianism by an anonymous source could cost a woman her government job, without appeal. A Senate subcommittee ruled in 1950 that homosexuals should not ever be recruited to government because homosexuality was "contrary to the normal accepted standards of social behavior"; also, they should not be employed because, in a cold war environment, lesbians and gay men could be extorted and therefore become security risks. Even the Left was reluctant to defend homosexuals in the face of this onslaught. Informants were everywhere, causing lesbians to lead a double life and encouraging intense introversion.[38]

Author Margaret Cruikshank also chronicles the wartime experiences of homosexuals, but she believes it gave them the spirit to endure the hostile redbaiting and persecution of the McCarthy era that followed.[39] By the 1950s, every state had declared homosexual conduct illegal. Even the American Civil Liberties Union, usually the defender of last resort, did nothing until 1967 to challenge sodomy laws, and the popular press did less. The period of the feminine mystique, then, was for many lesbians as much a period of frustration as for stay-at-home wives, except that government worked in tandem with homophobes to promote an irrational and oppressive fear of homosexuality.

In response, most lesbians prior to the second wave still remained personally and politically attached to the idea of separateness, of finding spaces, however small, where they could at least be themselves. Wealthier lesbians, with the same goal in mind, became expatriates. But others longed for integration and were willing to behave with sufficient "femininity" to be accepted in a highly gender-polarized society. Even after the repressive 1950s gave way to the unisex counterculturalism of the 1960s, historian Faderman finds the lesbian subculture to have remained more conservative as a result of this habituation even than the heterosexual society in which it was embedded. Her conclusion is that, given the many faces of homophobia in America, well into the 1960s lesbians did not feel they could demand any rights at all.[40]

In 1955 this slowly began to change with the founding of the first lesbian organization, Daughters of Bilitis, named after a poem to a young girl by the lesbian poet Sappho. DOB was intended to be a private social group providing middle-class lesbians with an alternative to the gay bar scene, but the organization soon became involved in "improving the lesbian image" more publicly.[41] Not that "coming out" was yet possible in that era, but in the city of San Francisco DOB members felt they could provide a monthly open forum about lesbianism without taking undue risks. By 1970, Abbott and Love report, DOB's nonactivist position no longer fulfilled the needs of many lesbians. But for fifteen years, during some of the most virulent homophobia the country has ever known, it provided a "home away from home" where women could come together and better understand their lesbian identity.[42]

Five years earlier, in 1950, a small group of southern California men formed the Mattachine Society, devoted to group consciousness-raising of male homosexuals from a Marxist point of view. This occurred, of course, at the height of McCarthy's anticommunist purges, so the Mattachines were, so to speak, taking two formidable tigers by the tail. These and other like-minded groups called themselves "homophiles" in an effort to obscure their sexual preference since it was that aspect of their identity that was so fraught with danger for them and so despised by others. From 1950 to 1969 there may have been as many as five thousand organized "Homophiles."[43]

Homophobia was no longer at its zenith in 1969, but the police harassment of patrons of the Stonewall Inn, a gay bar in New York City, on June 28 of that year was a kind of watershed for lesbian and gay liberation. The police attack and three subsequent nights of rioting that followed led to the founding of a grassroots movement different from any gay or lesbian organization that had previously existed. Never again after "Stonewall" would homophobia drive homosexuals underground. Modeled on "Black Pride," the idea was to change the stigma attached to being gay into a source of pride for gay rights activists. Henceforth gay and lesbian politics would not just defend a lifestyle but, much in the way civil rights and anti–Vietnam War activism had done, would also provide a thoroughgoing critique of American society and its values. Two aspects of the new movement emerged right away. First, coming out became both a goal and a strategy (people who came out would do so as a political act, relinquishing their invisibility). Second, Stonewall brought lesbian and gay politics out in the open.[44]

Note that the Stonewall incident occurred virtually simultaneously with the birth of the second wave of feminism, and this simultaneity propelled large numbers of lesbians into liberation politics. Because of heterosexism in the women's movement and sexism in gay liberation, Radicalesbians was formed in New York; the Furies Collective in Washington, D.C.; and Gay Women's Liberation in San Francisco. Although gay men and lesbians had much in common, their priorities were never the same. Gay men primarily wanted freedom from harassment; Radicalesbians wanted an end to patriarchy.[45]

By the time the next wave of homophobia was unleashed, with the New Right's rise to power in the late 1970s and 1980s, the liberation communities were too powerful and too widespread to be destroyed. Even in 1976 when Anita Bryant, a former Sunkist Orange promoter, led a citizen's movement to repeal gay rights ordinances in Dade County, Florida, and in 1978 when Proposition 6 in California (the Briggs Initiative) sought to prohibit gays from teaching in the public schools, gays and lesbians were able to campaign openly against these measures. The Briggs Initiative, in fact, stimulated the most advanced gay organizing campaign in history and a victorious rejection by 60 percent of the voters, even though the victory cost gay supervisor Harvey Milk and San Francisco's Mayor George Moscone their lives. The two men were assassinated three weeks later by a former supervisor who favored the Briggs Initiative.[46]

Lesbianism and Feminism Today

Feminism and lesbianism eventually came to accept that they had one common goal: the eradication of sexism in all its manifestations.[47] But for many young women, the presence of homosexual women in feminist organizations—particularly on college campuses—provided one more reason for that odd refrain, "I'm not a feminist, but I support equal rights." Speaking for many young feminists in the early years, Ellen DuBois, an activist and a scholar, told Alice Echols of her personal reaction to the coming out of lesbians and the emergence of lesbian issues in the movement. Many young women of the time might have lamented the same: "I felt finally I had found a movement where I didn't have to worry about whether or not I was attractive or whether or not men liked me. . . . And just as I was beginning to feel [that] here at last I could forget all of that, sex once again reared its ugly head."[48]

Ellen DuBois later distanced herself from this remark. But therein lay some truth. "In the 1970s," writes Cruikshank, who in 1992 attempted a long view of the two prior decades, "gay identity was so novel and compelling that it tended to overshadow one's other identities."[49] From her research, she concludes that the "high-energy public lesbianism" of the 1970s was followed by a less political and more private phase, sometimes called "lifestyle lesbianism," in the 1980s. And as lesbianism became less shocking, "newcomers did not need to feel radical fervor in order to join its ranks."[50] In fact, coming out for many young and not so young lesbians was more of a private journey of personal acceptance than a political decision.[51]

As a result, in the 1980s and afterward many women new to lesbianism no longer regarded themselves as members of an oppressed group. They did not join political organizations or identify with a broad lesbian community; rather, they chose membership in smaller social groups.[52] But in December 1991 when it was revealed in *The Advocate*, a national gay magazine, that NOW president Patricia Ireland lived (at separate times) with both a husband and a female companion, it was obvious that lesbianism could still be used to stigmatize. This time it was the *New York Times Magazine* and not *Time* that published a "second look," asking whether Ireland, because of her sexuality, could legitimately speak for today's women.[53] "The equality of rights movement cannot afford such leadership," wrote *New York Times* columnist William Safire a month later.[54]

Whether or not lesbians chose to be political, the Ireland incident made it quite clear that, in America at least, lesbianism could still be used to taint feminism. As reported in a survey of the media coverage of the disclosure, the American public appeared unwilling to accept either a lesbian or a bisexual spokesperson for NOW.[55] It was, as Gloria Steinem observed during the furor, the Kate Millett story all over again. But clearly, twenty years had made the movement less defensive. Even under pressure, Ireland refused to label herself a lesbian, a bisexual, or anything else, and the NOW organization came to its leader's defense. Ireland continued to speak constructively of the connection between lesbianism and the feminist movement.

The feminist homophobia of the 1968–1971 period has been replaced by a feminism more self-conscious of its diversity and of the many ways in which sexuality is "politicized" in this culture. In a roundtable discussion of feminism staged by *Ms.* magazine in 1993, Naomi Wolf, author of *Fighting Fire with Fire;* Gloria Steinem, founder of *Ms.* and the National Women's Political Caucus; bell hooks, author of eight books, including *Ain't I a Woman*; and Urvashi Vaid, former executive director of the National Gay and Lesbian Task Force explored the relations of feminism and lesbianism.[56] They suggested that the media continues to label strong women "dykes," using homophobia to hurt the feminist cause. To counter this, the feminist movement needs to think of ways to respond when homosexuality is used as a weapon against all women. The one common cause that unites feminists and feminist lesbians, said Steinem, is the need to depoliticize sexuality.[57]

Feminist leaders have finally come to understand, as Steinem put it, that the requirement that all sex take place within patriarchal marriage and be directed toward having children "is a problem for feminists as well as lesbians." Nevertheless, activists continue to assert that lesbian feminists differ from heterosexual feminists in their priorities, that heterosexual feminists want the rights and privileges men enjoy, whereas lesbian feminists are fighting first and foremost for the right to be themselves.

Lesbian Rights: A Balance Sheet

The American Psychiatric Association's 1985 decision to remove homosexuality from the category of mental illness, the solidarity generated in the male homosexual community by the AIDS epidemic, and the national debate on gays in the military during the 1990s have all contributed to increased public awareness of the size, diversity, and extent to which homosexuals in the United States contribute to the American economy and are present in a wide variety of American institutions. This is not to say that homophobia has been displaced. The appearance of antigay ordinances on the ballot in Colorado and Oregon in the early 1990s belies that claim. But there have been significant gains in access for gays and lesbians and in equal treatment. Although many lesbians are still "closeted," there is far less cultural denial. The "don't ask, don't tell, don't pursue" policy in the nation's military is for many an unsatisfactory arrangement, but the acknowledgment and guarded acceptance of homosexual men and women in the armed services could not even have been contemplated twenty years ago.

Limited success, however, as in the women's movement, may have robbed gay and lesbian rights of its revolutionary fervor. At least some of the leadership is worrying about this. Barbara Smith, commenting in *The Nation* about the future of the lesbian and gay rights movements, joins Urvashi Vaid in complaining that a once radical movement has given way to "an assimilationist civil rights agenda."[58] "Unlike the early lesbian and gay movements, which had both ideological and practical links to the left, black activism and feminism, . . . [gay rights activists today are no longer] building unified, ongoing coalitions that challenge the system [or to] prepare for revolutionary change."[59] And as the gay and lesbian rights effort becomes more mainstream, the most visible spokespeople in the movement are more likely to be upper class, professional, and white.

Lesbians are also reexamining their place in American politics and their priorities. "Are we the women's part of the gay movement or the lesbian part of the women's movement?" the head of the National Gay and Lesbian Task Force, Torie Osborn, is quoted in *Newsweek* as asking.[60] In that same issue, Ellen Carton, of the Gay and Lesbian Alliance Against Defamation, worries publicly that lesbians are taking care of everybody else's issues but their own. Indeed, in recent years lesbians have contributed to issues least likely to affect them personally, such as AIDS and abortion. Now, according to *Newsweek*, lesbians are ready to "cast off their role as handmaidens to other activists and stake their own claims."[61] These include pay equity, day care, artificial insemination (which lesbians sometimes employ when they wish to become mothers), and breast cancer research. But of all the issues, the one that is most central to lesbian life is that of the lesbian family.

What Is the "Family" Anyway?

Among the many deprivations lesbians have had to endure under patriarchy have been not just restrictions on their "freedom to live and love exactly as they pleased" but also denial of the real, tangible benefits of family: financial security (including health and insurance benefits of a partner), recognition in the home, and maternal power.[62] That is because, as Abbott and Love observed more than twenty-five years ago, lesbians refuse to be part of the "sexist system." Abbot and Love wrote then: "It is acceptable for a man to do without women, as in men's clubs, sports, or the army, but it is never acceptable for a woman to be without a man. A woman is defined in relationship to men and family. A female without a man and a family is not considered complete. . . ."[63] Note the language—"a female without a family"—even in prolesbian women's writing in the 1970s. A female not living within a patriarchal family was assumed to be living without family at all.

According to law and custom, lesbian families did not exist. Lesbians could not legally marry (form permanent domestic partnerships), share households, file taxes jointly, or claim insurance protection as dependents. Worst of all, birth mothers and their life partners did not have a protected right to live with (or adopt) their children. "Spousal" and "parental" rights continued to be interpreted within the patriarchal meaning of those terms.[64] But what if "the family," in its patriarchal form, was not the only configuration of adults responsible for one another and for offspring? Lesbians and feminists insisted they were not "antifamily"; rather, they were for recognition of a wider variety of "family life."

The political Right, however, usurped the family issue as its own. Not content to battle ERA alone, Phyllis Schlafly formed the Pro-Family Coalition during the feminists' Houston convention in 1977. This coalition was explicitly both antifeminist and antigay and fueled a growing backlash against lesbian and gay rights on several fronts.[65] By calling her group "pro-family," Schlafly intentionally misrepresented the feminist/

lesbian position. Feminists and lesbians were not antifamily but critical of the patriarchal roots of the American family. Schlafly knew that but preferred to play the fear-of-change card in her politics.[66]

Against this background, lesbian family issues moved to the forefront of the lesbian/feminist agenda. In 1989 a New York Court of Appeals ruled that a gay couple living together for ten years must be considered a family under New York City rent-control regulations, a step in the direction of "marriage rights" that commentator Andrew Sullivan, author of *Virtually Normal,* believes is the next most important political issue (after the military ban) for homosexuals.[67] Lesbian and gay marriages are being performed in some religious "commitment ceremonies" by certain local churches (Quakers, Church of Christ, United Methodist), but not yet with denominational support. Reformed Jewish rabbis now recognize same-sex partnerships. Some Presbyterian ministers bless same-sex partnerships, but this is not yet widespread.

A bill to outlaw same-sex marriage (called the Defense of Marriage Act) made its way through Congress in spring 1996. Not even the president, who supported gay rights in the military, would or could oppose it. Nevertheless, fueled by the publicity given Sharon Kowalski, a woman disabled in an automobile accident whose lesbian partner was refused permission (by the disabled woman's parents) to be her official guardian,[68] more and more cities and states are recognizing domestic partnerships. In San Francisco couples may file an affidavit declaring that they have a committed relationship, live together, and agree to be responsible for each other's basic living expenses, or they can receive a certificate defining themselves as a nonprofit "family association."[69] Although Congress voted in 1996 (a presidential election year) to restrict the term *marriage* to heterosexual unions, elsewhere in that same year (in Boulder, Colorado, for example) provision was made whereby gay and lesbian couples could register their relationships with city government. With artificial insemination making it possible for lesbians to become birth mothers with or without the participation of a known father, thousands of lesbians have given birth to infants, leading to new child-custody issues when lesbian couples divorce. Like heterosexuals of both sexes, lesbians want to experience the joys along with the challenges of family life. Lesbians are pro-family, too.

Twenty-five states still have sodomy laws on the books, which, although they were intended to criminalize male homosexual acts, are also used to prosecute lesbians. Even when unenforced, they legitimize homophobia and the criminality of private consensual sex. These laws are constantly being challenged, most recently in Michigan and Texas. While antigay local ordinances come and go, little or no counseling is available for gay children or adolescents in schools.

Whether homosexuals will ever constitute a "suspect category," that is, have the special constitutional protection guaranteed women and minorities, will have to be decided by the Supreme Court.[70] In the meantime, as with gender discrimination, federal, state, and local statutory protection is the next best thing. No matter how much consciousness-raising is done, no matter how much tolerance for diversity is encouraged, no matter how much outreach homosexuals do, until the deprivation of their rights is legally actionable, there is no guarantee that their rights will be observed.

11

Third-Generation Issues

ISSUES ON WHICH FEMINISTS DO NOT AGREE

IN THE HEADY FIRST DOZEN YEARS of the revival of feminism in America, differences between women—by class, by race, by position in or out of the labor force, by age, by marital status, even by political affiliation—seemed less significant than a shared sense of previous isolation and a powerful agenda for change. As noted in Chapter 6, it was their overriding desire to be of service to other women that radicalized the relatively privileged women appointed to John Kennedy's fifty state commissions. Similarly, a sense of unfulfillment (after reading Friedan's *Feminine Mystique*) gave housewives some solidarity with the much younger women in the student Left who were coming to realize that "liberation politics" did not include them. Thus were very different women united under feminism's banner in the early years.

At the level of theory, there were, of course, differences among socialist, radical, and liberal women who came to their own brands of feminism through prior political influence; no amount of gender solidarity could erase real social-class differences among women in the degree and kind of oppression they experienced. But except for some concern that equal rights would threaten protective legislation, the policies that came to be championed in pursuit of role equity were so obviously necessary and long overdue that there was little disagreement as to where to go for political redress and how to get there (see Chapter 7).[1] Second-generation issues, which involved role change, took on greater urgency as the movement matured and, as we have seen in Chapter 8, were considerably more controversial. But again, with only a few exceptions, the Equal Rights Amendment, equal access to school-sponsored sports, affirmative action, and an end to sexual harassment served to unite feminists even more.

Such would not be the case with third-generation issues, issues on which feminists could and did forcefully disagree. With hindsight, it was probably inevitable that once equal access to jobs, pay, credit, and education was legislated, once abortion was at least protected by law and women could begin to take more control of their lives, it would be harder to get activists to follow a single "feminist" path through the next set of issues. But on which issues would feminists divide? That was not so obvious. Working through those issues myself in the 1970s and 1980s, I came to believe that issues such as women in the military, pornography, comparable worth, the Mommy Track, and unwed motherhood challenged feminists to come to grips with differences in outlook and priorities that had not surfaced before.

Women and the Military: Conflict over Combat and the Draft

In many respects the opportunities afforded women after the U.S. military was formally integrated in 1973 confounded the age-old issue of what ought to be a *feminist* position on militarism and war. On the one hand, as NOW would argue in supporting women's right to be drafted, equal rights involve equal responsibility, a responsibility that includes the nation's defense as well. (The argument for service in an offensive military machine would have been a little harder to make.) Moreover, since the U.S. military affords technical training and upward mobility for many Americans, particularly the nation's disadvantaged, women deserve to be eligible for these privileges, too. Finally, given women's skills and professional dedication, an armed force that excludes half the population is weaker than it has to be. For all these reasons, NOW applauded the elimination of the women's-only branches of the military in 1973 and, once President Carter raised the issue of conscription six years later, went on record in support of women's equal right to be drafted even if this involved participation in combat.[2]

On the other hand, there is a long antiwar, antimilitarist tradition among women. Long before they went to battle for their own rights, women weighed in on the side of peace against war and cut their political teeth, one might say, on that opposition. From the wives in Aristophanes' *Lysistrata*—the first connubial refusniks, who at first would not satisfy their husbands' sexual wants so long as their husbands went to war (but later caved in)—to the establishment during World War I of the Women's International League for Peace and Freedom, the history of women's pacifism is long, honorable, and international. American women, for their part, mounted antiwar demonstrations against every war America fought, from the Mexican War to World War II, and America's entry into that war, as you may recall from Chapter 3, was opposed by Jeannette Rankin, the first woman ever elected to the House of Representatives. Finally, as historian Amy Swerdlow documents in her book about the 1960s Women Strike for Peace (WSP), women were not only against war but also at the forefront of the several antinuclear weapons campaigns.[3]

"Peace," then, was traditionally (if not exclusively) a woman's issue. But as liberal feminism extended its claims on behalf of women to the inner sanctums of power, peace no longer appeared (to some at least) to be a feminist issue.[4] Women's activism on behalf of peace led too easily, it was thought, to an essentialist point of view, namely, that women are more pacific by nature than men. Indeed, Swerdlow, in whose person feminism, scholarship, and pacifism come together, admits that the women who rallied against nuclear weapons in the late 1950s "were searching for a space in which their moral, political, and *maternal* stance could be translated into action [italics added]."[5] And it was their maternalism, she thinks, that in an era when pacifism was especially suspect made them surprisingly effective. She writes, "By exposing the contradictions between mothers' responsibility for preserving life and the state's nuclear recklessness, [Women Strike for Peace] was able to gain public support for its attacks on such sacrosanct military and political institutions as the Pentagon, NATO, and the House Un-American Activities Committee."[6]

Ten years after Women Strike for Peace (WSPers, as Swerdlow calls them), second-wave feminism was in ascendance, and from the perspective of women's interchangeability with men, some feminists found the WSPers' style of protest retrogressive. Consider the latter's underlying claims. A first has to do with women's maternalism: that as "givers of life," women are more eager to preserve life than men. A second rests on women's vulnerability: that as the "weaker sex," they and their children suffer more (even more than men in the field) in times of war.[7] A third presumes women's moral superiority (an issue fraught with traps, as I have already documented in Chapter 2) and promises specifically that in a world run by women, there would be no more war. How could such views be reconciled with the feminists' position that apart from reproduction, women are interchangeable with men?

Yet when mainstream feminists rejected the woman-as-peace-lover argument, they risked cooptation, as Kathy Jones reminds us in her critique of NOW's support for women in the draft.[8] Thus were drawn the lines that would divide feminists on this issue. Not only were *equality* and *difference* opposed, but also there were deep divisions on the larger question embedded in women and the military—namely, was there a purpose in liberating women if they were only to become soldiers? As Bella Abzug said at the time, "The excessive focusing on the issue of [women and the] draft diverted attention from [what should have been] the real debate about what [justifies] drafting anyone."[9]

The pro- and antidraft issue was not just theoretical. President Jimmy Carter had come to the White House in 1977 determined to carry out dé-tente with the Soviet Union. But the buildup of Soviet intermediate-range nuclear missiles on the USSR's western borders caused him to re-consider the size of the armed forces. Not yet ready to reauthorize conscription, the Carter administration did ask Congress for authority to have all eighteen-year-old males *register* in case a draft was needed. In the end a draft was not reinstated—the cold war ended ten years later—but in 1979–1980 the question of whether women would or should be drafted fueled a real debate. The Equal Rights Amendment was still making its way around the country, and the "combat exemp-tion" had been one of its sticking points. Phyllis Schlafly was using the military as an example of the absurdity of legislating unisex. The country was waiting to see what the largest feminist membership organization would do. NOW agonized internally, but eventually NOW's president, Judy Goldsmith, presented before Congress a position in favor of women's conscription.[10]

The draft was not the only issue. In the decade that followed, women's participation in the nation's armed forces climbed to 10 percent, with fewer and fewer combat exemptions;[11] West Point, Annapolis, and the Air Force Academy, the nation's officer-training academies, were all opened to women;[12] a Vietnam Memorial to the women who died in that war was erected on the Washington Mall; sexual harassment of women officers and enlisted personnel was exposed and new standards put in place;[13] and, whereas in 1984 vice-presidential candidate Geraldine Fer-raro had been considered by many to be unqualified for highest office because she had never served in the military, in 1993 a woman astro-physicist who had also never served, Sheila Widnall, professor of aero-nautical engineering from MIT, was appointed secretary of the Air Force (the first woman to act as civilian overseer of a military branch).

If the debate on military matters during the 1970s was whether women should be part of the peacetime military at all, the debate in the early 1980s was dominated by the sudden resurgence of the very real threat of nuclear war. Détente had given way to what the military calls "threat-whomping," and Americans of all political stripes were scared.[14] Against that backdrop, what difference did it make what kind of argu-ments women employed to achieve disarmament? Or whether equal rights for women were achieved at all? The threat of nuclear disaster in the early 1980s, like the Great Depression and World War II, could not help but trivialize women's issues as it drove people back to essentials. For some feminists, such as Eleanor Smeal, nuclear issues were a diversion from the real equity issues pertaining to gender and race.

Worst of all was the resurgence of "neomaternalism" in the service of world peace. Some British women in the late 1970s were so opposed to the deployment of American nuclear-tipped cruise missiles in Greenham, England, that they came from all over England, with children in tow, to stage rallies on the site. Eventually, they created a peace encampment for women only.[15] Their stance was emotional, their position unyielding. "All I have to know about cruise missiles," said a Greenham Encampment leader on a tour to raise money for the Encampment in the United States, "is that I will have to watch my child die [from radiation]."[16] At the same time, other women just as much in favor of disarmament were turning themselves into strategy experts so that they could debate the military on its own terms.[17] The dividing issue went beyond mere tactics: Were women to become knowledgeable about arms control, they might be seduced into the military's way of thinking about peace and war. Perhaps it was better to be just unutterably opposed.

My own activism during this period was an effort to bring outsiders in—at least into the debate about weapons. Thinking that what women needed was a guide to nuclear weapons and strategic thought, three collaborators and I wrote a book with women peace activists in mind that came out in 1982 called *What Kinds of Guns Are They Buying for Your Butter? A Beginner's Guide to Defense, Weaponry, and Military Spending.* Later, I mounted two slide shows, "Know Your Weapons" and "Know Your Defense Budget," which were circulated to women's groups.[18] But as far as my coauthors and I could ascertain, peace activists were not as interested in having detailed descriptions of nuclear delivery systems as they were in their gut feelings; nor were they willing to consider a viable defense strategy based on a nonnuclear alternative. Only antinuclearist Helen Caldicott of Physicians for Social Responsibility, who brought a mother's passion together with a scientist's understanding of the issues, succeeded in teaching her audiences about nuclear arms while rousing their ire.[19]

In time, a feminist analysis of the entire situation finally emerged, focused on the nuclear arms race and its justification rather than solely on the dangers of nuclear war. Carol Cohn, a feminist invited to a weapons briefing session at MIT, later described in chilling detail the way strategic thinkers both *sexualized* and *domesticated* the nuclear weapon.[20] In an angry book called *Missile Envy,* Helen Caldicott accused men on both sides of the Iron Curtain of risking the human race to pursue a kind of macho competition.[21] But although women were becoming more and more active as strategic professionals, the 1980s threat of nuclear war came and went without a significant transformation of the language or rhetoric of traditional peace politics as practiced by women. Pacifists continued to focus on the horrors of war; strategists, on the insiders' work of political and military planning so that war would not be a viable option.

In a post–Cold War environment, feminists are still divided on military issues, but the divisions cut differently from before. For example, what are the lessons from the 1991 Persian Gulf War for feminist politics? On the one hand, there was a surge of war fervor in the United States during the brief 100 days of that war, and women participated just as much as men in displaying yellow ribbons of support for U.S. soldiers. What is a feminist to make of that? On the other hand, the Persian Gulf was the first war to which a large number of uniformed women (forty thousand) were sent. Women were so visibly a part of the effort that news commentators back home could no longer talk about "our *boys* in Riyadh" or "our *men* in uniform." Even though few were in direct line of fire, many women died in one costly barracks bombing in Saudi Arabia and on medical missions. Meanwhile, some of the women scheduled to go to the front—trained military personnel—balked (even got pregnant by intention) at being separated from their families. Several had to be dishonorably discharged. What was a feminist to make of that? Was this an indication of female inferiority or of how dehumanizing any war must be?

In many ways, however, military business was conducted as usual: Women were conspicuously absent from the generals' strategy planning staffs where military decisions were made. Cynthia Enloe, in her postscript to that war, observes that "gender politics" was more complicated than ever.[22] How were American feminists supposed to think about Iraqi women, who, with their children, bore the brunt of the allied bombing and who in another time and context American feminists would have embraced? How were American feminists to think about the Kuwaiti women, whose (husbands') sovereignty the allies were defending but who themselves could not vote or participate in politics? Yes, they were victims of invasion and later of rape by their occupiers, but so were their imported Asian servants. No wonder Enloe entitles her chapter "The Gendered Gulf."[23]

Comparable Worth

During the 1980s, pay equity was redefined by many feminists to mean not just equal pay for equal or substantially equal work (the language used in the 1963 Equal Pay Act—see Chapter 7) but also equal compensation for jobs of "equal value" to the employer. This shift reflected a growing concern that the equal pay legislation did not go far enough. Women continued experiencing lower pay and occupational segregation on the basis of their gender.[24] Moreover, the wage gap between fully employed men and fully employed women did not seem to be diminishing fast enough despite legislation and many court settlements. Women on average (that is, across all occupations) were still earning between $0.64 and $0.70 for every $1 men earned. Advocates of the new idea of comparable worth argued that this wage gap was the result of wage discrimination by individual employees *and* of the artificially lower value assigned to "women's work."

The idea that women's work is lesser work is so internalized in this country that it takes special rethinking to imagine how a particular function would be compensated in a gender-unbiased society. Take nursing, for example. There are, of course, senior nurses, specialized nurses, and head nurses. But whatever their "value" to the patient or in the managing hospital, female nurses tend to be less well paid than other medical personnel, including laboratory technicians.[25] Why is this? Nurses have patient *welfare* under their jurisdiction, doctors and other specialists are said to be responsible for patient *cure*, but patient welfare is valued less than patient cure. But who decides that patient cure is not directly dependent on patient welfare? Even when working conditions are compared, there is less compensation for nursing care than for the hazards of other occupations.

In most areas of the United States child care workers, to take another example, are paid about the same wage as parking attendants, as if caring for a child and "caring" for an automobile had the same value to society. Indeed, the pattern in all wage determinations in industrial society is to assign a higher value to the care and handling of machinery and instrumentation than to the care and handling of people. One of the several considerations in wage determination is the negative value of the "loss" to the company or organization if the job is not done properly. It is easier to calculate the financial loss resulting from the mishandling of a machine than from the loss of, say, customer goodwill. Hence, the care and cultivating of goodwill, often in the hands of a trusted secretary, may be less well compensated than the care of a computer. That women's work tends to involve people and public relations and is therefore less well paid is said to be coincidental. It just so happens that women choose this work, and it just so happens that the work they choose is lower paid. The classic example, quoted in much of the literature on pay equity, is that of municipal tree trimmers. Tree trimmers are laborers without advanced training who work out of doors and at some physical risk. These men are paid significantly more by municipalities than (mostly female) librarians who hold master's degrees.

If a comparable worth policy were implemented, it would mean that job categories in which women predominate would be revalued, presumably upward, to allow for better pay.[26] Men's wages would not be lowered but would remain either the same or rise more slowly. The procedure for making a comparable worth adjustment would consist of revising the job evaluation criteria that are generally used within large organizations to assign "points" and comparative values to different jobs. The underlying issue in the scheme is *job worth:* what it is, how it is determined, and to what extent that determination rests on traditional views of the *value* of what men and women do.

Why do feminists disagree on comparable worth? It appears to some that efforts to raise standards and compensation in the "pink-collar ghetto" could make the ghetto too cozy. Public efforts (money and policy) should be used, these feminists argue, to retrain women instead into nontraditional (that is, male-dominated) occupations.[27] These feminists see occupational segregation by gender, not merely inadequate pay for traditional women's work, to be at the root of the problem. Thus, the provision of comparable worth—that is, better pay for the work that women are traditionally assigned—would not better women's job prospects in the long run.

Table 11.1 and Figure 11.1 show how little occupational segregation by gender has changed since 1975, especially as regards the clerical, farming, forestry, fishing, and transportation industries. In 1990 more than 45 percent of all employed women worked in service retail. Even where occupations seem to be well integrated by gender, that appearance may belie considerable segregation in subfields. Take sales, for example. Although sales in general is well integrated, there is considerable segregation within sales by product. Sales of furniture, automobiles, computers, and computer products, for example, are largely done by men; sales of lesser-cost products (which affect salary and commission, of course) are women's work. Among women managers, race complicates upward mobility still more.[28]

Some feminists are not opposed to comparable worth adjustments in theory but express two other fears: first, that comparable worth may be so thorny and difficult to implement (how does one actually compare the value of goodwill to the value of a mainframe computer?) that it will absorb feminist energies and drain feminist credibility; second, that the issue of comparable worth could spark a backlash against pay equity in all its variants by working men and their families, who depend on a wage based on traditional evaluation. Phyllis Schlafly has already played this card. In a series of brochures, testimony, and Eagle Forum–sponsored conferences, she began attacking comparable worth as early as 1983. A typical broadside featured inflammatory descriptions such as "Comparable Worth Will FREEZE Your Wages" and "The looniest idea since Looney Tunes."[29]

In Schlafly's analysis (based on a court case against the state of Washington), the application of new job evaluation criteria *reduces* the points

TABLE 11.1 Women as a Percentage of All Civilian Employees in Selected Occupations by Race and Hispanic Origin, 1990

Occupation	Percent Females All Races	Percent White Female	Percent Black Female	Percent Hispanic Origin Female
Secretaries	99.0	89.5	7.5	5.1
Textile sewing machine operators	89.2	66.5	14.6	18.0
Health aides, except nursing	84.8	65.6	17.0	4.7
Waitresses	80.8	74.2	3.3	4.3
Production inspectors, checkers, and examiners	52.2	42.4	7.9	4.5
Bus drivers	51.5	42.4	8.6	2.3
Financial managers	44.3	41.3	1.8	1.0
Assemblers	43.5	34.1	7.3	5.6
Computer programmers	36.0	30.6	2.4	1.0
Precision food [handlers]	32.7	25.3	6.7	3.1
Insurance sales	32.6	29.3	2.6	1.3
Stock handlers and baggers	25.0	21.9	2.2	2.3
Farm workers	21.0	19.0	1.3	4.2
Physicians	19.3	16.2	0.5	0.5
Laborers, except contruction	18.7	14.4	3.7	1.9
Police and dectectives	13.9	9.8	3.9	0.8
Electrical and electronic equipment repairers	8.7	6.4	1.8	0.3
Engineers	8.0	7.0	0.1	0.3
Coonstructions trades	1.9	1.7	0.1	0.1
Total, all occupations	45.4	38.7	5.0	3.0

SOURCE: U.S. Bureau of Labor Statistics, *Employment and Earnings*, January 1991. Reprinted from *The American Woman, 1992–1993: A Status Report*, Paula Ries and Anne J. Stone, eds. (New York: W. W. Norton, 1993), p. 332.

Industry

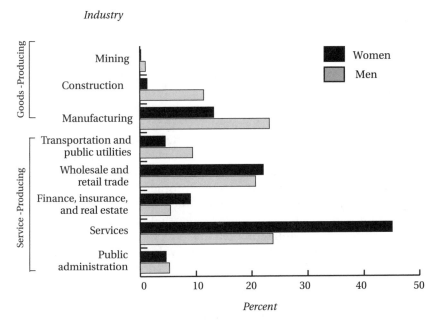

FIGURE 11.1 Workers in Goods-Producing and Service-Producing Nonfarm Industries by Sex, 1990. SOURCE: U.S. Bureau of Labor Statistics, *Employment and Earnings*, January 1991, Table 27. Reprinted from *The American Woman, 1992–1993: A Status Report*, Paula Ries and Anne J. Stone, eds. (New York: W. W. Norton, 1993), p. 331.

allowable in the "working conditions" category, a category that favors men's work, in exchange for an *increase* in the "mental demands" category, a category that favors some women's work. The upshot, warned Schlafly, would be a freeze in men's wages to pay for the upgrade in women's. Her brochure ends: "If you are a blue-collar man or woman, 'comparable worth' advocates have targeted YOU for a WAGE FREEZE because they think you are overpaid! They want bureaucrats to decide how much your job is 'worth.'"

Her list of the soon-to-be "wage frozen" includes plumbers, electricians, policemen and firemen, truck drivers, mechanics, maintenance men, and construction workers. And in testimony before Congress, Schlafly elaborated still more on the matter of unfair comparisons: "One of the techniques . . . is devaluing of the physical and working-condition factors so important to blue-collar jobs. This devaluation . . . is the inevitable result of integrating white-collar and blue-collar jobs in the same [system]."[30] Feminists opposed to comparable worth as a strategy surely do not feel comfortable on the same side of any issue as Phyllis Schlafly, but there they are.

The Mommy Track

Since 1950 the workforce participation of mothers of preschool-age children has quadrupled. More women are better educated, relationships between the sexes have relaxed, and fewer children, later childbearing, and changing attitudes about married women's capabilities in the workforce have all contributed to gains for women workers. But in addition, as has already been noted in Chapter 4, economic necessity has transformed the American family. Women today are driven to work by the need to support their families as single parents or to make ends meet in two-paycheck families. Particularly for the lower-income mother, the "dual career"—that is, the need to work both at home and in the workforce—has limited her employment options. Many poor or unmarried mothers, eager to have the job security, health and retirement benefits, and upward mobility that come with full-time jobs, cannot compete with other job applicants because of time constraints. Therefore, they take a disproportionate share of part-time, underpaid employment in the retail service sector. A child's illness, especially in a single-parent family, can mean the difference between a full week's pay and no pay at all. Absent federally supported child care, a mother's first obligation is to her children.

Among professional workers, child care can be purchased, but there are times in the average mother's life when a part-time or at least a less stressful job week is preferable. Yet professional job slots are predicated on a non-family-oriented lifestyle (even, said some feminists in the early days, on the presumption that a working man and his wife together will fulfill a "two-person career," as it takes a hostess, suitcase packer, laundress, and so forth and a working husband to move him ahead in certain careers).[31] How, then, can a woman accommodate motherhood and work? In January 1989 Felice Schwartz, a founder and longtime director of Catalyst, a nonprofit national organization concerned with women and business, published an article in the *Harvard Business Review* outlining what she thought was a solution.[32] Although she never used the term "Mommy Track," her proposal was to provide some breathing space on the professional fast track for women employees raising children at home. Almost immediately her idea was denounced in the press as nothing less than an excuse for employers to make women second-class citizens on the job.

Felice Schwartz had been working to integrate women into business for twenty-seven years when her proposed idea backfired. She and other Catalyst coauthors had published a book in 1972 provocatively entitled *How to Go to Work When Your Husband Is Against It, Your Children Aren't Old Enough, and There's Nothing You Can Do Anyhow.*[33] So her concern for women was undisputed. But how feminist was her proposed solution? She believed that if business leaders were given a variety of ways of using female talent, the workplace could be transformed. But, eager to be "like men," the women business students she frequently met with engaged in a "conspiracy of silence" about women's difficulties in combining a fast-track professional career with a family. In a book published three years after the controversy erupted, Schwartz recalled that telling the truth about women was dangerous because, young women believed, any discussion of their family needs would reinforce the biases that corporate leaders still hold; the net result would be to keep women down.[34]

Indeed, in interviewing female MBAs about to go on the job market in 1990, Schwartz found them to be unwilling to wear their wedding rings to an interview. Even employed professional women would delay announcing their pregnancy when in negotiation for a promotion or at some other critical juncture in their career. Others were returning to work soon after childbirth, even if they were not sure they wanted to. These young women were struggling with the unwritten code of business: that nurturing a family is antithetical to nurturing a career.[35]

What Schwartz wanted for women was flexibility. Had she talked about male employees' need for "family time," she might not have been so criticized. But, as she argued later, most senior (male) executives would not have been able to relate to that option since, "with few exceptions, they never played a big role in the daily lives of their families."[36] (Her unwillingness to confront this issue made feminists especially angry.) Schwartz saw women as needing options, not men. Not all women would select the "career-and-family" path, as opposed to the "career-primary" road, but some women might for a limited period of time.[37] Rather than lose their services altogether, she wanted managers to realize that business would benefit, as would their women employees. It would be a win-win situation.

The term "Mommy Track" was definitely not Schwartz's. Six months before writing the *Harvard Business Review* article, Schwartz sent a letter (never published) to the *New York Times* criticizing the paper for using the term in a story entitled "Women in the Law Say Path Is Limited by 'Mommy Track.'" The story reported on women lawyers unable to make headway in firms when they cut back on work to have time for their families. But for many feminists, the Mommy Track, by whatever name, was odious. Betty Friedan, interviewed by the *Los Angeles Times,* soon after the article was cited, called Schwartz's categories "dangerous," a sort of "retrofeminism." Even author Sylvia Ann Hewlett, who wanted to restore motherhood to its rightful place in women's lives, resented the implication of Schwartz's proposal, namely, that children are "a woman's issue."[38] In *Ms.* Barbara Ehrenreich and Deirdre English dismissed Schwartz's essay as "a tortured muddle of feminist perceptions and sexist assumptions that should never have been taken seriously." Even the *New York Times* criticized Schwartz editorially for her proposal.[39]

In her retrospective, Schwartz attributed the intensity of the attacks on her idea to a deep-rooted feminist ambivalence in the early years of the second wave of feminism on the subject of women's "differences" from men.[40] Yet the issue would not go away. In 1985 the Korn/Ferry survey revealed that, even though 83 percent of American women have children, only 39 percent of female corporate leaders do (compared to 97 percent of males in comparable positions).[41] Writing in 1995, Elizabeth Fox-Genovese supported something like a Mommy Track as well.[42] Schwartz's point was and still remains that "employers will not be able to effectively advance women until they accept maternity as the predictable, manageable event it can be."[43]

The controversy over Schwartz's ideas, whether misrepresented by the media or not, suggests how divided feminists were over the suggestion that working women needed special consideration. Even more significant, the Mommy Track seemed to many to be an issue for middle-class white women to work out. The majority of working women enjoyed no options at all. They had to work, and they had to take care of their families, and no employer was going to make it easier for them to do either, certainly not to do both.

Pornography

Many feminists consider pornography to be the quintessential feminist issue since it is the primary mechanism linking sex and violence and therefore sex and control of women by men. Where feminists diverge is on the assessment of what is pornography, how to measure its impact, and, above all, how to make it go away. Complicating the "free-speech" aspect of the issue is that fact that not only does pornography degrade women in its scripted fantasies, but also the industry abuses and exploits real women to get its products made. Feminists investigating commercial sex in the 1970s found that the industry particularly preyed on vulnerable women. The brave few who came forth to testify described levels of coercion and abuse that made the scripts look tame. "Linda Lovelace," of the infamous "Deep Throat" series of pornographic films, was an unwilling performer in the films, and she was kept a prisoner and tortured when she did not submit. Lovelace was not unique; hers was simply the best publicized case.[44]

People on all sides of the issue have difficulty defining pornography but tend to recognize it when they see it. When Margaret Atwood was researching her novel *Bodily Harm*, she talked to a journalist for whom "anything involving naked bodies and sex" was pornographic. But for most feminists, pornography is more than what is "obscene."[45] Pornography degrades the women it displays; it also may incite viewers to commit violence against women. "Women getting their nipples snipped with garden shears" was Atwood's threshold.[46] After finishing her book, she became an antipornography activist.

Pornography became a feminist issue in the same way rape emerged from the closets of shame and was suddenly seen to be "political" both in its origins and its practice (see Chapter 8). Kate Millett's analysis of the erotic in Henry Miller made it clear to her readers that what was sexy for men in Miller's novels—namely, women wanting to be taken in the way objects are consumed—was for women not sexy at all. But feminists Andrea Dworkin and Catharine MacKinnon gave pornography a theoretical grounding that, like Brownmiller's theory of rape, put it squarely on the feminists' action agenda.[47] For MacKinnon and Dworkin, the basis of women's subordination has to do not just with childbearing and childrearing but also with sexuality itself. "Sexuality is to feminism what work is to Marxism, that which is most one's own, yet most taken away," MacKinnon wrote in 1982. "[It is] the primary sphere of male power . . . the linchpin of gender inequality."[48]

Sociologist Scott McNall agrees that the wielding of power over women is central to pornography's appeal:

> Pornography "says" that sex is under male control. It is men who will decide when sex will take place, and with whom. . . . The sexually alive woman (meaning one who decides for herself who, when, and how) is threatening, and pornography is about control of sexuality. . . . Sex becomes commodified not merely in the sense that it can be purchased, but also in the sense that one is dealing with a totally alienated being—one separated from, out of control of, her body. . . . Pornography is purchased sex, and the implication for men is that women can be bought.[49]

Owing to our nation's Puritan (antipleasure) tradition, the production and distribution of "obscene" materials were for a long time prohibited by law. Books such as Henry Miller's *Tropic of Cancer* and James Joyce's *Ulysses*, published without incident in Europe, could not be brought out in America for many years, despite their literary merit. In 1973, pressured by artists and free-speech advocates alike, the U.S. Supreme Court finally modified the legal definition of obscenity to allow for "frank sexual description" in literary works. Although it was not the Court's intention, women-degrading pornography flourished after this decision.[50] With the invention of the videotape just ten years later, pornographic films became a difficult-to-control medium for the depiction of increasingly violent acts against women.

The first reported feminist action against pornography was initiated by a group of San Francisco women in 1976 in response to a disturbing increase in the number of pornographic distributors in that city. Two years later the San Franciscans encouraged a group of New York feminists to found Women Against Pornography. Their strategy was to tour porno shops in groups to show uninformed women what pornography is really like. As with rape and abortion, the first step in activism was to raise awareness among women of the extent of pornography.

For once, the government appeared to share these concerns. In 1985 President Reagan created a commission to investigate pornography and to recommend how the government should deal with it. When in 1986 the Meese Commission delivered its report, it found pornography to be both "harmful" and "a social menace."[51] The commission recommended increased obscenity prosecution through amendment of federal and state laws and through linkage of all the prosecuting agencies involved. Many more federal funds were spent prosecuting obscenity cases than ever before. The Supreme Court restricted sexually explicit telephone services—the 900 number was another new form of public pornography—and federal licensing agreements were rewritten to restrict television programming.

One complication for antiporn feminists is their discomfort at finding themselves on the same side of an issue that attracts conservatives. Gayle Rubin, anthropologist and essayist, in search of a "radical theory of the politics of sexuality," reports that the antipornography movement in the United States is largely populated by the New Right and by those who want to turn the clock back on women's emancipation.[52] Another complexity is the potential conflict between regulating pornography and restricting free speech. That position is enunciated by the Feminist Anti-Censorship Task Force (FACT). For FACT, *depictions* of sexual depravity and violence are simply not the same thing as the actual acts. Therefore, pornography should not be prosecuted as a form of violence. FACT is also opposed to the various antiporn local ordinances that antiporn feminists Andrea Dworkin and Catharine MacKinnon have tried to implement. FACT fears that once these ordinances are in place, local courts will be able to interpret them any way they want. Even writing about sexuality, in books and manuals such as *Our Bodies, Ourselves*,[53] could be targeted for censorship in certain localities if there was no agreed-upon way to differentiate the erotic from the obscene.[54]

Free speech is the feminist issue, argued New York State NOW's president Marilyn Fitterman at the time of the debate on the "Pornography Victims' Compensation Act" in 1992.[55] "Censorship has been, throughout history, the single most widely used tool for 'protecting' women from birth control, abortion, sexual satisfaction, and non-heterosexual relationships," wrote Fitterman to Catharine MacKinnon in regard to that bill.[56] And, indeed, that measure and some of MacKinnon and Dworkin's local ordinances attracted vocal and sustained opposition from Betty Friedan, Gloria Steinem, and many other well-known feminists.

Other feminists nevertheless believe that the issue of the secondary effects of pornography on women is the way to get around the free-speech issue. Experiments with audiences in Scandinavia, Atwood tells us, demonstrate that there is a link between the viewing of a film with sexual violence and the will to do violence when the audience leaves.[57] Atwood concedes that pornographic materials should not be confused with the acts themselves, so she would have pornography regulated like hate literature and alcohol abuse. (She is from Canada, where such matters are more easily regulated than they are here.) Not all feminists would be satisfied with regulated pornography, however. Dworkin and MacKinnon, the two feminists who have made pornography a cause cèlébre, take the position that government has a *compelling interest* (the legal term that justifies limitations on citizens' rights) to stop the manufacture and distribution of pornographic materials. For Rubin, this kind of antiporn legislation is not feminist but regressive, the "most retrogressive," she writes, "this side of the Vatican."[58]

Rubin sees two "feminist" positions on the issue of pornography and one unstable middle position slowly evolving between them. "Prosex" feminists, as Rubin labels them, are opposed to antiporn legislation on the grounds that the defense of sexual pleasure is a form of "erotic justice."[59] Antiporn feminists, thinks Rubin, consider "sexual liberation" a way for males to extend their access to women previously unavailable to them. These are very different views of sexuality, and not surprisingly, they lead to very different strategies for handling pornography. Women have a right to be angry at the way they are depicted in commercially available sex products, Rubin concedes. But, as she reminds us, sexism was not invented by pornographers. "The sex industry reflects the sexism that already exists in society as a whole."[60]

Most feminists would probably agree with this middle position. But in the real world of politics, one has to take a stand. By enlarging the definition of obscenity, the Meese Commission opened the door to censorship of a wide range of materials, including erotic photography. Eight years later, in 1993, certain members of Congress attacked a photographic exhibit of Robert Mapplethorpe's work, commissioned by the federally funded National Endowment for the Arts, as sexually explicit; the museum closed the show. No wonder the unintended alliance between antipornography feminists and conservatives makes feminists uncomfortable. But feminists such as Dworkin and MacKinnon are undeterred. They would like to codify into law a "feminist definition of pornography" that would make pornography that is degrading to women punishable *twice*—first as pornography, second as sex discrimination.

Instead of dividing feminists, pornography might have been the occasion for feminists to gain a fuller understanding of sexual oppression in all its various guises. Gayle Rubin thinks it still might accomplish this. With pornography infecting the Internet, the issue is likely to get even more complicated before it is solved. Whether a viable middle position on the issue will emerge remains to be seen.

When Illegitimacy Becomes Legitimate

A combination of the sexual revolution, the relaxation of historical barriers to "illegitimacy," and alternate family formations has caused an enormous increase in the numbers of children born out of wedlock and/or living during most of their childhood in single-parent households. Most of their parents are previously married women awarded custody in divorce proceedings. But a growing number of children have never-married parents and are "illegitimate" in the technical sense of that term. It could be argued, and is by many feminists, that "legitimacy" and "illegitimacy" are outmoded, socially constructed categories that ought to be buried along with the traditional marriage contract. But the growing number of children brought up in single-parent families, as well as the growing documentation that they are poor, and likely to stay poor, and to have behavioral, social, and school-related problems, has ushered in a debate, even among feminists, as to what is "best" for children, as well as for young women without money or a decent education.

Among the generation of young people who came of age after World War II, 80 percent grew up in families with both biological parents present. By 1980 only 50 percent fit that pattern, and if current trends continue, "less than half of all children born today will live continuously with their own mother and father throughout their childhood."[61] So begins a reconsideration of divorce, single parenthood, legitimacy, and illegitimacy in the United States by Barbara Dafoe Whitehead, published under the provocative title "Dan Quayle Was Right." The reference in the title is to a remark made by Quayle when running for vice-president on the Republican Party's 1992 ticket. Seeking the support of the "family values" constituency, Quayle took the then-popular television character "Murphy Brown" (played by the even more popular Candace Bergen) to task for flaunting an out-of-wedlock birth as part of the series.

"Murphy Brown" and many of her fans replied tartly that having a baby without a husband represented a "higher level of maternal devotion and sacrifice" than having a baby with a husband.[62] Instead of boosting the ticket, Quayle's offhand remark may have cost him votes. In the eyes of many, he appeared foolish, stuffy, old-fashioned, and even hostile to the full emancipation of women. But the issue did not go away.

Reports of underachievement, emotional instability, sexual abuse, and criminal behavior among children who grow up in single-parent families can only partially be explained by the confluence of poverty and illegitimacy. The problem of what one writer calls "life without father"[63] reveals that "just as motherhood no longer defines adult womanhood, fatherhood has declined as a norm for men."[64]

Whitehead traces the growing acceptance of single-parent families, including those headed by never-married mothers, to three assumptions that took hold coincidentally with the second wave of feminism. First, divorce was often "better" for everyone, including the children, than holding together a failed marriage. Second, women in a more equitable society could find work that would permit them to support their children on their own. And third, the much-maligned "nuclear family" was only one of several acceptable ways for adults and children to cohabit.[65] Carol Stack's *All Our Kin,* published in the 1970s, reinforced those views.[66] Daniel Moynihan's controversial counterview, at least for the African-American family, was largely criticized as "racist,"[67] but by the 1980s longitudinal surveys of children from such alternative families had begun to surface, and an altogether different picture from Carol Stack's emerged, one that reinforced Moynihan's findings.[68] Particularly disturbing to some feminists were data like the following: Daughters of single parents are 53 percent more likely to marry as teenagers, 111 percent more likely to have children as teenagers, 164 percent more likely to have a premarital birth, and 92 percent more likely to dissolve their own marriages—all of which would increase welfare dependency.[69]

Not all this can be blamed on single parenting alone. The failure of the nation to enforce child support (see Chapters 8 and 14) is one main source of family poverty in America; permanently low-wage occupations, another. After divorce, the average annual income of mothers and children is $13,500 for whites and $9,000 for nonwhites, as compared with $25,000 for white nonresident fathers and $13,600 for nonwhite nonresident fathers. Several studies have shown that whatever the previous marital arrangement, only 20 percent of unmarried mothers, white and nonwhite, receive child support of any amount. But the sense of entitlement to motherhood among women of all social classes is an issue that has divided feminists. There is a growing impatience with welfare dependency, particularly with teenage mothers from families already on welfare who have additional children out of wedlock. The issue sets feminists in favor of changing welfare requirements intended to discourage illegitimacy against feminists who want welfare payments to be indexed to family size.

Three issues are in contention here: (1) whether teenage mothers continue to bear children because they have coolly calculated the financial benefits of pregnancy (an increase in welfare payments) or simply because they are sexually active, (2) whether early childbearing is a cause or a measure of poverty, and (3) how to reduce the numbers. Sociologist Kristin Luker, who clarified the politics of abortion in 1984 by studying women on both sides of the issue,[70] in 1996 did a major empirical study of teenage pregnancy to get some answers. So long as teenagers are sexually active, she concluded, the most effective way to reduce the chance that they will have children is to assure that they have access to contraception and abortion.[71]

But that is not what most Americans and some feminists believe. When the state of New Jersey passed new welfare legislation in 1992 that eliminated extra cash payments (though not food stamps and Medicaid) for the children born to women already on welfare, NOW's Legal Defense and Education Fund unsuccessfully sued the state on the grounds that such legislation was "punitive."[72] NOW was joined by the American Civil Liberties Union (ACLU) and the Legal Council of New Jersey, which took the position that *children* should be supported no matter what and that intergenerational poverty and the dysfunctions that result from it are the result of inadequate funding, not of illegitimacy or insufficient mothering. But as Jacqueline Tencza, a spokeswoman for the Department of Human Services expressed the matter in New Jersey's defense of its new law, the intent of the "family cap" was to "send a message about personal responsibility—if you have a child while on welfare, be sure you can care for that child both emotionally and financially."[73] As the NOW lawsuit made its way through the courts, other states developed "child exclusion" or family cap legislation during the same period, and polls showed the public divided on the issue quite as much as feminists, depending on whether the survey framed the question in terms of "irresponsible women" or "innocent children." With welfare reform continuing to be contested in the late 1990s, these divisions are unlikely to be healed.

Conclusion

As feminists struggled with third-generation issues, the differences that divided them were often rooted in feelings too powerful to be ignored. Women who felt passionately about peace could not bring themselves to study war and war's weapons; nor could they celebrate the integration by gender of the nation's armed forces. Women who wanted the workforce to accommodate marriage and motherhood found the Mommy Track too restrictive. Free-speech adherents were prepared to tolerate pornography, however degrading and dangerous to women, for the same reasons that the American Civil Liberties Union defends the free speech rights of Nazis and skinheads. But other feminists could not bring themselves to do so.

Should lower-income teenage mothers be punished for having more babies because these babies are doomed to replicate their mothers' lifetime welfare dependency? Why not? say some feminists. Is it not more important that low-income women stay in school? say others. NBC reporter Betty Rollin feels passionately that some disincentives to illegitimacy must be legislated.[74] Those who brought the suit against the state of New Jersey for limiting a woman's welfare payments in the case of additional births feel as passionately that just as women must be guaranteed the right not to have children, so the right to bear children must be guaranteed as well.

African-American feminist Audre Lorde used to say that feelings are the "spawning grounds for radical ideas" because "feelings lead to ideas, and ideas lead to action."[75] But passion makes compromise difficult, and politics—even feminist politics—had to be practical to succeed. Feminist theory provided much of the rhetoric for disagreement. Could feminist theory and feminist scholarship provide some meeting ground as well?

12

New Theory, New Scholarship

FEMINIST THEORY AND FEMINIST POLITICS were deeply entwined from the beginning of the second wave. And no wonder. It was Kate Millett's theory about how politics and culture came to be male dominated and male defined that led to her startling conclusion that after the suffrage era governments in Western Europe and America reared back from the specter of women's self-emancipation and *conspired*, as it were, to reverse the flow. And it was this conspiracy, she argued, and not women's fears or fantasies, that had put women back in their place.[1]

Millett knew her history. There had been women's movements all over Europe in the early twentieth century that had succeeded, in Germany and Great Britain as well as in the United States, in winning the vote for women. But soon thereafter in Italy, in Germany, and to some extent in France and England, fascist parties emerged that featured racist and antifeminist elements in their ideologies.[2] German Nazism was more explicitly hostile to women's equality than Soviet communism, which also came to power in the 1920s. But both movements set out to erase the gender solidarity that had bound European women to one another across economic, class, and national boundaries during the suffrage era. Once the Nazis brutally eliminated all political opposition in the mid-1930s, women (even otherwise privileged Aryan women) were relegated once again to *Kinder, Kuche, Kirche*—children, kitchen, and church. For the Soviets and their Maoist and neo-Marxist cousins in China and elsewhere, women were given titular "equality" but were expected to subsume their revolution within the larger goal of a classless, though not genderless, society.[3] The Nazis were overturned by the Allied armies, the Soviets eventually by history. But the stamp of the early twentieth century left its scars not just on the fallen or on the victims of concentration camps and the gulag but also on women's political coming of age.

In the United States the counterrevolution was somewhat more benign but no less destructive of women's rights and aspirations. Friedan called it the feminine mystique and placed blame on the Freudians, commercialism, and suburbanism in the period after 1945.[4] But in different ways, both *Sexual Politics* and *The Feminine Mystique* provided an important and mind-opening explanation for how it was that, in the face of new technologies that should have freed women in the industrial West from their age-old birthing and domestic burdens, women were still everywhere considered inferior to men.

The power of feminist theory, then and now, was its logic—unassailable if you allowed yourself to overturn basic premises about males and females in our society. Men do not operate individually in their relations with women. They behave as a kind of "ruling class," with the maintenance of their domination of women (patriarchy) as their primary goal. Women's assigned roles, then, are not an accident of history or the natural result of their biological and psychological sex differences. Nor are they the product of any individual man's desire to oppress a particular woman in a particular situation, as men do not have to operate as patriarchs to benefit from patriarchy. The way patriarchy works is to assign women roles—wife, mother, care-giver of the sick and the infirm, decorative (sex) object—which are invented and reinvented by every generation to keep women isolated, busy in the private realm, unable and unwilling to bond with one another, and out of power. From this it follows that the so-called differences between men's and women's intellects, temperaments, behaviors, and taste—all but women's essential reproductive functions—are socially constructed to justify gender-role assignments. Any woman or girl who balks at her assigned role or status, or who dares to cross the boundaries of approved feminine behavior, is therefore not "normal," certainly not desirable, and surely to be punished for life.

Feminist theory also exposed some of the glaring contradictions in the way patriarchy maintains itself. If, for example, women are naturally inferior, why the need to punish them when they step out of role? And if patriarchy itself is natural (as "natural" as it had once been argued slavery was), why the need for vigilance in enforcing gender roles? Yet patriarchs and the men and women who support the current system understand quite well how dangerous it is to raise even the mildest challenges to male-female roles.[5] That is why, as recently as 1995, a T-shirt sporting the phrase "Someday a woman will be President" was seen to threaten family values when it appeared on Wal-Mart shelves, causing the management to take it off the shelves temporarily.[6]

Another source of feminist theory's power was the shock and recognition it engendered. "Women will come out of the woods to hear

Friedan," I was told back in 1968 when I proposed bringing Betty Friedan to the Cornell campus, "and they will never be or act or think the same again." The same was true of Millett's audiences, Germaine Greer's, Ti-Grace Atkinson's, Shulamith Firestone's, Toni Morrison's, Florynce Kennedy's, Alice Walker's, Maya Angelou's, and, in time, Bella Abzug's, Gloria Steinem's, Dorothy Pitman Hughes's, and Eleanor Smeal's. "The women's movement is a teaching movement," said Florence Howe, a founder of women's studies and the Feminist Press in the early 1970s, and indeed, it was that as well. Even before the new scholarship on women unearthed forgotten literary, scholarly, and artistic treasures, and even before the disciplines were revised to eliminate gender bias, feminist theory led recruits through an unlearning of everything they had previously thought to be true so that they could take in the new.

Theory need not always be formal and philosophical to have an impact on politics and personal life. The young (and not so young) women who met together in consciousness-raising groups in the late 1960s and early 1970s worked their way through to an understanding of their own experiences that was just as much "theory driven," if not in as formal a language, as the works of Millett, Friedan, de Beauvoir, and Greer.[7] They were meeting together to try to fathom why it was that, despite their dreams, their "specialness," their participation in radical politics, and their education, they were still second class in the money they earned, second rate in the status they could claim, exploited at home, and, despite four decades of voting rights, relatively powerless at the polls.[8]

What Jane O'Reilley, writing in *Ms.* magazine, called a "click!" experience, feminist theorists explained as the result of "attentiveness of experience."[9] After absorbing some amount of feminist analysis, either through reading—and here the underground press was important—or through talk, a woman would experience a click! A smug remark, the downplaying of an aspiration, a door closing just as she was about to enter, a lover dismissive of her fondest dreams, would provide a transforming insight, the kind that energizes religious converts and distances them from everything they used to be. That there is a great distance between those who "get it" and those who do not was captured for all time during the Anita Hill–Clarence Thomas confrontation in the Senate Judiciary Committee in 1991 when Representative Pat Schroeder said of the senators unable to fathom Hill's delayed reaction to Thomas's alleged harassment, "They just don't get it!"

The impetus for black feminist theory came out of a different set of conditions and followed a more tortuous path. In a 1971 article entitled "The Role of Black Women in the Community of Slaves," Angela Davis offered an interpretation of the differential effects of racial oppression on men and women, expanded later in her book *Women, Race, and*

Class.[10] Since under slavery survival was a form of resistance, and since slave women were responsible for their families' survival, by extension black women must be credited for the entire culture's survival.[11] The larger point was that historians, white or African American, could not understand slavery without paying attention to differences in gender. According to sociologist Elizabeth Higginbotham and historian Sarah Watts, subsequent research into black women's history has flowed in large measure from Davis's insights.[12]

Black feminist theory grows out of "everyday actions and ideas," writes Patricia Hill Collins in *Black Feminist Thought,* and the "everyday" occurred largely at home.[13] The home is a particularly positive place for women in the African-American culture. In *Home Girls: A Black Feminist Anthology,* Barbara Smith employs the term *home* on several levels.[14] The home is the place where the black woman is surrounded by women who do everything necessary to maintain her. Home is also a community, a culture, and the locus of mother-daughter relations. Alice Walker's *The Color Purple,* first a Pulitzer Prize–winning novel, then a popular film, is a favorite example for Collins of home. Walker, she writes, brings to life the view that "the origins of contemporary black feminism [lie] in the lives of our mothers."[15]

Thus, it was difficult, though not impossible, for women of color to embrace a woman's movement whose practices appeared to be responsive only to the particular situation in which privileged, white, American-born women found themselves. Nevertheless, there was an "innate feminist potential," according to Barbara Smith, in black women's strength, particularly their ability to "function with dignity, independence, and imagination in the face of total adversity."[16] Perhaps *womanist* would be the better term to describe all this. Alice Walker thought so. So did Spelman College's president Johnnetta Cole.[17] In a political statement drafted in 1977 by the Combahee River Collective, an African-American feminist organization founded in Boston three years before, a multilayered strategy was proposed to deal with the "simultaneity of oppressions" of African-American women.[18] Instead of being paralyzed by all the work ahead, the collective believed that such a strategy could unite, rather than isolate, women of different races.

Some Early Divisions

Since theory loomed so large—as an impetus behind the forging of group identity among women and as a context for the feminist agenda—it is not surprising that there were disagreements over priorities. Many feminists would continue to agree throughout the period on the basics:

Sisterhood was "powerful," and American society was "sexist" (to borrow the titles of two widely read anthologies in the early 1970s).[19] Furthermore, women's roles were confining, unrealistic, and sexually charged. And, finally, many people benefited from women's unequal opportunities in life. In short, the nature of women's inequality would remain undisputed among most feminists. But the origins of women's differences, from one another as well as from men, would lead to competing explanations, different perspectives, different political priorities, and different scenarios for change.

For feminists who subscribed to the theory, for example, that controlling her body is a woman's most fundamental right, without which all other "equalities" and "opportunities" are meaningless, there could be no compromise on abortion. For feminists who believed that economic self-sufficiency, educational opportunity, freedom from sexual harassment, or the elimination of racism and classism is a precondition of "personhood," there would be different political alignments.

We have already seen how the issue of sexual preference divided feminists and not just because of the lavender menace. There were substantial disagreements among feminists then and now as to how prominent the whole issue of sexuality should be. In earliest writings, Millett had subsumed sexual relations under sexual politics: The relation of women to men was a power relation of which the sexual act, however romanticized, was little more than a means of making woman an object. By exerting masculine power over one woman, a patriarch was exerting power—on behalf of his gender—over all women. Later, Susan Brownmiller, in her history of rape, would extend that notion (which caused real discomfort to many good husbands and fathers) to this one: "When one man rapes, all men benefit."[20]

For Shulamith Firestone, the means of enslavement lay not in the sexual act itself but rather in "enforced" gestation. So in her "new world biology," women would have to be free first (and that is the point: what must come first) from the requirement of *bearing* children before they could be free for anything else. Firestone's theory represents an adaptation of Marx's dialectical materialism, with sex substituted for class.[21] In 1985 Margaret Atwood published *The Handmaid's Tale*, a grisly, futuristic account of a society in which healthy, fertile women are kept as slaves to bear children to a genetically damaged elite, making of Firestone's critique a fictionalized nightmare.[22]

Probably the first serious theoretical rift among second-wave feminists to have extensive political consequences came with a disagreement over whether abortion should be included in NOW's 1968 Bill of Rights. Foreshadowing the continued and costly battles to preserve woman's "right to choose" in the 1980s and 1990s, a group of NOW members, alike in every way to the founders except on the issue of abortion, broke away and created the Women's Equity Action League. Their defection was based on both their moral and religious qualms about the abortion act itself and on their belief that the issue would detract from educational and employment equity. According to their reading of sexual politics, educational opportunity and employment equity were more fundamental and hence more urgent.[23] In time, other divisions would surface, but in those first heady years it appeared as if feminism, in its exposure and analysis of our gendered society, was an idea whose time had finally come.

The New Scholarship

At least as important as feminist theory in the development of women's political consciousness was the blossoming of what came to be called "the new scholarship on women" and its extension into the classroom as women's studies.[24] In recent decades, as graduate education had opened up to women, they found that it was natural for them to "lay down their buckets where they were," in Booker T. Washington's famous words, to do research and to develop courses on women. But how were they to scope out a subject that was not cataloged in libraries under either "women" or "gender" and crossed disciplinary boundaries, where data were incorrect or incomplete and whole chapters were missing?[25] And how were women to integrate politics with scholarship—that is, to use feminist premises to throw light on the darker corners of history, literature, psychology, and sociology—without distorting truth when it was found? These questions and many more engaged feminist scholars as they set to work, starting in the early 1970s, to create a whole new academic content and methodology to inform the study of women.[26]

Their efforts proceeded on several levels. First, there was the subject itself waiting to be defined: Was the subject of the new scholarship women of all classes and origins, irrespective of their politics and their class? The answer to this was a resounding "yes," and scholars (some of them still graduate students) in all disciplines, including history, literature, the arts, and language, went to work looking for "lost women." With this work of "recovery" came criticism of the disciplines, specifically of how it was that these women had been lost in the first place.[27] Linda Nochlin, an art historian then working at Vassar College, dug passionately into the question, Why were there so few women artists? She found that, like Shakespeare's imaginary "sister" in Virginia Woolf's *A Room of One's Own*,[28] women artists had never had an equal chance with men to be educated or to exhibit. Forbidden admission to the great art schools (because they would be drawing from nude models), women were also prohibited from competing for commissioned work.[29]

As with white and European women, the absence of African-American women artists, writers, and intellectuals from mainstream history and culture was neither "accidental nor benign," according to Patricia Hill Collins.[30] How many students of American history had ever heard of Mary W. Stewart, Ida B. Wells, Mary Church Terrell, Anna Julia Cooper, Mary McLeod Bethune, and Ella Baker? How many knew that women of color in America had not been passive in the face of their oppression? Rather, they had been actively involved in abolition, suffrage, and the club movements, working to educationally advance their own people and to provide the social services and civil rights that would enhance their status.[31] Recovery of lost women would be at least as urgent for scholars of women of color, particularly since black studies was not nearly as sensitive to gender as to race.

Recovering Women's Fiction

If the discovery of loss by feminist students and academic scholars was painful, the work of recovery was invigorating. Feminist literary scholar Susan Koppelman, for example, single-handedly rediscovered four hundred women short story writers, not one of whom was referenced in any literary bibliography when Koppelman began her work in 1972. Out of her treasure trove have come seven collections of short stories by women, each organized around a theme, such as "mothers and daughters," "women's friendships," "the 'other' woman," and "battered women," to name but four.[32] Alice Walker, in looking for black women's voices to augment her fiction, returned to the work of Zora Neale Hurston, folklorist, novelist, and anthropologist, and helped reclaim Hurston's significant contribution to an Afrocentric feminist perspective.[33] Among other women of color, scholarship has offered revised views of Latina women, Native American women, and Asian-American women.[34]

The Feminist Press, founded by Florence Howe and Paul Lauter in 1970, was destined to play a critical role in recovering women's writing. The press was first conceived out of a failed effort by Howe, a teacher of literature at Goucher College in Baltimore, Maryland, to interest mainstream publishers in a series of critical feminist biographies. Howe had compiled a women's studies curriculum for her writing students at Goucher, intending to introduce them to women's writing and to encourage them in their own. But now she wanted to do more: workshops for parents and teachers, production of books and other materials for the classroom, and promotion of women writers. In time, the Feminist Press would achieve all three.[35]

Recalling the press's beginning on the occasion of its twenty-fifth anniversary in 1995, Howe remembered that it was in about 1970 that she realized that what she knew of "culture" was but half the story.[36] In researching the women's studies curriculum for students, the writer Tillie Olsen handed Howe a tattered photocopy of an anonymous novella called *Life in the Iron Mills,* published in an 1861 issue of the *Atlantic* magazine. As an experienced critic of literature, Howe, like Olsen, recognized the value of the piece and was stunned to learn that the novella, along with its author, Rebecca Harding Davis, was entirely unknown to modern readers and scholars.[37] In 1972 the Feminist Press republished the book as the first of its series of rediscovered feminist literary classics, with a biographical afterword by Tillie Olsen. Between 1982 and 1985 the volume went through nine printings.

With *Life in the Iron Mills,* the Feminist Press began the process of "restoring to its rightful place . . . the literature of women writers."[38] In 1973 the press published *Daughter of the Earth,* by Agnes Smedley, and *The Yellow Wallpaper,* by Charlotte Perkins Gilman, and began the search for the rights to Zora Neale Hurston's writings, eventually publishing the Alice Walker anthology of her work. By 1980 the Feminist Press had published fifty books. Although other presses would follow suit eventually, publishing "discovered" women writers, the press was the first to focus on African-American writers, publishing in rapid succession Paule Marshall's *Brown Girl, Brownstones* in 1981 and *Reena and Other Stories* in 1983; Dorothy West's *The Living Is Easy* and *But Some of Us Are Brave: Black Women's Studies* in 1982; and Louise Merriwether's *Daddy Was a Numbers Runner* and Sarah E. Wright's *This Child's Gonna Live* in 1986.[39] In 1980, with the help of the Ford Foundation, the Feminist Press expanded its search to encompass lost women writers around the world.

Challenging the "Canon"

Once a researcher had uncovered omissions, distortions, and trivialization in the discipline's treatment of women and women's issues, questions inevitably arose as to how the discipline itself had come to be biased against half the world's population. The denial of a public life to most women in most societies had, to be sure, denied them a public record as well. But even more subtle than the omissions were the distortions. In the groundbreaking essay "Did Women Have a Renaissance?" historian Joan Kelly contrasted women's and men's situations in the Italian city-states during the period in which the arts and humanities had

flowered there. Her essay raised important new questions as to historians' collective judgments about that era.[40]

Not surprisingly, the first efforts in the new scholarship were in fields
where women were already working: literature, history, anthropology,
sociology, and psychology. It was not that male scholars were entirely
absent. Carl Degler of Stanford was a historian of women before Gerda
Lerner became his student;[41] William Chafe produced an early and
widely read short history of the American woman from a revised point of
view,[42] and before feminists discovered the role of power within the family, sociologist William Goode had reanalyzed family dynamics in those
terms.[43] In the field of literature, Paul Lauter researched the absence of
women (and minority and working-class writers) from the agreed-upon
literary "canon," that bundle of "great" writers and poets who populated
college literature textbooks and dominated literary scholarship.[44] And
Robert Hemenway, a white male scholar, wrote the first modern literary
biography of African-American writer Zora Neale Hurston and arranged
for the publication of several new editions of her work.[45]

But the majority of the new feminist scholars were female and already
trained or being trained in their several disciplines. That is why the first
wave of revolution in new subject matter and in new treatment of old
subject matter took place in the fields in which women were already a
sizable minority.[46] Inspired by their feminism and encouraged by one
another, feminist scholars' productivity was prodigious. Then, as now, a
new variable, a necessary correction, or simply a fresh and hitherto unrecognized point of view was a great stimulant to research.[47] Questions
about women in history, literature, and agrarian and industrial societies
soon gave rise to larger questions about gender as a variable in psychology, sociology, anthropology, and philosophy, about the distribution of
roles and rewards based on sex in politics, economics, and, eventually,
science.

"Central to feminist scholarship," wrote Judith Stacey and Barrie
Thorne in a summary review of research in their own field of sociology
published in 1985, "is the belief in the deep importance of gender, not
only for understanding areas specific to the experiences of women . . .
but also for understanding class structure, the state, social revolutions,
or militarism."[48] In addition, feminists made cutting edge contributions
to the understanding of society and inspired better research in the subjects of organizations, occupations, deviance, criminology, health, and
stratification because they studied topics that had previously been de-
valued or studied in distorted ways. Feminists also helped revitalize the
research on mothering, housework, reproduction, rape, contraception
and abortion, marriage, divorce, widowhood, and the life cycle.[49]

Sociologist Scott McNall says feminism was immediately at home
within sociology because of sociology's connection to the social reform

movements of the 1960s. In turn, feminism enlarged sociological theory in its willingness "to examine the extent to which gender was historically constructed and a willingness to pay close attention to new sociological 'facts,' e.g., women were underpaid relative to men, etc. Class theorists, attempting to understand the nature and transformation of capitalist society, as well as the possibility of socialist societies, argued that class, race, and gender were similar constructs. The sociology of knowledge perspective was easily expanded to include a feminist world view."[50]

Other disciplines attracted feminist scrutiny. There were never as many academic women in philosophy as in history, literature, sociology, and law. But philosophy would eventually be dramatically altered by a feminist perspective, not only social and political philosophy but also epistemology and metaphysics.[51] Studies of what came to be called "the politics of language" also exploded, as linguists and linguistic philosophers on both sides of the Atlantic explored two related issues: sexism in language (the use of the generic *he* and *him* and its impact on perceptions of gender) and, along with Robin Lakoff from the University of California at Berkeley, sex differences in language use.[52]

Psychology was another field ripe for revision. We have already seen how the new feminists went after Freud and Freudianism. What was assumed by psychologists to be "normal" in male and female development turned out to be a function of a particular historical time and place. And, furthermore, the models were derived by and for men. Psychologists who studied "high achievers," for example, assumed them to be driven by some innate need for achievement, "n-ach" as it came to be known. Since high-achieving women did not appear to be similarly motivated, researchers simply did not include them in the populations they sampled. Had they done so, they might have discovered, as did psychologist Matina Horner in the late 1960s, that in school-successful females the "n-ach" was often constrained by an equally powerful opposite drive, which Horner called "fear of success."[53] The point is that, even though the standard model of high achievement might not apply to half the population, it was nevertheless taken to be true.

Other feminist psychologists, quite independent of Horner, located a tension in young women between a need for affiliation and a need for achievement, a tension that delayed their intellectual flowering. Only after affiliative needs were satisfied by marriage and childbearing could (some) women reconnect with earlier ambitions that had been put on hold.[54] Even mental illness needed to be redefined in terms of the new psychology. Women were being put away, concluded Phyllis Chesler, the author of the first major study of women and madness, for behavior that would be considered nondeviant—even laudable—in males.[55]

Rather than become mired in the debates over nature versus nurture, feminist psychology in more recent years has turned toward a focus on "gender polarization" and "androcentrism," which together provide the backdrop against which behavior is measured. Sandra Bem explores the way a culture's perceptions affect social reality in her book *The Lenses of Gender*. The significance of the differences between men and women, writes Bem, is not in their substance but in the way "androcentric institutions transform difference into disadvantage."[56]

While the recovery of suppressed women writers and scholars of earlier eras gave second-wave scholars and their students much to celebrate, the very fact that they had been "lost" brought insight into the effects of patriarchal culture on their work.[57] In *The Madwoman in the Attic*, literary scholars Sandra Gilbert and Susan Gubar described an "anxiety of authorship" that inhibited women writers in America and England from doing even more than they had done, an anxiety rooted in a historical denial of women's creativity in intellectual spheres.[58] Upon republishing nineteenth-century author Kate Chopin's novel *The Awakening*, Florence Howe and Emily Toth, Chopin's recent biographer, concluded that it was Chopin's audacity (not her lack of talent) in writing romantically about adultery that led late-nineteenth-century critics to dismiss her work.[59] Other literary studies of women characters in the hands of male writers (Coppelia Kahn's *Masculine Identity in Shakespeare* and Ruth Benson's *Women in Tolstoy*) documented and elaborated on Simone de Beauvoir's original insight that in Western Europe's intellectual history, woman was deprived of her humanity, her capacity to grow and develop, and instead was objectified or made a foil even of fictional men.[60]

Writing in 1988, Elizabeth Higginbotham and Sarah Watts summarized how the new scholarship on African-American women added to and changed black scholarship from the 1960s and 1970s. The emphasis of black scholarship prior to the women's movement was on what they call "paternalistic male leadership," and, they note, the paternalistic family was still unrecognized as an oppressive environment for black women.[61] But black history was not the only paradigm to be challenged. Studying low-income teenage girls in a St. Louis housing project, sociologist Joyce Ladner found that childbirth and childbearing played an altogether different role in black ghetto families than among the middle classes. Indeed, what appears "deviant" and even "pathological" to white social scientists, she concluded, might be a "very healthy and successful accommodation . . . to a set of very unhealthy conditions, given [black girls'] limited resources."[62]

In time, the paradigms and methodologies governing the hard sciences and mathematics came in for critical scrutiny as well. Why were there so few great women scientists? It turned out there were some, but they had either been denied an identity separate from their husbands or colleagues or had not been given appropriate recognition.[63] Almost typical was the story of crystallographer Rosalind Franklin, whose contribution to the discovery of the structure of DNA was never properly acknowledged.[64] Women had always been in mathematics and science, but these subjects are considered so "masculine" that it was thought "unnatural" for a woman to be doing mathematics and science at all, much less to be doing it as well or better than men.

Questions about the absence of women and girls from mathematics and science generated new studies of the culture of schooling and of the culture of science and mathematics itself.[65] Long before the American Association of University Women published in 1992 its searing critique *How Schools Shortchange Girls*,[66] feminist educator Bernice Sandler was documenting a "chilly climate" for young women in college classrooms.[67] Coeducation might appear to be more modern and advanced, but girls in single-sex environments were achieving more, particularly in fields that were considered to be better suited for men. And why were some fields considered better suited for men? Feminist analysts such as Ruth Bleier, Evelyn Fox Keller, and Nancy Merchant found science to have been overly "masculinized" in the seventeenth century.[68] Rationality divorced from feelings, a sharp separation between the knower and the known, and the scientific method itself, said these critics, redefined the relationship between investigator and nature in a way that made women feel less comfortable in science.

As feminist scholarship moved into the natural and social sciences, the central tenets of each of the disciplines came more and more under critical review. In paleo-anthropology, for example, the notion that "man the hunter" was the driving force in the development of human intelligence and culture had to be amended to include "woman the gatherer," and possibly even "woman the inventor of agriculture," since new research was documenting how important women were to every group's economic survival. Even more challenging to dominant themes of anthropology was biologist Ruth Hubbard's reminder in her book *The Politics of Women's Biology* that modern scholars cannot know what life was really like among ancient peoples because "behavior leaves no fossils."[69]

The field of family sociology had long been dominated by another central dogma, namely, Talcott Parsons's "structure-functionalism." Writing in the 1950s, Parsons defined the "functional" nuclear family as featuring separate, nonoverlapping, and inherently complementary roles played by husbands and wives and fathers and mothers.[70] (Friedan called this view "the functional freeze" in *The Feminine Mystique*.) In Parsons's classical formulation of his thesis, women's "expressive role" and men's "instrumental role" guaranteed consensus, stability, and continuity. But as Barrie Thorne and other feminist sociologists were to point out, Parsons's model suppressed questions of power and con-flict.[71] The notion of separate roles, like that of the nineteenth century's "separate spheres" for women and men, so permeated the dominant paradigms of social psychology that Erich Fromm, in his book *The Art of Loving,* assumed that the "healthy child" needs two entirely different kinds of parenting to succeed: "mother love," the totally accepting, un-conditional kind, and "father love," the kind that demands attainment in exchange for love—as if Mom and Dad or any loving adults in the child's environment could not possibly provide both.[72]

Even professional groups were seen to mirror the role divisions in the Parsonian family. Certain participants in small groups would assume the expressive, or female, role; others, the instrumental, or male, role even where the group was made up entirely of men.[73] Feminist scholars criticized structure-functionalism both for its artificial separation of functions, which were assumed to be not only different but also nonoverlapping, and its assignation of women to the expressive role in these models.

Anne Oakley's groundbreaking work in sociology in the 1970s led her to conclude (as had Thorne and Stacey) that there was no way to add women to the discipline without fundamentally changing the discipline itself. Oakley's subject, housework from ancient times to the present, was not even considered a legitimate "occupation" for sociological study before she began her research. Yet Oakley was able to analyze women's household work using models developed by sociologists of "working conditions" and "employers' behavior." Her contribution was to see that housewives and housework were part of a system for regulating women's lives.[74]

Feminist scholarship had a tremendous effect on the humanities as well, asking questions that went right to the heart of academic selectiv-ity and evaluation, such as why certain literary texts had greater "signifi-cance" than others. In the search for undervalued literary works, femi-nist scholars researched diaries and letters that in the past would not have been considered finished literary products. Historians, as noted, found whole periods of importance to women's history left out of stan-dard texts and proceeded to fill in the gaps. But even more fundamen-tally, feminist scholars demonstrated, in Ann-Louise Shapiro's classical formulation, "the ways in which the exclusion of women [from the disci-pline] shaped professional practice."[75] This was as true of anthropology, primatology, political science, and jurisprudence as of history, literature, and psychology. Through the lens of gender, as it came to be called, fem-inist scholars began to challenge both the canon of different disci-plines—the accepted body of knowledge that "belonged"—and the basis on which these canons were selected.

It was one thing to undertake new research on women; it was quite another to have it published, taken seriously, and eventually mainstreamed into the various disciplines under attack. Scholarship is institutionalized in American universities. Experimental and empirical work requires outside funding, and publication is "peer-reviewed," which means that leading scholars must agree that it has value before it is approved. The new scholarship on women not only broke new ground in methodologically unorthodox ways but, as we have seen, also challenged many of the central tenets of the existing disciplines. Who would publish the work? Could feminist scholars expect promotion and tenure; feminist writers, book contracts and royalties for their work? Three developments served to disseminate and to ensure a ready audience for the new scholarship on women: the establishment of a number of scholarly and semischolarly journals dedicated to women and gender studies, an exponential growth in courses and programs in women's studies,[76] and, not least, the launching of at least 125 feminist bookstores, their shelves full of books and periodicals by and about women—99 percent of which were published or republished after 1970.[77]

The Spread of Feminist Ideas

The argument of this chapter and the next is that feminist theory provided the energy, vision, and rationale for feminist politics and was in turn deepened, elaborated, and sometimes complicated by the new scholarship on women. What remains to be described is how all this new thinking and new research was diffused, and in record time. Florence Howe, of the Feminist Press, held the view, shared by many of us holding academic and teaching appointments at the time, that feminist theory and scholarship should not be limited to academics. Activists such as Charlotte Bunch, editor of *off our backs,* and journalists such as Phyllis Rosser and Lucy Komisar were making important contributions to both. Besides, feminist theory and scholarship needed to be communicated to women everywhere and in language they could understand.

Ever alert and responsive to trends, especially to a trend that involved sex and gender, the mainstream press and broadcast media gave the movement and the ideas behind it early and sustained attention. Some of this attention was voyeuristic, as when *Esquire* published in a double-page spread headshots of leading feminists over the cutline "They're cute when they're angry." Some of the coverage was inaccurate and unwanted, some of it openly hostile, such as *Time* magazine's write-up of Kate Millett's coming out or the unrelenting negative coverage of feminism as alternately neofascist and socialistic in the conservative press.

But in the beginning the attention was appreciated because it served to diffuse a great deal of information about feminism to the nonacademic and nonactivist population.

Journalist-turned-media critic Susan Faludi has ably documented how the media eventually turned against feminism, especially during feminism's second decade (the neoconservative 1980s).[78] By then, she argues, the media were giving widespread coverage to a barrage of poorly researched claims of feminism's excesses and its damaging effects on women's psyches without either acknowledging the flaws in these "studies" or providing equal time for rejoinders. But in the first decade or so, feminism, with its new thinking about women and gender roles, was a happening that the mainstream media could not ignore. Even the soaps *All in the Family, Maud,* eventually *Designing Women,* and *Murphy Brown* integrated feminist themes into their story lines and characterizations.

The existing images of women in advertising, children's literature, and popular culture were, of course, grist for feminist analysis. Eager to get the Equal Employment Opportunity Commission to prohibit sex-segregated want ads, for example, the newly organized NOW Legal Defense and Education Fund persuaded the American Advertising Council to distribute a set of powerful counterimages as a "public service."[79] So beginning in 1972, posterlike ads sporting such comments as "Hire him. He's got good legs," or "She's Golda Meier, but can she type?" appeared in a wide variety of magazines and newspapers and got people to notice and then to laugh at their own stereotypes.

Not long after, sociologist Lenore Weitzman completed a scholarly study of images of males and females in elementary school textbooks. Weitzman analyzed eight thousand pictures of boys, girls, adult men, and adult women that appeared in a series of widely used children's schoolbooks and were typical of other series of the 1960s and early 1970s. First, she coded the eight thousand pictures by age, gender, and race of subject; then by what the subjects were doing or experiencing; and finally (if there was more than one person in a picture) by who was in charge. From her quantitative analysis of the picture codes (and additionally by subject area) came an overwhelming finding: Children were being exposed to a gendered view of themselves and of the world, especially in science and math texts. Boys were overwhelmingly pictured as active investigators, girls and adult women as passive and dumber than males.[80]

When Weitzman reported to the NOW Legal Defense and Education Fund that sexism in children's textbooks went so far as to define (in a spelling text) vowels as "feminine" and consonants as "masculine" and to show puppet consonants pummeling puppet vowels to keep them in their place, she asked for and got funding to reproduce the original pictures in a slide show for distribution to parents, teachers, and publishers as one of several strategies for change.[81] Except that Weitzman was both scholar and popularizer in this instance, the example is typical of the period. Scholars provided the data, the analysis, and the documentation; popularizers laid out the consequences of patriarchy in delimiting women's social and political roles.

The Explosion

Between 1968 and 1973—the first five years of sustained and politically inspired new thinking about women—more than five hundred feminist publications appeared in the United States alone.[82] The majority began as newsletters produced by and for a specific group and filled with what Patrice McDermott, a historian of the feminist scholarly press, calls "heated manifestos."[83] But heated manifestos soon gave way to more substantive articles on feminist topics furthering a feminist analysis that was designed to lead to action. Ann Mather, who has studied the history of feminist periodicals, counts sixty newspapers, nine newspaper/magazines, and seventy-two magazines and journals appearing between 1968 and 1973—some kind of new feminist publication in all but seven states.[84]

Their titles convey their purpose and spirit. Out of Boston came *No More Fun and Games, Notes from the First Year*, and, out of new York, *Lilith*—named, according to its founding editor, for Adam's companion and alleged equal, the first female who did not make it to the Garden of Eden. Out of Washington came *off our backs*, which has lasted more than twenty-five years, as has *Sojourner* from Boston. In Boston, Iowa, Minneapolis, Salt Lake City, Raleigh-Durham, New York, Chicago, San Francisco, and Trumansburg, New York, book publishers sprang up with names such as Shameless Hussy Press and Crossing Press, which, even after mainstream publishers were accepting feminist writings, continued to publish radical feminist fiction, nonfiction, and poetry. Some periodicals came and went, but all had their devoted readers: *Sinister Wisdom, Common Lives/Lesbian Lives*, and *Chrysalis*. At this writing, *The Women's Review of Books* and *Belles Lettres* continue the fine tradition of introducing women's writing and taking it seriously.[85]

One other publication must be mentioned, even though it was a book, because it was done by a feminist collective and opened the subject of women's health from an unusual perspective. The book *Our Bodies, Ourselves* has been updated several times since it was first published in 1969 and has never been out of print. With sections entitled "Taking Care of

Ourselves," "Relationships and Sexuality," "Growing Older," and "Women and the Medical System," the Boston Women's Health Book Collective broke new ground in empowering women to understand and take control of their health. The purpose of *Our Bodies, Ourselves* was, and remains, to inform readers so that they can negotiate from strength with their medical practitioners. At least as important was the authors' emphasis on what women can do for each other.[86]

Even though these initial publications were largely the product of the women's liberation strand of the new movement, there were splits even among them on policy, politics, and priorities. These splits reflected emerging divisions between feminists who wanted to focus on mainstream political activism ("politicos") and those for whom a radical restructuring of American culture was a first priority.[87]

The first magazine to target a national audience of women who might be converted to feminism but who might not yet be affiliated with any feminist organization was *Ms.*, founded in late 1971.[88] The magazine was born in the minds of a group of New York City women journalists, editors, and graphic artists who had been marginalized and ghettoized, much like Betty Friedan in her freelance writing days, assigned to subjects that editors thought would interest women readers and not permitted to be part of the journalistic mainstream. At the organizing meeting I attended in spring 1971, the task of launching a glossy four-color national magazine seemed overwhelming. It would require hundreds of thousands of startup dollars and substantial advertising commitments to get even a first issue on newsstands everywhere. And none of the feminists in that room had access to that kind of money or corporate connections. Even Gloria Steinem, who had become relatively well known both as the woman who posed as a Playboy bunny to expose the Playboy Club's exploitation of its bunnies[89] and as a political activist on behalf of California's farmworkers and Robert Kennedy's antiestablishment presidential campaign, was not rich. But she was stalwart, as were the woman who was to become publisher, Patricia Carbine, Mary Thom, Letty Cotton Pogrebin, Dorothy Pitman Hughes, Suzanne Levine, JoAnn Edgar, and the magazine's long-term staff about the need for a feminist magazine.

An answer to how to finance a sample issue came when Clay Felker, the editor of *New York*, an upscale city magazine, offered to publish thirty pages of *Ms.* as a kind of "insert" in *New York* and then to add another 100 pages to create a separate preview issue for national distribution. Thus it was that on December 20, 1971, an issue of *New York* magazine appeared on newsstands and in unsuspecting subscribers' mail boxes including a thirty-page glossy supplement called *Ms.* (Wonder Woman graced the second issue's cover. See Illustration 12.1.)[90]

Illustration 12.1   Cover from an early issue of *Ms.* Reprinted by permission of *Ms.* Magazine, c. 1972.

The preview issue was an immediate and surprising success. Within a year *Ms.* had 350,000 subscribers or newsstand buyers and a readership of about 1.4 million. The magazine tended to focus on women's rights issues such as the ERA and legislative recourse to job discrimination, along with more "radical" concerns, including racism, lesbian love, welfare as a woman's issue, and reproductive freedom.[91]

Unlike the underground press, *Ms.* relied on advertising to keep the subscription price within the reach of most women, which raised issues within and outside the magazine about the conflict of women-as-constituency versus women-as-market.[92] McDermott says a few radical feminists criticized *Ms.* from the beginning for its "pervasive class bias," its "reliance on feminist media stars," and its "obsession with electoral politics." *Ms.* appeared to focus on sex-role conditioning rather than a systemic power analysis. In short, the radical press attacked *Ms.* for promoting women's rights in place of women's liberation.[93] Nevertheless, readers could find in *Ms.* a forum for a variety of ideas and solutions.

Ms. endured some rocky times, but the magazine's meaning for several "generations" of readers was captured in a collection called *Letters to Ms.* published in 1987.[94] As Gloria Steinem recalled in her introduction to the volume, many women wrote in the early years that they had felt "crazy" and "alone" until they found *Ms.* on their newsstands. One opined, fifteen years later, that she felt about *Ms.* the way she felt about her mother—sometimes angry, wanting her magazine to be perfect, but never wanting to be really separated from *Ms.*[95] The magazine had struck a chord.

Conclusion

Feminist theory was never a monolith. In the first edition of a popular women's studies textbook, equal weight is given to "liberal feminism," "radical feminism," "Marxist feminism," and "socialist feminism" as "alternative feminist frameworks."[96] But it was still possible in the first decade or so for feminists of a variety of persuasions to identify themselves as feminists and to work constructively together. Today, this is no longer the case. Not much remains of that first shared feminist vision, as fault lines already evident in early theoretical writings have become fissures, and fissures, fractures.[97]

13

Fissures into Fractures

IN 1993 WENDY KAMINER, a frequent and perceptive writer about feminism, took aim at what she thought to be an "identity crisis" in the movement.[1] Starting with poll data augmented by interviews, Kaminer reported that most women—even those who have benefited most from feminist achievements on their behalf—do not feel "comfortable" with feminism as an ideology. "Three decades of feminism and one Year of the Woman later," Kaminer wrote, "a majority of American women agree that feminism has altered their lives for the better." Yet the same polls suggested that a majority of women—two-thirds of those queried—hesitate to associate themselves with the movement. Kaminer's explanation shows how feminist theory over the past several decades managed both to unite and to divide American women. "To the extent that it challenges discrimination and other political exclusions of women, feminism is relatively easy for many women to embrace. It appeals to fundamental notions of fairness. ... But to the extent that feminism questions [women's] roles and the underlying assumptions about sexuality ... it poses an unsettling challenge that well-adjusted people instinctively avoid."[2]

Apart from the issue of roles and sexuality, "gender" itself is no longer as unifying as it once was; differences between women seem overwhelming. Kaminer quotes Susan McHenry, a former *Ms.* editor and founding editor of *Emerge*, a magazine for middle-class African-American women, as saying that African-American women experience both racism and sexism but consider the fight for racial justice to be primary. They think of feminism today as a "white women's movement" and prefer the term *womanist*, invented by author Alice Walker, to define their identity. Meanwhile, a whole new generation of so-called difference feminists, inspired by psychologist Carol Gilligan, author of *In a Different Voice*, have come of age who do not want to be "equal" if equality means becoming interchangeable with men.[3] Such women cherish women's specialness and find much to celebrate in what used to be taken as women's "weaknesses," such as a need to connect to others and a talent for "relational" work.[4]

For so-called relational or difference feminists, the personal and political have reversed themselves. Books describing "recovery" from self- or others-inflicted abuse and from "loving too much" far outnumber feminist political tracts in the women's studies sections of bookstores. Even Gloria Steinem appears to have shifted her focus to *The Revolution from Within* (the title of her 1992 best seller).[5] Responding to developments like these, some younger feminists (typified by author Katie Roiphe) are rejecting the original feminist analysis altogether. For Roiphe and those of her age whom she claims to represent, feminism's focus on rape and other abuses has turned it into a movement for "victims," not for people wishing to master their fate.[6]

We have seen how Phyllis Schlafly was able to capitalize on her followers' discomfort with women's liberation because she could equate it with loss of protection and status. But the members of the Eagle Forum (and she herself) were already conservative in their view of government, the family, and society. They preferred separate spheres for women that rested on clearly defined gender roles because they believed these contributed to stability. Any perturbation of the historically defined "order" that governs gender relations (which the new feminism seemed to them determined to undermine) would loosen the "web of obligation" that kept their children obedient and their husbands at home. But this does not explain why progressive women, the very sort who were originally drawn to feminism, have pulled back from a "gender-free" society. Nor does it explain why two-thirds of those Kaminer talked to—American women who have benefited and continue to benefit from feminism's achievements in the political arena and in the workplace—should be "sincerely ambivalent" about feminism's theory and goals, unless that ambivalence has been engendered by an antifeminist turn in media coverage.[7]

There is no way to convey the richness and complexity of the theoretical arguments that bear on these questions in a chapter of this length. Dozens of books with titles such as *Conflicts in Feminism, Contemporary Feminist Thought,* and *Paradoxes of Gender* (each with twenty or more pages of bibliographic references) have been written about the intricacies and controversies within feminist theory.[8] But feminist theory and feminist politics appear to have fractured most on how three basic questions are answered:

- Do women have to be (or become) the same as men to be equal? In the beginning it was assumed that there was no way to make up for the "deficits" or "disadvantages" of being born female other than to eradicate those differences and to be and behave more like men. But as feminist theory matured and women became more self-confident and more self-aware, the question was answered more and more in the negative.

- What is to be a "feminist" analysis of the family and most particularly of motherhood?
- Is there any single theory of gender that can incorporate the special needs and perspectives of women of different races, classes, and other ethnic groups in America or in the world?

The Do-We-Have-to-Be-the-Same-to-Be-Equal Issue

Initially, or so it appears in retrospect, most feminist theorists answered the question "Do women have to be the same as men to be equal?" with "probably so." Not maleness itself but the power men exercised was attractive to the high-achieving, mainly academic women who were writing theory at the time. Since gender differences were learned or "conditioned" by a society cast in a male model, unlearning and unconditioning were necessary first steps to equality. This is what liberation or emancipation meant: freedom from the constraints not just of gender stereotypes but also of gender itself, "free to be," as Letty Cotton Pogrebin wrote in her best-selling record album for children, "you and me." What the "liberated woman" would become, once free of stereotypes, was left somewhat to the imagination. After all, how could one know one's true self if that self had been artificially constructed in conformity to some gender ideal? Nevertheless, even when not explicitly stated, a genderless society seemed not only possible but also a desirable feminist outcome. Women were not essentially *different* from men, only *disadvantaged* in ways that an enlightened society could correct.

Research by psychologists Inge and Donald Broverman seemed to affirm this point of view. When asked to define mental health, the Brovermans reported, professionals held different standards for men and women. In other words, the experts' view of mental health was just as arbitrary and socially constructed as feminists were finding maleness and femaleness to be in other contexts.[9] Independence, for example, was considered a desirable adult trait and was appropriate to mentally healthy males but not to mentally healthy females. This left females with nowhere to go but to take on "male" traits in order to be treated as adults. Another view, of course, was to question why it was that only "female" traits were deviant. Maleness could be just as much a distortion as femaleness. Some feminists would eventually take this position, but not immediately.

Feminists who answered the sameness and equality question in the affirmative came to be known as "rights-oriented" or liberal feminists.[10] For liberal feminists, writes Cynthia V. Ward in a recent recounting of the argument, "sex discrimination is an aberration, an externally imposed collectivization of women that violates liberal ideals of equal concern and respect for all persons as individuals."[11] Feminism's task is to make this clear to men so that once unequal treatment is corrected, women's assigned (or constructed) group identity will also disappear.

According to rights-oriented feminism, government and society simply need to be informed that women's full rights are missing. Since the barriers to women's power and prestige are artificial, and since liberal society is basically "enlightened," legal rights will inevitably be equalized. And once this is accomplished, women's "true" selves will emerge, selves that are equal to men's in their all-important capacities for autonomy and rationality. Logically, then, there should be no long-lasting woman's point of view, no need to conserve women's group identity, no need even for a long-standing feminist movement. Once inequality disappears, so will the differences (read: disadvantages) that women experience. And so liberal feminism was poised to work its way toward its own annihilation.[12]

Opposing views were not long in coming and rested on several distinctive levels of disagreement. Betty Friedan's plaint "Do we want to be equal to unfree men?" resonated with many of the 1960s counterculturalists streaming into the feminist movement, who found much to disavow in mainstream politics and culture. But the more serious challenge to rights-oriented liberal feminism and to the goal of a genderless society came from the work of Carol Gilligan on women's distinctive moral development, Nancy Chodorow's post-Freudian description of "womb envy" in men, Mary Field Belenky's and her colleagues' description of "women's ways of knowing," and dozens of popularizers of their writings from the mid-1970s onward.[13] What these thinkers had in common was the view that woman's nature is not something to be replaced but something to be maintained, indeed celebrated, for the sake both of women and society.

Such theoreticians, writes Ward, challenged the imperfect realization of equal rights and the root concepts of individualism. "[They] believe that liberal ideas . . . are not merely the wrong way to end sexual inequality but help to perpetuate it since they reflect *male ways of being*."[14] Radical feminists were also concerned that only women who are "similarly structured" to men—that is, career- and power-oriented women—would succeed when external barriers were removed. "The norm is already sex-specific," wrote Zillah Eisenstein in *The Female Body and the Law.*[15] Echoing Schlafly, these thinkers—particularly those who are concerned with sexual abuse and exploitation—saw the removal of traditional protections as contributing to women's greater vulnerability.

What remains is a reality check: Can feminism embrace the Gilligan-Belenky-Chodorow position that celebrates gender differences (even speaks favorably of a woman's culture) and still achieve equality in what is a society dominated by male values? In the much celebrated Sears case (*EEOC* v. *Sears Roebuck and Company*), where a woman employee brought suit against the giant retail company, claiming employment discrimination, two feminist scholars, Rosalind Rosenberg and Alice Kessler-Harris, testified on opposite sides.[16] Rosenberg, a professor of women's history at Barnard College, testified for Sears that women preferred low-risk, noncompetitive positions that did not interfere with family responsibilities.[17] Kessler-Harris, director of women's studies at Rutgers University, made the case for women's sameness on every work-related dimension. The court ruled in favor of the employer. As historian Joan Wallach Scott writes in her discussion of the case, after Sears, "'differences' would become inequality's explanation and legitimation."[18] Indeed, Catharine MacKinnon, in her discussion of difference and dominance, writes, "Difference is the velvet glove on the iron fist of dominance."[19]

Carol Gilligan's differences argument was not political in its origin. Rather, it was based on her research on girls' and boys' developing sense of justice, where she found considerable divergence between the two. Her findings were published just at the time when more and more women lawyers were becoming local, state, and federal judges and within a decade of the appointments of Sandra Day O'Connor and Ruth Bader Ginsburg to the Supreme Court. Politically, then, her book could have been devastating. If the Senate Judiciary Committee had thought that, irrespective of the cases at hand, the judgments of women justices would be fundamentally different from those of their male colleagues, would women have been appointed to the courts?[20]

It was, in fact, in the Supreme Court that the differences argument was finally put to rest, but not until feminist Ruth Bader Ginsburg, an appointee of President Clinton, was able to shape the Court's thinking on the subject. In the Court's June 1996 ruling (*United States* v. *Virginia*) on the legitimacy of state support for the all-male Virginia Military Institute, Ginsburg wrote in words that immediately made history, "Generalizations about 'the way women are,' estimates of what is appropriate for *most women,* no longer justify denying opportunity to women whose talent and capacity place them outside the average description."[21]

Despite threats like these, difference feminism has always been appealing. Recall how much people wanted to believe that a government elected by women would be more compassionate and less warlike than one elected by men alone during feminism's first wave and, in our discussion of women and the military, how hard it is for women, even in exchange for full citizenship, to give up their traditional pacifism. In the 1990s, especially among young college-age women, Gilligan's *In a Different Voice* and Belenky's *Women's Ways of Knowing* enjoyed an enormous popularity.[22] But we must ask the hard-nosed questions of difference or relational feminism: Does it not retard feminism's political agenda?[23]

Rethinking the Family

"Over the last three decades, the nuclear family has been at the very heart of the battle between progressive and conservative forces in the U.S." writes Karen Kahn, editor of the feminist publication *Sojourner* in her introduction to a collection of essays on the family from that journal published in 1995.[24] Kahn attributes this in part to the growing power and popularity of the religious Right, which promoted a pro-family ideology as part of its campaign against women's liberation, abortion, gay rights, and the other leftover "excesses" of the 1960s. But it is not only antifeminists who have come to the defense of the nuclear family. Within feminism itself—and feminist theory reflects this shift—there has been a sizable retreat from the original starting point on which liberal, radical, socialist, and Marxist feminists all agreed: that "the male-dominated, child-centered nuclear family was the single most important site of female oppression."[25] That consensus no longer obtains.

Kahn does a masterful job of reconstructing feminism's original view of the family. For white middle-class feminists to whom Betty Friedan's *The Feminine Mystique* appealed, it was "the oppressive nature of the ideology of domesticity which had flung women out of the work force and into suburban homes."[26] For radical feminists like Shulamith Firestone, ways had to be found, however extreme, to dismantle the patriarchal family. This was the reasoning behind her extreme notion that women should no longer gestate their young.[27] The family was further censured by early feminists for being a microcosm of the patriarchal state and for helping to socialize children to fit into a "gendered" world. As Kahn reminds us,

> As the primary site of gender socialization, the family was where girls and boys learned the rules of femininity and masculinity . . . [girls] to gain fulfillment from taking care of others, . . . [boys] to wield . . . power. Moreover . . . families kept women economically dependent on men.
>
> Not only were they expected to stay home and focus their entire lives on caretaking, women who did work were paid less than their male counterparts because they didn't need to support a family . . . [which made them]

vulnerable to violence, battering and incest, and to poverty in case of abandonment and divorce.[28]

Indeed, some radical feminist organizations felt so strongly about the reactionary nature of the family, as Molly Lovelock, another *Sojourner* writer, reported at the time, that they restricted the number of married women allowed into their political groups or made married women feel, in the early years, like "fish out of water."[29]

Because of feminists' deep distrust of the male-headed, wife-subordinated family, insufficient intellectual attention was given in the early days to the complex economics of marriage and to the difficulties of finding suitable alternate arrangements for bringing up children. There was a flurry of excitement in 1970 when Pat Mainardi and others proposed a system for assigning "wages for housework."[30] The Chase Manhattan Bank had at one point calculated that a typical Wall Street employee's wife worked 99.6 hours at home, for which $257.53 (1970 dollars) would be a fair weekly wage. But the question of who would pay the housewife's wage was never satisfactorily answered. The "family allowance" paid mothers by the British and some European governments is considerably less than $257.53 per week; for families not in poverty, it seemed hard to justify a government subsidy for the already well-off that would not burden the rest. Besides, on what basis would the subsidy be paid: income forgone by the mother who stayed at home (in which case the rich would get even richer) or numbers of children? With zero-population growth a concern during that same period, a money incentive for having more children was not likely to be popular. And the purer theoretical "solution"—namely, charging husbands (or even children in a delayed payment system) for the care of home and hearth—would further increase wives' and mothers' economic dependence on their families.[31]

As for government-supported child care, the argument foundered over real differences of opinion as to whether what was "good" for working mothers was always equally "good" for children and over the total cost of providing day care for all working mothers. In the face of a growing need for day care, as more and more women with small children entered the workforce, it was always easy for the pro-family Right to exaggerate cost estimates by arguing that if the government was going to subsidize day care for mothers who worked outside the home, it should pay the equivalent for child care performed by individual mothers in the home.[32] This mother subsidy caught feminists in one of the contradictions of their own thinking about the family: On the one hand, it provided at least in theory the "wages for housework" that some feminists had demanded, and on the other, it killed government-subsidized day care every time (which was its proponents' real intention) because it trebled the total estimated cost.

But the real challenge to the view that the family was the seat of the oppression of women came from feminists themselves and falls under four lines of rethinking. First, there was ever-growing and undeniable evidence that, while housework could be denigrated with some impunity, motherhood could not. Feminists quite as much as other women felt a special attachment to their children, which no amount of theorizing could deny. Second, a shift in sentiment occurred over surrogate motherhood occasioned by the Baby M case, which raised new threats to birth mothers owing to improvements in reproductive technologies that no one, including feminists, could have foreseen.[33] Third, there was some rethinking about the family led by influential feminist thinkers, who gave ringing reendorsements of family life as unique and irreplaceable. And fourth, it was undeniably true that for African-Americans, Latinas, Chicanas, and women of other ethnic minorities living in a racially charged society, the family was often the only source of resistance and support. With 47 percent of African-American families and 23 percent of Hispanic families headed by women, the whole notion of a "patriarchal family" needed modification if a feminist theory of the family was to have any meaning for women of color.

These four "deviations" (if you consider the family-as-the-seat-of-oppression to be the correct analysis) must be viewed against the backdrop of a pro-family political ascendancy in the Reagan and Bush years. Two feminist books published in the mid-1980s can be taken as one measure of change. Kristin Luker's prize-winning study of pro- and antiabortion advocates (among women), published in 1984, found that more than any other factor, a woman's attitude toward *motherhood* determined her stance on abortion. If motherhood was seen to be the most important and satisfying role open to her, she tended to be antichoice; if motherhood was seen as only one of several roles and a burden when defined as the only role, she tended to be pro-choice.[34] Clearly, there was no room for debate about the family on the Right.

But among feminists there was growing ambivalence. Writing about the family at about the same time as Luker was publishing her long-term study, a group of feminist scholars and theoreticians chose contributors who would give attention both to "the supportive and nurturant" as well as to "the oppressive side" of family life. Their title shows the loss of a feminist consensus on the family. They called their collection *Rethinking the Family: Some Feminist Questions* and acknowledged in their Introduction that they were "struggling" with a series of contradictions in feminist thinking about the family. Yet they held fast to the notion that agreement might be achieved and promised that a "more realistic and complex understanding [of] the family [would be] part of a larger program of social change."[35]

Mothering and Motherhood

It is not as if feminists had ignored mothering altogether. Rather, in books such as *Woman's Estate* and *The Reproduction of Mothering*, authors Juliet Mitchell and Nancy Chodorow found evidence that the assignment of mothering varies from culture to culture and era to era and that mothering as a full-time occupation is only a modern industrial phenomenon.[36] In the past mothers had to grow food as well as prepare it, construct clothing as well as select it, and with multiple pregnancies and many more children to bring up, spend much more time caring for their families. Thus, full-time mothering was never known in human history and might even be dysfunctional for all kinds of reasons. Indeed, Dorothy Dinnerstein in *The Mermaid and the Minotaur* and Nancy Chodorow in *The Reproduction of Mothering* found that women-exclusive mothering confined children as well as mothers in unhealthy ways.[37] In 1976 poet Adrienne Rich offered a way out of the "good motherhood/bad motherhood" dilemma by suggesting that motherhood exists in two forms, its natural form, mostly a positive experience for both mothers and children, and its institutional form, from which its negative aspects flow.[38] Throughout the 1970s, then, the discussion of motherhood among feminists was ongoing but still attentive to its negative side.

In 1981 Betty Friedan made public her growing doubts on the subject. Friedan had always been an integrationist as far as men were concerned; recall, she named NOW the National Organization *for* and not *of* Women. Nor was she a radical critic of the nuclear family. But in her 1981 book *The Second Stage*, she went further. She regretted that the family and, as she put it, "women's need to give and get love" had been "overlooked" by the movement.[39] What caused Friedan to distance herself even from her own earlier writings and to call for a "second stage" were several: "the way the rhetoric of women's lib was being used to justify increased divorce, explosion of rape, battered children, and the moral delinquency of the 'me' generation; . . . the way judges were shortchanging women [in divorce settlements] who had given over their own wage-earning years to their family's well being; and . . . the agonizing conflicts young and not so young women are facing or denying . . . as they come up against the biological clock."[40]

These concerns were real, but did they justify a dramatic remaking of the feminist agenda? Friedan thought so. She wanted to abandon the "personal is political" basis of feminist politics, to distance herself from what she now dubbed the "*feminist* mystique," and to accelerate feminism's "second stage."[41] Her book is not as carefully argued as her others, but it bears mentioning because the need for the "second stage," in her view, rested *entirely* on feminism's failure to appreciate the family. The family, she wrote, had to be "the new feminist frontier and motherhood its joyous expression"[42]—a far cry from the original feminist consensus on the family. Indeed, when Betty Friedan and NOW Legal Defense and Education Fund Coordinator Muriel Fox expressed these views at the 1979 National Assembly on the Future of the Family, some feminists accused Friedan and Fox of "reactionary family chauvinism."

But Friedan and Fox were not alone. Even radical theologian Mary Daly, who had shocked the country in the 1970s with her books challenging the maleness of God himself (*Beyond God the Father* and *Gyn/Ecology*), during this period wrote that the mother-child relationship is the primary relationship of all.[43]

Baby M

In 1987 a childless professional couple, William and Elizabeth Stern, contracted with Mary Beth Whitehead, a working-class mother, to carry to term a fetus fertilized by Stern's sperm. The contract was overseen by the Sterns' attorney, and a fee of $10,000 was settled upon. Further conditions governed the mother's health and prenatal care and the right of the Sterns to have the fetus aborted if amniocentesis showed the child to be in any way deformed. After the child was born healthy, to everyone's surprise the birth mother reneged on her contract and refused to hand the baby over to her legal "owners."[44]

The case seems to have accelerated feminist rethinking on birthing, motherhood, and reproductive technology. Sociologist Barbara Katz Rothman, herself a mother, was driven to write a book entitled *Recreating Motherhood* in response to the decision on the part of the courts to award Baby M to the surrogate parents.[45] Calling for a "feminist analysis of mothers and motherhood that is consistent with feminist politics and feminist theory," her book is a mélange of feminist and pronatalist thinking. In one section Rothman acknowledges that in a patriarchal society men *use* women to have *their* children, but, at the same time, she romanticizes pregnancy by talking about a "baby inside [that is] not so different from the baby outside." Such a blurring of the distinction between the fetus and the child could be used to undermine the legal case for abortion, especially when Rothman concludes that aborting a fetus is a means of "ending the relationship" between mother and child.[46]

By supporting the primacy of the birth mother's claim in the Baby M case, Rothman and other feminists who took that same position found themselves side by side with conservatives and religious fundamentalists. To be sure, they (in Rothman's words) had taken "very different paths to get there and [were] headed in very different directions." Only the feminists, for example, noted that in the argument over which would be the "fittest" family, money, class, and race loomed large. The Sterns were well educated and well off; Mary Beth Whitehead was neither. But if theory is to generate political alignments, these differences may not matter much. To justify the birth mother's rights, feminists found themselves reclaiming "maternal instincts."[47]

A Paean to the Family

By the end of the 1980s, the wheel seemed to have come full circle. While feminist theoretician Sara Ruddick, in the widely published and republished essay "Maternal Thinking," argued that the "most revolutionary change" in the institution of motherhood would be to include men equally in every aspect of child care, elsewhere in that same essay she asserted that "maternal thought exists for all women in a radically different way than for men."[48] "It is because we are daughters, nurtured and trained by women that we early receive maternal love with special attention to its implications for our bodies, our passions, and our ambitions."[49] Moreover, she argued, the assimilation of men into child care is *not* the primary social goal for mothers.[50] Rather (echoing the "women-are-morally-superior-to-men" arguments of the suffrage era), with women in power the public realm will be "transformed by maternal thought."[51]

Jean Bethke Elshtain's writing on the family was (and remains) even more influential (and controversial) than Ruddick's. Elshtain, first a political scientist at the University of Massachusetts, later holding named professorships at Vanderbilt University and the University of Chicago, has an international reputation as a political and moral theorist and a readership that extends far beyond that of many other women scholars. In the evolution of her own thinking, Elshtain was deeply moved by the plight in the 1980s of the "Mothers of the Disappeared," women who stood up to Argentina's most tyrannous government since that of Juan Perón, demanding the return of their children, most of them sons, who had been "disappeared" because of alleged political crimes. Like the mothers striking for peace in the 1950s in America, these women were strengthened and politicized by their maternal love for their children—not seeking to transcend their mother role.

Writing in the late 1980s, Elshtain began to talk about the intergenerational family as the locus of moral development, the "social form best suited to provide children with a trusting, determinate sense of place and ultimately a 'self.'" Moreover, contrary to much earlier feminist writing in which the patriarchal family was characterized as the wrong model for a democratic society, Elshtain found the family vital to democracy itself.[52] Her argument is interesting. Democratic society requires that the governed have a place to stand, somewhere safe and secure, from which they can criticize and eventually (as needed) assert their independence (their freedom) from government. While she accepts "plural possibilities" (nontraditional families and nontraditional lifestyles), Elshtain believes that the traditional family provides the kind of private, personal space on which the proper functioning of democracy depends. In the originally conceived "feminist utopias"—Firestone's "new world of biology" and Alison Jaggar's "families without sex roles"—Elshtain finds only "a world of lovelessness [where] women are oppressed at having to be women."[53] "Mothering is *not* a 'role' on par with being a file clerk, a scientist, or a member of the Air Force. Mothering is a complicated, rich, ambivalent, vexing, joyous activity which is biological, natural, social, symbolic, and emotional. . . . A tendency to downplay the differences . . . oversimplifies what can or should be done to alter things for women, who are frequently urged to change roles in order to solve their problems."[54]

Race, Ethnicity, and Multiculturalism

The book *Feminist Frameworks,* an overview of feminist theory that was widely used as a college text, first appeared in the mid-1970s. The second edition came out in 1984 and the third in 1993.[55] In the introductions and commentary to the third edition, editors Alison Jaggar and Paula Rothenberg offer a useful retrospective on the changes in feminist theory over the past twenty years. They write that there has been a lessening of feminism's reliance on any one theory to explain women's subordination. Feminists now question, for example, whether there exists a single "root cause" or single pattern of women's oppression or whether it is better to use a multiplicity of "lenses" and categories to explain women's subordination.[56] Part of the reason for this shift in focus, the editors believe, has been the growing significance of race, class, ethnicity, and sexual preference in feminist theory and politics. Indeed, if one compares the content of the first, second, and third editions of *Feminist Frameworks,* the biggest change has been the addition of writings on race, class, and ethnicity. In the 1993 edition, even global and multicultural feminism warrants a section.[57]

Feminist scholars, such as historian Gerda Lerner, who published one of the first collections of important documents in African-American women's history, were well aware that to ignore differences among

American women was to "distort reality."[58] Women of color, wrote Patricia Hill Collins, suffer a "matrix of domination."[59] But the challenge to feminist theory, reflected in the third edition of *Feminist Frameworks*, came mainly from women of color themselves. Feminist "essentialism"—the "all women are the same" because "all women have suffered the same" argument—not only "insults black women," in Angela Davis's words, but also represents a broken promise, "the promise to listen to black women's stories."[60] Indeed, when these "stories" found their way into print and into women's studies courses, they had a profound effect on both feminist theory and politics.

In 1995 a five-hundred-page anthology of African-American feminist thought was published that, for the first time, collected black women's nonfiction writing on gender as well as race-generated oppression from the early nineteenth century to the present. Although the editor, women's studies scholar Beverly Guy-Sheftall, offers an all-inclusive definition of feminism, within which the "interlocking nature of the oppressions" African-American women suffer can be explained, there is no denying from the material she anthologizes that black women find much to criticize in mainstream feminist theory.[61]

Guy-Sheftall chronicles in some detail the variety of ways in which African-American women have responded to the feminism of the second wave. Some were among the founding members of the National Organization for Women; others, concerned that the black liberation movement was not paying sufficient attention to black women's issues, founded the National Black Feminist Organization in 1973.[62] And Guy-Sheftall herself is comfortable with the term *feminist* and has an appointment at Spelman College in the field of women studies. But there is ample evidence in her anthology of how race blindness in mainstream feminist theory and incidents of racism in mainstream feminist politics led many black women to go their separate ways.

Feminism (meaning the second wave), writes bell hooks in Sheftall's anthology, did not emerge out of black women's experience, nor was it the product of those who are "most victimized by sexist oppression."[63] Rather, *The Feminine Mystique* and other liberal feminist writings (which, as hooks sees it, "dominate feminist discourse") take as their subject "the plight of a select group of college-educated, middle- and upper-class married white women—housewives bored with leisure, with the home, with children, with buying products, who wanted more out of life." The plight of white women is made to appear synonymous with a condition affecting all American women, continues hooks, which "deflected attention away from [its] classism, [its] racism, and [its] sexist attitudes toward the masses of American women."[64] In other words, liberal (that is, white women's) feminism has nothing to do with, nothing to say to, the majority of American women who work too hard to be frustrated by boredom and leisure.

Particularly obnoxious, from this point of view, has been white women's co-opting of the term *oppression* and their claim that "all women are oppressed," as if such factors as class, race, religion, and sexual preference do not determine the extent to which sexism will be an oppressive force.[65] For some women, terms such as *exploitation* and *discrimination* are more appropriate descriptors than "oppression." Hooks continues: "While it is evident that many women suffer from sexist tyranny, there is little indication that this forges a common bond among all women. There is much evidence substantiating the reality that race and class identity creates differences in quality of life, social status, and lifestyle that take precedence over the common experience women share—differences that are rarely transcended."[66]

Hooks recognizes that articles written in the early 1970s attempted to address a wider audience of women, not exclusively white, middle class, or college educated, but she believes this inclusiveness was not sustained. Partly it was the fault of "classism" in early feminist theory, partly an inability to see beyond "competitive, atomistic liberal individualism," and partly an unwillingness to encourage a diversity of voices, critical dialogue, and controversy in place of a feminist "party line." To some extent, white women feminists allowed themselves to accept the racist stereotypes of the superhuman black woman, says hooks. But the most serious flaw in feminist theory was its failure to go beyond the view that gender is the sole determinant of a woman's fate.[67]

African-American protest was soon joined by that of women of other ethnic and racial minorities. Wishing to give voice to a radical feminism of Third World women, Cherríe Moraga and Gloria Anzaldúa collected essays and poetry from a wide range of nonmainstream women writers and called their book *This Bridge Called My Back: Writings by Radical Women of Color.*[68] The book became a classic, not least because, as poet Audre Lorde expressed it, "the oppression of women knows no ethnic or racial boundaries, but that doesn't mean it is identical with those boundaries."[69] Radical women of color had much to say about the limitations of white women's feminism and the "limitations of race ideology to describe our total experience."[70] From her vantage point, Audre Lorde was convinced that "the master's tools will never dismantle the master's house," the title of her classic essay on the subject. Another writer was more cynical: "I think about all the white women I knew in San Francisco, women with master's degrees from Stanford University and cars that Daddy bought; women with straight white teeth and clear skins from thousands of years of proper nutrition."[71] How little, she implied, these women had in common with her.

Despite the ever-increasing readership for writers like these and, eventually, the willingness of major publishing houses to publish their works, the hoped-for alliance of African-American and Hispanic women with Asian-Pacific and Native Americans never materialized. By 1983 Moraga and Anzaldúa were despairing of a unified feminist movement of Third World women.[72] Differences of ethnicity, class, and sexual preference took their toll on women of color, too.

Acknowledgment of differences *among* women offered an important corrective to mainstream feminist theory but undermined it at the same time. For women of color, gender was simply *not* the sole determinant of their fate. "What we need to do is deal with *us* first. Then maybe we can develop a wimmins' movement that is more international in scope and universal in application," wrote Doris Davenport.[73] But the central tenet of feminist theory, from Millett onward, had been the centrality of gender as the source of all oppression. Gender was supposed to erase class, race, and other differences and unite all women. Without gender as the unifying bond, there was no way to stem the hemorrhage. Hispanic women—Latinas and Chicanas—suffered a particular kind of family control rooted in machismo that, as feminists, they had to confront. Native American women, living "encapsulated" in American cities, suffered multiple exclusions—not least the loss of their history and traditions.[74] And Asian-American women, daughters of immigrants, victims of incarceration during World War II, or ghettoized in Chinatowns, had their own ghosts to expunge.

In a burst of multicultural activism, the late 1970s and 1980s witnessed a myriad of conferences, newsletters, books, and testimonials from an ever more inclusive but at the same time fragmented women's movement.[75] It was no longer clear where "mainstream feminism" was situated and even whether it was still there. White feminists, however, did respond, late but sincerely.[76] Adrienne Rich offered an approach: White women did not create racism but have a responsibility for participating in or perpetuating its practice.[77] Never again would it be possible to convene a feminist conference, construct an anthology of feminist writings, or undertake scholarly research without acknowledging the lessons learned from women of color, namely, the impact of race and class on gender and that of gender on race and class.[78]

The challenge to gender as the common denominator of women's oppression occurred on several different levels at the same time and seemed to dovetail with a much larger literary and philosophical approach, postmodern, just then beginning to influence academic thought. Postmodernism takes the position that history and culture are "texts" from which endless interpretations (and no one better or more true than any other) are possible. As applied to the challenge of multiculturalism in feminism, this approach fueled skepticism as to whether *gender* could be used as an "analytic category" at all. Many feminists in the academy, most particularly those in the more theoretical and humanistic disciplines, were attracted to postmodernism precisely because it seemed to extend the feminist view that ideas, like gender itself, are socially constructed. Postmodernism, however, goes still further than many theoretical feminists were willing to go: no "idea" (not even feminism) is any better than any other. Multiplicity of interpretations, then, may result in what feminist philosopher Susan Bordo calls a "view from nowhere."[79] This certainly would not assist in the setting of a movement's political agenda.

There is no question that multiculturalism served to enlarge the feminists' agenda. Reproductive rights now included not only access to abortion but also protection from the "race genocide" of enforced sterilization. Issues relating to women now included the feminization of poverty, as women were understood to be the main victims of the economic shifts at play in the 1970s and 1980s, and a new understanding of the American welfare system documented how women are maintained in dependency.[80] As American feminists became better informed about the exploitation and abuse of women in the Third World, they passed resolutions at their conferences condemning "bride price" and enforced clitoridectomies, along with America's complicity, through its international aid programs, in maintaining male privilege in those countries.

President Jimmy Carter did not "get it" in 1979 when Bella Abzug, whom he had selected to be head of his Advisory Committee on Women, insisted that inflation, unemployment, and the federal budget were women's issues. (He fired her when she refused to give way.) Nor did the organizers of an April 9, 1989, pro-choice rally, which brought the largest number of women to Washington in a decade to protest the erosion of abortion rights, see that it was a missed opportunity. As Kip Tiernan and Fran Froelich wrote in *Sojourner* after the event, the rally failed to "stretch beyond reproductive rights to the [issue of] the economic dependence of an entire generation of women whose lives and those of their children are endangered." Whatever had happened to solidarity? "Has the world become so terribly complex that we are forced to deal with only one agony at a time?" the authors complained.[81]

Indeed, with the election of Ronald Reagan in 1980 and the imposition of "trickle-down" economics, the agonies would increase. Federal spending for the domestic safety net was sacrificed to a last spasm of cold war paranoia resulting in still more investments in military hardware. With appointments to the Supreme Court in the hands of Republican presidents for twelve years, the ERA, *Roe* v. *Wade*, affirmative action, and the rest of the liberal feminists' achievements began to be whittled away. Bella Abzug might write menacingly of a "gender gap" on the eve of Ronald Reagan's reelection campaign in 1984,[82] and Eleanor Smeal, founder of the Fund for the Feminist Majority, might warn of a comeuppance for Reagan-Bush Republicans at the polls, but feminist opposition to Reagan-Bush Republicanism remained isolated. Just when unity was needed most, there was not *one* feminism but many. The case could be made that, although attention to race, class, and ethnicity had been badly needed to correct fundamental oversights in feminist theory, multiculturalism came at the wrong time, just when the perceived unity and power of feminism as a whole would have mattered most.[83]

Bella Abzug's 1984 gender gap never materialized, at least not as Abzug and others had predicted. Analysis of exit polls revealed that Reagan was disproportionately popular (no doubt owing to his "stand tall" rhetoric) among male voters, which more than compensated for his minor losses among women. And by the end of the 1980s, it was also clear that Smeal's organization notwithstanding, there was no feminist majority. The debates over difference feminism, feminism and the family, and multiculturalism had certainly enriched feminist theory and led to an explosion of new and important feminist writings and scholarship. But in politics perceptions are reality, and the perception was that feminists were no longer united, which meant politically that feminism was no longer a force to be reckoned with.

14

Surviving the 1980s

THE 1980S DESERVE A CHAPTER OF THEIR OWN because, with the election of Ronald Reagan in 1980, feminism had to move quickly and gallantly from the offense to the defense. The demise of the Equal Rights Amendment—technically in 1982 but already prefigured in the late 1970s—was only a symptom of the nation's careening toward the political Right. With Ronald Reagan at the helm in the United States, another conservative, Margaret Thatcher (England's first woman prime minister but no friend to feminism) at the helm in Great Britain, and conservatives in power elsewhere in Europe, there began a dozen years of rollback, particularly in regard to the more controversial second-generation issues feminists had fought for. "What the Congress giveth, the Congress can anytime taketh away," pro-ERA activists had warned in their argument for an equal rights amendment. And, indeed, with a popular president reading (if not writing) the script, and a Congress, at least until 1986, strongly influenced by a surprisingly virulent antifeminist minority, some of the hardest-won legislation of the 1970s began to unravel in Congress. As more and more federal judges were appointed by the Reagan-Bush administrations,[1] the federal courts began to chip away or simply not enforce the hard-won rulings achieved by liberal activists in the previous two decades. And as Reagan and Bush replaced five out of the nine Supreme Court justices with people of their choice, the outlook for feminism looked grim indeed.[2]

Phyllis Schlafly, the "silent majorities," the born-again Christian Right, and the conservative "middle" achieved in the presidencies of Ronald Reagan and (to a lesser extent only because he exercised lesser power) George Bush what feminists had not believed possible. Recall that the 1977 Houston conference celebrating International Women's Year, a high-water mark for feminism, took place only three years before the election of Ronald Reagan. Yet women's rights were already eroding at that time. Most noticeably, ratification of the ERA was stalled. Two years after Houston, in 1979, with endorsement from President Jimmy Carter, feminists lobbied Congress to extend the deadline to 1982. But even before Reagan's election, it was obvious that the extension would make little difference. Abortion had been threatened in the 1970s by a series of federal and state statutes restricting public funding of abortions. The 1973 Supreme Court decision in *Roe* v. *Wade* guaranteed a woman's right to an abortion, but as later interpreted by the courts only women who could afford a private doctor could exercise that right. Feminists were torn by this inequity, but presumed that the 1973 Court decision would be inviolate, providing a firm floor for a woman's right to control her own reproduction.

The various attacks on reproductive rights were in one sense a boon: They generated widespread feminist response. In a period of feminist quiescence, with less visible activism, the various threats to abortion rights (now euphemistically called "women's right to choose") could always get out the troops. Thousands of women all over the country demonstrated against the Supreme Court's 1989 *Webster* decision and lobbied heavily against the 1992 *Casey* case. Whatever the shift in the political climate, and despite a large and increasingly vicious right-to-life movement, American women of all political stripes appeared unwilling to allow the abortion rights won under *Roe* to be rescinded, at least not without a fight.

Meanwhile, affirmative action—the requirement that employers make extra efforts to hire in accordance with the numbers of minorities and women in specific labor pools—continued to be challenged individually by white males and collectively by their unions. And the reach of Title IX into all aspects of educational equity (not just sports) continued to be stymied. The social wing of the New Right also organized what historian Susan Hartmann calls a "counter mobilization."[3] Calling her followers pro-family (as if all feminists were antifamily), Phyllis Schlafly opened a Washington office in 1982, signaling that she would be expanding her single-issue anti-ERA campaign to other issues. Calling sex education "the principal cause of teenage pregnancy," she and other New Right leaders mobilized in favor of the Family Protection Act in the 1982–1983 Congress. Introduced by Senator Roger Jepsen, a newly seated congressman of the New Right from Iowa, the Family Protection Act would have reestablished prayer in public schools, forbidden federal funding for school textbooks that portray women in other than traditional roles, repealed federal laws against child and spouse abuse, and prohibited coed sports.[4]

Not only was the New Right in ascendance, but for reasons that have yet to be fully understood, feminism also began to lose its luster and its freshness, its popularity and its power to convert. By the end of the Reagan/Bush era, the feminist "revolution" was in retreat. From the state houses to the talk shows, men and women of a variety of political persuasions felt freer than before to heap invectives upon feminism, blaming the movement and its followers for rising illegitimacy, increasingly open homosexuality, violence, and, inevitably, an undermining of family values.[5] Worse yet, women who continued to benefit from the overthrow of barriers to their advancement and their self-actualization were distancing themselves from the parent movement. Young women in particular seemed to gag on the word *feminism*. At best, they responded to questions about their politics with "I'm not a feminist, but . . ." At worst, they called it the "F word."

Women's progress in the 1980s, despite all of this, continued apace. Thus, the story of the 1980s cannot be told entirely in terms of legislative setbacks and judicial reversals. It is, rather, full of ironies small and large. The antifeminist President Reagan nominated the first woman ever to the Supreme Court in 1981. Although Sandra Day O'Connor was a political conservative, she was no stranger to discrimination and not unmindful of the ways in which women were disadvantaged in this society. As an outstanding graduate of Stanford Law School during the era of the feminine mystique, she was obliged to work at lower-level jobs than her male classmates, many of whom had graduated behind her academically in law school. On the Court, O'Connor showed herself to be more sensitive to women's issues and more committed to women's equality than had been expected. Hers was the swing vote in a number of Supreme Court decisions that could—had she voted with the conservatives—ended abortion rights forever.

Throughout the 1980s women continued to be elected to more and higher local, state, and federal offices.[6] This happened despite the fact that feminism was losing its cachet even among the Democratic Party (no longer hostage, as it had been in the 1970s, to womanpower) and even though young women were no longer as radical or as political as they had been in the past. The point is that as the women's Movement (with a capital *M*) diminished in formal organization, impact, and size, the movement of women (with a small *m*) in the workforce and in public life continued almost unabated. The exception was women in poverty. Indeed, the tenth anniversary issue of *Ms.*, published in 1982, featured an article by Barbara Ehrenreich and Karin Stallard called "The Nouveau Poor." If current trends continue, wrote Ehrenreich and Stallard, "by the year 2000 all of the nation's poor will be women and their children."[7]

The Feminization of Poverty

The analysis of poverty by gender represented a new way of looking at poverty in America. As the data on poverty began to find their way into feminist writings, a picture emerged of gender discrimination as well as layers of jeopardy affecting women of color, females heading house-holds, and older women abandoned by their husbands or left without adequate support when they were widowed.[8] In the United States, black and Hispanic single mothers suffer poverty rates 50 percent greater than those of their white counterparts, and black women are three times as likely as white women to be in the economically vulnerable position of single motherhood.[9] When the 1980s began, according to an analysis by economist Barbara Bergmann, 48 percent of single mothers were living below the official federal poverty level, of whom 63 percent were black and 41 percent white.[10]

The new analysis of poverty put the "costs" of parenthood into plain view.[11] Once upon a time, in our agrarian past, children were a source of income and security. The more children a family had, the more hands there were to work the farm or to help produce the goods and services needed in the home. The combination of industrialization and urban-ization (together called modernization by economists) has rendered children an economic burden rather than an economic boon. And living in America has made the situation worse. Alone among industrialized countries, the United States provides no universal allowance to offset the costs of childbearing or childrearing.[12] In America neither the gov-ernment nor employers provide child care for working mothers in intact families. As a result, single mothers with low wage expectancies find themselves caught in an impossible bind: either to work at low wages, which are reduced further in private child care arrangements, or to go on welfare, which in turn maintains them in poverty.

Poverty was not unknown in America. During the Great Depression of the 1930s, the widespread laying off of employed workers had threat-ened America's political stability and our nation's belief in unfettered capitalism itself. To deal with the impoverishment of workers and the costs to the nation of the vagaries and dangers of unemployment, the government had, under Franklin Delano Roosevelt, taken steps to create a set of bulwarks against poverty for regularly employed (mostly) men and women. Roosevelt's New Deal established mandatory old age insur-ance (social security), workman's compensation for injuries suffered on the job, protections against union busting, and federally mandated un-employment insurance, to which all employers had to contribute. These new requirements were explicitly designed to provide income security for retirees, disabled workers, and for workers laid off through no fault of their own. In addition to New Deal protections, former war veterans had, of course, additional benefits for short- and long-term health care.

Not considered at the time were the needs of homebound workers, namely, mothers. Married women were not yet a sizable proportion of the workforce, and divorced or abandoned women were not the government's priority. Indeed, except for widows and orphans, the reforms of the 1930s paid scant attention to women in poverty.[13] The work of child-drearing fell then and now under "income transfer" rather than "wages" and was therefore not protected either by unemployment or old-age insurance. It was only fifty years later that feminist economists began to understand that the "job" of housewife was a very "peculiar occupation" in terms of benefits and risks.[14] "By tradition and by law, the housewife is not counted as working for an 'employer.' The reward she gets for her work is not legally defined as a 'wage.' That reward may be access to goods and services rather than cash. . . . Because she has been considered to be merely an economic and social appendage of her husband, she was never taxed as other workers. Her old-age support was not arranged on the same basis as that of other workers."[15] So it is not surprising that traditional safety nets for employed men and women excluded women "employed" at home.[16]

As we have seen in the discussion of marriage and divorce, when fathers absent themselves or are unknown or unidentified, the costs of parenthood are even greater. Fewer than half of all divorced fathers pay any child support, and even those who do contribute, on average, much less than fathers in two-parent homes.[17] Of children born out of wedlock, only 19 percent have had paternity established, which means that child support cannot even be assigned to a working male. The feminization of poverty, then, is the accumulated result of the costs of parenthood, combined with women's lower wages and occupational segregation by gender. Together with the lack of any federal child care system or child allowance, many single mothers are catapulted onto the welfare rolls. But welfare is no protection against poverty. The cash benefits of Aid to Families with Dependent Children is below the poverty level in *all* states; in forty-one states it falls below 75 percent of the poverty level, even when the cash value of food stamps is calculated.[18] Since women more than men are welfare dependent, America's low level of aid to families with dependent children contributes to the feminization of poverty.

Poverty affects women at all stages of the life cycle. Owing to pension inequities and the accumulation of a lifetime of depressed earnings, 73 percent of the elderly poor are women.[19] With divorce on the rise, even more elderly women are likely to find themselves living alone on extremely limited incomes. The needs of such women, like those of the poor and minority women outside the labor force, had not been adequately addressed by the Equal Pay Act and Title VII. In the 1980s feminists finally turned their attention to this gap. With the help of the Congressional Caucus for Women's Issues and supported by Senator Dave Durenberger (R–Minn.) and Representative Geraldine Ferraro (D–N.Y.), a series of bills was introduced, known collectively as the Economic Equity Act (EEA). Supported by NOW, WEAL, the American Association of University Women, and other groups, the EEA was aimed at women in the lower economic rungs (women of color, poor, and working-class women) and covered pensions and retirement, unisex insurance, equitable economic responsibility between parents after divorce, and more extensive day care coverage for working parents. The act also addressed problems of divorced women and displaced homemakers not primarily as wives and mothers but as "autonomous individuals" in the public sphere.[20]

Although introduced as a package, the Economic Equity Act was treated piecemeal in the Congress. Instead of "titles" (as was the case with the 1964 Civil Rights Act and its 1972 educational amendments), the EEA provisions were introduced as separate bills during the 1980s. Some of them passed, and others did not. Two were passed by the Ninety-eighth Congress: retirement equity and collection of support payments. Pay equity or comparable worth, in contrast, remained a sticking point with legislatures. Much of the EEA's success was in the area of insurance. At the time, insurance fees and insurance scales were differentiated by age and sex, which made payouts in earned retirement income less for women (who, actuarial tables show, live longer) than for men, but the cost of automobile insurance for young adults was lower for girls. At first, the insurance industry opposed "unisex insurance" on the grounds that the administrative costs of the changeovers required would be too burdensome, but eventually the industry caved in under growing pressure.

Unlike unisex insurance, pension equity encountered almost no opposition, largely because costs can be passed on to pensioners or to their employers. The Retirement Equity Act of 1984 did much to equalize benefits for working women in private pension systems, but not much for people outside those systems. Geraldine Ferraro made pension equity a priority, and when the Republicans decided that they would not oppose pension equalization (their "gift" to women after the ERA had failed), all inequities by gender (age of "vesting," etc.) were removed, protection of benefits during maternity or paternity leave was assured, and states were given the authority to divide pension benefits between spouses upon divorce—an important corrective to a long-standing inequity that Lenore Weitzman had documented in her book *The Divorce Revolution.*[21]

But other economic issues, especially the ones that would have affected women in poverty, turned out to be more complicated. Feminists, led by Representative Patricia Schroeder, introduced a family and medical leave bill that would allow fathers as well as mothers to take unpaid leave for childbearing or childrearing emergencies. According to economist Heidi Hartmann, "Family leave" undifferentiated by sex represented a "maturing" of the women's movement.[22] But little of this new legislation affected women of color. In an article published in *The Nation* in 1989, Margaret Wilkerson and Jewell Handy Gresham argued that the phrase *the feminization of poverty* was a "distortion" since it underplayed the role of racial barriers to black employment, particularly among males. So long as black male unemployment remained at the 45 percent level, they wrote, the problems of poverty for women of color would not be comprehensively addressed simply by women-friendly legislation.[23]

Abortion

Roe v. Wade: *The Case*

In 1969 Norma McCovey, an unmarried woman with no particular skills and fewer resources, found herself pregnant and without many options. In her home state of Texas, as in all but two other states at the time, abortion was illegal according to state law. Texas women frequently went to Mexico for abortions, but McCovey did not have the money for the trip or for the illegal abortion that was then priced in Texas at $500. In her search for an adoption possibility, she was brought into contact with two Texas women lawyers, Linda Coffee and Sarah Weddington, who were trying to change the abortion law in Texas. They could not do this by simply going into court and asking a judge to overturn the law since there would not be a "cause of action." Instead, they needed to find a pregnant woman who would sue the state of Texas as a plaintiff. Norma McCovey did not know it at the time, but she would be the plaintiff in the 1973 landmark case that overturned all restrictive abortion laws in the United States, the "Jane Roe" in *Roe* v. *Wade*.[24]

Weddington and Coffee had not themselves suffered under the Texas abortion law. Unlike McCovey, who was politically unaffiliated, they were active feminists who wanted to do something for women. Abortion reform was in the air in the 1960s. "Problem pregnancy" groups had sprung up all over the nation to refer women to doctors who were willing to do abortions illegally. Until 1967 when California legalized abortion, and until New York State in 1969 repealed its abortion law outright, few thought the laws could be overturned. Most wanted abortion simply to be "liberalized," either through legislation or, when legislatures were recalcitrant, through the courts. To the extent that suing a state was discussed among abortion activists, it was always assumed that a physician would have to be the plaintiff since according to most state laws, only the doctor who performed the abortion could be prosecuted, not the woman herself. Coffee and Weddington's genius was to initiate a suit on behalf of a woman denied an abortion, making her the plaintiff. Another brilliant move was to argue that the Texas statutes (there were two that dealt with abortion) were unconstitutional under the Ninth Amendment, which reserves all powers not mentioned in the Constitution to the states. How did they make this connection? They did so by arguing (following the *Griswold* case in Connecticut)[25] that the reserved powers clause applied as well to individuals. That is why, they would argue, the Texas abortion statutes were unconstitutional: They abridged the constitutional right of citizens to decide in privacy when and whether to have children.[26]

Suit was brought in federal court in the U.S. Fifth Circuit in whose jurisdiction Texas fell. As the primary enforcer of Texas's statutes, the office of Henry Wade, Dallas district attorney, was the object of the suit (hence, the "Wade" in *Roe* v. *Wade*). At the hearing in federal court in spring 1970, lawyers for Wade's office tried to make the case that the state had a "compelling interest" in the life of the fetus; also, they argued that the Texas laws protected women from the prey of "scurrilous abortionists." Weddington countered that it was the state's restrictive legislation that gave rise to illegal and dangerous abortion mills. In the end, to everyone's surprise, federal Judge Irving Goldberg ruled the Texas abortion law unconstitutional because a woman's right to abortion was constitutionally protected under the amendments cited by the plaintiff.[27] The case was immediately appealed by the Texas attorney general and taken to the Supreme Court.[28]

Weddington and Coffee had not grounded their case against Attorney General Wade in any kind of feminist theory, but they had successfully solicited support from Texas women's groups in the first round of litigation. In the eighteen months between the Dallas decision and the presentation of their oral arguments before the Supreme Court in fall 1971, an enormous groundswell of feminist and liberal activity was generated. The National Abortion Rights Action League (NARAL) had been founded in 1968 to focus feminists' and others' attention on abortion, and as I have noted in Chapters 6 and 7, reproductive rights held a prominent place on NOW's 1968 Bill of Rights. NARAL carefully picked its issues and managed to stay afloat during the 1980s, even to grow and to expand.

The Supreme Court makes its decisions on the judicial merits of a case, but it could not help noticing that after Judge Goldberg's decision in the Dallas case, the abortion law reform movement had redirected itself to abortion law repeal. Money needed for the Supreme Court procedure was easily raised, and experts volunteered to help prepare the main and associated briefs. That Sarah Weddington, the young lawyer from Texas, remained the principal spokesperson in the case was remarkable. In comparable situations someone experienced in appearing before the Supreme Court would have been selected. But Weddington was an unusual and effective speaker, brilliant and persuasive, too.[29] On January 22, 1973, a year after oral arguments had been heard, the justices released their written opinion. Their verdict: the Texas statutes and, by extension, all comparable statutes in the fifty states that made abortion a criminal act were herewith unconstitutional.

The Court's judgment and the opinions rendered by the Justices were as far-reaching as they were surprising. Of the nine justices who heard the case, seven voted with the majority; three, including Chief Justice Burger, filed concurring opinions, and only two, William Rehnquist and Byron White, dissented. In the majority decision—a remarkable document written by Justice Harry Blackmun that recounted the entire history of abortion and the law—the Court established that a woman has a constitutionally protected right, but not an absolute right, to decide whether to terminate her pregnancy. The decision also established that the state has a "legitimate interest" in protecting potential human life—but only after "viability." Defined as the capacity of the fetus to sustain life outside the womb, viability was assumed to take place at about the end of the sixth month.[30] To incorporate the two considerations, Justice Blackmun offered a trimester framework: Up to the end of the first trimester, a woman has the right to make a private medical decision, with the help of her doctor and without interference from the state, about whether to continue with her pregnancy. During the second trimester, the state may choose to regulate abortion procedures in ways that are related to maternal health. For the third trimester, the state can ban abortions outright.[31]

Roe v. Wade: *The Aftermath*

In the first thirteen years after *Roe*, more women than anyone had predicted sought and obtained legal abortions. Because the procedure had previously been illegal, no one knew how many abortions had been performed annually before 1973. But now that abortion was legal, the numbers could be counted, and they indicated that all prior assumptions had been vast underestimates. The numbers fluctuated for a while—

sometimes as high as 1.5 million annually—but finally settled at 1 million per year, a number that would concern even those who had sought liberalization and repeal. But it was the antiabortion forces that fastened onto the numbers and made abortion the issue around which to organize a right-to-life political movement that enormously strengthened Phyllis Schlafly's StopERA and contributed mightily to the election of Ronald Reagan in 1980.[32]

The so-called right-to-life movement appeared for the first time during the New York State assembly's debate on abortion repeal in 1969, but until *Roe* was passed, it remained fairly quiescent. The movement appeared to be grassroots, but its growth and direction were firmly in the hands of certain religious and political leaders. Its strategy was to challenge the *Roe v. Wade* decision in every way possible. As early as 1976, lobbied by right-to-lifers in the Republican Party, the party debated abortion at its national convention—the first time it had ever been an issue before the platform committee of either party—and adopted an antiabortion plank. Local right-to-lifers pressed state legislatures to pass specific restrictive legislation that proabortion activists would have to challenge in court.[33] In the beginning, with the *Roe* justices still in place, the state-generated restrictions were for the most part struck down by the Supreme Court. The exceptions had to do with payment for abortion out of federal or state funds. It was easier for the antiabortionists in the early years to get majorities in Congress and in the Supreme Court to hold back public money from women wanting abortions than to reverse the 1973 decision itself.

The issue of public financing was critical. Between 1973 and 1986 nearly three hundred thousand abortions (33 percent of all abortions) were funded annually by Medicaid, a cooperative federal- and state-supported health subsidy for the poor. Antiabortionists in Congress could not, of course, overturn the Supreme Court's ruling, but they could restrict how federal funds would be spent. In 1976 the first of Representative Henry Hyde's annual amendments was passed, limiting the application of Medicaid funds to abortions unless the mother's life was in danger. The Hyde amendment was promptly challenged by a pregnant woman from Brooklyn, Cora McCrae. The justices did not rule on the McCrae case right away, but they did uphold a similar statute dealing with state funding of abortions—*Maher v. Roe*—in 1977 and eventually ruled against McCrae in 1979.[34]

Except for public financing, however, the Supreme Court was not prepared to limit access to abortion until much later. State restrictions tended to be struck down.[35] In 1976, for example, in *Planned Parenthood v. Danforth,* the Supreme Court ruled that the state of Missouri could not interfere with a woman's abortion decision by giving veto power to the father or, in the case of a minor, to her parents, these two being the critical provisions of a Missouri state law intended to limit access to abortion. Parental consent requirements appeared again in a citywide ordinance passed by Akron. And this time, in 1983, in *City of Akron* v. *Akron Center*, the Court upheld parental consent requirements for minors so long as there was a quick and confidential "judicial bypass" (some way to obtain speedy court approval if the parents were not available). A Pennsylvania law passed in the mid-1980s went too far for the Court. In 1986, in *Thornburgh* v. *American College of Obstetricians and Gynecologists*, the Court struck down the law requiring that a woman seeking an abortion be given a detailed description of fetal development and forbade Pennsylvania from imposing a fixed waiting period on a woman seeking an abortion.

But antiabortionists had time on their side. Their successes at the state level were widely viewed as a sign that *Roe* might eventually fall to their political ax. Indeed, in case after case a weakened majority for *Roe* on the Supreme Court came close to reversing the Court's own pro-choice decision by considering state limitations that restricted trimester abortions, gave parents rights over their minor daughters' desire to have abortions, and eliminated all manner of abortion counseling if conducted in federally supported clinical programs. At the same time, the conservatives had to be disappointed that a proposed human life amendment to the Constitution, even though it was backed by the National Conference of Catholic Bishops, was never able to muster the necessary two-thirds majority to get through Congress. Disappointing, too, was the fact that, even though the Reagan/Bush administrations were able to appoint Supreme Court justices opposed to abortion, the Court never did overturn *Roe*.

Instead, from 1981 to 1992 antiabortion was used as a "litmus test" in selecting judges in the federal court system. On the Supreme Court, the older justices were retiring and were replaced, one by one, with Reagan and Bush appointees supposedly opposed to *Roe*. By 1989 two new justices, Sandra Day O'Connor and Antonin Scalia, were in place. Taking advantage of the presumed loss of a *Roe* majority on the Court, the state of Missouri came back with another even more restrictive abortion law in 1989, which declared in its preamble that "the life of each human being begins at conception." The Missouri law prohibited the performance of abortions in state-funded hospitals and clinics and required a test of fetal viability in the *second* trimester—in clear violation of *Roe*. The Supreme Court voted five to four in *Webster* v. *Reproductive Services* to uphold the Missouri law. Even though the Court recoiled at rescinding *Roe* outright, the *Webster* case was seen by pro- and antiabortion forces as giving states back the power they had lost in *Roe* to write new restrictive abortion laws.

One justice must have disappointed the antiabortion forces. Sandra Day O'Connor, who as a Reagan appointee was expected to press for repeal of *Roe*, argued in *Webster* that a woman's decision should not be encumbered with any "undue burden." O'Connor's language signaled that she was not yet willing to overturn *Roe*. Nevertheless, antiabortion legislators in Louisiana, Utah, and Guam took the *Webster* decision to mean they could prohibit abortion within their state boundaries and passed antiabortion legislation within the year. Elsewhere, with increasing harassment (and later violence) perpetrated on abortion clinics, their patients, and their doctors, more and more abortion clinics were closing and fewer doctors were willing to be associated with them. Thus, even though *Roe* remained on the books, legal abortion during the 1980s was becoming more of a privilege for women of means than a right to which all American women could lay claim.[36]

The Reagan and Bush administrations had other ways of restricting abortion. They could employ executive rulings, and they did. To restrict federally funded women's health services from even advising women about abortion, the administration promulgated what became known as the "gag" rule. Title X of the Social Security Act supported Planned Parenthood clinics in many localities. Clearly, abortions could not be funded out of Title X money, so the clinics kept carefully separated accounts. Pregnancy counseling, however, was supported by federal moneys. The gag rule prohibited counselors from even mentioning the "A word" in their discussions with pregnant patients. Efforts made in Congress to overturn the administration's ruling were to no avail. And in May 1991 in *Rust* v. *Sullivan*, the Supreme Court ruled that it was constitutional for the government to restrict Title X–funded clinics from counseling women on abortion, even if the continued pregnancy threatened a woman's life or health.[37]

After *Webster*, two more liberal justices, Justices William Brennan and Thurgood Marshall, retired and were replaced by David Souter and Clarence Thomas, both presumed to be antiabortion appointees. Thereafter, even more states—some of which, such as Pennsylvania, had failed to get earlier laws through the courts—were emboldened to pass legislation restricting abortion. Pennsylvania's 1992 statute was extremely restrictive. The new Pennsylvania law required that the physician selected to perform the abortion meet with the patient twenty-four hours before the procedure and hand her a packet of state-mandated information. The "information packet" included the statement that if she continued the pregnancy, the father of the child would be forced to support her and the child—an assertion not founded in fact. A second requirement of the Pennsylvania law was that the husband of a married woman had to be informed of the impending procedure and by implication had to approve—a throwback to the nineteenth-century male parent's prerogative in abortion decisions. And in the case of minors, one parent at least had to formally consent. When the Planned Parenthood Association of Southeastern Pennsylvania sued state attorney general Robert P. Casey to bring the Pennsylvania statute before the Supreme Court, pro-choice forces again held their breath: Was *Casey* (*Planned Parenthood of Southeastern Pennsylvania* v. *Robert P. Casey*) to be the occasion for the overthrow of *Roe*?

As it turned out, *Roe* survived the *Casey* ruling just as it had survived *Webster.* But things continued to look grim. Justice Thomas, only one year into his lifetime tenure on the Supreme Court, wrote in his opinion upholding *Casey* that "as a matter of natural law, the fetus is a person." If affirmed, this would not only have allowed states to prosecute women for "murdering" their fetuses but, in the opinion of abortion legal scholar Sylvia Law, would have *required* states to do so.[38] Within six months of *Casey*, however, the Reagan-Bush era was over. President Bill Clinton and his activist wife, Hillary Rodham Clinton, were on record as supporting a woman's right to choose. Within two years the Clinton administration replaced two more retiring Supreme Court justices with feminist Ruth Bader Ginsburg and Stephen G. Breyer, no friend to the antiabortion forces. *Roe* had galvanized an anti–abortion rights movement and a substantial backlash against feminist principles, but these had failed in the end to recriminalize abortion.

Operation "Rescue"

What began as occasional on-site harassment of abortion clinics in the 1970s and 1980s became a full-fledged, direct-action, and sometimes violent obstructionism in the late 1980s and 1990s. Operation Rescue (later renamed the Christian Defense Coalition), led in turn by Keith Tucci and Randall Terry, claimed responsibility for tumultuous blockades, multiple arsons, and bombings and eventually were alleged to have precipitated, if not contracted, for the murders of two doctors, an abortion clinic receptionist, and another associate.[39] Calling abortion a plank of "Satan's agenda," Operation Rescue appeared to know no bounds. In 1994 the Supreme Court ruled that abortion clinic obstructionism was a crime of collusion under a federal racketeering statute, making it possible for clinics to call in federal marshals for protection.[40]

But in a society where doctors can choose whether or not to perform abortions, harassment and threats took their toll on the reservoir of goodwill that had sustained women wishing to end their pregnancies. In the mid-1990s fewer doctors were being trained to do the procedure and of those trained, fewer were willing to perform abortions.[41] For the many thousands of women living in rural areas not served by abortion clinics, women who would have to make costly child care arrangements or take unpaid leave from low-paying jobs to leave their home counties for a day or more, abortion might as well have been illegal.

After two decades of almost unrelenting battles over women's right to abortion, the end of the 1980s brought with it a hunger for compromise. Two books, Laurence Tribe's *Abortion: Beyond the Clash of Absolutes*, published in 1990, and Roger Rosenblatt's *Life Itself: Abortion in the American Mind*, published in 1992, sought some way of bridging the enormous gap between pro-choice and antichoice advocates.[42] A possible compromise would have recognized the moral value of the fetus while permitting abortion, would have increased financial support for women who choose to have children, and would have called for expanded sex education and the provision of contraceptives for teenagers. But in an analysis of the likelihood of compromise, feminist abortion scholar Sylvia Law sees little chance. "This is more than a debate about the status of the fetus," she told an audience of students and faculty at the University of California, San Diego, speaking in April 1992, the very day the *Casey* decision was to be handed down. "This is but the latest chapter in a debate over competing visions of the role of gender, of sexuality, and of the family."[43]

RU 486

Abortion has generated public debate because it touches on deeply held personal values and religious beliefs. For those who believe life begins at conception, the scraping of a few hundred cells from the walls of the uterus is more than a medical "procedure"; it is the taking of a life in formation. But it is also a matter for public scrutiny because so long as the procedure is invasive, a trained medical practitioner must assist. This means the decision to have an abortion needs to be conveyed to a second party, a doctor or a trained nurse practitioner, and the abortion itself is best done in a medical location. Thus, it is a quasi-public act. But suppose abortion could be done privately and without outside assistance. Then, except for procuring the pharmaceuticals involved, it would be a private act, harder to criminalize and harder yet to prevent. With hundreds of millions of dollars worth of illegal drugs entering this country every year, it was only a matter of time before a safe and effective abortion pill would have been invented and imported, therewith making "privacy" not only a constitutionally defended right but also a reality.

Only it did not happen quite that way. In 1980 scientists reported that a drug to abort fetuses in the first nine weeks of gestation was close to development in France. Soon thereafter, RU 486, as it was called, became available as an abortifacient in that country, in England, and in China and was expected to be approved for public use in the Netherlands and in three Scandinavian countries within the year. The advantage of this "pill" was that it induced abortion late enough for pregnancy to be certifiable and that it was safe and inexpensive. One hundred thousand French women took advantage of it, and Claude Evin, the French minister of health, hailed it as "the moral property of women."[44] Feminists and family planning specialists in the United States immediately began to campaign for its approval in this country. But by 1992 opposition to abortion was widespread, extending even to the White House. Calling it a "death drug" (National Right to Life Committee) and a "human pesticide" ("born-again" Christians), the Reagan and Bush administrations were able to stop all RU 486 research at the National Institutes of Health and to have the Food and Drug Administration (FDA) in 1989 proscribe its use and block its entry into this country.[45] Not until 1996 did the FDA begin reconsidering approval.

Many believe, along with Lawrence Lader, a longtime abortion advocate and author of a book about RU 486, that the pill may put the abortion issue to rest by swaying those who only "moderately" oppose abortion.[46] Polls show that only 15–20 percent of Catholics are opposed to all abortions. Since with RU 486 there is no "fetus" expelled (the pill works early and produces only a heavy menstrual flow), the term *abortion* may be eliminated altogether. Indeed, Dr. Etienne-Emile Baulieu, a developer of the pill in France, describes the process as "contragestion," a word he invented to mean "contraction of gestation" rather than "abortion." What RU 486 induces is something like a miscarriage, where the body sheds early embryonic materials, nothing like the lifelike fetus that antiabortionists like to show writhing in pain in videos and print materials.

Reproductive Rights More Broadly Defined

For more radical feminists, reproductive rights were never limited to the single issue of abortion. Pressure on poor women to be sterilized, temporarily or permanently through the injection of new drugs such as Norplant or Depo-Provera, should have generated among the women's movement the same kind of reaction as attacks against *Roe*. But for these broader issues, mainstream feminist support came more slowly. An example is the politics of worldwide population control. Radical feminists see population control as a way to "trade off" Third World women's rights in the interest of a "male-dominated, Eurocentric population policy."[47] Closer to home, proof that drugs and alcohol taken during pregnancy can damage the developing fetus (fetal alcohol or fetal effects syndrome) sets the rights of pregnant women against those of their fetuses in yet another way: Could pregnant addicts be legally incarcerated to prevent damage to the unborn child? And what effect would such policies have on a woman's right to abort? The Reagan administration found a wedge in all these discussions to prohibit medical research on fetal tissue transplantation, which might provide treatment for diseases such as Parkinson's and diabetes. But with amniocentesis and fetal therapy now standard practice, some feminists fear something new: a growing "competition" between the mother-to-be's well-being and that of her fetus.[48]

Conclusion

While feminists were kept busy putting out fires set by the Reagan and Bush administrations, they were inevitably distracted from the central policies of that administration, of which putting down women's liberation was but a side show.[49] Indeed, feminists were conspicuously absent from the main political stage. They played little role in the spate of mergers and acquisitions that increased big business's share of the economy and made investment bankers the most sought-after professionals of the decade. Nor were the many scandals of the 1980s (180 political appointees had to resign during Ronald Reagan's first six years) reported in the feminist press or discussed at feminist meetings. The savings and loan bailout, priced at $162 billion of taxpayer money, was similarly off the feminists' screen. It was as if the way business and politics are conducted in America is not a feminist issue.

The degradation of the environment, as the nation's environmental protection agencies were handed over to those who would despoil it, were protested by activist women working as members of environmental protection groups, some of them part of an "ecofeminist" movement. But three military involvements within twelve years—in Grenada, in Somalia, and in the Persian Gulf region—did not generate the overwhelming opposition that one might have expected from a movement dedicated to employing war only as a last resort. With the collapse of the Soviet Union at the end of the 1980s, and with it the hegemony of Soviet communism in Europe, one would have thought that such momentous events would have stirred organized feminism either to celebration or to concern. But while feminism was becoming more international, with contacts made in Mexico City, Nairobi, Copenhagen, and, eventually, Beijing, its priorities remained woman centered in the narrowest sense and local.

The U.S.-led invasion of Iraqi-occupied Kuwait in the Persian Gulf in 1991 is a case in point. Feminists had reason to celebrate as, for the first time in the nation's history, forty thousand uniformed women were involved in the front-line fighting forces. But one could criticize as well the underreporting of the devastating effects of allied bombing when it became clear that women and children were bearing the brunt of the high-tech attack on Iraq. Some 140,000 people were killed in the Persian Gulf War (80 Americans), but America cheered. Women were the first to join the yellow ribbon brigade, competing with one another in their desire to celebrate sacrifice and victory. But, as I have noted in Chapter 11, with few exceptions, feminists did not criticize this support. Nor did they widely promulgate a feminist analysis of the gender issues embedded in that war.[50]

What happened to poor people during the Reagan and Bush administrations was not limited to women. Indeed, there was a "racialization of poverty" in that era that was quite as devastating as the feminization of poverty. The two presidents allowed unemployment to replace inflation as the nation's number one economic problem and to hobble unions (beginning with the break-up of the air controllers' strike in 1981). Also, a new tax code was put in place that advantaged the rich. But many younger women benefiting from new professional opportunities, who might a decade before have joined a feminist protest group, appeared not to care.

In fact, despite the numbers of women who made political strides during the 1970s by way of the feminist movement, it is surprising how little impact feminism had in the 1980s on the nation as a whole. One factor must be the machismo that Reaganism consciously played to. Not only did the military budget climb to over $300 billion for the first (and last) time in the century, but also under Ronald Reagan and his secretary of defense the Pentagon entertained scenarios for "limited" nuclear war. Women were well represented in the antinuclear movement during the 1980s. Indeed, the idea for a "nuclear freeze"—a unilateral halt to nuclear weapons research, production, and deployment—was born in the mind of a remarkable woman, Randall Forsberg; and another woman, Australian-born pediatrician Helen Caldicott, transformed an organization, Physicians for Social Responsibility, into a powerful voice for nuclear sanity. But neither Forsberg nor Caldicott came out of the feminist movement, and few feminist groups (the exceptions were Women and Nuclear Disarmament and Mothers for Nuclear Disarmament) affiliated with the antinuclear campaigns. This is not to say that feminists were not opposed to the arms buildup; they were, but not as feminists. Recall Eleanor Smeal's remarkable assertion: "Peace is not a feminist issue." From her point of view, much of the history being made (or unmade, depending on your point of view) in the 1980s was merely a way of postponing gender equity.

One could invoke conspiracy theory and argue that the Reagan-Bush administrations *intentionally* set the antifeminist fires to keep feminists distracted with other matters, while increased military spending tripled the national debt and business got what was euphemistically called "regulatory relief." Certainly, a comparable strategy worked in disempowering the nation's unions. Or perhaps it was the increasing divisions within feminism itself that diffused its focus at this most crucial time. A more fundamental issue, however, has to do with what is *core* and what is *peripheral* in American feminism. In the beginning feminism insisted that the personal was political, meaning that power relations between the sexes—whether in marriage or on the job, whether supported by advertising or by tradition—deserved to be taken seriously and redressed in a public arena. But what if feminist politics was to be limited only to issues pertaining directly to sex and gender? Was the second wave becoming too self-absorbed to take its rightful place in the governing of the country? Was protest to remain its strategy of choice and not a stepping stone to participation? If, as Susan Hartmann uses the phrase, feminism was to proceed "from margin to mainstream," then mainstream issues, and not just gender inequity, deserved more of the feminists' attention.[51] At the end of the 1980s, these were the issues to ponder.

15

The End of a Movement

THREE DECADES HAVE PASSED SINCE the multiple strands of the second wave of feminism became a self-conscious movement for social and political change. Feminist theory provided the link that joined women of different classes, races, ages, and situations in life into an "us-versus-them" mentality. Sexual politics, as we have seen repeatedly, was not limited to electioneering. Nor did second-wave feminists lobby in the traditional sense of the term. They legislated, litigated, and, where possible, infiltrated the power structures; but at least as much effort—in true movement style—went into marching, sitting-in, bombarding the media, and offering a new vision of what relations between the genders could and should become.[1] It was not just a piece of the proverbial pie that women were after, but some fundamental changes in how the pie was put together in the first place.

A social movement for change is characterized by a high degree of intensity and single-mindedness rarely present in mainstream politics, save for the few short months of an election campaign and sometimes not even then. Campaign staffs must be paid to do the work. Movement people, in contrast, have to be reminded to "get a life" apart from their cause.[2] It was inevitable that the single vision of the second wave would eventually be diffused into several and that the energies of its pioneers would eventually give out. But it was hoped, certainly expected, that younger women, the beneficiaries of the changes being wrought, would stay the course.

Maybe they will. But the "Movement" as we knew it, loved it, and lived it in the 1960s and 1970s may well be over, even though "movement," in the more general sense of progress being made, is ongoing and probably at this late stage unstoppable. Ten years ago some commentators began talking ambiguously about postfeminism, as if the era of intensive feminist activism had already passed.[3] It was never quite clear whether by postfeminism they meant that feminists had made their point, that the time had come to relax the pressure, or that feminism was in retreat. At the time, Gloria Steinem stated there could be no postfeminism until and unless true equity for women in all realms was achieved. It was an interesting debate, pitting the pioneer generation against some younger women we might call feminists, even if they would not, who wanted, understandably, to forge ahead on their own terms.[4]

Making Change in America: What Have We Learned?

We may disagree on how to evaluate feminism in the post–Reagan-Bush era, but even as some women are making extraordinary inroads into arenas that until recently were exclusively male, the mood of the country is different now than it was coming out of the rebellious 1960s. If feminism is going to survive in the coming decades, it has to be different. The scale may already have tipped toward the inside, rather than the outside, of the political mainstream. But even as it does, there is a sense that anger, direct action, and protest continue to deserve a place in feminist politics, a view that cannot be attributed entirely to nostalgia. In this chapter I explore feminist strategies that worked—albeit not all the time and not always in the ways feminists expected—and strategies that may not work so well in the future, particularly if (as appears to be the case) feminism loses its center and with it the power to convert.

Playing the Political Game

It is commonly argued that the path to power in America is through party politics. How else can one achieve electoral office or influence those who legislate and enforce the nation's laws, except through the two major parties? As women matured in their professionalism, it seemed natural that the handful who populated state and national office when the second wave began would grow, and with them, the influence of feminism on the nation as a whole. Yet there was a powerful tradition of "outsider politics" in feminism. Although the nineteenth-century women's rights movement made suffrage a first priority, much of its political activity was outside the political arena. Before 1920 women effectively organized for peace, for maternal and child health benefits, even for birth control, with little or no assistance from the mainstream parties.

The second wave was similarly nonpartisan, in the narrowest sense of that term. Of the three strands that came together to form the feminist movement in the 1960s, only the members of the president's and later the state commissions on the status of women had been previously active within the political process. Friedan's housewives (who later made up the core of NOW) were not inside politics by habit or tradition. And the third strand, those younger women who came into the movement by way of the student Left, remained skeptical, even contemptuous, of the hurly-burly of election-dominated politics.

In actuality, there was a tradition of party activity among women. From 1920 onward certain middle-class and mostly white women participated in their political parties and, by dint of hard work and party loyalty, made their presence known and felt.[5] But until well into the second wave, the Republican and Democratic Parties treated their women loyalists largely as tokens and did not reward them with nominations and support for their electoral ambitions.[6] Moreover, as feminists correctly intuited, working in mainstream politics meant compromise, dilution of their energies, having to set aside the feminist agenda—sometimes even to deny certain aspects of it altogether—in order to win elections. And not least, mainstream politics meant having to work with men. To the extent that the second wave saw itself as a revolutionary movement, party political activity was for many a contradiction in terms.[7]

The parties saw things otherwise. Even after it became clear in the 1920s that the new women voters would not vote as a bloc, but rather in conformance with their social class and family members, they did vote and, as importantly, were willing and able to support the party of their choice in myriad ways. In 1938 after losing the presidency two times in a row, the Republican National Committee finally acknowledged the party's need to get out a woman's vote by creating the National Federation of Republican Women (the group for which Phyllis Schlafly was a failed candidate for president in 1966, before leaving to found the Eagle Forum). The establishment of this separate women's affiliate also coincided with new and important internal party rules: Women henceforth would hold an equal number of positions on the Republican Party's national and executive committees.[8] The Democratic Party did not follow suit until 1972, when a rule requiring equal numbers of delegates by gender to the national convention was adopted, in this instance in response to demands of feminists within the party.

Nevertheless, second-wave feminism as a movement owed its origins and support to forces outside of party politics and remained, as a movement, uncomfortable inside mainstream politics. Not until 1971, five years after the founding of NOW, did a group of feminists from both major parties join together in the National Women's Political Caucus expressly to encourage women of both parties to run for office. And even then, many of the then-leading feminists in NOW and women's liberation collectives stayed away, the NOW leadership fearing loss of membership to the new organization, the women's liberation collectives not particularly interested in elective office.

Most of the founders of the NWPC were already active in party politics. Tanya Melich, whose later defection from the Republican Party is detailed in her 1996 book *The Republican War Against Women*, was typical. She had a long history of activism within her party, as did Elly Peterson, vice-chair of the Republican Party, who joined her in the caucus. Bella Abzug, a Democratic member of Congress at the time, was also one of the founders, along with Gloria Steinem and Betty Friedan. Of the twenty-one founders, eleven were Democrats, two were Republicans, and eight were party unaffiliated. Many were actually new to the women's movement, but not to feminism in the broader sense of wanting to support other women. Melich felt she had always worked to elect Republicans and would continue to do so. Her intent in joining the caucus was "to elect Republican women who believed in feminist goals."[9]

Several of the founders and many of the three hundred political women who came to the NWPC's first meeting in July 1971 were Hispanics, Native American women, and women of color representing themselves and their minority constituencies. Among these were Fannie Lou Hamer of the Mississippi Freedom Democrats, Lupe Anguiano, and Shirley Chisholm (D–N.Y.). Chisholm's "conversion" to feminism was an interesting example of the "matrix of domination" Patricia Hills Collins talks about. The first African-American woman to be elected to the House of Representatives (in 1968), Chisholm won by beating James Farmer, like herself a great civil rights leader. Although Farmer was also African American, he gave himself points during his campaign against Chisholm (and hoped the voters would do the same) for being male. Chisholm's consciousness was raised, according to her later book about the "good fight," when Farmer "stressed in his campaign the need for a 'strong male image' and 'a man's voice in Washington.'" Arriving in the nation's capital to take her seat in 1969, Chisholm felt, according to historian Susan Hartmann, that the "sting of sexism" was stronger than the sting of racism.[10]

Women's status was on the rise at the 1972 Democratic National Convention, which took place only one year after the NWPC had been formed. Among the many "firsts" was Representative Chisholm's remarkable, if late-starting, campaign to be the candidate for president, as well as Texas legislator Frances ("Sissy") Farenthold's nomination from the floor (supported by more than four hundred delegates) to be the party's vice-presidential nominee. The candidate, George McGovern, chose Sargent Shriver instead and lost anyway to Richard Nixon. Nixon

will be remembered for other aspects of his presidency, but it is important for the record to note that the convention that nominated him featured the first woman keynoter of party convention history, Ann Armstrong, and that as president Nixon appointed a record number of
women to high office.[11] In his first State of the Union address, Nixon also
stated—another first—that "every woman should have the freedom to
choose . . . a career." He later vetoed the first comprehensive child care
bill ever passed by Congress on the grounds that child care threatened
"family stability," but he supported the ERA and in the 1972 amendments to the Equal Employment Opportunities Act (see Chapter 7) supported affirmative action as well.

By 1984, despite the loss of the ERA in the states, the feminist movement was strong enough (and the Democratic Party weak enough) to influence the Democratic Party's top ticket. Walter Mondale's selection of
Geraldine Ferraro to be his vice-presidential running mate won him the
awe and gratitude of feminists of both parties; more specifically, it gained
him the endorsement by NOW—its first of a national ticket. By then,
women were running and winning powerful offices around the country.
Democrat Ella Grasso won election—the first in her own right and not as
the widow of a deceased husband—to the governorship of Connecticut
in 1974, followed in the next two decades by Kay Orr of Nebraska, Dixie
Lee Ray of Washington, Madelyn Kunin of Vermont, Ann Richards of
Texas, and Christine Whitman of New Jersey. Republicans Millicent Fen-
wick of New Jersey, Nancy Johnson of Connecticut, and Virginia Smith of
Nebraska joined Democrats Pat Schroeder of Colorado, Yvonne Braith-
wait Burke of California, Barbara Jordan of Texas (the first woman of
color to keynote a national convention), Geraldine Ferraro of New York,
and Mary Rose Oakar of Ohio, among others, in the House. In 1978
Kansas Republican Nancy Landon Kassebaum became the only woman
elected to the Senate in recent times, later joined by Barbara Mikulski
(D–Md.), Dianne Feinstein and Barbara Boxer (D–Calif.), Paula Hawkins
(R–Fla.), Carol Mosely Braun (D–Ill.), Olympia Snowe (R–Maine), Patty
Murray (D–Wash.), and Kay Bailey Hutchinson (R–Tex.). Three organizations, the Women's Campaign Fund, Emily's List (for Democrats), and
WISH (for Republicans), joined the NWPC in furthering women's capac-
ity to get elected. They raised money specifically for women candidates.
Also assisting women candidates was the loosening of party control over
the nominating process. Women did better in direct primaries and open
meetings than in the traditional "smoke-filled back rooms."[12]

Many of the issues of importance to feminists are decided at the state
level. State office is also easier to win than national office. The cost of
campaigns is just a fraction of the cost of running for Congress, and
women who have family responsibilities, if elected, can work nearer to

their homes. Thus, state legislatures and state executive mansions became attractive targets for women willing to play the political game. In 1974 women held 8 percent of state legislative seats and sixteen seats in Congress. By 1986 those figures were 14.8 percent and twenty-four; in 1996, 21 percent of state legislators were women. But not all these women were feminists. I used to say, when asked in the 1970s about party politics, that my feminism "stopped at Louise Day Hicks," that is, my willingness to vote or work for a woman candidate did not supersede my fundamental political values. (Louise Day Hicks was a conservative woman who ran an anti–school desegregation campaign in Boston in the 1970s.) Indeed, with the ascendance of the New Right in politics, many women were selected by their parties to run on antiabortion and anti-ERA platforms. When the national Republican Party under Ronald Reagan reversed the party's decades-long support for both issues in 1980, feminist candidates within the party lost whatever power and influence they had painfully accumulated.[13]

It began to appear that the feminists who had been skittish about party politics had the right instinct after all. Despite sizable increases in the numbers of women running for and achieving electoral and appointed office during the 1970s and 1980s and the increasing power of women among Democratic ranks, Jimmy Carter consulted only his conscience and not his feminist friends in supporting the Supreme Court's decision in *Maher v. Roe* that government funds should not be used to pay for abortion. His rationale: "There are many things in life that are not fair." Carter also appointed to the all-powerful office of secretary of health, education, and welfare a man who was on record as opposing abortion.[14] The Republican Party in the Reagan era was even more baldly antifeminist. With the New Right virtually dictating party politics and the activism of Phyllis Schlafly's group within and without the Republican Party, it appeared that those feminists who had made concessions to their parties were never going to be rewarded. Indeed, Tanya Melich writes despairingly of how Republican feminists were tricked into believing that the Reagan era was over with the nomination of George Bush in 1988, only to be disappointed once again after his election.[15]

But the feminists who thought only women could further the feminist agenda were wrong, too. The period witnessed an outpouring of support—even at the expense of part of their constituencies—by many political men. The "good men" in politics on the ERA and other issues included Republicans and Democrats alike. On the Republican side were Barber Conable (N.Y.), Jacob Javits (N.Y.), Charles Mathias (Md.), Ted Stevens (Ala.), Howard Baker (Tenn.), Lowell Weicker (Conn.), Edward Brooke (Mass.), Robert Packwood (Oreg.), and John Heinz (Penn.) On the Democratic side were Birch Bayh (Ind.), Edward Kennedy (Mass.), Daniel Moynihan (N.Y.), Anthony Beilenson (Calif.), Paul Simon (Ill.), Tom Harkin (Iowa), Dale Bumpers (Ark.), and others. Interestingly, Robert Packwood's unswerving support for feminist issues over a twenty-year tenure in the Senate did little to keep him from committing sexual harassment or from being punished for it.

Like the "women's vote," which failed to materialize in the 1920s, the highly touted "gender gap" came and went in the 1980s and 1990s. Defined by political scientist Ethel Klein as "sex differences in voter choices and policy preferences," the gender gap never became the political two by four feminists could count on.[16] More women than men voted for Jimmy Carter in 1980, but then many more men than women voted for Ronald Reagan in that same election. Indeed, with his military buildup and "stand tall" rhetoric, Reagan appealed to macho men in ways the feminist political strategists had not anticipated.[17] Women may have favored Michael Dukakis more than men did—that is what the 25 percent gender gap meant in preelection polling in 1988. But the gap was insignificant since in the end 52 percent of women voted for George Bush.

Nevertheless, the entry of some feminists into mainstream politics was not without impact. Politics, with its bottom-line, winner-take-all dimensions, teaches some important lessons, one of which is that not all women are feminists and not all feminists are women. The Congressional Women's Caucus, first consisting solely of women in the U.S. House and Senate, opened its doors in 1981 to men who supported women's issues (and was renamed the Congressional Caucus on Women's Issues). For another, the very presence of women in important party positions and in a wide variety of elected offices demonstrated for all Americans that women could be just as competent (and on occasion just as incompetent, venal, and corrupt) as men.[18]

Politics brings with it—for better and for worse—immense visibility. Younger women growing up in the 1970s and 1980s, whatever their evolving political orientation, could not fail to notice the diversity of appearance, style, and views of women in public office. There were Geraldine Ferraro, pretty and powerful; Barbara Mikulski, scrappy and effective; Yvonne Braithwait Burke, pregnant during her first term in Congress; Patricia Schroeder, bringing up her two children over a twenty-year period in office. Governor Dixie Lee Ray of Washington was anything but glamorous. Indifferent to her appearance and lifestyle, once she left the governor's mansion, she holed up alone in her RV. Nancy Landon Kassebaum, in contrast, was the epitome of a lady, remaining cool and incorruptible under fire, voting her conscience every time. Patricia Roberts Harris joined the president's cabinet under Carter in 1977 as secretary of housing and urban development, the first African-American woman in history to do so. Who could ever say again that "all women are . . ."

Despite the divergence of their views on many issues, women in politics, whether elected or appointed, seemed always to be ahead of the crowd on children, peace, social welfare, and environmental issues. When Ferraro, in her much-celebrated debate with then-vice-presidential candidate George Bush in 1984, defended her lack of military service with the line "Do I have to have known war to love peace?" she partially closed a political door that had defined war service as a fitting (indeed the only) apprenticeship for leadership.[19]

However personally successful, women holding elective office in this period were also especially sensitive to women who were not like themselves, who were victims of dependency and abuse. Patricia Schroeder, for years a senior member of the House Armed Services Committee, worked hard to achieve both equal status for women in uniform and equalization of pensions for divorced spouses of military men. Ann Richards, as governor of Texas, offered selective amnesty to women incarcerated for life for having murdered violently abusive husbands. It was not just women running for elective office who were changing sex-role stereotypes, but also politician's wives. When Hillary and Bill Clinton became the "first couple" in 1992, they were just that, a modern couple, where in order to facilitate the husband's public service career, the wife had supported the family through her work as a lawyer. By the mid-1990s the new egalitarian marriage was not restricted to Democrats. Early in Bob Dole's 1996 campaign for president, Elizabeth Dole, who had taken leave from her job as president of the American Red Cross to assist him for the year, made it quite plain to her audiences that if he was elected, she would return to her job, the first First Lady to do so and, parenthetically, the first First Lady to make more money than her husband, the president himself.[20]

Such is the stuff not of revolution but of transformation. Nevertheless, many feminists—especially younger ones—found politics at worst corrupting, at best too slow. The lag rested, in large measure, on the fact that not all women voters agreed with the feminists on their goals and that large numbers of women eligible to vote chose not to do so. Even though, beginning in the 1980s, there was a sizable gender gap in favor of women in voter registration (on average, 1.13 percent more women were registered to vote than men),[21] voter participation was a problem. It took the National Women's Political Caucus nearly twenty-five years to make this problem a priority. In 1994 under the presidency of Harriet Woods, a former Missouri lieutenant governor and failed candidate for the U.S. Senate, the NWPC made voter registration of women a primary goal.

The Third Wave

The NWPC was not the only feminist organization to see that registering new voters was a necessary next step to overcoming the remaining barriers to women's equality and self-actualization. In the early 1990s groups of women in their twenties appeared willing, even quite proud, to call themselves "the third wave" and to identify as actual or spiritual progeny of second-wave feminism. One group, which included Rebecca Walker, daughter of feminist poet and novelist Alice Walker, and *Ms.* editor Barbara Findlen, claimed to have registered twenty-five thousand new inner-city voters in one year. Other young women (including high school girls) formed a myriad of on- and off-campus organizations. While these young women are no less feminist in their orientation, they have different priorities from the earlier strands of the movement. When reporter Joannie Schrof went looking for some of them to interview for an article about "feminism's daughters" for a 1993 roundup, she found WHAM (Women's Health Action and Mobilization), pressing for affordable health care for poor women, and FURY (Feminists United to Represent Youth), and YELL (Youth Education Life Line) campaigning for better sex education.[22] But although these young feminists appeared to build on elder feminists' concerns, they did not believe that anyone would take their issues as seriously as they did. So despite immense progress in the status of women during their lifetime, Schrof explained, they felt "betrayed."

> The vigor that third-wavers bring to feminism is fueled by both confidence and anger. While they have witnessed social change and believe they have the power to affect the status quo, young feminists . . . complain that they are inheriting a ravaged environment and a ruined economy; during their lifetimes, the AIDS epidemic has exploded, reports of violence against young women have risen nearly 50 percent and college tuition has skyrocketed. "We've been dumped on one too many times, and we've decided to take matters into our own hands."[23]

The thread that unites these disparate women's groups is their youth, with its special concerns and vulnerabilities: parental consent laws restricting abortion, systematic sexual abuse and violence against girls, date rape, anorexia and bulimia, poverty, and even the special circumstances that render young girls homeless. *3WAVE*, a news brief produced by the organization that takes the third wave as its name, tells readers that after parental consent laws went into effect in Minnesota, the birthrate for fifteen- to seventeen-year-olds increased 40 percent; that 8 million girls are sexually abused before they reach the age of eighteen; that one in ten adolescent girls suffers from anorexia or bulimia; and that forty thousand teenage girls drop out of high school each year because of pregnancy. Gender inequality in wages is mentioned but not featured in their material.[24]

Third-wavers are mindful that the second wave got the "reputation," earned or not, of being "hateful to men, focusing on too narrow a set of goals, and marginalizing minority and low-income women."[25] Inspired by feminists such as black poet Audre Lorde and Hispanic writer Gloria Anzaldúa, young feminists are looking to eradicate the image of feminism as a rich white woman's club.

Some second-wavers are put off by the criticism, even more by younger women's unwillingness to acknowledge their debt to the movement. Schrof tells of an intergenerational meeting at which, when asked what older feminists wanted from younger ones, the answer was "thank you." Nevertheless, there must be a sense of pride and affiliation when young feminist Barbara Findlen, in introducing a collection of her contemporaries' writings, describes what it was like to grow up in the shadow of the second wave:

> My feminism wasn't shaped by antiwar or civil rights activism; I was not a victim of the problem that had no name. Indeed, by the time I was discovering feminism, naming had become a principal occupation of feminists. Everywhere you looked feminists were naming things—things like sexual harassment, date rape, displaced homemakers, and domestic violence—[things] that used to be called, as Gloria Steinem pointed out, just life.
>
> In fact, born in 1964, I became a part of a massive, growing, vibrant feminist movement at the age of eleven—something that literally had not been possible for Gloria Steinem, Kate Millett, my older sisters, my mother, or any of my other feminist role models. While feminism has been around for as long as patriarchy, I came of age during one of those moments in history when the feminist movement was becoming so large, so vocal, and so visible that it could reach into and change the life of an eleven-year-old suburban girl.[26]

How typical is Barbara Findlen and her third-wave contemporaries? How likely is it that there will be a Movement or an equivalent feminist consciousness to inspire the next generation of young women?

From Margin to Margin

The feminist Movement is losing its center and its power to convert because for some years now feminism has been engaged in a self-destroying, casting-off process, distancing itself first from one set of constituents and then another. The risk is "remarginalization," and the tragedy is that this is occurring just when mainstreaming is in view.

In 1989 historian Susan Hartmann published a comprehensive history of American women in politics since 1960. She entitled it *From Margin to Mainstream* to convey the remarkable enlargement of women's participation in American political life during that period.[27] And, indeed, from my own interactions with women holding elected office, there is no question that prior to the women's movement political women were on the margin *even while serving.* At a meeting I attended of a sample of elected women state legislators called by Rutgers University's Center for American Women in Politics in 1972 (from which Jeane Kirkpatrick, a political scientist and later Ronald Reagan's ambassador to the United Nations, wrote a book),[28] anecdotal evidence of marginalization was overwhelming. I recall a legislator from the Midwest bemoaning the fact that she found it necessary to print her campaign literature on the backs of recipe cards, the kind housewives could file. Never married and childless, she needed to demonstrate to the voters that (as she put it) her cupboard was not as barren as her womb. Another legislator, well into her sixties and obviously experienced and talented, was forced, as she told her story, to give up her seat in the Georgia state house when her husband became a stroke victim. Even though she could do nothing for him at home, her constituents fully expected her to be at his side.

Grownup women told us at that meeting, held in the Pocono Mountains of Pennsylvania, that as a matter of course they would feign headaches during official trips with other state legislators in order not to be present and embarrass "the boys" when they chose to go to burlesques during their evenings out of town. And as for sex or even dating, there was no way to live a life not socially sanctioned and still retain the confidence of the voter. In retrospect, given the period during which these women were first elected—a period when the feminine mystique held sway—it is remarkable that they were sent to their state capitals at all. But there they were, older on average by twenty years than their male colleagues because for the women, state office was a mid- to late-life prize for decades of volunteering. For their male associates, the state house was supposed to be a stepping stone to higher office.

Hartmann's metaphor—from margin to mainstream—seems, then, to be an appropriate characterization of the sea change in American women's participation in the economy and in mainstream politics during the period she chronicles. But how well does this characterization work when applied to feminists and feminism itself? We have no way of knowing how future historians will assess the second wave of feminism. They might, as William O'Neill dubbed the first, describe it as having had a "rise" and "fall." But they might just as well conclude that, after remarkably widespread discussion and even acceptance of feminists' ideas and values, the traumas of the 1980s sent feminists back to the safety of the margin, convinced that mainstreaming would never work.

In contrast to Hartmann's view of American women in politics, feminists and feminism itself seem (at least to this observer) to be at risk of returning to the margin, which this time is self-defined and self-imposed. Unlike women's "outsider status" as described prior to the 1960s by feminist thinkers such as Simone de Beauvoir, this marginalization is not a condition created by men. Neither de Beauvoir nor anyone else in the early days thought women had *put themselves* on the sidelines of history and culture. But for whatever reasons, and they are certain to be complex, feminists in the late 1990s appear to be even more isolated. How did this happen? And what does it bode for the future?

Identity Politics

In retrospect, Kate Millett's theory opened the floodgates. Once sexual politics was understood to mean that female identity was socially constructed (for the purpose of maintaining male power and privilege), then it was only logical that other "identities" might be similarly constructed as well. It followed that once consciousness is raised, an oppressed group is uniquely entitled to define its own needs and goals. Daphne Patai and Noretta Koertge, in a controversial discussion of "identity politics" in their 1994 book *Professing Feminism*, explain the internal logic of this position and how it served to marginalize first one group of feminists and then another: "According to feminist epistemology, the knowledge produced by those in power (typically, white European males) inevitably reflects their partisan interests and is prejudicial to all those not in power. The knowledge needed for liberation must, therefore, be generated by the oppressed themselves. . . . It is assumed that the only way for an oppressed group to remedy its unsatisfactory situation is by single-mindedly pursuing the needs of its own members."[29]

As long as gender was the key variable in defining women's identity, the single-minded pursuit of the needs of its members served feminism well. But with time, other issues surfaced within feminism as certain groups felt especially stigmatized because of racial or national origins, physical disabilities, physical appearance, or sexual preference. As Patai and Koertge describe it: "Nearly everyone could lay claim to some need for special treatment. The result has been a degrading struggle among members of identity groups for the recognition of each group's oppression, generating an atmosphere of condemnation directed at anyone who could be labeled a member of a more privileged group . . . [and] a contest for 'most oppressed' status."[30]

Identity politics inevitably gives rise to exclusionary politics, and the first obvious exclusion was of men—not on the basis of what they thought or were willing to do but simply on the basis of gender. You may recall my own first encounter with separatism, when I asked Ti-Grace

Atkinson in 1969 to address our Cornell Conference on Women and was told she would not speak to a mixed audience. The participation of men in feminist organizations (except for NARAL) over the thirty-year period I have been chronicling has steadily decreased. Even in NOW, where co-founder Betty Friedan had gone out of her way to name the organization *for* instead of *of* women, male names no longer show up on NOW rosters or as bylines in the *National NOW Times.* The numbers of men taking women's studies classes, while never very large, also waned;[31] even when present, their participation came to be seen as "problematic." As one women's history professor told Patai and Koertge, "Once you've defined the world as a world of women and decided that men cannot be assimilated into the way in which you develop your theory and methodology . . . then you've already placed yourself in a curious contradiction to the whole concept of diversity."[32]

Soon it was not just males who were being cast off but also married women, white women, economically privileged women, physically able women, women who dressed "fashionably" or wore makeup, women who were thin, and women who had the great good fortune to have grown up in nonabusive families. One by one, groups that were said to be less oppressed than others were marginalized, until the great diversity that had characterized the movement in its early stages seemed a problem rather than a source of strength. As the history professor interviewed by Patai and Koertge put it: "There has to be respect for other people's decisions to live certain kinds of lives, whether it's to have children or not to have children, to be married to men or not to be married to men. These choices can't be seen as excluding someone from being a thoroughgoing feminist."[33] But in many circles they did.

The right to be free of socially stigmatizing identities remained, of course, a strong tenet of both women's liberation and gay liberation. But the notion that unless a person has been born into a certain ethnic group or body type, that person cannot think, feel, participate, or know something other people know is what identity politics is all about. Originally, the great insight that the personal is political gave feminists permission to deal politically with issues previously thought to be personal, such as marriage, divorce, reproductive freedom, or images in advertising. Identity politics reverses the equation: Now the political position one takes has to be grounded in a particular personal experience. Since no two people can possibly have identical personal experiences, it follows that political discourse between them, and cooperation and collaboration among groups of them, is not going to be easy, or as theorist Linda Alcoff puts it in an article on the identity crisis in feminist theory, there is no "room for maneuver."[34] Margaret Ferguson and Jennifer Wicke worry, too, about the required "matchup" between identities and experience, the "clicking" of invisible designations into place, the need to have "one or more of each." It is imperative, they write, "to resist identity as the sole criterion of either a feminist or a postmodern politics."[35]

Identity politics also leads to inhibition. The term *politically correct* has come to signify the opposite of the free range of ideas that characterized the women's movement in its early days. John Schlesinger, a British film director, speaking not particularly of feminism but rather of the impact of political correctness overall, believes that in the 1990s the degree of freedom of artistic exploration is far less than it was in the 1970s. Why? "Having to be politically correct," he said during a television interview in spring 1996, "is more inhibiting even than out-and-out censorship."[36]

Alienation and burnout are not the only causes. Women whose ambitions and opportunities were enlarged by the women's movement are now more interested in self-help and self-advancement than in confrontational activism. *Ms.* magazine—now a nonprofit quarterly instead of a monthly available on the nation's newsstands—has difficulty competing for readership with service magazines. Would-be members of NOW, NARAL, and NWPC often prefer to network locally with people like themselves. Mutual assistance appears to be the late-1990s version of sisterhood, and mentoring has replaced protest as the dominant theme. The Movement can still get thousands of people out onto the street when abortion is threatened. Indeed, a veritable "reunion" of second-wavers took place in my hometown of Tucson during a 5 A.M. vigil called when our Planned Parenthood clinic was threatened by Operation Rescue in 1992. But our feminist newspaper has few subscribers under fifty, and no one seems to be able to do anything about the problem.

What does this mean for change? Will the Movement be replaced by separate interest groups organized around specific issues or identities? Are there any commonalities left, apart from abortion, which can crosscut political affiliations? And if not, does it matter? Is movement (with a lowercase m) unstoppable, finally beyond the reach of another Great Depression, another war, another wave of right-wing conservatism? Many indicators certainly seem to suggest that there is no going back. Sports, which along with politics and the military, was one of the last bastions of men, if not fully integrated, is certainly in awe of women at the top. Just prior to the 1996 summer Olympics, *Newsweek* magazine ran a cover story about it that featured female athletes as the nation's "best hope for Olympic Gold."[37] More important than athletics, of course, for long-term economic independence of the average American family is how women are faring in the workplace.

Working Women

In 1994 the Women's Bureau of the Department of Labor took the pulse of working women in America, detailing the size, scope, and residual problems attending women's full-scale "migration from home to the workplace."[38] Of the 102 million women age sixteen and over in the United States in 1994, 60 million were in the civilian labor force, including people working and people actively looking for jobs. This was a record. Women already accounted for 46 percent of the total labor force (compared to 24.4 percent in the 1930s) and were projected to make up 48 percent in the year 2005. Not all women who wanted to work were working, however. Unemployment varied enormously depending on race, ethnicity, education, and training. According to the bureau's final report, unemployment for white women in 1994 was only 5.2 percent. However, 11 percent of black women and 10.7 percent of Hispanic women, at the time the survey was taken, were out of a job.

From a sample of 250,000 women selected to reflect race, ethnicity, age, geographical location, and education, a remarkably high 79 percent of those working claimed to "love" or "like" their jobs, but 58.5 percent experienced too much stress in managing their dual careers as workers, wives, and mothers. Stress was highest, according to the bureau's findings, among single mothers, professional women, managers, and women of color. However much they liked their work, 48.9 percent complained about not getting paid enough and 43.8 percent about too skimpy benefits, especially paid leave. More than 50 percent experienced continued inequality in regard to on-the-job training, opportunity for advancement (26 percent of women of color believed they were discriminated against in promotion), and distribution of responsibility. "I've been here thirty-two years and I'll never make management," wrote one respondent on the questionnaire in the box marked "other comments." "The glass ceiling is not even in view," wrote another.[39]

When salaries were tallied, the women's reasons for frustration over pay and benefits were clear. Seventy-five percent of the women working earned less than $25,000 in their most recent year of work. Many were still in low-wage and low-skills jobs, locked in the pink-collar ghettos, working as day care and nursing aides. And nearly one-quarter could expect no pension benefits at all. At their salary levels, 56 percent found paying for child care a problem even when they could locate a provider.

For the better educated, however, substantial progress had been made. Only 5 percent of the five thousand members of the Senior Executive Service in the federal government (comparable to chief executive officers and vice presidents in business and industry) were female in 1979; in 1994 that proportion had climbed to 17 percent. Would it go higher? It would not unless women learned to invest in their careers the way men did, opined Martha Krebs, a senior federal executive. Upon arriving in her position at the Department of Energy with the Clinton administration in 1993, Krebs had gone out of her way to identify women who were ready for promotion. But there were problems. The "best," she reported, had not got the same coaching and counseling as men; and many had not "taken responsibility for their own careers," she told an audience of women scientists and technical managers. Things would have to be different if the federal government's next set of goals was to be reached.[40]

Summing Up

On balance, Krebs is optimistic. She notes that the rationale for having women at all levels of government has changed in interesting ways over the past forty years. In the 1950s the issue was fairness; in the 1970s the argument was that equal opportunity was the law; in the 1990s employers are coming to realize that women are valuable to a business because they offer different points of view, new ideas, and new solutions.

We can be optimistic, too. What we stand for and do in this country affects other countries as well. In spring 1996 the giant Japanese firm Mitsubishi was challenged in the courts by a class-action suit alleging sexual harassment of women in the company's U.S.-based plant in Ohio. Shortly thereafter, women in the parent company in Japan were emboldened to complain of sexual harassment, too. The issue remains whether women anywhere can achieve social and economic equality with men by insisting that gender does not matter, while at the same time expecting concessions for their roles as wives and mothers. This is not just a theoretical issue. Kate Millett's *Sexual Politics* showed how women's status is linked politically to women's roles. The challenge, to borrow the language of feminist theorist Zillah Eisenstein, is to invent "a new version of equality" that no longer depends on everyone being the same.[41]

Some years after the French Revolution, poet William Wordsworth said of those heady years, "Twas bliss to be alive and to be young was very heaven." That sentiment could just as well be applied to the era in which the second wave of feminism burst upon the scene in the United States. Those of us who started out mimicking the breathy, childlike voices of Marilyn Monroe and Jacqueline Kennedy in an effort to be feminine and popular, and then went on to change history, feel more than a little lucky to have "been there" when feminism happened. Our souvenirs are the buttons, the film clips, the articles that first appeared in the underground press, and, of course, our memories. Marching, sitting-in, raising hell, were not exactly what our parents had in mind for us, any more than sisterhood with other women. But we learned how and we learned fast. Once we began speaking for ourselves, we discovered our voices were not naturally breathy any more than our bodies were ill-equipped for serious athletics. Speaking for us all early in the 1970s, Helen Reddy brought forth the essence of what the second wave of feminism meant to us: "I am woman," she sang lustily. "Hear me roar!"

Chronology

1830   Antislavery societies are active in this decade and the next.

President Andrew Jackson signs the Indian Removal Act, forcibly removing Native Americans from their land and herding them along what becomes known as the "Trail of Tears."

1838   Abolitionist Angelina Grimké remarks that she cannot make the contribution she is capable of making to the emancipation of the Negro slave until she is herself emancipated.

1840   Elizabeth Cady Stanton and Lucretia Mott travel to London as U.S. delegates to the World Antislavery Conference, where they are relegated to the nonvoting section of the meeting.

1848   New York State enacts Married Women's Property Acts.

A convention on women's rights is held at Seneca Falls, New York.

The United States wages war against Mexico and subsequently annexes Texas, New Mexico, Arizona, and California.

1850   Women such as Susan B. Anthony and Elizabeth Cady Stanton actively disseminate their views on suffrage and women's rights.

1852   The first women's rights convention to list suffrage as its goal is convened.

1861   The Civil War begins.

1865   The Civil War ends.

The Thirteenth Amendment to the Constitution emancipates slaves in the United States.

1868   The Fourteenth Amendment to the Constitution guarantees that all Americans have "equal protection" under the law.

1870   The Fifteenth Amendment to the Constitution extends male suffrage to African Americans.

1880   Jim Crow laws in the South prevent African Americans from voting.

The typewriter is invented in this decade.

1890   African-American journalist and publisher Ida B. Wells launches an anti-lynching crusade.

The National American Women's Suffrage Association is formed (from the National Women's Suffrage Association and the American Women's Suffrage Association) to work on getting the vote for women.

The first U.S. Census finds that 1.2 million women are working outside the home.

1893 The state of Colorado allows women to vote, the first state in the union to do so.

1896 The National Association of Colored Women is founded.

1907 On a wave of "anti-immigrant" fervor, a bill is introduced in Congress that compels a woman who marries a foreigner to adopt her husband's citizenship.

The Supreme Court under Chief Justice Louis Brandeis allows to stand a number of laws protecting children and women in the workplace.

1911 The term *feminism* is first used.

1912 The federal Children's Bureau is established.

1914 World War I begins.

1916 Jeannette Rankin (R–Mont.) is the first woman elected to Congress.

1917 The communist revolution occurs in Russia.

1918 World War I ends.

Jeannette Rankin is defeated in her bid for reelection because she voted against U.S. entry into World War I.

1919 Congress passes the Nineteenth Amendment to the Constitution, granting women the right to vote. The amendment is ratified by three-fourths of the states on August 26, 1920.

1920 The League of Women Voters is formed by Carrie Chapman Catt.

The Women's Bureau of Department of Labor is established.

The Women's Joint Congressional Committee, a loose coalition formed by the League of Women Voters to lobby for women's issues, is created.

1921 Congress passes the Sheppard-Towner Maternity and Infancy Protection Act, introduced into Congress by Jeannette Rankin in 1918.

The U.S. open-door immigration policy ends.

1922 The Cable Act is passed, which guarantees a woman's nationality independent of her husband's.

1923 The Equal Rights Amendment to the Constitution is first introduced into Congress.

1924 Congress passes an amendment to the Constitution, introduced in 1922, to give Congress the power to regulate child labor. (By 1930, only six states have ratified the amendment.)

1929 The U.S. stock market crashes.

1930 The Great Depression takes hold of the United States, and women lose many gains.

1932 The National Economic Act (the first of several bills initiated by the Roosevelt administration to deal with the economy) makes it illegal for both husband and wife to work for the federal government. (The law is in force until 1937.)

1935   *Sex and Temperament in Three Primitive Societies,* by Margaret Mead, is published.

Congress passes the Social Security Act, which establishes federally guaranteed survivors' benefits for widows and dependent children.

1938   After the loss of two presidential elections, the Republican Party acknowledges the need to attract women voters by creating the National Federation of Republican Women. (Democrats follow suit in 1972.)

Congress passes the Fair Labor Standards Act, establishing standards for minimum wage and employment of children.

1940   Jeannette Rankin, the first woman member of Congress, is reelected to Congress.

1941   President Franklin D. Roosevelt signs Executive Order 8802, which bars discrimination by race or national origin in companies doing business with the federal government.

World War II begins.

1942   Women's branches are established in the military.

Jeannette Rankin is defeated in her bid for reelection because she voted against U.S. entry into World War II.

1945   World War II ends.

The Equal Pay for Equal Work bill is first introduced into Congress by Robert Taft (R–Ohio) and Claude Pepper (D–Fla.) (it is finally passed in 1963).

1950   A Senate subcommittee rules that homosexuals should not be recruited to government.

California men form the Mattachine Society, devoted to consciousness-raising of male homosexuals.

1952   Phyllis Schlafly fails in her first bid for Congress.

1953   *The Second Sex,* by Simone de Beauvoir, is published (originally published in French in 1949).

Sexual Behavior in the Human Female, by Alfred C. Kinsey, sees publication.

1954   The Supreme Court decides in *Brown* v. *Board of Education* that separate but equal facilities impede equal opportunity, thereby clearing the way for desegregation of public education in primary and secondary schools.

1955   In Montgomery, Alabama, a bus boycott is led by Reverend Martin Luther King, Jr.

The Daughters of Bilitis, the first lesbian organization, is founded.

1960   The Student Nonviolent Coordinating Committee is founded in the South by African Americans to protest civil rights violations.

1961   President John F. Kennedy establishes the first President's Commission on the Status of Women, chaired by Eleanor Roosevelt.

Birth control pills are approved for marketing in the United States.

1963   *American Women*, the report of the Presidential Commission on the Status of Women, is published.

President John F. Kennedy appoints the permanent Citizens' Advisory Council on the Status of Women. (Eventually, fifty parallel state commissions are also established.)

A march on Washington, D.C., for civil rights takes place.

Congress passes the Equal Pay for Equal Work Act.

The Feminine Mystique, by Betty Friedan, sees publication. (Five million copies are sold by 1970.)

President John F. Kennedy is assassinated in Dallas, Texas.

1964   Congress passes the Civil Rights Act, including Title VII, which prohibits discrimination in employment on the basis of race, color, religion, national origin, or sex.

The Equal Employment Opportunity Commission is created to enforce Title VII of the Civil Rights Act.

Hundreds of students converge on the South to assist in voter registration during what is called "Freedom Summer."

1965   President Lyndon B. Johnson signs Executive Order 11246, which requires companies doing business with the federal government to undertake affirmative action in hiring minorities.

Sonia Pressman Fuentes is appointed EEOC counsel and begins to press for amelioration of sex discrimination in employment.

In a case taken up by the EEOC, stewardesses Dusty Roads and Nancy Collins charge American Airlines with sex discrimination.

"Jane Crow and the Law: Sex Discrimination and Title VII," by Mary Eastwood and Pauli Murray, is published in the *George Washington Law Review*.

Civil rights workers Casey Hayden and Mary King distribute a memo about sexual inequality within the civil rights movement.

A paper titled "Women's Liberation—a Step Beyond Rights" is laughed off the floor at a Students for a Democratic Society meeting.

1966   Fifty state Commissions on the Status of Women meet in Washington, D.C., to compare their findings.

The National Organization for Women is founded.

NOW petitions the EEOC to ban the sexual categorizing of employment advertisements.

Funding for family planning is made available through President Lyndon B. Johnson's Department of Health, Education, and Welfare.

Phyllis Schlafly fails to win the presidency of the National Republican Women's Federation.

1967   The Chicago Women's Liberation Group is formed, perhaps the first in the country to use the term "liberation."

New York Radical Women is founded, the first radical feminist group.

President Lyndon B. Johnson signs Executive Order 11375, which extends affirmative action to women.

The American Civil Liberties Union first challenges sodomy laws.

The EEOC holds hearings on sex discrimination.

California legalizes abortion.

1968   Eugene McCarthy launches an anti–Vietnam War campaign for president.

The Democratic National Convention is held in Chicago, Illinois.

Richard Nixon is elected president of the United States.

New York Radical Women begins a process of sharing stories that later becomes known as "consciousness-raising."

New York Radical Women protests the Miss America Pageant in Atlantic City, New Jersey.

The NOW Bill of Rights is published, prompting some women to resign over legalization of abortion.

The Women's Equity Action League is established as a spinoff from NOW.

Martin Luther King Jr. is assassinated.

The Poor People's March on Washington is organized by the Welfare Rights Organization.

Feminist publications begin to appear in the United States (500 between 1968 and 1973).

Shirley Chisholm (D–N.Y.) is elected the first African-American woman to the House of Representatives.

The National Abortion Rights Action League is formed.

The first national women's liberation conference held in Chicago.

1969   The Conference on Women is held at Cornell University.

The John Birch Society calls women who demonstrated at the Miss America Pageant in 1968 "communists."

Rita Mae Brown and others resign from New York NOW over the issue of lesbianism.

A rebellion by homosexual patrons of Stonewall Inn in New York City against treatment by police launches the gay and lesbian rights movement.

The Boston Women Health Book Collective publishes *Our Bodies, Ourselves: A Book by and for Women* (in print ever since).

New York Radical Feminists is formed.

New York repeals its abortion law.

1970 The Equal Rights Amendment to the Constitution is reintroduced into Congress.

The first large-scale women's studies course, "The Evolution of Female Personality," is offered at Cornell University.

Sexual Politics, by Kate Millett, is published.

Naomi Weisstein's paper "'Kinder, Kuche, Kirche' as Scientific Law: Psychology Constructs the Female," which criticizes traditional psychology's attitude toward women, is published.

Time publishes a women's liberation issue with Kate Millett on the cover.

Sit-ins at *Newsweek* and *Ladies Home Journal* are staged to protest discrimination against female workers. (An antidiscrimination suit is filed later against *Time*, *Life*, *Fortune*, and *Sports Illustrated*.)

The North American Indian Women's Association is founded.

Comisión Feminil Mexicana is founded by Chicana feminists.

The First Women's Equality Day is organized by Betty Friedan.

The United Nations designates the 1970s as the "Women's Decade."

California is the first state to adopt a "no-fault" divorce law.

Bella Abzug (D–N.Y.) is elected to Congress.

Phyllis Schlafly fails in her second bid for Congress.

Congress passes the Public Health Service Act, which provides funds for family planning for low-income women.

The first "lesbian purge" of national NOW occurs.

The radical group Redstockings, affiliated with the Gay Liberation Front and eventually Radicalesbians, is founded.

The Second Congress to Unite Women is convened.

The Feminist Press is started by Florence Howe and Paul Lauter.

Sisterhood Is Powerful, edited by Robin Morgan, sees publication.

Pat Mainardi proposes a system of assigning "wages for housework."

The Women's Equity Action League files lawsuits against several universities for sexual discrimination.

The United Auto Workers is the first major labor union to support the Equal Rights Amendment.

The first national women's liberation conference in Great Britain occurs.

1971 There is a second "lesbian purge" of NOW.

A few months later, NOW's second convention votes in favor of a "pro-lesbian" resolution.

The first national Chicana conference is held.

New York Radical Women organizes the first of three public "speak-outs" on rape.

Woman in Sexist Society: Studies in Power and Powerlessness, edited by Vivian Gornick and Barbara K. Moran, is published.

The Female Eunuch, by Germaine Greer, is published in the United States.

Ms. magazine first appears as an insert to *New York* magazine.

The National Women's Political Caucus is formed to assist women in getting elected to political office.

President Richard M. Nixon vetoes the Comprehensive Child Development Act, which would have established federally funded day care centers.

1972   The first conference of Puerto Rican women is convened.

President Richard M. Nixon establishes the National Commission on Consumer Finance to study inequities in credit industry.

The Equal Rights Amendment passes both houses of Congress. (Ratification by three-fourths of the states is required by 1979.)

Congress passes Title IX of the 1972 Educational Amendments to the Civil Rights Act to enforce sex equity in education.

Congress passes the Equal Employment Opportunity Act, which prohibits sex discrimination in employment.

Phyllis Schlafly forms StopERA.

Sappho Was a Right-on Woman: A Liberated View of Lesbianism, by Sidney Abbott and Barbara Love, sees publication.

The Feminist Press begins publication of the *Women's Studies Newsletter* (later renamed the *Women's Studies Quarterly*).

The Feminist Press republishes *Life in the Iron Mills*, by Rebecca Harding Davis, the first in a series of rediscovered feminist literary classics.

Ms. magazine publishes its first full issue in spring.

Texas legislator Frances ("Sissy") Farenthold is nominated from the floor of Democratic National Convention to be the party's vice presidential nominee.

The Republican National Convention features its first woman keynoter, Ann Armstrong.

Shirley Chisholm runs as a candidate for the Democratic Party's nomination for president of the United States.

Prostitutes organize into a union, COYOTE (Call Off Your Old Tired Ethics).

The Ms. Foundation is created to support women's projects.

The League of Women Voters declares its support of the Equal Rights Amendment.

1973   The National Black Feminist Organization is established.

The Supreme Court decides *Roe* v. *Wade,* establishing a woman's right to abortion.

The Supreme Court rules that sex categorizing in employment advertisements is unconstitutional.

The American Federation of Labor–Congress of Industrial Organizations declares its support of the Equal Rights Amendment.

Thirty states ratify the Equal Rights Amendment (eight states to go for passage).

Phyllis Schlafly claims that StopERA has several thousand members and is active in twenty-six states.

The U.S. military formally integrates itself by eliminating women-only branches.

Congress appoints the first female page in the House of Representatives.

The Supreme Court modifies the legal definition of obscenity to allow for "frank sexual description."

The Feminist Press publishes *Daughter of the Earth,* by Agnes Smedley, and *The Yellow Wallpaper,* by Charlotte Perkins Gilman.

American Telegraph and Telephone agrees to end discrimination in women's salaries and pay retroactive compensation to women employees.

NOW begins a public service advertising campaign on equality for women.

Singer Helen Reddy wins a Grammy Award for her song "I Am Woman."

1974   The Coalition of Labor Union Women is founded.

The Association of Mexican-American Women is founded.

New York State ends the requirement for corroboration in rape cases.

Congress passes the Equal Credit Opportunity Act forbidding racial or sexual discrimination in the credit industry.

Congress passes the Women's Educational Equity Act to develop nonsexist curricula and nondiscriminatory vocational programs.

Democrat Ella Grasso is elected governor of Connecticut, the first woman to be elected governor in her own right.

1975   Much of the 1968 NOW Bill of Rights is accomplished.

Against Our Will: Men, Women, and Rape, by Susan Brownmiller, is published.

The United Nations sponsors its First International Conference on Women, in Mexico City, Mexico.

Federal employees' salaries are subject to garnishment for child support and alimony.

The first women's bank is opened in New York City.

Signs: Women, Culture, and Society, a journal devoted to the new scholarship on women, begins publication by the University of Chicago Press.

Time magazine features twelve women as "Man of the Year."

1976   The United Nations Decade for Women begins.

West Point, Annapolis, and the Air Force Academy open admissions to women.

Representative Henry Hyde (R–Ill.) attaches an abortion exclusion clause (and continues to do so annually) to the federal appropriations bill, prohibiting federal Medicaid money to be used for abortion.

The Supreme Court rules in favor of General Electric, deciding that the company's failure to cover pregnancy-related disability is nondiscriminatory.

The Supreme Court in *Planned Parenthood* v. *Danforth* rules that Missouri cannot interfere with a woman's abortion decision by giving veto power to the father.

A movement to repeal gay rights ordinances in Dade County, Florida, is led by singer Anita Bryant.

The first reported feminist action against pornography takes place in San Francisco.

ERAmerica is formed to work on ratification of the Equal Rights Amendment.

The National Alliance of Black Feminists is founded in Chicago.

Dr. Benjamin Spock revises *Baby and Child Care* to eradicate sexual bias.

1977   The First National Women's Conference, held in Houston, Texas, is chaired by Bella Abzug.

Phyllis Schlafly forms the "Pro-Family Coalition" during the Houston women's conference.

The Public Works Employment Act is passed, reserving a portion of federal contracts for firms with 51 percent female boards of directors.

A political statement by the Combahee River Collective, an African-American feminist organization in Boston, asserts the "simultaneity of oppressions" of African-American women.

Patricia Roberts Harris becomes the first African-American woman to be secretary of housing and urban development in President Jimmy Carter's cabinet.

The National Women's Studies Association is founded.

The Supreme Court in *Mahler* v. *Roe* upholds a state's right to refuse Medicaid payment for abortions.

1978   The Supreme Court in *Bakke* v. *University of California Regents* decides that race cannot be used as an exclusive criterion for admission to public higher education.

Congress passes the Pregnancy Discrimination Act to prohibit discrimination against pregnant women in all areas of employment.

Proposition 6 in California (the Briggs Initiative) to prohibit gays from teaching in California schools is put on the ballot and is defeated.

Women Against Pornography is founded in New York City.

Congress extends the ratification deadline for the Equal Rights Amendment to June 30, 1982.

One hundred thousand demonstrators march on Washington, D.C., to support ratification of the Equal Rights Amendment.

1979   The Moral Majority is founded by television evangelist Jerry Falwell.

President Jimmy Carter fires Bella Abzug from the Advisory Committee on Women when she insists that inflation, unemployment, and the federal budget are women's issues.

Five thousand feminists march against pornography in New York City.

1980   Ronald Reagan is elected president of the United States.

The United Nations sponsors the Second World Conference on Women, in Copenhagen, Denmark.

New Equal Employment Opportunity Commission guidelines on sexual harassment are published.

The Republican platform drops support of the Equal Rights Amendment for the first time in forty years. The party also goes on record against abortion.

The Feminist Press has published fifty books in its efforts to restore the literature of women writers "to its rightful place."

Scientists in France report the development of a drug to abort fetuses in the first nine weeks of gestation. Later known as RU 486, the pill is blocked from entry into the United States by the Food and Drug Administration.

1981   The Congressional Women's Caucus renames itself the Congressional Caucus on Women's Issues and opens its doors to men who support women's issues.

Sandra Day O'Connor is appointed the first woman to the Supreme Court.

The Second Stage, by Betty Friedan, sees publication.

1982   *In a Different Voice*, by Carol Gilligan, is published.

The Equal Rights Amendment fails to gather the requisite number of states for ratification.

The Equal Rights Amendment is reintroduced into Congress.

Phyllis Schlafly opens an office in Washington, D.C., to expand her work beyond opposition to the Equal Rights Amendment.

Roger Jepsen (R–Iowa) introduces into Congress the Family Protection Act, which would reestablish prayer in the schools, forbid federal funding for school textbooks that portray women in nontraditional roles, repeal federal laws against child and spouse abuse, and prohibit coed sports. The act does not pass.

Ms. magazine's tenth anniversary issue publishes an article, "The Nouveau Poor," by Barbara Ehrenreich and Karin Stallard, that claims that "by the year 2000 all of the nation's poor will be women and their children."

1983   Sally Ride becomes the first American woman in space.

The Economic Equity Act is introduced into Congress, two titles of which are eventually passed reforming support payments and retirement benefits.

The Supreme Court in *City of Akron* v. *Akron Center* upholds parental consent requirements for minors seeking abortions.

1984   The Supreme Court in *Grove City College* v. *Bell* rules that only those programs funded directly with federal money need provide sex equity.

Democratic presidential candidate Walter Mondale chooses New York Representative Geraldine Ferraro as his vice presidential running mate.

Bella Abzug predicts a "gender gap" on the eve of the presidential election.

Congress passes the Retirement Equity Act to equalize benefits for women in private pension systems.

1985   The United Nations sponsors the Third International Conference on Women, in Nairobi, Kenya.

The Reagan administration unsuccessfully tries to eliminate Executive Order 11246 (see 1965).

The American Psychiatric Association removes homosexuality from the category of mental illness.

1986   The Meese Commission finds pornography "harmful" and a "social menace."

The Supreme Court rules in favor of Sears in *EEOC* v. *Sears Roebuck & Co.*

The Supreme Court in *Thornburgh* v. *American College of Obstetricians and Gynecologists* strikes down a requirement that a woman seeking an abortion be given a detailed description of fetal development.

1987   *Real Rape,* by Susan Estrich, is published.

William and Elizabeth Stern contract with Mary Beth Whitehead to carry a fetus to term. Whitehead later decides to keep the child, who becomes known as "Baby M."

1988   Congress passes the Civil Rights Restoration Act to restore full coverage of Title IX, reversing the Supreme Court's decision in *Grove City* v. *Bell* (see 1984).

1989   New York City extends rent-control regulations to cover gay couples living together for ten years or more.

Felice Schwartz publishes an article in the *Harvard Business Review* suggesting an alternative way for women with children to retain their professional careers, later dubbed the "Mommy Track."

The Supreme Court in *Webster* v. *Reproductive Services* upholds the constitutionality of Missouri's prohibition against the use of public funds for abortion.

1990   Congress passes the Americans with Disabilities Act, prohibiting discrimination on the basis of disability.

1991   At his confirmation hearing, Supreme Court Justice Clarence Thomas is accused by his former special assistant Anita Hill of sexual harassment.

A storm greets NOW president Patricia Ireland's revelation that she lives with a female companion.

New Jersey eliminates extra cash payments for children born to women already on welfare. NOW's Legal Defense and Education Fund sues on the grounds that such legislation is punitive.

The American Association of University Women publishes a searing critique called *How Schools Shortchange Girls.*

The Supreme Court in *Rust* v. *Sullivan* rules that the government can restrict Title X–funded clinics from counseling women on abortion.

The Supreme Court affirms that the government can deny foreign aid to overseas health organizations that promote abortion.

1992   The Supreme Court in *Planned Parenthood of Southeastern Pennsylvania* v. *Robert P. Casey* affirms a woman's right to abortion but allows certain restrictions based on a state's "compelling" interest in potential human life.

Colorado and Oregon pass antigay ordinances (overthrown by the Supreme Court in 1996).

1993   Congress passes the Family and Medical Leave Act, giving men and women protected, unpaid leave to respond to family emergencies.

The Tailhook scandal surfaces, in which naval aviators are accused of lewd behavior toward female naval officers at an annual convention.

Public Law 93-647 establishes a federal service to locate parents delinquent in child support payments.

Shannon Faulkner is admitted to The Citadel, only to be rejected when her gender is discovered.

Sheila Widnall, a professor of aeronautical engineering from MIT, is appointed secretary of the air force.

Members of Congress attack the National Endowment for the Arts–supported exhibit by photographer Robert Mapplethorpe as sexually explicit.

1994   The National Women's Political Caucus makes voter registration of women a primary goal.

The Supreme Court rules that obstruction of an abortion clinic is a crime.

1995   The United Nations sponsors the Fourth International Conference on Women, in Beijing, China.

The Office of Civil Rights continues to revise regulations for Title IX, enacted in 1972.

The University of California Board of Regents ends affirmative action in admissions, hiring, and contracting at all campuses.

Wal-Mart removes from its shelves, on the grounds that it is "antifamily," a T-shirt that reads, "Someday a woman will be President." The management later reverses itself.

1996   A U.N. tribunal indicts eight Bosnian Serb military and police officers in connection with rapes of Muslim women as prosecution for war-related crimes.

Senator Robert Packwood (R–Ore.) resigns his Senate seat in the wake of numerous allegations of sexual harassment.

The Supreme Court rules that The Citadel and the Virginia Military Institute must open admissions to women.

A sexual harassment class-action suit is brought against giant Japanese firm Mitsubishi.

Notes

Preface

1. See Chapter 9 for more on Phyllis Schlafly; Elizabeth Fox-Genovese, *Feminism Is Not the Story of My Life: How Today's Feminist Elite Has Lost Touch with the Real Concerns of Women* (New York: Doubleday, 1995); and Sylvia Ann Hewlett, *A Lesser Life: The Myth of Women's Liberation in America* (New York: Warner Books, 1986).

2. Personal communication from editor and writer Amy Loyd.

3. Martha Weinman Lear, "The Second Feminist Wave: What Do These Women *Want?*" *New York Times Magazine,* March 10, 1968, 24.

4. Catharine R. Stimpson categorized the tasks of women's studies in this form in frequent presentations between 1970 and 1973.

5. The course title was "The Evolution of Female Personality: Its History and Prospects" and was offered in the Department of Human Development and Family Studies thanks to the sponsorship of two professors in that department: Harold Feldman and Joy Osofsky.

6. Mariam Chamberlain, *Women in Academe: Progress and Prospects* (New York: Russell Sage Foundation, 1988).

7. *Female Studies I,* later extended by the Committee on Women of the Modern Language Association and others to twelve individual volumes on women's studies. For a collection of women's studies course syllabi, see Wendy Kolmar and Patricia Vogt, eds., *Selected Syllabi for Women's Studies Courses* (College Park, Md.: National Women's Studies Association, 1996). For a narrative look at women's studies graduates, see Barbara F. Luebke and Mary Ellen Reilly, *Women's Studies Graduates: The First Generation* (New York: Teachers College, 1995).

8. Sheila Tobias and Lisa Anderson, "What Really Happened to Rosie the Riveter?" in Linda Kerber and Jane deHart Mathews, eds., *Women in America: Refocusing Our Past* (New York: Oxford University Press, 1972), 354–373; Sheila Tobias, *Overcoming Math Anxiety* (New York: Norton, 1978); Jean Elshtain and Sheila Tobias, eds., *Women, Militarism, and War: Essays in History, Politics, and Social Theory* (Lanham, Md.: University Press of America, 1990), 163–185.

9. E. J. Dionne, *They Only Look Dead: Why Progressives Will Dominate the Next Era* (New York: Simon and Schuster, 1996), 312.

10. Catharine A. MacKinnon, *Only Words* (Cambridge, Mass.: Harvard University Press, 1993).

11. See Katie Roiphe, *The Morning After: Sex, Fear, and Feminism on Campus* (Boston: Little, Brown, 1993); and Naomi Wolf, *Fire with Fire: The New Female*

Power and How It Will Change the 21st Century (New York: Random House, 1993).

Chapter 1

1. Margaret Mead, *Sex and Temperament in Three Primitive Societies* (New York: William Morrow, 1935). See also Michele Rosaldo and Louise Lamphere, eds., *Women, Culture, and Society* (Stanford, Calif.: Stanford University Press, 1974).

2. Mead, *Sex and Temperament*, 55. Anne Oakley has updated Mead's work and found even more evidence of role and trait variability by gender. See Anne Oakley, *Sex, Gender, and Society* (London: Temple Smith, 1978). See also Jane F. Collier and Michele Z. Rosaldo, "Politics and Gender in Simple Societies," in Sherry Ortner and Harriet Whitehead, eds., *Sexual Meanings: The Cultural Construction of Gender and Sexuality* (Cambridge: Cambridge University Press, 1981), 275–329.

3. "Matriarchy" is sometimes confused with "matrilinearity." Matriarchy means rule by women; matrilinearity means that power and/or property is inherited through the mother's line. True matriarchy is rare; societies organized around matrilinearity are not.

4. Kate Millet, *Sexual Politics* (New York: Simon and Schuster, 1990), 23–58.

5. Dale Spender, in her reconsideration of the classic feminist texts, also considers *Sexual Politics* to be one of the "foundation stones" of feminist theory. See Dale Spender, *For the Record: The Making and Meaning of Feminist Knowledge* (London: Women's Press, 1985), 33.

6. Patriarchy is often defined by feminist scholars as the institutionalization of male self-interest.

7. The following analysis is from Millett, *Sexual Politics*, 23–58.

8. Ibid.

9. Virginia Woolf, *Three Guineas* (London: Hogarth Press, 1938).

10. Eighteen years later, Cynthia Epstein, reviewing sociological research, finds Millet's thesis still relevant. She writes, "Dichotomous systems of thought serve the existing power structures and organization of society by reinforcing the notions of 'we' and 'not we.'" Cynthia Epstein, *Deceptive Distortions: Sex, Gender, and the Social Order* (New Haven: Yale University Press, 1988), 233–235.

11. Jane O'Reilly coined the term *click!* experience in her article "The Housewife's Moment of Truth," *Ms.* (Spring 1972):54–55, 57–59.

12. See Stewart C. Gilmore, "Aging of Geophysicists," *Eos* 65, no. 20 (1984):353–354.

13. Linda Nochlin, "Why Have There Been No Great Women Artists?" *Art News* 69 (January 1971):22–39.

14. This insight is well represented in the writings of women of color. This particular formulation is from bell hooks, *Ain't I a Woman: Black Women and Feminism* (Boston: South End Press, 1981), 136–140. Bell hooks is a pseudonym for Professor of English Gloria Watkins. She writes her name without capital letters. References to her in this book reflect this preference.

15. For a discussion of the variables of class, race, and ethnicity as regards women's work, see William H. Chafe, *The Paradox of Change: American Women in the Twentieth Century* (New York: Oxford University Press, 1991).

16. hooks, *Ain't I,* 1–86.

17. Ibid., 159–196.

18. Johnnie Tilmon, a founder of the National Welfare Rights Organization, cited in Karen Anderson, *Changing Woman: A History of Racial Ethnic Women in Modern America* (New York: Oxford University Press, 1996), 212.

19. Friedrich Engels and Karl Marx, *The Communist Manifesto* (New York: Oxford University Press, 1992).

20. Aileen S. Kraditor, *The Ideas of the Woman Suffrage Movement: 1890–1920* (New York: Norton, 1981).

21. Carol Gilligan, *In a Different Voice: Psychological Theory and Women's Development* (Cambridge, Mass.: Harvard University Press, 1982).

22. Mary F. Belenky, B. M. Clinchy, N. R. Goldenberger, and J. M. Tarule, *Women's Ways of Knowing: The Development of Self, Voice, and Mind* (New York: Basic Books, 1986).

Chapter 2

1. Gerda Lerner, *The Grimké Sisters from South Carolina: Rebels Against Slavery* (Boston: Houghton Mifflin, 1967). See also the description of Angelina Grimké's conversion in Catharine Stimpson, *Where the Meanings Are: Feminism and Cultural Spaces* (New York: Methuen, 1988), 16–19.

2. Kristin Luker, *Abortion and the Politics of Motherhood* (Berkeley and Los Angeles: University of California Press, 1984), 11–39.

3. See Linda K. Kerber's discussion of how the property promised married women if they stayed loyal to the colonies during the Revolutionary War (after their husbands left for Canada to join the British) was denied them after 1800 in "May All Our Citizens Be Soldiers and All Our Soldiers Citizens: The Ambiguities of Female Citizenship in the New Nation," in Jean Bethke Elshtain and Sheila Tobias, eds., *Women, Militarism, and War: Essays in History, Politics, and Social Theory* (Lanham, Md.: University Press of America, 1990), 89–102.

4. The term *feminism* was first used in the early twentieth century and is not usually associated with the nineteenth century's women's rights movement. Historian Nancy Cott dates the first usage of that term to about 1911. I use the term here generically. See Nancy F. Cott, *The Grounding of Modern Feminism* (New Haven: Yale University Press, 1987), 11–16.

5. Lerner, *The Grimké Sisters*; and Harriet Beecher Stowe, *Uncle Tom's Cabin; or, Life Among the Lowly* (Boston: Houghton Mifflin, 1879).

6. The conflicts between social reformers and the suffragists is examined in William L. O'Neill, *Everyone Was Brave: The Rise and Fall of Feminism in America* (Chicago: Quadrangle Books, 1969).

7. Quoted in Stimpson, *Where the Meanings Are,* 17.

8. Sara Evans, *Personal Politics: The Roots of Women's Liberation in the Civil Rights Movement and the New Left* (New York: Vintage Books, 1980). See also Jo Freeman, *The Politics of Women's Liberation* (New York: Longman, 1975).

9. Eleanor Flexner, *Century of Struggle: The Women's Rights Movement in the United States*, rev. ed. (Cambridge, Mass.: Belknap Press, 1975), 78–102. See also Lois W. Banner, *Elizabeth Cady Stanton: A Radical for Woman's Rights* (Boston: Little, Brown, 1980); and Ellen Carol DuBois, ed., *Elizabeth Cady Stanton, Susan B. Anthony: Correspondence, Writings, Speeches* (New York: Schocken Books, 1981).

10. Later in the century, freed Negroes would organize their movement for the betterment of the people of their race in similar fashion. Called the "Convention" period in African-American history, leaders traveled the country speaking out on racial equality and founding chapters of their organizations as they went. See Louis Lomax, *The Negro Revolt* (New York: Harper, 1962).

11. "A Feminist Friendship: Elizabeth Cady Stanton (1815–1902) and Susan B. Anthony (1820–1906)," in Alice S. Rossi, ed., *The Feminist Papers* (New York: Columbia University Press, 1973).

12. There are many excellent histories and studies of women of color in America. On African-American women, see Paula Giddings, *When and Where I Enter: The Impact of Black Women on Race and Sex in America* (New York: Bantam Books, 1984); and bell hooks, *Ain't I a Woman: Black Women and Feminism* (Boston: South End Press, 1981). On Mexican-American women, see Margarita B. Melville, ed., *Twice a Minority: Mexican-American Women* (St. Louis: Mosby, 1980). On Native-American women, see Rayna Green, *Women in American Indian Society* (New York: Chelsea House Publishers, 1992). On Asian-American women, see Elaine H. Kim, *With Silk Wings: Asian-American Women at Work* (San Francisco: Asian Women United of California, 1983).

13. Harriet Tubman is one of a number of well-known exceptions. See Sarah H. Bradford, *Harriet Tubman* (New York: Corinth Books, 1961).

14. Marta Cotera, "Feminism: The Chicana and Anglo Versions," in Melville, ed., *Twice a Minority*, 220.

15. hooks, *Ain't I*, 136.

16. Ibid., 15–49.

17. Lillian Smith, *Killers of the Dream* (New York: Norton, 1949).

18. Calvin Herndon, *Sex and Racism in America* (New York: Grove Press, 1965).

19. Karen Anderson, *Changing Woman: A History of Racial Ethnic Women in Modern America* (New York: Oxford University Press, 1996), 7.

20. Giddings, *When and Where*, 65.

21. Flexner, *Century*, 190.

22. Ibid.

23. Melville, ed., *Twice a Minority.*

24. Ibid., 192.

25. Giddings, *When and Where*, 95.

26. Ibid., quoting nineteenth-century activist Anna Julia Cooper, 96.

27. Ibid., 97.

28. Ibid.

29. Quoted in ibid., 98.

30. This was a right that virtually disappeared in the South after 1876 with the imposition of literacy tests and poll taxes under so-called Jim Crow laws and did

not reappear until the Voter Registration Act, passed nearly ninety years later in 1965.

31. For an excellent discussion of this issue, see Ellen Carol DuBois, *Feminism and Suffrage, 1848–1869* (Ithaca: Cornell University Press, 1978), 53–104.

32. For a discussion of black women's ambivalence on the subject, see hooks, *Ain't I*, 3.

33. Giddings, *When and Where*, 65.

34. DuBois, *Feminism*, 189–196.

35. The 1848 Seneca Falls Convention did not list women's suffrage as a right.

36. Quoted in Rita Simon and Gloria Danziger, *Women's Movements in America* (New York: Praeger, 1991), 12.

37. Interestingly, both Democratic and Republican Party platforms endorsed women's suffrage in 1916, but the amendment did not pass until Republicans gained control of Congress in 1919. Twenty-nine of the thirty-five state legislatures that voted to ratify were Republican dominated. Also, Teddy Roosevelt embraced women's suffrage in his third-party run in 1912 against William Taft and Woodrow Wilson.

38. Carrie Chapman Catt, *Woman Suffrage and Politics: The Inner Story of the Suffrage Movement* (New York: Scribner's, 1923).

39. Edith Hoshino Altbach, *Women in America* (Boston: Heath, 1974), 122, commenting on the failure of the Nineteenth Amendment to guarantee suffrage; Marta Cotera, "Feminism," 223, commenting on the significance of the 1974 amendments.

40. This section borrows heavily from Aileen S. Kraditor, *The Ideas of the Woman Suffrage Movement, 1890–1920* (New York: Norton, 1981), 43–74.

41. As late as 1894, Elizabeth Cady Stanton, who had convened the original women's rights convention in 1848 and was still active in the movement, wrote a pamphlet with that statement as its title. Quoted in Kraditor, *The Ideas*, 45.

42. See ibid., 219–248.

43. O'Neill, *Everyone Was Brave*, 70. See also Kraditor, *The Ideas*, 163–218.

44. Kraditor, *The Ideas*, 163–218.

45. O'Neill, *Everyone Was Brave*, 273.

Chapter 3

1. Susan Ware, *Beyond Suffrage: Women in the New Deal* (Cambridge, Mass.: Harvard University Press, 1981).

2. Estelle B. Freedman, "The New Woman: Changing Views of Women in the 1920s," in Lois Scharf and Joan M. Jensen, eds., *Decades of Discontent: The Women's Movement, 1920–1940* (Westport, Conn.: Greenwood Press, 1983), 21–42.

3. These protections were called collectively "protective legislation" and are discussed in Chapter 4.

4. Freedman, "The New Woman," 27. Other revisionist history works consulted for this chapter include: Gerda Lerner, "New Approaches to the Study of Women in American History," *Journal of Social History* 3 (Fall 1969):53–62;

William Henry Chafe, *The Paradox of Change: American Women in the Twentieth Century* (New York: Oxford University Press, 1991); Eugenia Kaledin, *Mothers and More: American Women in the 1950s* (Boston: Twayne, 1984); Leila J. Rupp and Verta A. Taylor, *Survival in the Doldrums: The American Women's Rights Movement, 1945 to the 1960s* (New York: Oxford University Press, 1987); Susan Ware, *Holding Their Own: American Women in the 1930s* (Boston: Twayne, 1982); and Blanche Wiesen Cook, *Eleanor Roosevelt* (New York: Viking Press, 1992).

5. Jo Freeman, unpublished ms on the history of women's participation in the political parties. Noted here as Freeman, I–4.

6. Quoted in William L. O'Neill, *Everyone Was Brave: The Rise and Fall of Feminism in America* (Chicago: Quadrangle Books, 1969), 266.

7. Freeman, I–3.

8. Quoted in Freeman, I–1–1.

9. Freeman, I–1–3. A typical annual lobbying effort was for funds for the Children's Bureau, established in 1912, and the Women's Bureau, established in 1920.

10. By 1921, Rankin was no longer a member of Congress. She was defeated in November 1918 after voting against U.S. entry into World War I. She was re-elected to Congress in 1940 but defeated again in 1942 after voting against the country's involvement in World War II.

11. Freeman, I–1–3.

12. Ibid., I–1–4.

13. Ibid., I–1–5.

14. O'Neill, *Everyone Was Brave*, 265.

15. Ibid., 267.

16. Ibid., 274–275. Mrs. Oliver Belmont is referred to only by her husband's name.

17. These included women on the Right such as Phyllis Schlafly as well as feminists who thought the second wave had neglected motherhood, such as Sylvia Ann Hewlett, *A Lesser Life: The Myth of Women's Liberation in America* (New York: Warner Books, 1986).

18. Freeman, I–4–1.

19. Ibid.

20. Emma Wold, "Equal Rights in the Legislatures of 1925," *Equal Rights*, October 24, 1925, 295, cited in Freeman, I–3.

21. The story is related in Freeman, I–1–6/7.

22. Descriptions of what these women did is often accompanied by photographs: Betsy Ross darning the first American flag; Amelia Bloomer wearing the Turkish pantaloons she invented that gave women much more mobility than the huge, bustling skirts they used to wear; Carrie Nation, a die-hard temperance activist wielding her hatchet in the destruction of saloons; and finally Eleanor Roosevelt, President Roosevelt's able ambassador and champion of human rights, seated reading stories to little children.

23. Ware, *Beyond Suffrage*, 79. Even after the repeal of Section 213, however, and as late as 1939, banks, insurance companies, and public utilities continued to maintain restrictions on the employment of married women.

24. The late venerable magazine editor Norman Cousins wrote in 1939: "There are approximately ten million people out of work in the United States today. There are also ten million or more women married or single, who are job

holders. Simply fire the women who shouldn't be working anyway, and hire the men. Presto! No unemployment. No relief roles. No Depression." Quoted in Lillian Faderman, *Odd Girls and Twilight Lovers: A History of Lesbianism in Twentieth-Century America* (New York: Penguin, 1992), 96.

25. Sheila Tobias, "Shifting Heroisms: How Men Use Their War Service in Politics," in Jean B. Elshtain and Sheila Tobias, eds., *Women, Militarism, and War: Essays in History, Politics, and Social Theory* (Lanham, Md.: University Press of America, 1990), 163–185.

26. Ibid.

27. Ibid.

28. Susan Faludi, *Backlash: The Undeclared War Against American Women* (New York: Doubleday, 1991).

Chapter 4

1. In the first census taken of Americans, in 1890, 1.2 million women (largely immigrant women and American-born women of color) were working outside the home.

2. Barbara R. Bergmann, *The Economic Emergence of Women* (New York: Basic Books, 1986), 199–200.

3. Susan M. Hartmann, *The Home Front and Beyond: American Women in the 1940s* (Boston: Twayne, 1982), 86. For a fuller discussion of black women's employment, see Teresa Amott and Julie A. Matthai, *Race, Gender, and Work: A Multicultural History of Women in the U.S.* (Boston: South End Press, 1991).

4. Technically "free," they were in fact in bondage (peonage) to the landowner because of debt. As criminal codes were rewritten in the South to make indebtedness and vagrancy grounds for incarceration, black families, men and women alike, found themselves tied to the land quite as much as they had been during slavery. (See forthcoming book by James C. Clarke, *The Lineaments of Wrath*.)

5. For a detailed history of the employment patterns of racial-ethnic women in the United States, see Karen Anderson, *Changing Woman: A History of Racial Ethnic Women in Modern America* (New York: Oxford University Press, 1996), 67–184.

6. See Louise Kapp Howe, *Pink-Collar Workers* (New York: Putnam, 1977).

7. See Virginia Slims advertisements, which commonly feature women in Gibson Girl attire.

8. For a sophisticated but readily accessible analysis of women and work, see Francine Blau and Marianne Ferber, *The Economics of Women, Men, and Work*, 2d ed. (Englewood Cliffs, N.J.: Prentice-Hall, 1992).

9. These data are taken from ibid., 5.

10. American women of color and women from recently immigrated families may have had a 90 percent workforce participation during this entire period. Amott and Matthai, *Race, Gender*. Today married women take only one to four years out of employment to begin a family.

11. Paula Giddings, *When and Where I Enter: The Impact of Black Women on Race and Sex in America* (New York: Bantam Books, 1984), 142–148.

12. Sheila Tobias and Lisa Anderson, "What Really Happened to Rosie the Riveter?" in Linda Kerber and Jane DeHart Mathews, eds., *Women's America: Refocusing the Past* (New York: Oxford University Press, 1982), 354ff.

13. Black, migrant, and immigrant women always worked. See Anderson, *Changing Woman*, 92–122.

14. In 1800, the average American woman had eleven pregnancies, of which seven or eight were live births and of which six lived to adulthood. Between 1800 and 1900, the birthrate of American women fell by 40 percent. After World War II, on average (the period of the feminine mystique being an exception), a woman could expect that of her two or three pregnancies, all would live into adulthood.

15. Molly Haskell, *From Reverence to Rape: The Treatment of Women in the Movies* (Baltimore: Penguin, 1973).

16. Under the Social Security Act of 1935, until amended in 1977, old age and survivors' insurance provided a dependent wife with a pension equal to one-half of her husband's, but only after he retired and if the couple had divorced, only if the marriage had lasted twenty years. In 1977, the marriage duration requirement was changed to ten years. Although working women have the same pension rights through their employment as men, it is still the case that a *homemaker* cannot get a pension from social security *in her own right*. See Dorothy McBridge Stetson, *Women's Rights in the USA: Policy Debates and Gender Roles* (Pacific Grove, Calif.: Brooks/Cole, 1991), 243.

17. Alice Kessler-Harris and Karen Brodkin Sacks, "The Demise of Domesticity in America," in Lourdes Beneria and Catharine R. Stimpson, eds., *Women, Households, and the Economy* (New Brunswick, N.J.: Rutgers University Press, 1987), 65. See also Heidi I. Hartmann, "Changes in Women's Economic and Family Roles in Post World War II United States," in Beneria and Stimpson, eds., *Women*, 33ff.

18. See Ann Corinne Hill, "Protection of Women Workers and the Court: A Legal Case History," *Feminist Studies* 5, no. 2 (Summer 1979):247–273.

19. Myra Wolfgang, as reported by Eileen Shanahan, "Women Unionists Score Equality Plan," *New York Times*, September 10, 1970.

20. This section draws from the author's research, described in Tobias and Anderson, "What Really Happened?"; from the oral history of individual women war workers edited by Sherna Berger Gluck, *Rosie the Riveter Revisited* (New York: New American Library, 1987); and more generally from Karen Anderson, *Wartime Women: Sex Roles, Family Relations, and the Status of Women During World War II* (Westport, Conn.: Greenwood Press, 1981); Leila Rupp, *Mobilizing Women for War: German and American Propaganda, 1939–1945* (Princeton: Princeton University Press, 1978); Susan Hartmann, *The Home Front and Beyond: American Women in the 1940s* (Boston: Twayne, 1982), esp. 77–99; and Maureen Honey, *Creating Rosie the Riveter: Class, Gender, and Propaganda During World War II* (Amherst: University of Massachusetts Press, 1984).

21. Gluck, *Rosie*, 21.

22. Hartmann, *The Home Front*, 90–91.

23. The quotations in this section are taken from Connie Field, *The Life and Times of Rosie the Riveter*, motion picture (Franklin Lakes, N.J.: Clarity Educational Productions, 1980).

24. The entire workforce was reduced temporarily after the war while factories retooled for civilian work. But the shutdowns were only temporary and postwar unemployment (which was feared during the war) never materialized.

25. Hartmann's figures are 2.5 million additional women workers in heavy industry, representing an increase of 140 percent. Women increased their share of office work as well; manufacturing was better paid and, given unionization, should have been more secure. See Hartmann, *The Home Front*, 86, 88.

26. Marta Cotera, "Feminism: The Chicana and Anglo Versions," in Margarita B. Melville, ed., *Twice a Minority: Mexican-American Women* (St. Louis: Mosby, 1980), 225.

27. Tobias and Anderson, "What Really Happened?"

28. Ibid.

Chapter 5

1. Betty Friedan, *The Feminine Mystique* (New York: Norton, 1963).

2. Personal communication to the author.

3. Simone de Beauvoir, *The Second Sex* (New York: Knopf, 1953); first published as *Le Deuxieme Sexe* in 1949. Somewhat later treatments of the subject from an American point of view are Elizabeth Janeway, *Man's World, Woman's Place* (New York: Dell, 1971); and Carolyn Heilbrun, *Reinventing Womanhood* (New York: Norton, 1979).

4. Betty Friedan, *It Changed My Life: Writings on the Women's Movement* (New York: Random House, 1976). For an American view of "woman as outsider," see Heilbrun, *Reinventing Womanhood*, 37–70.

5. Susan Faludi, *Backlash: The Undeclared War Against American Women* (New York: Crown, 1991), 51.

6. Ibid., 51–53.

7. See Sheila Tobias, "Shifting Heroisms: How Men Use Their War Service in Politics," in Jean Bethke Elshtain and Sheila Tobias, eds., *Women, Militarism, and War: Essays in History, Politics, and Social Theory* (Lanham, Md.: University Press of America, 1990), 163–185.

8. Five million copies sold between 1964 and 1970.

9. Betty Friedan may have exaggerated her "housewife" status to identify with the women she wrote about in *The Feminine Mystique*. See Karen J. Winkler's account of Daniel Horowitz's work in *The American Quarterly*, which has sparked a controversy about the roots of Friedan's own feminism in her labor and progressive political activism prior to the 1960s. Karen J. Winkler, "Relooking at the Roots of Betty Friedan's Feminism," *Chronicle of Higher Education*, April 5, 1996, A10.

10. Juliet Mitchell, *Woman's Estate* (New York: Pantheon, 1971).

11. See Naomi Wolf, *The Beauty Myth* (London: Chatto and Windus, 1990).

12. John Bushnel, "Student Culture at Vassar," quoted in Friedan, *The Feminine Mystique*, 151–152.

13. Ibid.

14. Lost source. Personally communicated to the author in about 1958.

15. Friedan, *The Feminine Mystique*, 227.

16. Francine du Plessix Gray, *Soviet Women: Walking the Tightrope* (New York: Doubleday, 1989); and Dorothy Atkinson, Alexander Dallin, and Gail Warshofsky Lapidus, *Women in Russia* (Stanford: Stanford University Press, 1977).

17. Talcott Parsons and Robert F. Boles, *Family Socialization and Integration* (New York: Free Press, 1955).

18. Karen Horney, *Feminine Psychology* (New York: Norton, 1937).

19. Naomi Weisstein, "'Kinder, Kuche, Kirche' as Scientific Law: Psychology Constructs the Female," in Robin Morgan, ed., *Sisterhood Is Powerful* (New York: Random House, 1970), 228ff.

20. Friedan's summary of Freudian views of women in *The Feminine Mystique,* 115–120.

21. Friedan saw Freud's theory as "solipsistic," meaning self-identified, and so merely an extension of the narrow experience he had had as a firstborn male child in nineteenth-century Vienna.

22. See also Juliet Mitchell, *Psychoanalysis and Feminism* (New York: Penguin Books, 1974).

23. Marynia F. Farnham and Ferdinand Lundberg, *Modern Woman: The Lost Sex* (New York: Harper and Brothers, 1947).

24. Quoted in Friedan, *The Feminine Mystique,* 120.

25. Ibid.

26. Freud-bashing is no longer limited to feminists. The entire "talking therapy" and its basis in Freud's theory of personality are under review. See Paul Gray, "The Assault on Freud," *Time,* November 29, 1993, 46–51.

27. Bruno Bettelheim, quoted in Weisstein, "'Kinder,'" 229–230.

28. Erik Erikson, quoted in ibid.

29. Joseph Rheingold, quoted in ibid., 129–130.

30. There has been a great deal of writing since the 1970s on feminism and psychoanalysis, in this country and particularly in France. Mitchell, *Psychoanalysis;* Nancy Chodorow, *The Reproduction of Mothering: Psychoanalysis and the Sociology of Gender* (Berkeley and Los Angeles: University of California Press, 1978); and Elaine Marx and Isabelle de Courtivron, *The New French Feminisms* (New York: Schocken Books, 1981), review and contribute to that discussion. After the initial wholesale rejection of Freudianism, some feminists revised their assessment. Most important, there has been fast improvement, even "feminist approaches," to the clinical treatment of women patients. For an intelligent defense of Freud, see Elizabeth Young-Bruehl, *Freud on Women: A Reader* (New York: Norton, 1990), Introduction; for one more critical, see Edith Kurzweil, *Freudians and Feminists* (Boulder: Westview Press, 1995).

31. Gerden Lerner traces efforts to keep women in their place to preliterate societies in *Women and History,* vol. 1: *The Creation of Patriarchy,* and vol. 2: *The Creation of Feminist Consciousness* (New York: Oxford University Press, 1986 and 1993, respectively). See also Sheila Ruth, *Take Back the Light: A Feminist Reclamation of Spirituality and Religion* (New York: Rowman and Littlefield, 1994), Appendix.

Chapter 6

1. Historian Daniel Horowitz is at pains to show Betty Friedan's own roots in left-wing labor journalism. See Karen J. Winkler's account of David Horowitz's

work in the *American Quarterly,* in "Relooking at the Roots of Betty Friedan's Feminism," *Chronicle of Higher Education,* April 5, 1996, A10.

2. See Jo Freeman, *Social Movements of the Sixties and Seventies* (New York: Longman, 1983), 19ff.

3. A good but brief summary of the commissions' work can be found in Leila J. Rupp and Verta A. Taylor, *Survival in the Doldrums: The American Women's Rights Movement, 1945 to the 1960s* (Columbus: Ohio University Press, 1990), 167–174.

4. Quoted in ibid., 169.

5. Ibid.

6. An exception to almost all of this was Pauli Murray, a young black member of the commission, who urged the members to get the Supreme Court to begin interpreting the equal protection clause of the Fourteenth Amendment to guarantee women's equality.

7. *American Women: The Report of the President's Commission on the Status of Women* (Washington, D.C.: GPO, 1963; Margaret Mead, ed., *American Women: The Report of the President's Commission on the Status of Women and Other Publications of the Commission* (New York: Scribner's, 1965); Susan Hartmann, *From Margin to Mainstream: American Women and Politics Since 1960* (New York: Knopf, 1989), 52.

8. *American Women.*

9. Hartmann, *From Margin,* quoting Pauli Murray, 53.

10. Jo Freeman, *The Politics of Women's Liberation* (New York: Longman, 1975); Sara Evans, *Personal Politics: The Roots of Women's Liberation in the Civil Rights Movement and the New Left* (New York: Vintage Books, 1980); Pamela Allen, *Free Space: A Perspective in the Small Group in Women's Liberation* (Ojai, Calif.: Times Change Press, 1970); Rita Simon and Gloria Danziger, *Women's Movements in America* (New York: Praeger, 1991); and Louise A. Tilly and Patricia Guin, eds., *Women, Politics, and Change* (New York: Russell Sage, 1992). For the story in England, see Ann Coote and Bea Campbell, *Sweet Freedom and the Struggle for Women's Liberation* (London: Pan Books, 1982).

11. My own activism took place during summer 1963 when I worked with an "Upward Bound" program in a previously segregated school system in Charleston, South Carolina, living with an African-American family, and in summer 1964 when I traveled through Virginia, North Carolina, Georgia, Alabama, and Mississippi interviewing civil rights activists and studying their programs.

12. Evans, *Personal Politics,* 82.

13. Flora Davis, *Moving the Mountain* (New York: Simon and Schuster, 1991), 73.

14. Ibid.

15. Freeman, *The Politics,* 44–70. See also Hartmann, *From Margin,* 48–71; Myra Marx Ferree and Beth B. Hess, *Controversy and Coalition: The New Feminist Movement* (Boston: Twayne, 1985), 45–70; Alice Echols, *Daring to Be Bad: Radical Feminism in America, 1967–1975* (Minneapolis: University of Minnesota Press, 1989), 103–137; and Ginette Castro, *American Feminism: A Contemporary History* (New York: New York University Press, 1990).

16. Casey Hayden and Mary King, "Sex as Caste," appeared in two parts in the radical periodical *Liberation* (April and December 1966).

17. Davis, *Moving*, 77.

18. Evans, *Personal Politics*, 160, quoting James Weinstein.

19. Paula Giddings, *When and Where I Enter: The Impact of Black Women on Race and Sex in America* (New York: Bantam Books, 1984), 302.

20. Naomi Weisstein, "Woman as Nigger," in a collection of early women's liberation papers, collected and published "underground" by Jo Ann Gardner (Pittsburgh: KNOW Press, 1967); *off our backs* is a Washington, D.C.-based newspaper still being published in 1997; *Up from the Pedestal: Selected Writings in the History of American Feminism* is the title of a volume of early essays edited by Aileen S. Kraditor (Chicago: Quadrangle, 1968); "Bread and Roses" is the title of a journal and a group in Boston.

21. Evans, *Personal Politics*, 160.

22. In the traditional telling of this story, Smith is the villain, indifferent to women's rights, presenting the amendment as a maneuver to scuttle Title VII. Smith, however, had supported the Equal Rights Amendment as early as 1943 and was in receipt of a letter from the National Woman's Party urging him to add "sex" to the bill. Historians Rupp and Taylor conclude from their review of interviews and other new findings that "Smith's motives in all of this are not totally clear. While it is certainly true that he wanted to defeat the Civil Rights Act, . . . his legislative assistants reported that he would not have voted for something in which he did not believe." Rupp and Taylor, *Survival*, 177. For other versions of the story, see Hartmann, *From Margin*, 53–56. A longer scholarly account can be found in Carl M. Brauer, "Women Activists, Southern Conservatives, and the Prohibition of Sex Discrimination in Title VII of the 1964 Civil Rights Act," *Journal of Southern History* 49 (February 1983):41–51.

23. Hartmann, *From Margin*, 55, quoting Brauer.

24. Such was the case with the passage of the massive and complex Social Security Act of 1935. An entire new Social Security Administration was created to enforce the act.

25. Sonia Fuentes, unpublished talk, n.d.

26. Mary Eastwood and Pauli Murray, "Jane Crow and the Law: Sex Discrimination and Title VII," *George Washington Law Review* 34, no. 2 (1965):232–256.

27. As quoted in Hartmann, *From Margin*, 58. See also Patricia G. Zelman, *Women, Work, and National Policy: The Kennedy-Johnson Years* (Ann Arbor, Mich.: UMI Research Press, 1982), 92–105.

28. Toni Carabillo, "A Passion for the Possible," in Toni Carabillo et al., *The Feminist Chronicles: 1953–1993* (Los Angeles: Women's Graphics, 1993), 15.

29. Founding documents of NOW.

30. I and the thirty or so women who organized the Conference on Women at Cornell University in winter 1969, to which Betty Friedan of the second strand and Kate Millett and other women's liberationists from the third strand were both invited, established our own Finger Lakes chapter of NOW that spring. Needless to say, we were not aware of the "strand" analysis at the time. But we did have a sense that we were "making history." Gloria Steinem remembers my calling to invite her to the Cornell conference not as a feminist—neither she nor I would have called ourselves that in 1969—but as a presswoman to cover what I called, with some prescience, "the story of the decade."

31. The league may have thought itself "less controversial," but soon after, member Bernice Sandler challenged two hundred major universities in the country to meet federal "affirmative action guidelines" in women's employment. See Chapter 8.

32. Dorothy Haener and other union women from the United Auto Workers stayed with NOW despite some personal misgivings about Title VII. Later, the UAW heartily supported Title VII.

33. Pamela Allen, *Free Space: A Perspective on the Small Group in Women's Liberation* (Washington, N.J.: Times Change Press, 1970). The technique was already known as a means of community organizing through the writings of Paulo Freire, *Pedagogy of the Oppressed* (New York: Seabury Press, 1970).

34. See Germaine Greer, *The Female Eunuch* (London: MacGibbon and Kee, 1970); and Dale Spender, *For the Record: The Making and Meaning of Feminist Knowledge* (London: Women's Press, 1985).

35. Nan Robertson, *The Girls in the Balcony: Women, Men, and the New York Times* (New York: Random House, 1992).

36. "In 1971, a New York newspaper wrote of Judge Mildred Loree Lillie, 'In her mid-50s, she still has a bathing beauty figure.' Judge Lillie made the news as a possible nominee for the Supreme Court." Davis, *Moving*, 108–109.

37. Ibid., 17.

38. Ibid.

39. Ibid., 16.

40. Aileen Hernandez became the second president of NOW.

41. Patricia Ireland, NOW's president from 1991 to the present, began her work life as a flight attendant.

42. Giddings, *When and Where*, 299–304.

43. Writer Toni Morrison has won both the Pulitzer and the Nobel Prizes for her work.

44. Toni Morrison, "What the Black Woman Thinks About Women's Lib," *New York Times Magazine*, August 22, 1971, 15, quoted in Giddings, *When and Where*, 307.

45. Quoted in ibid., 309.

46. At the peak of the National Black Feminist Organization, it had two thousand members in ten chapters.

47. Gloria I. Joseph and Jill Lewis, *Common Differences: Conflicts in Black and White Feminist Perspectives* (New York: Doubleday, 1981), 69.

48. Ibid., 66–68.

49. Hartmann, *From Margin*, 38.

50. Marta Cotera, "Feminism: The Chicana and Anglo Versions," in Margarita B. Melville, ed., *Twice a Minority: Mexican-American Women* (St. Louis: Mosby, 1980), 227.

51. William Chafe, *American Women in the Twentieth Century* (New York: Oxford University Press, 1991), 238.

Chapter 7

1. This analysis is borrowed in part from that of Joyce Gelb and Marian Lief Palley's role equity/role change distinctions as laid out in *Women and Public*

Policies, rev. ed. (Princeton: Princeton University Press, 1987). The third "generation" of issues is my own contribution.

2. Equal Credit Opportunity Act, 1974. See ibid., 61ff, for an entire chapter on the Equal Credit Opportunity Act.

3. Felice N. Schwartz, "Management Women and the New Facts of Life," *Harvard Business Review* 65, no. 1 (1989):65.

4. Note the title of Sara Evans's history of the birth of women's liberation, *Personal Politics: The Roots of Women's Liberation in the Civil Rights Movement and the New Left* (New York: Random House, 1979).

5. National Organization for Women Bill of Rights in 1968 (adopted at the 1967 National Conference, here reprinted by permission of the National Organization for Women)

> I. Equal Rights Constitutional Amendment
> II. Enforce Law Banning Sex Discrimination in Employment
> III. Maternity Leave Rights in Employment and in Social Security Benefits
> IV. Tax Deduction for Home and Child Care Expenses for Working Parents
> V. Child Day Care Centers
> VI. Equal and Unsegregated Education
> VII. Equal Job Training Opportunities and Allowances for Women in Poverty
> VIII. The Right of Women to Control Their Reproductive Lives
> We Demand,

I. That the United States Congress immediately pass the Equal Rights Amendment to the Constitution to provide that "Equality of rights under the law shall not be denied or abridged by the United States or by any State on account of sex" and that such then be immediately ratified by the several States.

II. That equal employment opportunity be guaranteed to all women, as well as men, by insisting that the Equal Employment Opportunity Commission enforce the prohibitions against sex discrimination in employment under Title VII of the Civil Rights Act of 1964 with the same vigor as it enforces the prohibition against racial discrimination.

III. That women be protected by law to insure their rights to return to their jobs within a reasonable time after childbirth without loss of seniority or other accrued benefits and be paid maternity leave as a form of social security and/or employee benefit.

IV. Immediate revision of tax laws to permit the deduction of home and child care expenses for working parents.

V. That child care facilities be established by law on the same basis as parks, libraries and public schools adequate to the needs of children, from the pre-school years through adolescence, as a community resource to be used by all citizen from all income levels.

VI. That the right of women to be educated to their full potential equally with men be secured by Federal and State legislation, eliminating all discrimination and segregation by sex, written and unwritten, at all levels of education including college, graduate and professional schools, loans and fellowships and Federal and State training programs, such as the Job Corps.

VII. The right of women in poverty to secure job training, housing and family allowances on equal terms with men, without prejudice to a parent's right to remain at home to care for his or her children; revision of welfare legislation and poverty programs which deny women dignity, privacy and self-respect.

VIII. The right of women to control their own reproductive lives by removing from penal codes the laws limiting access to contraceptive information and devices and laws governing abortion.

6. Feminist think tanks were very important in providing the research for bills and testimony, for public education and court challenges. The earliest, still in existence, is the Center for Women Policy Studies in Washington, D.C. But many others were funded by private foundations and affiliated with colleges and universities. Another model was the "project" or "commission" on women or women's issues set up within an existing organization, such as the American Council on Education and the Association of American, and the "Federal Women's Programs" established during the 1970s in every federal agency.

7. Susan Faludi ably chronicles the shift in *Backlash: The Undeclared War Against American Women* (New York: Crown, 1991).

8. In 1981, the Department of Health, Education, and Welfare was dissolved, and two new departments were created, the Department of Education and the Department of Health and Human Services.

9. The importance of Susan Brownmiller's book *Against Our Will: Men, Women, and Rape* (New York: Simon and Schuster, 1975), a history and sociological analysis of rape, cannot be overestimated. For an analysis of the changes in rape law, see Susan Estrich, *Real Rape: How the Legal System Victimizes Women Who Say No* (Cambridge, Mass.: Harvard University Press, 1987).

10. The most complete analysis of the shifting arguments for paying women less than men is provided by Alice Kessler-Harris, *A Woman's Wage: Historical Meanings and Social Consequences* (Lexington: University Press of Kentucky, 1990).

11. For a brief discussion of the history of the Equal Pay Act, see Rita Simon and Gloria Danziger, *Women's Movements in America* (New York: Praeger, 1991), 45–67.

12. For the story of women journalists' efforts to achieve job and pay parity at the *New York Times*, see Nan Robertson, *The Girls in the Balcony: Women, Men, and the New York Times* (New York: Random House, 1992).

13. Eileen Shanahan, "Equal Rights Plan for Women Voted by House, 350–15," *New York Times*, August 11, 1970, embedded in a story on passage of the Equal Rights Amendment for the first time in the House.

14. The full title was *Alert: Women's Legislative Review.* The founding editors were the late Poppy Palewski and Harriette Behringer. Other statewide publications were far larger in size and longer in duration than *Alert. The Clarion: Southern Arizona's Feminist Forum* has been publishing for twenty years; Utah, New Jersey, North Carolina, and, of course, the major cities were known for the lively journalism of their local feminist publications. The total number is probably unknown, although the *Ms.* Foundation maintained files for a while.

15. AT&T was "picked" as a target by the EEOC both because so many complaints had already lodged against it with the commission (eighteen hundred by 1971) and because it was part of a "consolidation strategy" authored by EEOC

commissioner William H. Brown. The company's visibility as an industrial giant was no doubt also a factor. See Eileen Shanahan, "Four–Six Giant Companies Being Picked as Feds Target on Discrimination," *New York Times*, July 30, 1973.

16. In an early and chilling feminist analysis of "life in the telephone company," writer Eleanor Langer revealed to middle-class women the regimented and oppressive treatment of telephone operators. Eleanor Langer, "Inside the New York Telephone Company," in William L. O'Neill, ed., *Women at Work* (Chicago: Quadrangle Books, 1972), 307ff.

17. Because telephone operators could be promoted only to supervisors of other operators, all other management pathways were closed to them.

18. *Weeks* v. *Southern Bell*, March 1969, Georgia Appeals Court ruling.

19. The main impact of affirmative action for minorities was in the building trades. For women, it would be in professional and technical job categories.

20. See Richard Lester's argument against affirmative action in universities in *Antibias Regulation of Universities: Faculty Problems and Their Solutions* (New York: McGraw-Hill, 1974).

21. Gelb and Palley, *Women and Public Policies*, 61–92.

22. Ibid.

23. Ibid., 82.

24. Details about the conference are taken from Caroline Bird and the members and staff of the National Commission on the Observance of International Women's Year, *What Women Want: The Official Report to the President, the Congress, and the People of the United States on the National Women's Conference at Houston, Texas, November, 1977* (Washington, D.C.: GPO, 1978).

Chapter 8

1. See Joyce Gelb and Marian Lief Palley, *Women and Public Policies*, rev. ed. (Princeton: Princeton University Press, 1987), for a full discussion of the difference between role equity and role change issues.

2. See the Shannon Faulkner case, discussed later in this chapter.

3. Susan Brownmiller, *Against Our Will: Men, Women, and Rape* (New York: Simon and Schuster, 1975), 403.

4. Ibid., 439.

5. Phyllis Chesler, "What Is Justice for a Rape Victim?" *On the Issues* (Winter 1996):12ff.

6. Marlise Simons, "For the First Time, Court Defines Rape as War Crime," *New York Times*, June 28, 1996.

7. The term *date rape* first appeared in an article by Karen Barett, "Date Rape: A Campus Epidemic," *Ms.* (September 1982):48–51.

8. Susan Estrich, *Real Rape: How the Legal System Victimizes Women Who Say No* (Cambridge, Mass.: Harvard University Press, 1987), 130.

9. Norman Podhoretz, "Rape in Feminist Eyes," *Commentary* 92, no. 4 (October 1991):29.

10. Twenty-seven percent of college-age women told survey researcher Mary Koss of the University of Arizona Medical School, Department of Psychiatry, that

they had experienced sexual assault. Neil Gilbert, a professor of social welfare at the University of California, Berkeley, challenged these figures. See Neil Gilbert, "The Phantom Epidemic of Sexual Assault," *The Public Interest* (Spring 1991):54; Neil Gilbert, "The Campus Rape Scare," *Wall Street Journal*, June 7, 1991, editorial page; and Neil Gilbert, "The Wrong Response to Rape, *Wall Street Journal*, June 29, 1993, editorial page.

11. This last is Katie Roiphe's argument. In *The Morning After: Sex, Fear, and Feminism on Campus* (New York: Little, Brown, 1993), Roiphe argues that the issues of date rape and sexual harassment have turned the movement into "victim feminism."

12. This sentence is taken from Katha Pollitt's critical review of Roiphe, *The Morning After*, in "Not Just Bad Sex," *New Yorker*, October 4, 1993, 223.

13. Catherine MacKinnon, *Sexual Harassment of Working Women* (New Haven: Yale University Press, 1979), 217–218.

14. Quoted in *Sexual Harassment: Research and Resources* (New York: National Council for Research on Women, November 1992), 3–4. In 1986, the Supreme Court, in *Meritor Savings Bank* v. *Vinson*, upheld the EEOC guidelines, ruling unanimously that sexual harassment violated Title VII.

15. Stephanie Riger, "Gender Dilemmas in Sexual Harassment Policies and Procedures," *American Psychologist* 46, no. 5 (1991):497.

16. In addition to news magazine coverage, two books summarize the event, albeit from different sides: Jane Mayer and Jill Abramson, *Strange Justice: The Selling of Clarence Thomas* (Boston: Houghton Mifflin, 1994); and David Brock, *The Real Anita Hill: The Untold Story* (New York: Free Press, 1993).

17. Jill Abramson, "Women's Anger About Hill-Thomas Hearings Has Brought Cash into Female Political Caucuses," *Wall Street Journal*, January 6, 1992.

18. Anita Hill, "The Nature of the Beast," *Ms.* (January-February 1992):32, 33.

19. Anna Quindlen, "The Perfect Victim," *New York Times*, October 16, 1991.

20. See Nancy Gibbs, "An Ugly Circus," Jill Smolowe, "He Said, She Said," and Richard Lacayo, "A Question of Character," *Time*, October 21, 1991, 35, 36–40, and 43–44, respectively.

21. For more on the Tailhook scandal, see Melissa Healy, "140 Officers Faulted in Tailhook Sex Scandal," *Los Angeles Times*, April 24, 1993.

22. Mayer and Abramson, *Strange Justice*, 352.

23. As reported in *Time*, October 21, 1991, 63.

24. See profile of Healy in the *Washington Post Magazine*, June 21, 1992, 9–13.

25. Frances Lynch, Pima County Justice, as reported in *Arizona Daily Star*, October 9, 1995.

26. From Anita Hill's testimony, quoted in Mayer and Abramson, *Strange Justice*, 97.

27. Louise F. Fitzgerald and A. J. Ormerod, "Breaking Silence: The Sexual Harassment of Women in Academia and the Workplace," in F. Denmark and M. Paludi, eds., *Handbook of the Psychology of Women* (New York: Greenwood Press, forthcoming).

28. These figures are quoted in *Sexual Harassment*, 10.

29. Susan Faludi, author of *Backlash: The Undeclared War Against American Women* (New York: Crown, 1991), quoted in *Time*, October 21, 1991, 53.

30. The issue of no-fault and its economic consequences for women is comprehensively summarized by Lenore J. Weitzman, *The Divorce Revolution: The Unexpected Social and Economic Consequences for Women and Children in America* (New York: Free Press, 1985); and by Frank F. Furstenberg and Andrew J. Cherlin, *Divided Families: What Happens to Children When Parents Part* (Cambridge, Mass.: Harvard University Press, 1991).

31. Weitzman, *The Divorce Revolution*, 16–19.

32. Ibid., 27–28.

33. The study, done by Greg J. Duncan and Saul D. Hoffman, is cited in Furstenberg and Cherlin, *Divided Families*, 50.

34. Weitzman, *The Divorce Revolution*, 143. See also Cynthia Fuchs Epstein, *Deceptive Distinctions: Sex, Gender, and the Social Order* (New Haven: Yale University Press, 1988), 205.

35. The Supreme Court, in *Orr v. Orr* (1979), decided in favor of such a husband in finding an Alabama state law unconstitutional that provided that *only* husbands could be required to pay alimony. The statute was found unconstitutional, even without the ERA, because it provided "differential treatment on the basis of sex."

36. Weitzman, *The Divorce Revolution*, 393–394.

37. Typically within one year after divorce, 20 percent of fathers comply only partially with child support requirements, and 42 percent make no payments. By the tenth year after divorce, only 13 percent of fathers comply fully. Economist Barbara Bergmann concludes that "the poor state of child support enforcement has made the acceptance of the custody of a child a financially punishing experience for women." Barbara Bergmann, *The Economic Emergence of Women* (New York: Basic Books, 1986), 249.

38. Called the "runaway pappy bill," the legislation was pushed by President Gerald Ford, who himself had been abandoned by his father.

39. California's 50 percent divorce rate in 1970—far ahead of the rest of the nation—is now the average in the United States and in Europe.

40. In the 1990s, no-fault divorce itself came under fire. Governors and legislatures in three midwestern states—Michigan, Iowa, and, to a lesser extent, Illinois—proposed changing divorce laws to make it more difficult for families to separate. Some proposals would require a mandatory waiting period of at least one year, during which couples would have to undergo counseling to see if the marriage could be saved. See Myriam Marquez, "Promoting Loveless Marriages over Divorce Is in Vogue," *Arizona Daily Star*, January 12, 1996.

41. Gelb and Palley, *Women and Public Policies*, 93, 112. Susan Hartmann, *From Margin to Mainstream: American Women and Politics Since 1960* (New York: Knopf, 1989), 110.

42. Opponent Michael Levin promotes this misunderstanding in his chapter "Sports," in *Feminism and Freedom* (New Brunswick: Transaction Books, 1988), 208ff.

43. Gelb and Palley, *Women and Public Policies*, 109.

44. Hartmann, *From Margin*, 109.

45. Gelb and Palley, *Women and Public Policies*, 119.

46. The Supreme Court's decision rested on its interpretation of Congress's "intent" in passing the education amendments in the first place, not on any constitutional question. Hence, a new statute clarifying Congress's intent was sufficient to "overthrow" the previous decision. This would not have been possible had the Court stated that federal interference in college programs was unconstitutional. See Project on the Status and Education of Women, "The Restoration of Title IX: Implications for Higher Education" (Washington, D.C.: Association of American Colleges, 1989).

47. The coalition was led by the Leadership Conference on Civil Rights and the National Coalition for Women and Girls in Education.

48. She won the suit but left the academy soon after the school year began, citing exhaustion (her male classmates were unrelenting in their challenges to her). The Citadel thought it had won, but the following year six young women with unambiguous female first names followed Shannon Faulkner's steps and applied. For more on the case, see George Hackett and Mark Miller, "Manning the Barricades," *Newsweek*, March 26, 1990, 18.

49. This view has been provided the author by Bernice Sandler, formerly director of the Project on the Status and Education of Women at the Association of American Colleges in Washington, D.C., and Ramon Villareal of the Office of Civil Rights, Department of Education, Denver region.

50. The enforcement agency in this sense is the Office of Federal Contract Compliance in the Department of Labor.

51. A more legitimate complaint was the increased effort to locate labor pools, do the internal counts and comparisons, and write reports—an increase in paperwork and staff time. Particularly hard hit were the smaller businesses.

52. For an analysis of the differences in the impact of civil rights and affirmative action on black women in the professions, see Natalie J. Sokoloff, *Black Women and White Women in the Professions* (New York: Routledge, 1992). For a 1995 update on the benefits of affirmative action for women, see Bob Cohn, Bill Turque, and Martha Brant, "What About Women? Affirmative Action: The White House Searches for Ways to Regain Control of a Treacherous Issue," *Newsweek*, March 27, 1995, 22–25.

53. The Public Works Employment Act of 1977 reserved a portion of federal contracts for firms whose boards of directors were 51 percent female.

54. Reported in Cohn, Turque, and Brant, "What About Women?" With one-third of MBA students made up of women in the mid-1990s, these figures are likely to go up. One eloquent African American sees affirmative action as having been essential to educated professionals like himself. Stephen L. Carter, *Reflections of an Affirmative Action Baby* (New York: Basic Books, 1991).

55. Occupational segregation—defined as job categories in which 90 percent or more of the jobs are held by one sex—remains substantial in the U.S. workforce and worse than in many other industrialized countries. See Francine Blau and Marianne Ferber, *The Economics of Women, Men, and Work* (Englewood Cliff, N.J.: Prentice-Hall, 1986), Table 6.6, 167.

56. Carol G. Carson and Faye J. Crosby, "Rx: Affirmative Action," *Smith Alumnae Quarterly* (Winter 1989):12.

57. A strong case for affirmative action's inefficiency (in terms of overall cost and loss of productivity) is made by Michael Levin, *Feminism and Freedom*, 112–126.

58. See *University of California Regents* v. *Bakke*, 1978, later, substantially modified in the 1996 *Hopwood* decision, which prohibited the use of racial preference in admissions.

59. In the 1987 decision in *Johnson* v. *Transportation Agency*, the Court allowed an affirmative action plan at the transportation agency to stand. But in 1989, in five separate cases, the Supreme Court reversed itself again, making it easier for employers to prevail in employment discrimination cases. Typical was *Wards Cove Packing Co.* v. *Atonio* and *Patterson* v. *McLean Credit Union*, which made it harder for employees to prevail in sex and race discrimination complaints.

60. Kathryn J. Rodgers, "Affirmative Action: A Women's Issue," *NOW Legal Defense and Education Fund* (Fall 1995):2.

61. *Newsweek*, March 27, 1995, 22.

62. Feminists have not shied away from a class analysis. See Chapter 11 for a brief discussion of Marxist feminists and socialist feminists. For examples, see Angela Y. Davis, *Women, Race, and Class* (New York: Random House, 1981); and Heidi Hartmann, "Capitalism, Patriarchy, and Job Segregation by Sex," *Signs* 1, no. 3, part 2 (1976):773–776. For an earlier study, see Juliet Mitchell, *Woman's Estate* (New York: Pantheon, 1971).

63. Because few feminists oppose abortion and because abortion has become a banner for antifeminism, it is to my way of thinking a second-generation issue (one on which feminists agree) rather than a third-generation issue (one on which even feminists disagree). For both overview and details on the politics of abortion, see Kristin Luker, *Abortion and the Politics of Motherhood* (Berkeley and Los Angeles: University of California Press, 1984). Sarah Weddington, *A Question of Choice* (New York: Putnam, 1992); Marian Faux, *Roe v. Wade* (New York: New American Library, 1988); and Laurence H. Tribe, *Abortion: The Clash of Absolutes* (New York: Norton, 1990). For a detailed history of the issue, see Chapter 14.

64. Beginning in 1976, Representative Henry Hyde, a Republican from Illinois, successfully attached an abortion exclusion to every federal appropriation bill, making it impossible to use federal moneys—through Medicaid—to pay for abortions.

65. See Gelb and Palley, *Women and Public Policies*, 162–174, for an excellent recounting of the events.

66. Ibid., 68.

Chapter 9

1. For more discussion of the divisions among earlier feminists on the Equal Rights Amendment, consult Nancy Cott, *The Grounding of American Feminism* (New Haven: Yale University Press, 1987); and William L. O'Neill, *Everyone Was Brave: The Rise and Fall of Feminism in America* (Chicago: Quadrangle Books, 1971).

2. Eileen Shanahan's reporting of the debates in the House and Senate for the *New York Times* are must reading for feminists and scholars. Beginning in 1970, Shanahan was to bring the arguments to a far wider public than would ordinarily have heard about them—and on page 1 of her newspaper. See Eileen Shanahan, "Equal Rights Plan for Women Voted by House 350–15," *New York Times*, August 11, 1970; and subsequent coverage during 1970, 1971, and 1972.

3. Ibid.

4. The states rescinding approval of the ERA were Nebraska, Tennessee, Kentucky, Idaho, and South Dakota.

5. For a more extensive discussion of the failure to ratify the ERA, see Jane Mansbridge, *Why We Lost the ERA* (Chicago: University of Chicago Press, 1986); Mary Frances Berry, *Why ERA Failed* (Bloomington: Indiana University Press, 1986); and Donald G. Mathews and Jane Sherron De Hart, *Sex, Gender, and the Politics of ERA* (New York: Oxford University Press, 1990).

6. Susan M. Hartmann, *From Margin to Mainstream: American Women and Politics Since 1960* (New York: Knopf, 1989), is an exception. See 130–152.

7. The main book-length biography of Phyllis Schlafly is Carol Felsenthal, *Phyllis Schlafly: The Sweetheart of the Silent Majority* (Garden City, N.Y.: Doubleday, 1981). Felsenthal, a Chicago-based journalist, started out as a detractor but became, as she reports it herself in her book, an admirer of Schlafly's. The book eventually had Schlafly's stamp of approval. When it went out of print (the original publisher was Doubleday), Schlafly complained that the "libbers" had threatened to boycott bookstores that carried the book. Since that time, her office makes it readily available at cost out of her own printing establishment, Père Marquette Press. Thus, the biography can be considered quasi-authorized.

8. I like to think it was me whom she was asked to debate because at the time I was actively promoting feminism around the state of Connecticut.

9. Barbara Ehrenreich, *The Hearts of Men* (New York: Doubleday, 1983), 152.

10. From Felsenthal, *Sweetheart*, as quoted in ibid., 153.

11. Ibid.

12. Ibid., 155.

13. Ibid., 156.

14. Berry, *Why ERA Failed*, 65.

15. From a taped speech of Phyllis Schlafly's circa 1976 in author's possession.

16. From a classic speech on audiotape given by Phyllis Schlafly in Georgia to a group of churchgoing women in 1979.

17. Ibid.

18. Even as the federal ERA was failing, many state ERAs were passed in the 1970s. Having the ERA in sixteen state constitutions required divorce courts in those states to recognize homemakers as financial contributors to the value of the home upon divorce; Schlafly, however, managed to deflect that fact and play instead on her followers' overarching fear of divorce. See Flora Davis, *Moving the Mountain* (New York: Simon and Schuster, 1991), 389.

19. Rebecca E. Klatch, *Women on the New Right* (Philadelphia: Temple University Press, 1987), 24.

20. Schlafly, *The Power of the Positive Woman*, quoted in Ehrenreich, *The Hearts*, 148.

21. Ibid., 148–149.

22. From the classic Schlafly speech.

23. Ibid.

24. Klatch, *Women on the New Right,* 24.

25. Ibid., 34. It follows logically that social conservatives will subscribe to pre-scribed gender roles; laissez-faire conservatives might permit gender roles to vary with individuals.

26. Ibid., 180–181.

27. Eileen Shanahan, "Opposition Rises to Amendment on Equal Rights," *New York Times,* January 15, 1973, 1.

28. Similarly, NOW's membership grew to an all-time high during the final "ERA Countdown Campaign" year in 1982.

29. Johnnie Tilmon was a founder of the National Welfare Rights Organiza-tion. Her phrase was widely quoted by, among others, Wilma Scott Heide, NOW's second president, in many speeches.

30. Ehrenreich, *The Hearts,* 152.

31. Pamela Johnston Conover and Virgina Gray, *Feminism and the New Right* (New York: Praeger, 1983), 68–69.

32. See Kristin Luker's analysis of these women in *Abortion and the Politics of Motherhood* (Berkeley and Los Angeles: University of California Press, 1984).

33. Davis, *Moving,* 394.

34. See Mansbridge, *Why We Lost.*

35. The original list is taken from Eileen Shanahan, "Equal Rights Amendment Approved by Congress," *New York Times,* March 23, 1972; and Eileen Shanahan's news opinion article, no title, *New York Times,* March 23, 1972.

36. See Kathleen Jones's review of this debate in "Dividing the Ranks: Women and the Draft," in Jean B. Elshtain and Sheila Tobias, eds., *Women, Militarism, and War: Essays in History, Politics, and Social Theory* (Lanham, Md.: Rowman and Littlefield, 1990), 105–122; see also Chapter 11.

37. Mansbridge, *Why We Lost.*

38. Adrienne Rich, *Of Woman Born* (New York: Norton, 1976); Mary Belenky et. al., *Women's Ways of Knowing: The Development of Self, Voice, and Mind* (New York: Basic Books, 1986); Carol Gilligan, *In a Different Voice: Psychological Theory and Women's Development* (Cambridge, Mass.: Harvard University Press, 1982); Jean Bethke Elshtain, *Public Man, Private Woman* (Princeton: Princeton Univer-sity Press, 1981); and Betty Friedan, *The Second Stage* (New York: Summit Books, 1981). See Chapter 13 for more on this revisionism.

Chapter 10

1. A description of that debate and its aftermath is included in a report by Car-oline Bird and the National Commission on the Observance of International Women's Year, *What Women Want: The Official Report to the President, the Con-gress, and the People of the United States on the National Women's Conference at Houston, Texas, November 1977* (Washington, D.C.: GPO, 1977), 64.

2. Ibid., 78–80.

3. That footage was employed even after the ERA had been lost. In a campaign for a statewide ERA in Iowa, for example, where the footage appeared (on certain

Iowa television stations and not on others), voting for the state's ERA was negative.

4. The term *sexual preference* is not liked by some writers, notably Adrienne
Rich, but I use it interchangeably with other synonyms in this chapter.

5. Many lesbian feminists believed their resistance to traditional female roles,
their independence from men, and their strong bonding with women coincided
with the goals and theory of the women's movement. Indeed, as early as 1970
lesbian feminists Sidney Abbott and Barbara Love went further: For lesbians,
"women's liberation is not an intellectual or emotional luxury but a personal imperative." Sidney Abbott and Barbara Love, *Sappho Was a Right-on Woman: A
Liberated View of Lesbianism* (New York: Stein and Day, 1972), 135. Heterosexual
feminists reciprocated, Abbott and Love write. Chapters on lesbianism were included in the first three feminist anthologies published in the early 1970s: Robin
Morgan, ed., *Sisterhood Is Powerful* (New York: Vintage, 1970); Sookie Stambler,
ed., *Women's Liberation: Blueprint for the Future* (New York: Ace, 1970); and Vivian Gornick and Barbara Moran, eds., *Woman in Sexist Society: Studies in Power
and Powerlessness* (New York: Basic Books, 1971).

6. Cruder still was Rita Mae Brown's claim that "you can't build a strong movement if your sisters are out there fucking with the oppressor." Quoted in Alice
Echols, *Daring to Be Bad: Radical Feminism in America, 1967–1975* (Minneapolis: University of Minnesota Press, 1989), 232.

7. Quoted in Flora Davis, *Moving the Mountain* (New York: Simon and Schuster, 1991), 263.

8. Ibid., 262–263. Sidney Abbot and Barbara Love provide more details of this
first confrontation between lesbian feminists and the National Organization for
Women. In the press release issued by the Congress to Unite Women, two lesbian
affiliates were deleted by an unnamed NOW official, and a prolesbian motion
was later tabled. Sidney Abbott and Barbara Love, "Is Women's Liberation a Lesbian Plot?" in Gornick and Moran, eds., *Woman*, 614–616.

9. Quoted in Gornick and Moran, eds., *Woman*, 615.

10. Abbott and Love make this observation regarding their definition of sexism, which they apply to the preference for heterosexuality over homosexuality
quite as much as to the elevation of one gender over the other: "Sexism emerges
from making reproduction rather than personal pleasure or personal development the goal of sexual intercourse." Quoted in Gornick and Moran, eds.,
Woman, 604. Rita Mae Brown, as part of the radical lesbian separatist group the
Furies, did a similar sort of critique of heterosexism, or "a form of domination
based on the assumption that heterosexual sex was the only 'natural' kind . . .
[and] that every woman was either bound to a man or wished she were." Furies
member Charlotte Bunch called heterosexism "a cornerstone of male supremacy." Quoted in Davis, *Moving*, 270.

11. Echols, *Daring*, 264–265.

12. Ibid.

13. Davis, *Moving*, 269.

14. For a history of lesbians and the reaction to lesbianism in the United
States, see Lillian Faderman, *Surpassing the Love of Men: Romantic Friendship
and Love Between Women from the Renaissance to the Present* (New York: William
Morrow, 1981); and Lillian Faderman, *Odd Girls and Twilight Lovers: A History of*

Lesbian Life in Twentieth-Century America (New York: Penguin, 1992). Other important books on the subject of lesbianism and feminism include Karla Jay and Allen Young, eds., *Out of the Closets: Voices of Gay Liberation* (New York: Douglas Book, 1972); Nancy Myron and Charlotte Bunch, eds., *Lesbianism and the Women's Movement* (Baltimore: Diana Press, 1975); and Jill Johnston, *Lesbian Nation: The Feminist Solution* (New York: Simon and Schuster, 1973).

15. Ti-Grace Atkinson, "Lesbianism and Feminism," in Phyllis Birkby, ed., *Amazon Expedition: A Lesbian Feminist Anthology* (Albion, Calif.: Times Change Press, 1973), 11.

16. This was her response to marchers wearing lavender armbands at the 1976 Women's Equality Day, as she recalled the event and her response in 1976. Betty Friedan, *It Changed My Life* (New York: Random House, 1976), 158.

17. This story is told in Davis, *Moving,* 268.

18. Ibid.

19. Ibid., 267–268.

20. Friedan did not join the press conference. In her retrospective *It Changed My Life,* written a decade later, she remembered: "I begged them not to do it. I said the women's movement was too important to too many people . . . to be sacrificed to such a cause. . . . I was sure it would boomerang into an era of sexual McCarthyism" (159).

21. For a discussion of the politics of these events, see Echols, *Daring,* 219; and Davis, *Moving,* 267–268. For the exact wording of the "Constitution on Lesbian Feminist Liberation," adopted by the National Conference of NOW in 1971, see Judith Papachristou, ed., *Women Together: A History in Documents of the Women's Movement in the U.S.* (New York: Knopf, 1976), 250. The constitution asserts the right "of every woman to express her sexuality in any way she chooses" and the intention of the organization to "confront and disarm the attitudes and institutions that attempt to limit these rights."

22. Friedan's resistance may have had its roots in her own lack of understanding as to what lesbianism is about. Consider her remark about the women's movement having nothing to do with "denouncing the love of men." In fact, many lesbians will say that for them lesbianism is more about loving women than about denouncing men.

23. The title of this section is an expression used in the defense of Oscar Wilde during his trial for sodomy (1895–1897) and is from a poem written by his lover.

24. Sometimes writers became quite metaphoric in describing the "abnormality," as with "a masculine soul heaving in a female bosom," attributed to Richard von Krafft-Ebing, *Psychopathia Sexualis,* as quoted in Carroll Smith-Rosenberg, "Discourses of Sexuality and Subjectivity: The New Woman, 1870–1936," in Martin Duberman, Martha Vicinius, and George Chauncey Jr., eds., *Hidden from History: Reclaiming the Gay and Lesbian Past* (New York: New American Library, 1989), 270.

25. Faderman, *Odd Girls,* 42, 130. See also Faderman, *Surpassing.* For essays on lesbian and gay history more generally, see Duberman et al., eds., *Hidden.*

26. Michel Foucault, *History of Sexuality* (New York: Pantheon, 1978), vol. 1; Smith-Rosenberg, "Discourses."

27. Faderman, *Surpassing*, 239–253.

28. Ibid., 239, quoting German psychologist Carl von Westphal.

29. Carroll Smith-Rosenberg, "The Female World of Love and Ritual: Relations Between Women in Nineteenth-Century America," *Signs* 1, no. 1 (1975):9ff.

30. Quoted in Faderman, *Odd Girls*, 13.

31. Faderman, *Surpassing*.

32. Faderman, *Odd Girls*, 53.

33. Writer Adrienne Rich argues that a child's primary attachment is to his or her mother and that it is our heterosexist and patriarchal society that has replaced this "natural" bond to the female with the heterosexual one. She posits a "compulsory heterosexuality" mechanism working in society to maintain this replacement. Adrienne Rich, "Compulsory Heterosexuality and Lesbian Existence," in *Blood, Bread, and Poetry: Selected Prose, 1979–1985* (New York: Norton, 1986), 23–75.

34. Faderman, *Odd Girls*, 100.

35. Ibid., 119.

36. Audre Lorde, *Zami, a New Spelling of My Name* (Freedom, Calif.: Crossing Press, 1982), as quoted in Faderman, *Odd Girls*, 130. See also Margaret Cruikshank, *The Gay and Lesbian Liberation Movement* (New York: Routledge, 1992).

37. Kinsey's work appeared in two famous reports: Alfred C. Kinsey, Wardell Baxter Pomeroy, and Clyde Eugene Martin, *Sexual Behavior in the Human Male* (Philadelphia: Saunders, 1948); and Institute for Sex Research and Alfred C. Kinsey, *Sexual Behavior in the Human Female* (Philadelphia: Saunders, 1953). The reports were based on 18,500 individual interviews, which indicated a more variegated sexual behavior among the average American population. His studies have since been criticized for sampling and interviewing irregularities, but their "eye-opening" value to social science cannot be dismissed.

38. Faderman, *Odd Girls*, 141. For a discussion of McCarthyism in general, see 139–158.

39. Cruikshank, *The Gay and Lesbian Liberation Movement*, 61–68, 147.

40. This entire section has benefited from Faderman's masterful history of the period. Her *Odd Girls* and *Surpassing* are essential reading for anyone wishing to understand the history and politics of female homosexuality in America.

41. Ibid., 146.

42. Sidney Abbott and Barbara Love, "Is Women's Liberation a Lesbian Plot?" reprinted in Gornick and Moran, eds., *Woman*, 613.

43. Eric Marcus, *Making History: The Struggle for Gay and Lesbian Equal Rights, 1945–1990* (New York: HarperCollins, 1992), 90–92.

44. This description of Stonewall is taken from John D'Emilio, "Gay Politics and Community in San Francisco Since World War II," in Duberman et al., eds., *Hidden*, 466.

45. Faderman, *Odd Girls*, 211.

46. D'Emilio, "Gay Politics," 470.

47. In the mid-1970s the National Women's Political Caucus, an organization founded to support women in elective office, issued a position paper supporting nondiscrimination against lesbians in employment, housing, and educa-

tion. In a 1975 constitution, the National Women's Agenda, which included such traditional groups as the Girl Scouts and the YWCA, also expressed officially its support for lesbian rights. See Faderman, *Odd Girls*, 212–213.

48. Quoted in Echols, *Daring*, 217.

49. Cruikshank, *The Gay and Lesbian Liberation Movement*, 76.

50. Ibid., 157.

51. Personal communication from a young lesbian, 1993.

52. Cruikshank, *The Gay and Lesbian Liberation Movement*.

53. Jane Gross, "Does She Speak for Today's Woman?" *New York Times Magazine*, March 1, 1992, 16.

54. Quoted in Donna Minkowitz, "The Newsroom Becomes a Battleground," *The Advocate*, May 19, 1992, 36. Ireland tells her story in Patricia Ireland, *What Women Want* (New York: Dutton, 1996), 225–242.

55. Ibid.

56. Urvashi Vaid has since written a book on the gay and lesbian liberation movement: *Virtual Equality: The Mainstreaming of Gay and Lesbian Liberation* (New York: Anchor Books, 1995).

57. Gloria Steinem (and others) in *Ms.* (September-October 1993):35–36.

58. Barbara Smith, "Where's the Revolution?" *The Nation*, July 5, 1993, 12–15.

59. Ibid., 13.

60. Barbara Kantrowitz and Danzy Sanna, "The Power and the Pride," *Newsweek*, June 21, 1993, 56.

61. Ibid., 55–56.

62. Abbott and Love, in Gornick and Moran, eds., *Woman*, 610.

63. Ibid., 611.

64. Even the African-American family, touted by white sociologists as "matriarchal," was based on male privilege and power. Bell hooks, in writing about her own upbringing in a segregated southern community, notes that, although the African-American male may have been "silent" much of the time, when he spoke, his word was law. Bell hooks interviewed by Cornell West, in bell hooks and Cornell West, *Breaking Bread: Insurgent Black Intellectual Life* (Boston: South End Press, 1991), 69.

65. Examples include the antimunicipal gay ordinance campaign in Dade County in 1976; the Briggs Initiative, which, had it passed in California in 1978, would have deprived any practicing homosexual of employment in the public school system; "Save our Children" and "Save Our Moral Ethics" campaigns elsewhere in the country; and loss of rights to cohabit rental properties. For a summary of this backlash, see Faderman, *Odd Girls*, 200–201.

66. For further discussion of Schlafly's politics and strategy, see Chapter 9.

67. Andrew Sullivan, "The Politics of Homosexuality," *New Republic*, May 10, 1993, 24–37. See also Andrew Sullivan, *Virtually Normal: An Argument About Homosexuality* (New York: Knopf, 1995).

68. See Davis, *Moving*, 274–275, for a short summary of the Sharon Kowalski case.

69. Ibid.

70. Race in all cases and gender in some cases are considered suspect classifications by the Court, which means that any differentiation made on the basis of race or gender is suspect and has to be especially justified.

Chapter 11

1. An exception is the disagreement between the fifty state commissions and more radical women as to the issue of sex-segregated want ads, a disagreement that led to the creation of the National Organization for Women. See Chapter 6.

2. A good summary (and critique) of the arguments employed by liberal feminists in defense of registering women for the draft can be found in Kathy Jones, "Dividing the Ranks," in Jean B. Elshtain and Sheila Tobias, eds., *Women, Militarism, and War: Essays in History, Politics, and Social Theory* (Lanham, Md.: University Press of America, 1990), 125–127.

3. Amy Swerdlow, *Women Strike for Peace: Traditional Motherhood and Radical Politics in the 1960s* (Chicago: University of Chicago Press, 1992). A contrasting view is presented by Jean Bethke Elshtain, who points out in her various writings that it would be wrong to conclude that *all* women oppose war or that they are not complicit in their sons' and lovers' enthusiasm for it. Jean Bethke Elshtain, *Woman and War*, (New York: Basic Books, 1987).

4. Eleanor Smeal, then ex-president of national NOW, speaking on the subject in the late 1970s, said publicly, "Peace is not a feminist issue." Heard personally by the author.

5. Swerdlow, *Women Strike*, 3.

6. Ibid. The actions of WSP were in part responsible for the 1963 Atmospheric Test Ban, a bilateral agreement between the United States and the Soviet Union that banned aboveground nuclear testing. The ban did not lead, however, to disarmament since nuclear weapons continued to be developed and tested underground. Indeed, derisively, the late Alva Myrdal, an international expert on disarmament, called the 1963 treaty merely a kind of "environmental protection act," not a step toward peace. Alva Reimer Myrdal, *The Game of Disarmament: How the U.S. and Russia Run the Arms Race* (New York: Pantheon, 1976).

7. Susan Brownmiller, *Against Our Will: Men, Women, and Rape* (New York: Simon and Schuster, 1975), details how embedded rape is in war.

8. This summary borrows heavily in language and argument from that of Jones, "Dividing the Ranks," 127ff.

9. Quoted in ibid., 129.

10. See "Prepared Statement of Judy Goldsmith on Behalf of the National Organization for Women, Inc.," quoted in ibid., 134 n. 5.

11. See the author's account of women missileers working in the fully integrated front-line nuclear deterrent in Sheila Tobias, "Armed and Dangerous," *Ms.* (August 1988):63–67.

12. For a mixed review of the Air Force Academy's efforts to integrate women, see Judith Stiehm, *Bring Me Men and Women: Mandated Change at the U.S. Air Force Academy* (Berkeley and Los Angeles: University of California Press, 1981).

13. In the well-publicized Tailhook scandal, a group of naval aviators were charged with lewd behavior toward women at a conference. Cited in Jane Mayer and Jill Abramson, *Strange Justice: The Selling of Clarence Thomas* (New York: Houghton Mifflin, 1994), 352.

14. This was the period in which Jonathan Schell's *The Fate of the Earth* (New York: Knopf, 1982), an antinuclear tract, sold one hundred thousand copies (1980–1981) and 142,000 Americans in New York (in June 1982) and hundreds of

thousands in Europe marched in favor of nuclear disarmament. The movie *The Day After* also contributed to a growing concern, bordering on hysteria, about nuclear war.

15. See Dorothy Thompson, ed., *Over Our Dead Bodies* (London: Virago Press, 1983); Alice Cook and Gwyn Kirk, Greenham Women Everywhere (Boston: South End Press, 1984); and Barbara Harford and Sarah Hopkins, eds., *Greenham Common: Women at the Wire* (London: Woman's Press, 1984).

16. Personal communication to the author.

17. Randall Forsberg and Helen Caldicott are two notable women who studied military strategy.

18. Sheila Tobias, Peter Goudinoff, Stefan Leader, and Shelah Leader, *What Kinds of Guns Are They Buying for Your Butter?: A Beginner's Guide to Defense, Weaponry, and Military Spending* (New York: William Morrow, 1982). The construction and distribution of the slide shows were supported by a special "national security" grant from the American Association of University Women.

19. Although Caldicott began as a member of Physicians for Social Responsibility, she believes herself to have been edged out by the organization's male-dominated board. She later founded Women and Nuclear Disarmament, finding in her women followers more sympathy and support than from the men. See the Physicians for Social Responsibility's book by Ruth Adams and Susan Cullen, *The Final Epidemic: Physicians and Scientists on Nuclear War* (Chicago: Educational Foundation for Nuclear Science, distributed by University of Chicago Press, 1981). See also Helen Caldicott, *Missile Envy* (New York: William Morrow, 1984).

20. Carol Cohn, "'Clean Bombs' and Clean Language," first published in the *Bulletin of the Atomic Scientist*, later republished in Elshtain and Tobias, eds., *Women, Militarism*, 33–55.

21. Caldicott, *Missile Envy.*

22. Cynthia Enloe, *The Morning After: Sexual Politics at the End of the Cold War* (Berkeley and Los Angeles: University of California Press, 1993), 161–200. See also Sheila Tobias, "Connecting the Dots," *Women's Review of Books* (November 1993):21, a review of *The Morning After.*

23. Enloe, *The Morning After.* For an update on women and the military, see Ruth H. Howes and Michael R. Stevenson, eds., *Women and the Use of Military Force* (Boulder: Lynne Rienner, 1993).

24. See Louise Kapp Howe, *Pink-Collar Workers* (New York: Putnam, 1977); and *Nine to Five* (Farmington Hills, Mich.: CBS-FOX, 1980).

25. Male nurses are, on average, paid more than female nurses because they achieve head nurse status disproportionately to their numbers.

26. Mary Rose Oakar (D–Ohio) introduced legislation aimed at the federal government's own job evaluation policy, asking for a study of what would be the cumulative budgetary impact of adjusting federal wages according to a comparable worth analysis. The states of Washington and Oregon did the same. But in the end comparable worth turned out to be too difficult to implement, and the issue has essentially been shelved.

27. This analysis comes from Sharon Bernstein Megdal and Sheila Tobias, "An Economist and a Feminist Look at Comparable Worth," *Arizona Labor Market Information Newsletter* 10, no. 2 (February 1986):1–2. For further reading on the

comparable worth issue, see Heidi I. Hartmann, *Comparable Worth: New Directions for Research* (Washington, D.C.: National Academy Press, 1985); Barbara Bergmann, "Pay Equity: How to Argue Back," *Ms.* (November 1985):112; and Sara M. Evans and Barbara J. Nelson, *Wage Justice: Comparable Worth and the Paradox of Technocratic Reform* (Chicago: University of Chicago Press, 1989).

28. Elizabeth Higgenbotham, "Employment for Black Professional Women in the Twentieth Century," in Christine Bose and Glenna Spitzer, eds., *Ingredients for Women's Employment Policy* (Albany: State University of New York Press, 1987), 73–91.

29. "Will Comparable Worth Freeze Your Wages?" (Alton, Ill.: Eagle Forum, [1984 or 1985]).

30. See Phyllis Schlafly, Testimony Before the Compensation and Employee Benefits Subcommittee of the House Post Office and Civil Service Committee, May 30, 1985, reprinted in the *Phyllis Schlafly Report* (July 1985):1. Schlafly's Eagle Forum Education and Legal Defense Fund held a two-day conference on comparable worth October 17–19 1983, the proceedings of which are published in Phyllis Schlafly, ed., *Equal Pay for Unequal Work* (Alton, Ill.: Eagle Forum, 1983).

31. Hannah Papaneck, "Men, Women, and Work: Reflections on the Two-Person Career," *American Journal of Sociology* 78 (1973):89–97.

32. Felice Schwartz, "Management Women and the New Facts of Life," *Harvard Business Review* 67, no. 1 (January-February 1989):65–77.

33. Felice N. Schwartz, Margaret H. Schifter, and Susan S. Gillotti, *How to Go to Work When Your Husband Is Against It, Your Children Aren't Old Enough, and There's Nothing You Can Do Anyhow* (New York: Simon and Schuster, 1972).

34. Felice N. Schwartz, *Breaking with Tradition: Women and Work, the New Facts of Life* (New York: Warner, 1992), 141.

35. Ibid., 11–21.

36. Ibid., 138.

37. Ibid., 128

38. Sylvia Ann Hewlett expressed these views about motherhood in *A Lesser Life: The Myth of Women's Liberation in America* (New York: Warner, 1986).

39. Schwartz, *Breaking with Tradition*, 135.

40. Ibid., 138.

41. Cited in ibid., 65.

42. See Mary Gordon's review of Elizabeth Fox-Genovese, *"Feminism Is Not the Story of My Life": How Today's Feminist Elite Has Lost Touch with the Real Concerns of Women* (New York: Doubleday, 1995), in *New York Times Book Review*, January 14, 1996, 9.

43. Schwartz, *Breaking with Tradition*, 50.

44. Linda Lovelace was in real life Linda Marchiano. Her "jailer" was her then husband and manager. See Rosemarie Tong, *Feminist Thought* (Boulder: Westview Press, 1989), 119.

45. Erotic artifacts and narratives, totems, and fetishes appear to be universal—at least that is the impression a visitor to the Kinsey Institute in Bloomington, Indiana, takes away with her. But it is noteworthy that except for Japanese and Anglo-American materials, where sexual violence is celebrated, artifacts

from other cultures are lewd but not degrading. (These impressions are taken from an invited tour of the Kinsey collection taken by the author in 1987.)

46. Margaret Atwood, "Pornography," in Donald Hall and D. L. Emblen, eds., *A Writer's Reader* (New York: HarperCollins, 1991), 37–38.

47. Andrea Dworkin, *Pornography: Men Possessing Women* (New York: Perigee, 1979).

48. Catharine A. MacKinnon, "Feminism, Marxism, Method, and the State: An Agenda for Theory," *Signs* 7, no. 3 (Spring 1982):516, 529, 533, as quoted in Alison M. Jaggar, *Feminist Politics and Human Nature* (Totowa, N.J.: Rowman and Allenhead, 1983), 270, 105. Later MacKinnon wrote specifically about pornography. See Catherine MacKinnon, *Only Words* (Cambridge, Mass.: Harvard University Press, 1993).

49. Scott McNall, "Pornography: The Structure of Domination and the Mode of Reproduction," in Scott McNall, ed., *Current Perspectives in Social Theory* (Greenwich, Conn.: JAI Press, 1983), 4:194.

50. Flora Davis, *Moving the Mountain* (New York: Simon and Schuster, 1991), 328–331.

51. *Report of the U.S. Commission on Obscenity and Pornography* (Washington, D.C.: GPO, 1986).

52. Gayle S. Rubin, "Thinking Sex: Notes for a Radical Theory of the Politics of Sexuality," and "Afterword," in Linda S. Kaufman, ed., *American Feminist Thought at Century's End* (Cambridge, Mass.: Blackwell, 1993), 3–64.

53. Boston Women Health Book Collective, *Our Bodies, Ourselves: A Book by and for Women* (New York: Simon and Schuster, 1982), is a guide to women's health. See Chapter 12.

54. Local ordinances prohibiting pornography were introduced in Minneapolis, where the mayor vetoed it twice, and Indianapolis, where the law was struck down in federal court. Davis, *Moving,* 328–329. See also Rosemarie Tong, "Feminism, Pornography, and Censorship," *Social Theory and Practice* 8, no. 1 (Spring 1982):1–17.

55. The "Pornography Victims' Compensation Act," never passed by the full Senate but voted out by the Senate Judiciary Committee, would have given alleged victims of pornography the right to sue producers, distributors, and sellers of "obscene material" if the sex offender could have been shown to have been exposed to these materials before committing some violent act against women or children.

56. Quoted in Karen DeCrow, "Being a Feminist Means You Are Against Sexism, Not Against Sex," *New York Law School Law Review* 38, nos. 1–4 (1993):364.

57. Atwood, "Pornography," 41.

58. Rubin, "Thinking Sex," 37.

59. Ibid.

60. Ibid., 35–36.

61. Barbara Dafoe Whitehead, "Dan Quayle Was Right," *Atlantic* 271, no. 4 (April 1993):47.

62. Ibid., 55.

63. David Popenoe, *Life Without Father: Compelling New Evidence That Fatherhood and Marriage Are Indispensable for the Good of Children and Society*

(New York: Martin Kessler Books/Free Press, 1996). See also David Blankenhorn, *Fatherless in America: Confronting Our Most Urgent Social Problem* (New York: HarperCollins, 1995).

64. Whitehead, "Dan Quayle," 58.

65. Ibid., 60–61.

66. Carol B. Stack, *All Our Kin: Strategies for Survival in a Black Community* (New York: Harper and Row, 1974).

67. Daniel P. Moynihan, *The Negro Family: The Case for National Action* (Washington, D.C.: GPO, 1965); reprinted in Rainwater Yancey and William Yancey, *The Moynihan Report and the Politics of Controversy* (Cambridge, Mass.: MIT Press, 1967).

68. Sarah McLanahan and Irwin Garfinkel, *Single Mothers and Their Children: A New American Dilemma* (Washington, D.C.: Urban Institute Press, 1986). See also Judith Wallerstein, *The California Children of Divorce Study*, later published with Sandra Blakeslee as *Second Chances: Men, Women, and Children a Decade After Divorce* (New York: Ticknor and Fields, 1989).

69. Cited in Whitehead, "Dan Quayle," 62. Hillary Clinton is more generous to single-parent families, but no less of the opinion that "children deserve the benefit of what society has traditionally considered to be male and female traits and skills to meet their physical, emotional, and intellectual needs, and to offer them models for a range of human behaviors." Hillary Rodham Clinton, *It Takes A Village and Other Lessons Children Teach Us* (New York: Simon and Schuster, 1996), 203.

70. Kristin Luker, *Abortion and the Politics of Motherhood* (Berkeley and Los Angeles, University of California Press, 1984).

71. Kristin Luker, *Dubious Conceptions: The Politics of Teenage Pregnancy* (Cambridge, Mass.: Harvard University Press, 1996), as reviewed in Kai Erikson, "Scandal or Scapegoating?" *New York Times Book Review*, September 1, 1996, 10–11.

72. Martha Davis, attorney in the suit, personal communication to the author. The suit was lost in 1995 at the district level and then in August 1996 on appealed to the Third Circuit Federal Appeals Court. See Sarah Kershaw, "Welfare Law Is Upheld," *New York Times*, August 10, 1996.

73. Ibid.

74. Betty Rollin is an NBC correspondent who has covered the issue for the network. The statement referred to here is a personal communication to the author.

75. Quoted in Tong, *Feminist Thought*, 237.

Chapter 12

1. Kate Millett, *Sexual Politics* (New York: Simon and Schuster, 1969), 24–58.

2. See Berenice A. Carroll, *Liberating Women's History: Theoretical and Critical Essays* (Urbana: University of Illinois Press, 1976).

3. Claudia Koonz, *Mothers in the Fatherland: Women, the Family, and Nazi Politics* (New York: St. Martin's Press, 1986); Hilda Scott, *Does Socialism Liberate*

Women? Experiences from Eastern Europe (Boston: Beacon Press, 1974); William Mandel, *Soviet Women* (New York: Anchor, 1975); Francine du Plessix Gray, *Soviet Women: Walking the Tightrope* (New York: Doubleday, 1989).

4. Betty Friedan, *The Feminine Mystique* (New York: Norton, 1963).

5. See Lionel Tiger, *Men in Groups* (New York: Random House, 1969); Norman Mailer, *The Prisoner of Sex* (Boston: Little, Brown, 1971); and George Gilder, *Sexual Suicide* (New York: Quadrangle, 1973), for examples of how writers, in response to feminist theory, reasserted the desirability and inevitability of male domination.

6. Artist Ann Moliver Ruben, the shirt's designer, was told by a Wal-Mart buyer that the shirt's message "goes against Wal-Mart's family values." For a summary of the incident, see "Wal-Mart Apologizes for Dropping T-shirt," *Los Angeles Times*, September 24, 1995.

7. Catherine MacKinnon, writing in "From Practice to Theory," *Yale Journal of Law and Feminism* 13, no. 20 (1991):13, defines consciousness-raising as "using a group-based approach to discovery of the truth about women's situation."

8. For more details on women's political activity before, during, and after the second wave, see Jo Freeman's study of women in the political parties, in preparation; and Ruth Mandel, "The Political Woman," in Sherri Matteo, eds., *American Women in the Nineties: Today's Critical Issues* (Boston: Northeastern University Press, 1993), 34ff.

9. Jane O'Reilley, "The Housewife's Moment of Truth," *Ms.* (Spring 1972):54–55, 57, 59; Teresa de Lauretis, *Feminist Studies, Critical Studies* (Bloomington: Indiana University Press, 1986), 9.

10. Angela Davis, "The Role of Black Women in the Community of Slaves," *Black Scholar* 3, no. 4 (December 1971):2–15.

11. Angela Davis, *Women, Race, and Class* (New York: Random House, 1981).

12. Elizabeth Higginbotham and Sarah Watts, "New Scholarship on Afro-American Women," *Women's Studies Quarterly* 16, nos. 1–2 (Spring-Summer 1988):12–21.

13. Patricia Hill Collins, *Black Feminist Thought: Knowledge, Consciousness, and the Politics of Empowerment* (New York: Routledge, 1990).

14. Barbara Smith, ed., *Home Girls: A Black Feminist Anthology* (New York: Kitchen Table, Women of Color Press, 1983). See also *Conditions Five: The Black Women's Issue* 2, no. 2 (Autumn 1979), edited by Lorraine Bethel and Barbara Smith.

15. Alice Walker, *The Color Purple* (New York: Washington Square Press, 1982). The quotation is from Smith, *Home Girls*, l.

16. Smith, *Home Girls*, xxiv.

17. Johnnetta Cole, president of Spelman College, and many other African-American women prefer the term *womanist*, coined by Alice Walker, to *feminist*. See Johnnetta B. Cole, *Conversations: Straight Talk with America's Sister President* (New York: Doubleday, 1993).

18. Cited in Smith, *Home Girls*, xxxii.

19. Robin Morgan, ed., *Sisterhood Is Powerful* (New York: Vintage, 1970); and Vivian Gornick and Barbara K. Moran, eds., *Woman in Sexist Society: Studies in Power and Powerlessness* (New York: Basic Books, 1971).

20. Susan Brownmiller, *Against Our Will: Men, Women, and Rape* (New York: Simon and Schuster, 1975), 15.

21. Shulamith Firestone, *Dialectic of Sex* (New York: Bantam, 1970).

22. Margaret Atwood, *The Handmaid's Tale* (Boston: Houghton Mifflin, 1985). Not so fictional might be contracts with Third World women to partially gestate and then abort healthy fetuses as a way of permitting the industrial world to "harvest" fetal brain tissue for the cure of certain diseases—a view that has united some feminists and antiabortion activists in an effort to restrict research on fetal tissue.

23. Later WEAL reversed itself and supported abortion rights.

24. Women's studies is sometimes called feminist studies. The "new scholarship on women" was selected by Catharine Stimpson, a professor of English and the founding editor of *Signs: Women, Culture, and Society* (published since 1975 by the University of Chicago Press), as the most appropriate name for what feminist scholars were engaged in.

25. When Susan Brownmiller began her research on rape, she rarely found the subject "woman" in any of the catalog listings. Brownmiller, *Against Our Will*. Feminist librarians would soon change this.

26. For an early description of the origins of women's studies, see Catharine Stimpson, *Women on Campus: The Unfinished Liberation* (New Rochelle, N.Y.: Change, 1975). See also Florence Howe, "Feminist Scholarship: The Extent of the Revolution," *Change* 14, no. 3 (April 1982):12–20.

27. See Joanna Russ, *How to Suppress Women's Writing* (Austin: University of Texas Press, 1983); and Dale Spender, *Women of Ideas and What Men Have Done to Them* (Boston: Pandora, 1988).

28. Virginia Woolf, *A Room of One's Own* (New York: Harcourt Brace Jovanovich, 1957). The salient section is reprinted in Elaine Showalter, *Women's Liberation and Literature* (New York: Harcourt Brace Jovanovich, 1971), 186ff.

29. Linda Nochlin, "Why Have There Been No Great Women Artists?" *Art News* (January 1971):22–39, reprinted in Diane Apostolos-Cappadona and Lucinda Ebersole, *Women, Creativity, and the Arts: Critical and Autobiographical Perspectives* (New York: Continuum Press, 1995), 44–69.

30. Collins, *Black Feminist Thought*, 5.

31. African-American women's history is in the process of being reclaimed. See, for a few examples, Paula Giddings, *When and Where I Enter: The Impact of Black Women on Race and Sex in America* (New York: William Morrow, 1984); Jacqueline Jones, *Labor of Love, Labor of Sorrow: Black Women, Work, and the Family from Slavery to the Present* (New York: Basic Books, 1985); Dorothy Sterling, ed., *We Are Your Sisters: Black Women in the Nineteenth Century* (New York: Norton, 1984); Deborah Gray White, *Ar'n't I a Woman: Female Slaves in the Plantation South* (New York: Norton, 1985); and Sharon Harley and Rosalyn Terborg, *Afro-American Woman: Struggles and Images* (Port Washington, N.Y.: Kennikat Press, 1978). Among the new biographies, see Marilyn Richardson, *Maria W. Stewart: America's First Black Woman Political Writer* (Bloomington: Indiana University Press, 1987).

Other "reclaimers" of black women's history and scholarship are Gloria T. Hull, Patricia Bell Scott, and Barbara Smith, eds., *All the Women Are White, All the*

Blacks Are Men, But Some Of Us Are Brave (New York: Feminist Press, 1982); Maxine Baca Zinn and Bonnie Thornton Dill, *Women of Color in U.S. Society* (Philadelphia: Temple University Press, 1994); and Beverly Guy-Sheftall, *Words of Fire: An Anthology of African-American Feminist Thought* (New York: New Press, 1995).

32. Susan Koppelman, *Old Maids: Short Stories by Nineteenth-Century U.S. Women Writers* (Boston: Pandora Press, 1984); *The Other Woman: Stories of Two Women and a Man* (New York: New American Library, 1984); *Between Mothers and Daughters: Stories Across a Generation* (New York: New American Library, 1985); *"May Your Days Be Merry and Bright" and Other Christmas Stories by Women* (Detroit: Wayne State University Press, 1988); and *Women's Friendships: A Collection of Short Stories* (Norman: University of Oklahoma Press, 1991).

33. Alice Walker, *In Search of Our Mothers' Gardens* (New York: Harcourt, Brace, 1983).

34. See Cherríe Moraga and Gloria Anzaldúa, eds., *This Bridge Called My Back: Writings by Radical Women of Color* (New York: Kitchen Table, Women of Color Press, 1983).

35. In 1971 the press published its first book, *The Dragon and the Doctor,* by Barbara Danish, a children's story about a girl doctor who mends a sick dragon's tail with the help of her younger brother, a nurse. Later that year the press moved to the newly established College at Old Westbury of the State University of New York, where Florence Howe had been appointed professor of humanities. In 1972, to serve the new women's studies movement, the press began publishing the *Women's Studies Newsletter,* expanded and later renamed the *Women's Studies Quarterly.* The Feminist Press is now associated with the City University of New York.

36. Florence Howe, "Here's to the Next Twenty-Five," in *Re-visioning Feminism Around the World* (New York: Feminist Press, 1995), 6.

37. Ibid.

38. Ibid.

39. Ibid.

40. Joan Kelly, "Did Women Have a Renaissance?" in *Women, History, and Theory: The Essays of Joan Kelly* (Chicago: University of Chicago Press, 1984). See also Joan Wallach Scott, *Gender and the Politics of History* (New York: Columbia University Press, 1988), part 1.

41. Gerda Lerner, *The Majority Finds Its Past: Placing Women in History* (New York: Oxford University Press, 1979).

42. William Chafe, *The American Woman* (New York: Oxford University Press, 1972); William Chafe, *Women and Equality* (New York: Oxford University Press, 1977).

43. William J. Goode, *The Family,* 2d ed. (Englewood Cliffs, N.J.: Prentice-Hall), 1964.

44. Paul Lauter, *Reconstructing American Literature* (Old Westbury, N.Y.: Feminist Press, 1983). W. W. Norton, publisher of the much-used *Norton Anthology of Literature,* soon thereafter published Sandra Gilbert and Susan Gubar's *The Norton Anthology of Literature by Women* (New York: Norton, 1985). See also Cathy N. Davidson and Linda Wagner-Martin, eds., *The Oxford Companion to Women's Writing in the United States* (New York: Oxford University Press, 1995).

45. Many feminist scholars, white and women of color, were reading old editions of Zora Neal Hurston's work and urging republication even before Robert Hemenway produced his biography. See Alice Walker's edited anthology, *I Love Myself When I Am Laughing . . . and Then Again When I Am Looking Mean and Impressive* (Old Westbury, N.Y.: Feminist Press, 1979). See also Robert Hemenway, *Zora Neale Hurston: A Literary Biography* (Urbana: University of Illinois Press, 1980).

46. For the distribution of women doctorates in American universities at about this time, see Helena Astin, *The Woman Doctorate in America: Origins, Career, and Family* (New York: Russell Sage, 1969). For a description of academic women of a decade earlier, see Jessie Bernard, *Academic Women* (University Park: Pennsylvania State University Press, 1964).

47. Often, the feminist point of view illuminated whole periods and literary genres that previously had not been taken seriously. See Annette Kolodny's germinal work on the frontier in American literature drawn from her study of women writers: *The Land Before Her* (Chapel Hill: University of North Carolina Press, 1984).

48. Judith Stacey and Barrie Thorne, "The Missing Feminist Revolution in Sociology," *Social Problems* 32, no. 4 (April 1985);311.

49. Ibid.

50. Personal communication from sociologist Scott McNall to the author.

51. See Sheila Ruth, "Methodocracy, Misogyny, and Bad Faith: Sexism in the Philosophical Establishment," *Metaphilosophy* 10, no. 1 (January 1979):48–61.

52. See Casey Miller and Kate Swift, *Words and Women* (Garden City, N.Y.: Anchor Press, 1976); and Robin Lakoff, *Talking Power: The Politics of Language* (New York: Basic Books, 1990). See also Dale Spender, *Man Made Language* (London: Routledge, 1980).

53. Matina Horner, "Women's Fear of Success," quoted in "Sex and Success," *Time*, March 20, 1972, 46.

54. Juanita Williams, *Psychology of Women: Behavior in a Biosocial Context* (New York: Norton, 1977). See also Debra Kaufman and Barbara Richardson, *Achievement and Women* (New York: Macmillan, 1975).

55. Phyllis Chesler, *Women and Madness* (New York: Harcourt Brace Jovanovich, 1972).

56. Sandra Lipsitz Bem, *The Lenses of Gender: Transforming the Debate on Sexual Inequality* (New Haven: Yale University Press, 1993), 189.

57. See Alice Rossi, *The Feminist Papers from Adams to de Beauvoir* (New York: Columbia University Press, 1973), which made available to students and scholars the classic writings on feminism, many of which had long been out of print. New recovery works included new interpretations of the lives and works of pioneer suffragists; see, for example, Lois W. Banner, *Elizabeth Cady Stanton: A Radical for Women's Rights* (Boston: Little Brown, 1980). See also Ellen Carol DuBois, ed., *Elizabeth Cady Stanton, Susan B. Anthony: Correspondence, Writings, Speeches* (New York: Schocken Books, 1981); and Andrea Moore Kerr, *Lucy Stone* (New Brunswick, N.J.: Rutgers University Press, 1992). This revived history also included studies of women's participation in eras in which women had been thought not to have had a public role. See Linda Kerber, *Women of the Republic: Intellect and Ideology in Revolutionary America* (Chapel Hill: University of North Carolina Press, 1980).

58. Sandra Gilbert and Susan Gubar, *The Madwoman in the Attic* (New Haven: Yale University Press, 1979).

59. Kate Chopin, *The Awakening* (New York: Capricorn, 1964); Emily Toth, *Kate Chopin: A Life of the Author of* The Awakening (New York: William Morrow, 1990).

60. Elaine Showalter characterizes studies of men's writing as "feminist critique" and the recovery and analysis of women's writing as "feminist criticism." See Elaine Showalter, *Speaking of Gender* (New York: Routledge, 1989). See also Coppelia Kahn, *Man's Estate: Masculine Identity in Shakespeare* (Berkeley and Los Angeles: University of California Press, 1981); and Ruth Benson, *Women in Tolstoy* (Urbana: University of Illinois Press, 1973).

61. Higginbotham and Watts, "New Scholarship," 14.

62. Joyce Ladner, *Tomorrow's Tomorrow: The Black Woman* (Garden City, N.Y.: Doubleday, 1971), xxiv. Ladner's research grew out of a study of "social and community problems in public housing areas" sponsored by the National Institute of Mental Health in 1964.

63. Londa Shiebinger, *The Mind Has No Sex: Women in the Origins of Modern Science* (Cambridge, Mass.: Harvard University Press, 1989). There are dozens of new biographies of women scientists that show how they continue not to be appropriately recognized. See Evelyn Fox Keller, *A Feeling for the Organism: The Life and Work of Barbara McClintock* (San Francisco: Freeman, 1983); and Ruth Lewin Sime, *Lise Meitner: A Life in Physics* (Berkeley and Los Angeles: University of California Press, 1996).

64. Ann Sayre, *Rosalind Franklin and DNA* (New York: Norton, 1975). See also the comparable story of physicist Lise Meitner, as reported in compelling detail in Sime, *Lise Meitner.*

65. See Sheila Tobias, *Overcoming Math Anxiety* (New York: Norton, 1994), 72–106. See also Elizabeth Fennema and Gilah Leader, *Gender and Mathematics* (New York: Teachers College Press, 1990).

66. *How Schools Shortchange Girls* (Washington, D.C.: American Association of University Women, 1995). See also Myra Sadker and David Sadker, *Failing at Fairness: How America's Schools Cheat Girls* (New York: Scribner's, 1994).

67. Roberta M. Hall and Bernice Resnick Sandler, *The Classroom Climate: A Chilly One for Women?* (Washington, D.C.: Association of American Colleges, 1982).

68. Ruth Bleier, *Feminist Approaches to Science* (New York: Pergamon Press, 1986); Evelyn Fox Keller, *Reflections on Gender and Science* (New Haven: Yale University Press, 1985); and Nancy Merchant, *The Death of Nature: Women, Ecology, and the Scientific Revolution* (San Francisco: Harper and Row, 1980). For a more general feminist critique of science, see Sandra Harding and Jean O'Barr, eds., *Sex and Scientific Inquiry* (Chicago: University of Chicago Press, 1984); and Sandra Harding, *Whose Science? Whose Knowledge?* (Ithaca: Cornell University Press, 1991).

69. Ruth Hubbard, *The Politics of Women's Biology* (New Brunswick, N.J.: Rutgers University Press, 1990), 102–104.

70. Talcott Parsons, *Social Structure and Personality* (New York: Free Press, 1970). See also Talcott Parsons and Robert F. Bales, *Family, Socialization, and Integration Process* (New York: Free Press, 1955).

71. Quoted in Stacey and Thorne, "The Missing Feminist Revolution," 307.

72. Erich Fromm, *The Art of Loving* (London: Allen and Unwin, 1957), reissued in paperback in 1985 by HarperCollins. Sociologist Jessie Bernard saw "stroking" as the all-pervasive women's function, in *Woman and the Public Interest* (Chicago: Aldine/Atherton, 1971), 688–104. The assignment of nonoverlapping spheres of loving was absorbed by a generation of family sociologists, notably Daniel Moynihan, who attributed lack of vocational ambition on the part of young black males to the absence of "conditional love" in their fatherless families. Daniel P. Moynihan, *The Negro Family: The Case for National Action* (Washington, D.C.: GPO, 1965), reprinted in Rainwater Yancey and William Yancey, *The Moynihan Report and the Politics of Controversy* (Cambridge, Mass.: MIT Press, 1964).

73. Parsons, *Social Structure*.

74. See the following three books by Ann Oakley: *Sociology of Housework* (New York: Oxford University Press, 1974); *Housewife* (New York: Penguin, 1976); and *Woman Confined: Toward a Sociology of Childbirth* (New York: Oxford University Press, 1980).

75. Ann-Louise Shapiro, "History and Feminist Theory," in Ann-Louise Shapiro, ed., *Feminists Revision History* (New Brunswick, N.J.: Rutgers University Press, 1994), 1.

76. According to a recent survey of campus trends conducted by the American Council on Education, over two-thirds of all universities, nearly half of all four-year colleges, and about one-fourth of all two-year institutions now offer women's studies courses. In addition, there are over 50 centers or institutes for research on women, 625 special programs on women's studies, numerous professional journals for the publication of the new knowledge, and more than 100 feminist bookstores across the country. For a collection of recent syllabi, see Wendy Kolmar and Patricia Vogt, eds., *Selected Syllabi for Women's Studies Courses* (College Park, Md.: National Women's Studies Association, 1996). For a description of the growth of women's studies, see Mariam Chamberlain, "The Emergence and Growth of Women's Studies Programs," in Sara E. Rix, ed., *The American Woman: A Status Report* (New York: Norton, 1991), 315ff. What happened to the first generation of women's studies graduates is documented in Barbara F. Luebke and Mary Ellen Reilly, *Women's Studies Graduates: The First Generation* (New York: Teachers College Press, 1995).

77. Two reference books ably summarize much of the work done by women scholars: Helen Tierney, ed., *Women's Studies Encyclopedia* (New York: Peter Bedrick Books, 1991); and Davidson and Wagner-Martin, eds., *The Oxford Companion to Women's Writing.* "Writing" is the Oxford collection is defined more broadly than just "literature."

78. Susan Faludi, *Backlash: The Undeclared War Against American Women* (New York: Crown, 1991).

79. For issues of public concern, such as civil rights and environmental preservation, the Advertising Council regularly requests unpaid space in print media and unpaid time in broadcast media for materials provided by public interest groups selected for this one-time, cost-free exposure.

80. Weitzman's study was published in booklet form by the National Education Association in 1973. See Lenore Weitzman and Diane Rizzo, "Sex-Role

Stereotypes in Elementary School Textbooks" (Washington, D.C.: National Education Association, 1973). For a comparable study of pictures in books for elementary-age children, see Women on Words and Images, "Dick and Jane as Victims" (Princeton: Women on Words and Images, 1975). The group analyzed 134 elementary school textbooks published by sixteen separate publishers and found similar sex role–socialized messages.

81. In 1976, invited to talk in Yugoslavia, Czechoslovakia, and Hungary (then still part of communist East Europe) on the subject of "American feminism," I decided to take the Weitzman slide show with me because it captured the way in which American feminism was exposing our society to its own deep-seated biases. In conversations with teachers, child development experts, and children's publishers in all three countries, I discovered that gender bias in their textbooks was just as common but not yet acknowledged.

82. Ann Mather, "A History of Feminist Periodicals," *Journalism History* 1 (Autumn 1974):82. For a then-current compilation of feminist and lesbian periodicals and publishers, see Andrea Fleck Clardy, *Words to the Wise: A Writer's Guide to Feminist and Lesbian Periodicals and Publishers* (Ithaca: Firebrand Press, 1987).

83. Patrice McDermott, *Politics and Scholarship: Feminist Academic Journals and the Production of Knowledge* (Urbana: University of Illinois Press, 1994), 29–30.

84. Mather, "A History," 82.

85. *The Women's Review of Books,* published since 1983 by the Wellesley College Center for Research on Women, has been of singular importance in disseminating feminist scholarship and books bearing on feminist topics intended for a wider readership. In any one year, hundreds of books that might not be reviewed as seriously (or at all) elsewhere are assigned to able feminist writers for thoughtful reviews; careful indexing of titles, authors, and reviewers helps glue widely dispersed authors and readers together.

For the online reader, magazines for girls and women, called girl-zines, henzines, tan-zines, and e-zines, began to appear in the mid-1990s.

86. From the contents, preface, and introduction to Boston Women Health Book Collective, *Our Bodies, Ourselves: A Book by and for Women* (New York: Simon and Schuster, 1984).

87. McDermott describes these splits in *Politics and Scholarship,* 17–41.

88. Cited in ibid., 30–31.

89. Gloria Steinem, "A Bunny's Tale," *Show* (May 1963, June 1963), reprinted as "I Was a Playboy Bunny," in Gloria Steinem, *Outrageous Acts and Everyday Rebellions* (New York: Signet, 1983), 33ff.

90. The term *Ms.* to denote women without reference to their marital status was just then becoming the preferential salutation for feminists. But the *New York Times* and other leading newspapers and magazines would continue to use Miss and Mrs. for many years. Ms. was at the time an inspired choice of title.

91. At the same time that Steinem and Carbine founded *Ms.,* they founded two support organizations to extend their feminist activism: the Ms. Foundation and the Woman Action Alliance.

92. McDermott, *Politics and Scholarship,* 30–31.

93. Ibid.

94. Mary Thom, ed., *Letters to Ms.: 1972–1987* (New York: Henry Holt, 1987).

95. Gloria Steinem, Introduction to ibid., xi–xii.

96. Alison M. Jaggar and Paula S. Rothenberg, eds., *Feminist Frameworks* (New York: McGraw-Hill, 1978).

97. Early fault lines showed up in disagreements over whether women's studies should be more "activist" or more "learning" oriented, over allegations of "elitism" among feminist scholars, and over a real ambivalence about academe in general. See Catharine Stimpson, "What Matter Mind: A Theory About the Practice of Women's Studies," *Women's Studies* 1 (1973):293–314, reprinted in Catherine Stimpson, *Where the Meanings Are: Feminism and Cultural Spaces* (New York: Methuen, 1988), 38–53.

Chapter 13

1. Wendy Kaminer, "Feminism's Identity Crisis," *Atlantic* 272, no. 4 (October 1993):51.

2. Ibid., 52.

3. Carol Gilligan, *In a Different Voice: Psychological Theory and Women's Development* (Cambridge, Mass.: Harvard University Press, 1982).

4. Kaminer, "Feminism's Identity," 62

5. Gloria Steinem, *The Revolution from Within: A Book of Self-Esteem* (Boston: Little, Brown, 1992).

6. Katie Roiphe, *The Morning After: Sex, Fear, and Feminism on Campus* (Boston: Little, Brown, 1993).

7. Kaminer, "Feminism's Identity," 62. For evidence of the media backlash from the mid-1970s on, see Susan Faludi, *Backlash: The Undeclared War Against American Women* (New York: Crown, 1991).

8. Marianne Hirsch and Evelyn Fox Keller, eds., *Conflicts in Feminism* (New York: Routledge, 1990); Hester Eisenstein, *Contemporary Feminist Thought* (Boston: Hall, 1983); Judith Lorber, *Paradoxes of Gender* (New Haven: Yale University Press, 1994). For a more general introduction, see Rosemarie Tong, *Feminist Thought: A Comprehensive Introduction* (Boulder: Westview Press, 1989); and Linda S. Kauffman, ed., *American Feminist Thought at Century's End: A Reader* (Cambridge, Mass.: Blackwell, 1993).

9. Inge K. Broverman, Donald M. Broverman et al., "Sex Role Stereotypes and Clinical Judgments of Mental Health," *Journal of Consulting and Clinical Psychology* 34 (1970), cited in Phyllis Chesler, *Women and Madness* (New York: Harcourt Brace, 1989), 67–68.

10. See Zillah Eisenstein, *The Radical Future of Liberal Feminism* (Boston: Northeastern University Press, 1986); Zillah Eisenstein, *The Female Body and the Law* (Berkeley and Los Angeles: University of California Press, 1989); Alison Jaggar, *Feminist Politics and Human Nature* (Totowa, N. J.: Rowman and Allenheld, 1983); and Alison Jaggar and Paula Rothenberg, *Feminist Frameworks: Alternative Theoretical Accounts of the Relations Between Women and Men*, 3d ed. (New York: McGraw-Hill, 1993), 113ff.

11. Cynthia V. Ward, "The Radical Feminist Defense of Individualism," *Northwestern University Law Review* 89, no. 3 (1995):872.

12. Ibid.

13. Carol Gilligan, *In a Different Voice*; Nancy Chodorow, *The Reproduction of Mothering* (Berkeley and Los Angeles: University of California Press, 1978); Mary Field Belenky et al., *Women's Ways of Knowing: The Development of Self, Voice, and Mind* (New York: Basic Books, 1986).

14. Ward, "The Radical Feminist Defense," 873.

15. Eisenstein, *Female Body*, as quoted in Michele Barrett and Anne Phillips, eds., *Destabilizing Theory: Contemporary Feminist Debates* (Cambridge: Polity Press, 1992), 19.

16. Joan Wallach Scott, *Gender and the Politics of History* (New York: Columbia University Press, 1988), 168–177.

17. Jon Weiner, "Women's History on Trial," *The Nation*, September 7, 1985, quoted in Katha Pollitt, "Are Women Morally Superior to Men?" *The Nation*, December 28, 1992, 802.

18. Scott, *Gender*, 171. For additional reading on the arguments of Rosenberg and Kessler-Harris, see Ruth Milkman, "Women's History and the Sears Case," *Feminist Studies* 12 (1986):394–395.

19. Catharine A. MacKinnon, *Towards a Feminist Theory of the State* (Cambridge, Mass.: Harvard University Press, 1989), 219.

20. Carol Gilligan, *In a Different Voice*, argues that, although adult women have a different sense of justice than do men, theirs is equally valid. A critique of difference feminism close to mine is provided in Cynthia Fuchs Epstein, *Deceptive Distortions: Sex, Gender, and the Social Order* (New Haven: Yale University Press, 1988), 165–186.

21. Cited in Linda Greenhouse, "Military College Can't Bar Women, High Court Rules," *New York Times*, June 27, 1996.

22. Belenky et al., *Women's Ways of Knowing*.

23. This questions has been debated among feminist political theorists such as Susan Moller Okin and Zillah Eisenstein. For a further discussion of the question, see Barrett and Phillips, eds., *Destabilizing Theory*, 19–25; and Pollitt, "Are Women Morally Superior?" 799–807.

24. Karen Kahn, ed., *Front-Line Feminism, 1975–1995: Essays from Sojourner's First Twenty Years* (San Francisco: Aunt Lute Books, 1995), 131–137. A more extensive discussion of this issue, closely linked to my analysis, can be found in Judith Stacey, "Are Feminists Afraid to Leave Home?" in Juliet Mitchell and Ann Oakley, eds., *What Is Feminism? A Reexamination* (New York: Pantheon, 1986), 208–237. See also Epstein, *Deceptive Distortions*, 187–214.

25. Kahn, ed., *Front-Line Feminism*, 131.

26. Ibid.

27. Shulamith Firestone, *The Dialectic of Sex* (New York: William Morrow, 1970).

28. Kahn, ed., *Front-Line Feminism*, 132.

29. Molly Lovelock, "Married Feminists: Fish Out of Water," *Sojourner* (March 1978), reprinted in Kahn, ed., *Front-Line Feminism*, 137ff.

30. Pat Mainardi, "The Politics of Housework," in Robin Morgan, ed., *Sisterhood Is Powerful* (New York: Vintage, 1970), 447–455.

31. Barbara Bergmann, *The Economic Emergence of Women* (New York: Basic Books, 1986), 209–212, criticizes this position.

32. This was one of Phyllis Schlafly's many arguments against day care. See Phyllis Schlafly, *Who Will Rock the Cradle?* (Alton, Ill.: Eagle Forum, 1989).

33. See Phyllis Chesler, *Sacred Bond: The Legacy of Baby M* (New York: Times Books, 1988).

34. Brian Barry and Samuel L. Popkin, Introduction to Kristin Luker, *Abortion and the Politics of Motherhood* (Berkeley and Los Angeles: University of California Press, 1984), xi.

35. Barrie Thorne and Marilyn Yalom, eds., *Rethinking the Family: Some Feminist Questions* (New York: Longman, 1982), 20. Stacey also dealt with this issue in "Are Feminists Afraid?"

36. Juliet Mitchell, *Woman's Estate* (New York: Vintage, 1973); Chodorow, *The Reproduction of Mothering.*

37. Dorothy Dinnerstein, *The Mermaid and the Minotaur* (New York: Harper and Row, 1976); and Chodorow, *The Reproduction of Mothering,* as summarized in Thorne and Yalom, *Rethinking the Family,* Introduction.

38. Adrienne Rich, *Of Woman Born,* (New York: Norton, 1976).

39. Betty Friedan, *The Second Stage* (New York: Summit Books, 1981), 22.

40. Ibid., 15, 22

41. Ibid., 27, 28.

42. The full quotes are "The new frontier where the issues of the second stage will be joined is I believe the family, that same trampled bloody ground. . . . The right to choose has to mean not only the right to choose not to bring a child into the world against one's will, but also the right to have a child joyously, responsibly, without paying a terrible price. . . . [Women] need to feel good about being a woman." Ibid., 83, 86–87.

43. Mary Daly, *Beyond God the Father: Toward a Philosophy of Women's Liberation* (Boston: Beacon Press, 1973); Mary Daly, *Gyn/Ecology: The Metaethics of Radical Feminism* (Boston: Beacon Press, 1978).

44. Eventually, the Sterns won the child, and Mary Beth Whitehead had to be satisfied with visiting rights. The fact that the birth mother may have had financial motives in her change of heart does not make the case any less interesting or important for feminist thinking on the family.

45. Barbara Katz Rothman, *Recreating Motherhood: Ideology and Technology in a Patriarchal Society* (New York: Norton, 1989).

46. Ibid., 26–26, 101, 106.

47. Ibid., 240, 249, 241.

48. Sara Ruddick, "Maternal Thinking," in Thorne and Yalom, *Rethinking the Family,* 89.

49. Ibid.

50. Ibid., 90

51. Ibid.

52. Jean Bethke Elshtain, *Power Trips and Other Journeys: Essays in Feminism as Civil Discourse* (Madison: University of Wisconsin Press, 1990), 47, 60.

53. Elshtain's reference to Firestone's "world of lovelessness," ibid., 46. Her characterization of "women oppressed by having to be women," ibid., 47, is a reference to Jaggar, *Feminist Politics,* 132.

54. Jean Bethke Elshtain, *Public Man, Private Woman* (Princeton: Princeton University Press, 1981), 243, quoted in Tong, *Feminist Thought*, 33.

55. Jaggar and Rothenberg, eds., *Feminist Frameworks*.

56. See, for example, the theme of Karen Anderson's study *Changing Woman: A History of Racial Ethnic Women in Modern America* (New York: Oxford University Press, 1996), 9: "There is no one pattern in the ways women of color have struggled for equality."

57. Ibid., ix.

58. Gerda Lerner, ed., *Black Women in White America: A Documentary History* (New York: Random House, 1972); Gerda Lerner, "Conceptualizing Differences Among Women," first given as a keynote address for the Lowell Conference on Women's History, March 2, 1988, and published in Jaggar and Rothenberg, eds., *Feminist Frameworks*, 231ff.

59. Patricia Hill Collins, *Black Feminist Thought: Knowledge, Consciousness, and the Politics of Empowerment* (Boston: Unwin Human, 1990), quoted in Maxine Baca Zinn and Bonnie Thornton Dill, eds., *Women of Color in U.S. Society* (Philadelphia: Temple University Press, 1994), 9.

60. Angela Davis, *Women, Race, and Class* (New York: Vintage, 1983).

61. Beverly Guy-Sheftall, *Words of Fire: An Anthology of African-American Feminist Thought* (New York: New Press, 1995), xiv.

62. Ibid., 14–15.

63. Bell hooks, "Black Women: Shaping Feminist Theory," in Guy-Sheftall, ed., *Words of Fire*, 270.

64. Ibid.

65. Ibid., 273.

66. Ibid., 272–273.

67. Ibid., 274–276, 280.

68. Cherríe Moraga and Gloria Anzaldúa, eds., *This Bridge Called My Back: Writings by Radical Women of Color*, 3d ed. (New York: Kitchen Table, Women of Color Press, 1983).

69. Audre Lorde, "The Master's Tools Will Never Dismantle the Master's House" in *Sister Outsider: Essays and Speeches by Audre Lorde* (Freedom, Calif.: Crossing Press, 1984), 110ff.

70. Moraga and Anzaldúa, eds., *This Bridge*, 105.

71. Chrystos, "I Don't Understand Those Who Have Turned Away from Me," in ibid., 68.

72. See Preface to ibid., iii.

73. Doris Davenport, "The Pathology of Racism: A Conversation with Third World Wimmin," in ibid., 90.

74. The term *encapsulated* is taken from a study by Jennie R. Joe and Dorothy Lonewolf Miller, "Cultural Survival and Contemporary American Indian Women in the City," in Zinn and Dill, eds., *Women of Color*, 185–202.

75. Guy-Sheftall's "selected bibliography" of African-American women's writing is thirteen pages long. Additional bibliography of Hispanic, Native American, Asian, Third World, and immigrant women can be found in ibid.

76. See Paula Rothenberg's anthology, *Race, Class, and Gender in the United States: An Integrated Study* (New York: St. Martin's Press, 1992); and a collabora-

tion by Gloria Joseph and Jill Lewis, *Common Differences: Conflicts in Black and White Feminist Perspectives* (Boston: South End Press, 1981).

77. Dale Spender, *For the Record: The Making and Meaning of Feminist Knowledge* (London: Women's Press, 1985), 199, paraphrasing Adrienne Rich from her 1980 essay "Disloyal to Civilization: Feminism, Racism, Gynephobia."

78. See the subtitle of Paula Giddings's history of black women published in 1984. Paula Giddings, *When and Where I Enter: The Impact of Black Women on Race and Sex in America* (New York: William Morrow, 1984).

79. Susan Bordo, "Feminism, Postmodernism, and Gender Skepticism," in Anne C. Hermann and Abigail J. Stewart, eds., *Theorizing Feminism: Parallel Trends in the Humanities and Social Sciences* (Boulder: Westview Press, 1994), 458–481. For other views, see Linda J. Nicholsen, ed., *Feminism/Postmodernism* (New York: Routledge, 1990).

80. Bergmann, *The Economic Emergence*, 238ff.

81. Kip Tiernan and Fran Froelich, "Homelessness: Crisis or Chronic Condition?" *Sojourner* (June 1989):114.

82. Bella Abzug with Mim Kelber, *Gender Gap* (Boston: Houghton Mifflin, 1984).

83. Many alternative cases could be made as well. Faludi, *Backlash*, blames the media for the inability of feminism to mount an electoral revolt during the Reagan-Bush years. Others might argue that the feminists who had first become active in the 1970s were simply burned out.

Chapter 14

1. Ronald Reagan alone filled 50 percent of the vacancies on federal courts in his eight years of office.

2. Sandra Day O'Connor joined the Court in 1981; Antonin Scalia, in 1986; Anthony M. Kennedy, in 1988; David H. Souter, in 1990, and Clarence Thomas, in 1991.

3. Susan M. Hartmann, *From Margin to Mainstream: American Women and Politics Since 1960* (New York: Knopf, 1989), 130.

4. The Family Protection Act was never passed.

5. Perhaps the most vocal of these was Rush Limbaugh, who labeled feminists "FemiNazis" in his widely popular daily talk show.

6. Ruth Mandel, director of the Center for the American Woman and Politics at Rutgers University, found in 1981 that of elected officials in the United States, approximately 10 percent were female. Ruth B. Mandel, *In the Running: The New Woman Candidate* (New York: Ticknor and Fields, 1981), 3.

7. Barbara Ehrenreich and Karin Stallard, "The Nouveau Poor," *Ms.* (July-August 1982):217. See also Diana B. Dutten, "Poorer and Sicker: Legacies of the 1980, Lessons for the 1990s," in Shirley Matteo, ed., *American Women in the Nineties: Today's Critical Issues* (Boston: Northeastern University Press), 98–138.

8. Arlene Scadron, *On Their Own: Widows and Widowhood in the American Southwest* (Urbana: University of Illinois Press, 1985).

9. Quoted in Gertrude S. Goldberg and Eleanor Kremen, "The Feminization of Poverty: Discovered in America," in Gertrude S. Goldberg and Eleanor Kremen,

eds., *The Feminization of Poverty: Only in America?* (New York: Greenwood Press, 1990), 5.

10. Barbara R. Bergmann, *The Economic Emergence of Women* (New York: Basic Book, 1986), 227ff.

11. Older analyses of poverty in America, such as Michael Harrington, *The Other America: Poverty in the United States* (New York: Macmillan, 1962), had noted the vulnerability of "consumer units," as Harrington called them, "headed by women" but did not single out women per se as a special target of poverty. This was typical. See 175–191.

12. See comparisons in Sylvia Ann Hewlett, *A Lesser Life: The Myth of Women's Liberation in America* (New York: Warner, 1986).

13. Today only 10 percent of fatherless children typically have lost their fathers through death.

14. Bergmann, *The Economic Emergence*, 199.

15. Ibid.

16. These 1930s laws also excluded farmworkers and domestic workers, causing hardship and economic exploitation for both.

17. Goldberg and Kremen, "The Feminization of Poverty," 35.

18. Ibid.

19. Joyce Gelb and Marian Lief Palley, *Women and Public Policies* (Princeton: Princeton University Press, 1982), 176.

20. Hartmann, *From Margin*, 187.

21. Lenore J. Weitzman, *The Divorce Revolution: The Unexpected Social and Economic Consequences for Women and Children in America* (New York: Free Press, 1985).

22. Hartmann, *From Margin*, 161.

23. Wilkerson and Gresham's article is reprinted in Alison M. Jaggar and Paula S. Rothenberg, *Feminist Frameworks: Alternative Theoretical Accounts of the Relations Between Women and Men*, 3d ed. (New York: McGraw-Hill, 1993), 297–304. See also Ruth Sidel, *Women and Children Last: The Plight of Poor Women in Affluent America* (New York: Viking, 1986).

24. The story of how Linda Coffee and Sarah Weddington found Norma McCovey and each other is well told in Marian Faux, *Roe v. Wade: The Untold Story of the Landmark Supreme Court Decision That Made Abortion Legal* (New York: Macmillan, 1988), 3–4.

25. In *Griswold* v. *Connecticut* (1965), the Supreme Court struck down a Connecticut law barring couples' use of contraception on privacy grounds, paving the way for the possibility that the Court might acknowledge the right of privacy as grounds for abortion.

26. Faux, *Roe v. Wade*, 197.

27. Ibid., 151–152.

28. A chronology of events can be found in Bo Schambelan, annotator, *Roe v. Wade: The Complete Text of the Official U.S. Supreme Court Decision* (Philadelphia: Running Press, 1992), vii–xi. There is also a tape recording of the arguments in *Roe* v. *Wade*, produced and distributed in the series *May It Please the Court* and edited by Peter Irons, professor of political science, University of California, San Diego.

29. Sarah Weddington has written her own memoir of the case. Sarah Weddington, *A Question of Choice* (New York: Putnam, 1992).

30. If the woman's life was in danger, abortion could be performed even after viability.

31. Schambelan, annotator, *Roe v. Wade*, x. Along with *Roe*, the Court concurrently decided a parallel case, *Doe* v. *Bolton*, specific to Georgia's abortion law.

32. Another contribution of the abortion controversy to long-term political developments in the United States was the emphasis by abortion foes on this single issue over and above party and other affiliations. Like the environmentalists' "dirty dozen," antiabortion organizers would identify friends and enemies based on this one issue and throw their weight behind their friends, further weakening party loyalty among voters and elected officials alike.

33. By the late 1970s, the right-to-life movement was providing financial and other assistance to elect new state legislators who promised to make pro-life legislation their first priority.

34. Laurence Tribe, *Abortion: The Clash of Absolutes* (New York: Norton, 1990), 153–155. See the *Maher* case in summary in Schambelan, annotator, *Roe v. Wade*, 104.

35. Tribe, *Abortion*, 10ff.

36. For a discussion of these developments, see Flora Davis, *Moving the Mountain: The Women's Movement in America Since 1960* (New York: Simon and Schuster, 1991), 453–470.

37. A month later in a case brought by Planned Parenthood against the federal government's Agency for International Development, the same Court affirmed the federal government's right to deny foreign aid to overseas health care organizations that promote abortion as a means of family planning.

38. Sylvia Law, talk on reproductive rights, on the day *Casey* was decided, at University of California, San Diego, April 1992.

39. Between 1977 and 1983 there were eight bombings and eighteen arsons reported to the National Abortion Federation. For a briefer period, 1984–1986, there were a reported twenty-four bombings and twenty-one attacks. Loretta Ross, "Abortion Terrorists: Guerrillas in the Midst," *Sojourner* (December 1994), reprinted in Karen Kahn, ed., *Front-Line Feminism: 1975–1995* (San Francisco: Aunt Lute Books, 1995), 209.

40. On January 24, 1994, the U.S. Supreme Court broadened application of the 1970 federal Racketeer-Influenced and Corrupt Organizations Act, making abortion protesters liable for prosecution.

41. Abortion services are not available in 83 percent of counties in the U.S. See Ross, "Abortion Terrorists," 211.

42. Tribe, *Abortion*; Roger Rosenblatt, *Life Itself: Abortion in the American Mind* (New York: Random House, 1992).

43. Law, "Reproductive Rights."

44. Lawrence Lader, *RU 486: The Pill That Could End the Abortion Wars and Why American Women Don't Have It* (Reading, Mass.: Addison-Wesley, 1991), 17.

45. Ibid., Introduction.

46. Ibid., 27.

47. Asoka Bandarage. "A New and Improved Population Control Policy?" *Sojourner* (September 1994), reprinted in Kahn, *Front-Line Feminism*, 217.

48. Ruth Hubbard, Nachama Wilker, and Marsha Saxton, "Of Fetuses and Women," *Sojourner* (April 1987), reprinted in ibid., 246.

49. Ironically, all the while the Reagan forces were railing against the "new woman," the president himself relied more and more on the speechwriting skills of one of them, Peggy Noonan.

50. Cynthia Enloe is an exception. See Cynthia Enloe, *The Morning After: Sexual Politics at the End of the Cold War* (Berkeley and Los Angeles: University of California Press, 1993), 161ff.

51. Hartmann, *From Margin*. See Chapter 15 for further discussion of this issue.

Chapter 15

1. A movement, according to Jo Freeman, is characterized not by participation but by protest. Jo Freeman, *The Politics of Women's Liberation* (New York: Longman, 1975); and Jo Freeman, ed., *Social Movements of the Sixties and Seventies* (New York: Longman, 1983).

2. Freeman points out that it is a social movement's lack of legitimacy that makes it dependent on its members' unwavering commitment. *The Politics*, 72.

3. Claudia Willis, "Women Face the '90s," *Time*, December 4, 1989, 81. *Time* itself declared the movement "hopelessly dated."

4. See a debate in print between Sheila Tobias and Wanda Urbanska, "Pre-, Pan-, or Post? Views on the Future of Feminism," *Comment* 14, no. 2 (October 1983):1. There are, of course, some young women who happily call themselves feminists.

5. Personal communication to author from political scientist Jo Freeman.

6. Martin Gruberg, *Women in American Politics* (Oshbos, Wis.: Academe, 1968), estimates that 6 million women did volunteer work either for Kennedy or for Nixon in the 1960 presidential campaign—well before the second wave of feminism began.

7. Alice Paul's National Woman's Party, an attempt to rally women around third-party candidates, was one response to this dilemma. However, it did not succeed.

8. For a history of these developments, see Tanya Melich, *The Republican War Against Women: An Insider's Report from Behind the Lines* (New York: Bantam, 1996), 3–17.

9. Melich, *The Republican War*, 16.

10. Shirley Chisholm, *The Good Fight* (New York: Harper and Row, 1973), quoted in Susan M. Hartmann, *From Margin to Mainstream: American Women and Politics Since 1960* (New York: Knopf, 1989), 68.

11. Among them was Barbara Franklin, the first "point person" on women's issues to have access to the president since Franklin Delano Roosevelt's administration.

12. These developments are ably analyzed in Hartmann, *From Margin*, 86–89. See also Ruth Mandel, "The Political Woman," in Sherri Matteo, ed.,

American Women in the Nineties: Today's Critical Issues (Boston: Northeastern University Press, 1994), 34–78.

13. Melich, *The Republican War,* 119–278. See also Anne N. Costain, "After Reagan: New Party Attitudes Toward Gender," *Annals of the AAPSS,* 515 (May 1991):125–144.

14. Secretary Joseph A. Califano. Califano's HEW also was so lax in enforcing Title IX of the 1972 education amendments that several feminist organizations had to jointly sue the agency to get enforcement.

15. Melich, *The Republican War,* 261–278.

16. Ethel Klein, *Gender Politics* (Cambridge, Mass.: Harvard University Press, 1984), 28. For more details on how women voted in various elections, see Carol Mueller, ed., *The Politics of the Gender Gap* (Newbury Park, Calif.: Sage, 1988), and Sandra Baxter and Marjorie Lansing, *Women and Politics: The Visible Majority* (Ann Arbor: University of Michigan Press, 1983), 179–214. In *Gender Gap* (Boston: Houghton Mifflin, 1984), Bella Abzug and Mim Kelber predicted a sizeable gender gap in the 1984 presidential elections. The prediction finally came true in the 1996 elections.

17. Evidence of the prevalence of the new machismo was the sales figures of Robert Bly, *Iron John: A Book About Men* (Reading, Mass.: Addison-Wesley, 1990), which is alleged to have been the best-selling nonfiction book the year (1987) that it was first published. The book describes a mythological journey of initiation into manhood that takes place, according to Bly, only when men separate themselves from women (most especially their mothers). Bly argues that the Industrial Revolution pulled boys from their fathers and placed them in compulsory schooling, where their teachers, most of them female, stunted their manhood.

18. The Clinton administration nominated women for 30 percent of ninety-one positions on the federal bench, more than the Bush (9 percent), Carter (8 percent), and Reagan (6 percent) administrations' female nominations combined. *Political Woman* 2, no. 10 (August-September 1994):7.

19. The benefits of war service in politics is documented in a comparison of the campaign rhetoric employed by politicians coming out of World War II with that of the men who ran for public office after Vietnam. Sheila Tobias, "Shifting Heroisms: How Men Use Their War Service in Politics," in Jean Bethke Elshtain and Sheila Tobias, eds., *Women, Militarism, and War: Essays in History, Politics, and Social Theory* (Lanham, Md.: University Press of America, 1990), 163–186.

20. A case for abolishing the U.S. First Lady altogether is made by feminist Germaine Greer in her 1995 analysis of Hillary Clinton's role and reputation. Germaine Greer, "Abolish Her," *New Republic,* June 26, 1995, 21–27.

21. Center for American Women in Politics, "Sex Differences in Voter Turnout" (New Brunswick: Eagleton Institute, Rutgers University, July 1995), 1.

22. Joannie M. Schrof, "Feminism's Daughters," *U.S. News and World Report,* September 27, 1993, 70–71.

23. Ibid.

24. *3WAVE* (New York: THIRD WAVE, n.d.).

25. Schrof, "Feminism's Daughters," 71.

26. Barbara Findlen, Introduction to Barbara Findlen, ed., *Listen Up: Voices from the Next Feminist Generation* (Seattle: Seal Press, 1995), xi.

27. Susan Hartmann, *From Margin to Mainstream: American Women and Politics Since 1960* (New York: Knopf, 1989), documents the remarkable engagement of women in American political life in the period chronicled here. The title of this section is a play on her title.

28. Jeane J. Kirkpatrick, *Political Woman* (New York: Basic Books, 1974).

29. Daphne Patai and Noretta Koertge, *Professing Feminism: Cautionary Tales from the Strange World of Women's Studies* (New York: Basic Books, 1994), 51.

30. Ibid.

31. The ratio of men to women in women's studies courses and programs, though unknown, appears to be small. Even where a course in women's or gender studies is required, few men go on to take a second one. My own efforts to attract male students to two courses on gender and politics at a California university in the 1980s and early 1990s yielded at most 15 percent, but sometimes 7 percent, males.

32. Patai and Koertge, *Professing Feminism*, 54.

33. Ibid.

34. Linda Alcoff, "Cultural Feminism Versus Post-Structuralism: The Identity Crisis in Feminist Theory," *Signs* 13, no. 3 (Spring 1988):417.

35. Margaret Ferguson and Jennifer Wicke, eds., *Feminism and Postmodernism* (Durham, N.C.: Duke University Press, 1994), 6.

36. Heard personally by the author.

37. Frank Deford, "Year of the Women: Why Female Athletes Are Our Best Hope for Olympic Gold," *Newsweek*, June 10, 1996, 62–82.

38. Women's Bureau, *Working Women Count* (Washington, D.C.: Department of Labor, 1995).

39. Heard personally by the author during a presentation given by a representative from the Women's Bureau at a meeting of women in the Department of Energy, Brookhaven National Laboratory, May 7, 1996.

40. Martha Krebs, ibid.

41. Zillah Eisenstein, *The Female Body and the Law* (Berkeley and Los Angeles: University of California Press, 1989), quoted in Michele Barrett and Anne Phillips, *Destabilizing Theory: Contemporary Feminist Debates* (Cambridge: Polity Press, 1992), 19.

About the Book and Author

AS ONE OF THE MAIN PLAYERS in the second wave of feminism, Sheila Tobias returns to Kate Millett's central tenet, "sexual politics," and argues that it can still unite progressive men and women around a common set of goals. Providing a map of a complex terrain, Tobias details "generations" of issues, each more radical and therefore harder to tackle than the ones before. She sets the story in two contexts: feminism's own evolving strategies and America's political landscape. Even though her passion for feminism remains, she is not unwilling to critique the sisterhood and herself for failing to see, for example, that not every woman would be a feminist or every man an enemy. In the heady first years, feminists forgot that deeper even than gender is the liberal/conservative divide in American politics.

From the origins of the movement through feminist theory and new scholarship on women, Tobias traces the political history of the second wave and its comeuppance at the hands of Phyllis Schlafly's StopERA—coincidental with the nation's careening toward the Right. Somehow, feminism survived the 1980s, but by having to fight brush fires throughout the Reagan-Bush presidencies, the movement lost some of its breadth and much of its taste for the mainstream. Because of her activism and her feeling for the period she chronicles, Tobias is at once inside and outside the issues of sexual preference, pornography, the draft, the Mommy Track, comparable worth, affirmative action, reproductive rights, and the challenges of equality versus difference.

For the past twenty-five years, Sheila Tobias has been an academic as well as an activist. She participated in many feminist gatherings from the Congress to Unite Women in 1970 to the Berkshire Conference of Women Historians in 1993. Former board member of the NOW Legal Defense and Education Fund, her friends and comrades-in-arms include Kate Millett, Gloria Steinem, Betty Friedan, Wilma Scott Heide, Gerda Lerner, Lenore Weitzman, Eleanor Smeal, and Florence Howe. While associate provost at a previously all-male college, Connecticut's Wesleyan University, Tobias began researching women's avoidance of mathematics, resulting in the bestseller *Overcoming Math Anxiety*, recently re-released. She is also the author (with Jean Bethke Elshtain) of *Women, Militarism, and War* (1990) and seven other books on math, science, testing, and defense policy. Her books have been widely reviewed in the *New York Times*, *Choice*, the *American Way*, *Glamour*, and the *Washington Post*. She works as a consultant to universities on math and science education, equity issues, and women's studies.

Index

Abbot, Sidney, 157, 163, 167
Abortion, 2, 94, 131–133, 146, 292(n63)
  in communist countries, 67
  court cases, 227, 235–238, 249
  and employment, 133
  and federal funding, 235
  and fetal tissue, 241, 305(n22)
  and NOW Bill of Rights, 194–195
  and Operation Rescue, 238–239, 257
  restrictive laws, 236–238
  right-to-life movement, 235–238,
    317(n32)
  and RU 486, 239–240
  and teenage pregnancy, 187–188,
    236, 238, 252–253
  and theory, 194
  and viability, 234
  See also Reproductive rights; *Roe* v.
    Wade
Abzug, Bella, 107, 109, 159, 173, 224,
  225, 247
ACLU. *See* American Civil Liberties
  Union
Acquired immune deficiency
  syndrome (AIDS), 146, 166
Advocate, The, 165
Affirmative action, 74, 96, 102–106,
  227
  company plans, 127–128
  and equal opportunity, 126, 127,
    130
  and executive orders, 126, 127
  and white women, 128–130
African-American women
  and corporate management,
    128–130
  employment of, 43, 44, 52–53, 56,
    279(nn4, 10)

  and family, 216, 298(n64)
  feminist theory, 192–193
  and NOW, 221
  and scholarship, 196, 200
  voting rights, 22, 276–277(n30)
  See also Hispanic-American
    women; Women of color
*Against Our Will: Men, Women, and
  Rape* (Brownmiller), 113
AIDS. *See* Acquired immune
  deficiency syndrome
Alcoff, Linda, 256
Alert, 100
Alexander, Dolores, 156
Amendments to the Constitution
  Ninth, 233
  Thirteenth, 20, 22–23
  Fourteenth, 22–23, 24, 50, 126
  Fifteenth, 22–23, 24
  Nineteenth, 25
American Association of University
  Women (AAUW), 201, 231
American Civil Liberties Union
  (ACLU), 162, 188
American Telephone and Telegraph
  Company (AT&T), 91, 101–102,
  103, 143
American Women's Suffrage
  Association, 23
Anderson, Lisa, 55, 56
Anthony, Susan B., 13, 14, 16, 17, 23,
  24, 27
Anzaldúa, Gloria, 222, 223, 253
Armstrong, Ann, 248
Asian-American women, 223
Atkinson, Ti-Grace, 158, 159, 255–256
Atmospheric Test Ban Treaty, 139,
  299A(n6)

and age limit, 89
and lawsuits, 97
and preferential treatment, 128
and pregnancy, 133
and sexual harassment, 114–115
See also Civil Rights Act of 1964
Title IX, 111, 152, 227, 291(n46)
and sports, 123–125
Title X, 237
Toth, Emily, 200

Unions, 51, 52, 55–56, 92, 242
African-American, 104
airline, 87–88

Vaid, Urvashi, 165, 166
Vietnam War, 76–78, 79
Virginia Military Institute, 126, 213
Voter registration, 25, 76, 251

Walker, Alice, 193, 196, 197, 209
Walker, Rebecca, 252
Ward, Cynthia V., 212
Washington, Mrs. Booker T., 21
Watts, Sarah, 193, 200
WEAL. *See* Women's Equity Action
League
Weddington, Sarah, 109, 232–234
Weeks, Loreen, 102
Weisstein, Naomi, 69
Weitzman, Lenore, 120–121, 204–205,
231
Welfare, 90, 187, 188, 224, 230
See also Poverty
Wells, Ida B., 20–21
Whitehead, Barbara Dafoe, 186–187,
218

Whitehead, Mary Beth, 218–219,
313(n44)
Wisconsin Equal Rights Act, 35–36
WJCC. *See* Women's Joint
Congressional Committee
Wold, Emma, 36
Wolfgang, Myra, 51, 71
Womanism, 193, 209
Women of color
differences between, 222–223
and employment, 258
and family, 216
and politics, 247
and population control, 240–241
powerlessness of, 18
and second wave of feminism,
89–92
See also African-American women;
Hispanic-American women
Women's Bureau, 71, 73, 74, 99,
257–258
Women's Educational Equity Act, 122
Women's Equity Action League
(WEAL), 85, 97, 105, 109, 195, 231
Women's Joint Congressional
Committee (WJCC), 31–33, 36–37
Women's liberation, 76–80
in other countries, 87
See also Feminism
Women's studies, 195, 309(n76)
Women Strike for Peace (WSP), 172,
299(n6)
Woolf, Virginia, 4, 195
Woolley, Mary, 161
World War II, 39–40, 51–57
WSP. *See* Women Strike for Peace